KIN

To be re

Trade and transport

Thomas Stuart Willan

J. West 1946

W. H. Chaloner   Barrie M. Ratcliffe   *editors*

Trade and transport

Essays in economic history in honour of T. S. Willan

Manchester University Press

Rowman and Littlefield

© MANCHESTER UNIVERSITY PRESS 1977

Published by Manchester University Press
Oxford Road, Manchester M13 9PL

ISBN 0 7190 0680 5

USA
Rowman and Littlefield
81 Adams Drive, Totowa, N.J. 07512

ISBN 0-8476-6013-3

British Library cataloguing in publication data

Trade and transport.
  1. Great Britain – Commerce – Addresses, essays, lectures
  I. Willan, Thomas Stuart II. Chaloner, William Henry
  III. Ratcliffe, Barrie Michael
  380'.0941   HF3504

  UK ISBN 0-7190-0680-5
  US ISBN 0-8476-6013-3

Printed in Great Britain
at the Alden Press, Oxford

Computerised phototypesetting by
G. C. Typeset Ltd., Bolton, Lancashire

Contents

Introduction

T. S. Willan's career is memorable, and for two reasons. The first is that he personifies the Manchester school of history. He spent almost his entire teaching career at Manchester, from his arrival as an assistant lecturer in 1934 until his retirement from the Chair of Economic History in 1974, a Chair he held for eleven years. His work in early modern English economic history typifies all that is best in Manchester historiography: scholarship, a profound knowledge of sources, a respect for the complexity of the past, a clarity of exposition. The bibliography of his works that follows is but one indication of his contribution; another is the respect and admiration of other scholars in the field.

There is a second reason why T. S. Willan's career is worthy of mark: the man himself. As teacher, colleague and friend he possesses a rare combination of qualities: ineffable modesty, gentlemanliness, humanity. Past undergraduates remember his lectures not merely for the high standards they set but for the dry humour they contained; research students recall his untiring interest and concern. Colleagues remember a gentle, retiring man who was all the more effective for being so, for nobody mastered the intricacies of university administration so reluctantly and yet so well, no one could so damningly express disapprobation with a gentle sigh, or be so influential in committee and still be so frugal with words in a profession so profligate with them. He is, in sum, a man who inspires respect and affection.

A group of his ex-students, ex-colleagues, friends, seeking to demonstrate *their* respect and affection, have written the following essays in his honour. The essays deal with either trade or transport, themes central to T. S. Willan's work, and their authors dedicate them to him.

W.H.C.
B.M.R.

A chronological list of the writings of T. S. Willan

'The parliamentary surveys for the North Riding of Yorkshire', *Journal of the Yorkshire Archaeological Society*, Part 123, vol. XXXI, 1933, pp. 224–89.

River Navigation in England, 1600–1750, Oxford University Press, 1936; new impression with minor corrections, Frank Cass, 1964.

'Bath and the navigation of the Avon', *Somerset Archaeological and Natural History Society, Proceedings of the Bath and Bristol branch*, 1936, pp. 139–40.

'The navigation of the Thames and Kennet, 1600–1750', *Berkshire Archaeological Journal*, vol. XL, 1936, pp. 146–56.

'Salisbury and the navigation of the Avon', *Wiltshire Archaeological and Natural History Magazine*, vol. XLVII, 1937, pp. 592–4.

'Yorkshire river navigation, 1600–1750', *Geography*, vol. XXII, 1937, pp. 189–99.

'The river navigation and trade of the Severn valley', *Economic History Review*, vol. VIII, 1st ser., November 1937, pp. 68–79.

The English Coasting Trade, 1600–1750, Manchester University Press, 1938; reprinted with a new preface, 1967.

'Chester and the navigation of the river Dee, 1600–1750', *Journal of the Chester and North Wales Architectural, Archaeological and Historic Society*, vol. XXXII, 1938, pp. 64–7.

'River navigation and trade from the Witham to the Yare, 1600–1750', *Norfolk Archaeology*, Norfolk and Norwich Archaeological Society, vol. XXVI, 1938, pp. 296–309.

With E. W. Crossley, joint editor of *Three Seventeenth-century York-shire Surveys* (Yorkshire Archaeological Society Record Series, vol. 104, 1941).

The Navigation of the Great Ouse between St Ives and Bedford in the Seventeenth Century (Publications of the Bedfordshire Historical Record Society, vol. XXIV, 1946).

'Some Bedfordshire and Huntingdon wage rates, 1697–1730', *English Historical Review*, vol. LXI, 1946, pp. 244–9.

'A Bedfordshire wage assessment of 1684', *Bedfordshire Historical Record Society Publications*, vol. XXV, 1947, pp. 129–37.

'Trade between England and Russia in the second half of the sixteenth century', *English Historical Review*, vol. LXIII, July 1948, pp. 307–21.

The Navigation of the River Weaver in the Eighteenth Century, Manchester University Press, on behalf of the Chetham Society for the publication of remains historical and literary connected with the palatine counties of Lancaster and Chester, 3rd ser., vol. III, 1951.

The Muscovy Merchants of 1555, Manchester University Press, 1953.

'The Russia Company and Narva, 1558–81', *Slavonic and East European Review*, vol. XXXI, No. 77, June 1953, pp. 405–19.

'Some aspects of English trade with the Lavant in the sixteenth century', *English Historical Review*, vol. LXX, July 1955, pp. 399–410.

The Early History of the Russia Company, Manchester University Press, 1956; reprinted, 1968.

Studies in Elizabethan Foreign Trade, Manchester University Press, 1959; reprinted, 1968.

(Ed.) *A Tudor Book of Rates* [text of *The Rates of the Customs House*, printed in London in 1582], Manchester University Press, 1962.

'The Justices of the Peace and the rates of land carriage, 1692–1827', *Journal of Transport History*, vol. V, November 1962, pp. 197–204.

The Early History of the Don Navigation, Manchester University Press, 1965.

An Eighteenth-century Shopkeeper: Abraham Dent of Kirkby Stephen, Manchester UniversityPress, 1970.

The Inland Trade: Studies in English Internal Trade in the Sixteenth and Seventeenth Centuries, Manchester University Press, 1976.

The Cumbrian iron industry
in the seventeenth century

Measured by the number of blast furnaces working, Cumbria was the least important region of the iron industry in the seventeenth century: in Cumbria there was just one in existence in the 1690s.[1] Studies of the seventeenth-century industry have therefore made little mention of the area. The thesis that English iron production declined during the late seventeenth and early eighteenth centuries was reinforced by claims that the industry was starved of charcoal. When Professor Flinn and Dr Hammersley showed that these positions were no longer tenable, that more sites produced more iron between 1660 and 1760, and that charcoal was, generally speaking, available, it was because of its eighteenth-century blast furnaces that Cumbria received attention.[2] Since the publication of Flinn's article in 1959 a number of detailed pieces of work, although mainly concerned with the industrial archaeology of the Cumbrian industry, have suggested that there was a considerable expansion of smelting capacity throughout the seventeenth century. While this expansion is not sufficient to promote Cumbria from the bottom of the national production table, it is certainly of significance as one growth sector in a locality often thought of by historians as economically backward in the century. The present essay surveys the Cumbrian industry, looking at smelting capacity, the availability of raw materials in the form of charcoal and ore, and the marketing of finished iron. Two facets of this industry are then examined in detail: the mining and sale of iron ore, and the entrepreneurs who ran the industry.

The discovery, dating and examination of smelting sites have progressed considerably in the last two decades from a sound base established by some of the late nineteenth-century antiquarians.[3] The best recent general survey is the chapter by Mr Davies-Shiel in *The Industrial Archaeology of the Lake Counties* (1969), briefly updated in 1971;[4] a

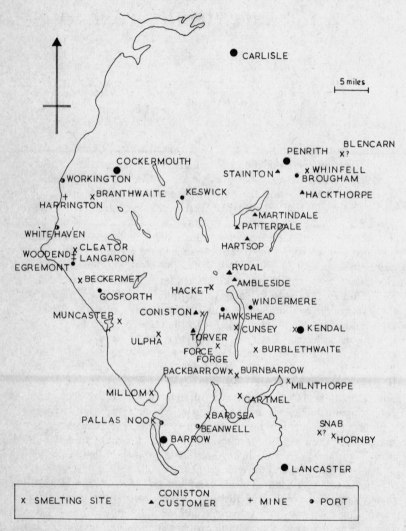

● CARLISLE

5 miles

BLENCARN
PENRITH   X?
COCKERMOUTH   STAINTON ▲   X WHINFELL
● WORKINGTON   BROUGHAM
+ ×BRANTHWAITE   ● KESWICK   ▲HACKTHORPE
HARRINGTON
                                         ▲MARTINDALE
WHITEHAVEN   ×PATTERDALE
WOODEND ×CLEATOR   HARTSOP
       ×LANGARON
EGREMONT   ▲RYDAL
    ×BECKERMET   ▲AMBLESIDE
  ● GOSFORTH   HACKET×
                          WINDERMERE
MUNCASTER   CONISTON▲×
       ×   ▲ HAWKSHEAD
           ULPHA   ×TORVER ×CUNSEY ×● KENDAL
            × FORCE×
              FORGE   × BURBLETHWAITE
       BACKBARROW× × BURNBARROW
                            ×MILNTHORPE
  MILLOM ×   ×CARTMEL
PALLAS NOOK ●   ×BARDSEA
            ● BEANWELL   SNAB
        ● BARROW   X? ×HORNBY
                    ● LANCASTER

┌───┐
│   CONISTON   │
│ × SMELTING SITE   ▲ CUSTOMER   + MINE ● PORT │
└───┘

Fig. 1.1   Smelting sites in Cumbria in the seventeenth century.

fuller, published record of sites is awaited. In the meantime it is clear that, from a number of sixteenth-century bloomeries and, perhaps, one bloomsmithy, the industry in Cumbria expanded throughout the seventeenth century. At least four bloomsmithies – Burnbarrow, Force Forge, Cunsey and Hacket – were built or rebuilt between 1600 and 1630. Burnbarrow, in the parish of Cartmel, ceased work about 1622; the other three continued in operation throughout the century.[5] At the same time, there was another works operated in the parish by the Preston family at Cark Shaws; this was still working in 1685. Fell Foot, close to Hacket, was certainly in operation by 1675, and perhaps as early as 1624. There was a 'forge' at Coniston probably before the Civil War, certainly in 1653; this was working in 1674, and Charles Russell, the hammerman, was still at Coniston in 1713. A bloomsmithy at Burblethwaite was in existence certainly by 1682, and perhaps in the early 1670s. In 1685 a bloomsmithy was built at Backbarrow. No accurate date can be put on a bloomsmithy at Bardsea. In Lonsdale, on the Lancashire–Westmorland border, there was a works at Hornby, certainly between 1635 and 1640. In south Westmorland there was a 'forge' at Kendal in 1606 and a bloomsmithy at Milnthorpe between 1653 and 1688–92; one also at Cunswick in 1674. In north Westmorland an ironworks was in operation at Brougham certainly between 1619 and 1623, and in 1647; this works was probably in continuous operation from 1619 to 1650. In west Cumberland the bloomsmithy at Ulpha was built in 1625, and it is described as working in 1671; this was probably 'Mr. Huddleston's forge', working in 1636 and referred to in a deed of 1640. The family also operated an ironworks at Millom in the last decade of the century. The family of Irton of Irton had a 'forge' working in 1636, probably in the Wasdale–Eskdale area. William Pennington of Muncaster built a bloomsmithy at Muncaster in 1636. There was one at Cleator by 1688, if not by 1670. Farther north in Cumberland, no reliable date can be put on bloomsmithies at Beckermet and Branthwaite, but there was one at Brigham, near Keswick, in operation from 1624. According to Davies-Shiel there were about thirty-four bloomsmithies in Cumbria, mostly operating after 1603, the last one being built at Stony Hazel (Furness) in 1718; there were in addition some three hundred bloomery sites operating from Romano-British times, but mainly between 1550 and 1645. Furthermore Schubert has shown the existence of a blast furnace at Cleator in 1694. Until 1957 the first blast furnace in the area was thought to be that built at Backbarrow (Furness) in 1711. The problem of proving continuity of working at these sites remains. Until Davies-Shiel's evidence is published, suffice it to say that Cunsey, Force Forge, Coniston, Milnthorpe, Hacket, Muncaster Head and Brigham at least can be shown to have been working for large parts of the century. Each of these bloomsmithies produced about twenty-five tons of bar-iron in a year. Multiplied by ten, the number of sites certainly known to be working in 1660, this would give a regional production figure of about 250 tons a year,[6] compared with Hammersley's estimate of national production in blast furnaces of nearly 18,000 tons.[7]

This increase in the smelting capacity of the area was undoubtedly facilitated by adequate supplies of charcoal and ore in the locality, although the price of these commodities was, perhaps surprisingly, high. Dr Hammersley has revised the view that lack of fuel was a major problem for the industry on a national level. For Cumbria he has convincingly argued that wood supplies were more than adequate to meet demand, despite the alleged depredations of the Keswick–Coniston copper industry in the seventy-odd years before 1640. Hammersley does not rule out local charcoal shortages, unless a proper coppicing system was practised.[8] There is evidence of coppicing in Furness in the sixteenth and seventeenth centuries.[9] Documentary evidence assembled by Miss Kipling suggests no lack of wood in the Windermere area in the seventeenth century.[10]

More specific evidence is available to show that individual ironworks were well supplied with wood. Far from the Keswick–Coniston copper works causing a shortage of charcoal, a report of 1616 on the works pointed to adequate supplies within sixteen miles of Keswick. Included amongst these resources were the woods of the Earl of Cumberland.[11] It is no surprise, then, to learn that by 1619 the Earl had started an ironworks at Brougham to utilise his timber supplies. There was plenty of wood available for the Muncaster Head works in 1636, obtained by its builder, William Wright, in Eskdale. When Wright's purchase was exhausted William Pennington was ready to use £800 worth of wood at Wasdale belonging to the Earl of Northumberland for the Muncaster works.[12] In Furness, between 1658 and 1663, B. G. Awty has shown that there was no difficulty in obtaining wood for Force Forge, although the price of charcoal, and the localities from which it was obtained, did vary. In 1658 and 1659 Sir Daniel Fleming of Rydal, lord of the manor of Coniston, was supplying wood from his Coniston estates to the ironworks at Coniston owned by the Kirkby family.[13] Two inventories of ironworks owners – Christopher Philipson, esquire, of Calgarth, d. 1634 (with an interest in Cunsey), and Sir George Midleton of Leighton, d. 1673 (joint owner of Milnthorpe) – record stocks of wood and charcoal in hand, suggesting that they had adequate supplies. Midleton further bequeathed standing woods worth £500 to his wife for use at Milnthorpe.[14] The use of alternative smelting fuels does not automatically indicate a charcoal shortage. Peat was used in the early eighteenth century at two Lakeland works for the supposedly higher quality of iron it produced.[15] The 1692 patent of Thomas Addison of Whitehaven for a coal-smelting process, under the patronage of Sir John Lowther of Whitehaven, is probably evidence of an attempt by coal owners to increase demand for their product.[16]

Iron ore, like charcoal, was readily available, yet the mining of iron ore has not attracted much attention. Fell says little that is pertinent to the seventeenth century except to trace descent of the ownership of mining rights. His local patriotic fervour for Furness led him to discount evidence of ore exports from west Cumberland assembled by H. A. Fletcher and J. D. Kendal in the nineteenth century. Dr Wood's pioneering thesis on west Cumberland heavy industry, and Davies-Shiel's work in *The Industrial Archaeology of the Lake Counties*, rely almost entirely on these nineteenth-century gleanings for their comments on the seventeenth century.[17]

In west Cumberland a small number of works were close to iron mining sites; in Furness and south Westmorland smelting sites were quite a distance from ore supplies. Most of the Furness and south Westmorland smelting sites obtained their ore from Furness, but the transport of ore was neither easy nor cheap. At Force Forge between 1658 and 1663 much of the ore came from the Adgardley–Stainton area. Circa 1620 a mixture of land and water transport – on Windermere – was used to bring ore to Cunsey.[18] It is possible that quantities of haematite from Langaron, Egremont, were smelted by William Wright at Cunsey or Force Forge; ore from Little Langdale was also perhaps used at these sites, and at Hacket. However, only two small loads of ore are known to have definitely been sold to Furness smelters from the mine at Langaron, Egremont, between 1635 and 1658. William Wright may have used ore from Langaron, Egremont, at Brougham, near Penrith, in the 1630s; apparently he was planning to use ore from Woodend, Egremont, at Blencarn, near Penrith, in 1667. In west Cumberland itself ore was led from Langaron, Egremont, to the Muncaster Head bloomsmithy, which also apparently used the closer supplies of ore in Eskdale.[19] The cost of transporting ore to a smelting site is nowhere clearly stated, except at Force Forge, where the cost was about 4s per quarter from Plain Furness overland between 1658 and 1663. The price of ore plus transport in particular may have made ore an expensive commodity for the Lakeland iron industry. In most other English smelting areas in the seventeenth century furnaces and mines were close together. Many Wealden works were near to their ore supplies, and those that were distant were regarded as uneconomic.[20] In the Midlands Sir Francis Willoughby's works at Oakmoor and Codnor were close to ore supplies, but at Middleton ore was more expensive and was brought from as far away as ten miles.[21] In south Yorkshire at the end of the seventeenth century most of the furnaces were within one mile of the outcrop of ore.[22]

The amount of ore used at Cumbrian smelting sites was not great. Detailed accounts show that about 140 tons per annum were sent from the Langaron mine at Egremont to Muncaster Head between 1638 and 1658. At Force Forge between 1658 and 1663 some 400 tons were purchased, but there was an unknown stock of ore in hand in 1658.[23]

Now there were at least ten bloomsmithies like Muncaster Head in
operation in 1660. If we assume that these ten each consumed, say, 150
tons of ore per annum, then total consumption would be 1,500 tons. The
mines at Stainton in Furness and Langaron, Egremont, were each
capable of producing in excess of 800 tons a year in the 1650s and '60s.
There were other mining sites in Furness besides that at Stainton, for
which no figures are available. Likewise we have no indication of
quantities mined in Little Langdale, at Woodend, near Egremont, and at
Millom towards the end of the century. Iron ore was also mined at
Harrington, near Workington, and on the Pennine fells, in the east of
Lakeland, although there is no certain evidence of mining here in the
second half of the century, and the quality of the ores was lower than that
of haematite. In other words, mining productivity in the area could easily
cope with local demand, even as that demand increased towards 1700. In
these circumstances iron ore owners would welcome a healthy trade
outside the area, especially since, as will be shown below, all the
indications are that iron ore could be a profitable commodity.

This increase in the smelting capacity of an area well supplied with
charcoal and ore was most likely an attempt to exploit the local market
for iron, which, in the late sixteenth and early seventeenth centuries was
supplied with Spanish iron, and, in the seventeenth century, some Irish
iron. There is no evidence of new large-scale metallurgical industries
requiring iron giving rise to this increase in smelting capacity.[24] Demand
for iron came from the coal and other mining industries of the area,
which were expanding throughout the century. Although Keswick copper
works closed by 1640, new lead mines were developed in the Derwent
Fells area in the following decade. B. G. Awty's forthcoming work on
Force Forge, in Furness, shows how little of the iron produced there went
outside Cumbria, and most of that went only into lowland Lancashire.
Indeed, in 1658 and 1659 most of the iron produced went to smiths in
Cumberland, with some to smiths in Westmorland and Furness.
Attempts to boost sales by 'commercial travelling' on the part of Thomas
Rawlinson, who managed the works, failed, and the most effective
marketing technique was the establishment in 1661 of a 'shop' at
Wellhead, close to Force Forge. A second shop was established in 1663,
probably at Ulverston. The effect of these was to increase the amount of
iron sold to customers from the vicinity of Force Forge and to decrease
the size of individual transactions. Altogether, between 1658 and 1663
most of the iron was sold into Cumberland. The fact that many of
Rawlinson's customers in Cumberland were Friends like himself does not
necessarily explain why so high a proportion of Force Forge's iron was
sold there. Such a pattern of dispersed sales may have been normal, for
fragmentary evidence of iron sales from Coniston works in 1653 suggests
that sales to customers relatively distant to the works were not unusual.
The debt book of Richard Harrison, of Martindale, who was steward

to the Fleming family of Rydal, lords of the manor of Coniston, lists sales to smiths at Stainton near Penrith (Cumberland), Martindale, Hackthorpe, Hartsop and Patterdale, all in north Westmorland.[25] Closer to Coniston, iron was supplied to John Braithwaite of Ambleside in Westmorland (a chapman) for resale, and to smiths at Rydal (Westmorland) and Torver (Furness), as well as to one or perhaps two smiths of Coniston. Harrison's role seems to have been that of financier rather than middleman, and he was perhaps a partner in the Coniston works. Evidence of the sale of Spanish and Irish iron imported into Workington by Sir Patricius Curwen between 1629 and 1632 accords with the pattern of sale of locally produced iron. Most of the iron went to a Workington smith, George Willis, and some to a Cockermouth resident, Henry Dalton, who could loosely be described as a merchant.[26] Apart from John Braithwaite of Ambleside chapmen do not seem to have been important in the marketing of iron, as they certainly were in the Midlands, and as they had been in marketing Keswick copper. Later in the century iron could be purchased in towns in the area. Formal arrangements for the sale of Force Forge iron existed at Kendal[27] and at Lancaster, where ironmongers and whitesmiths were responsible. It would not be surprising if iron was purchased for use in mining industries of the area, but the evidence for this is disappointingly slight. William Pennington purchased iron for use at Langaron mine before his own bloomsmithy at Muncaster Head was built, but later Pennington sold iron from this works to the lead miners of the Derwent Fells area.[28] Finally, there is little evidence for the export of iron by sea from Cumbria, or even overland to Scotland. Certainly small amounts of *English* iron are mentioned in the port books for the Cumbrian coast, and also in the books dealing with the overland trade through Carlisle. But there is no proof that this iron had been made locally. The account book of the Fell family contains one instance of the sale of Force Forge iron to a Quaker in the Isle of Man, and one instance of the sale of iron in Cornwall.[29] Given the competition of English, Spanish, Irish and, increasingly, Swedish iron, this situation is not unexpected; the Cumbrian industry contented itself with supplying established local needs in the seventeenth century. Unless local demand for iron expanded in keeping with the expansion of smelting capacity the Cumbrian iron industry must have been very competitive.

Unfortunately a detailed survey of the industry to test this hypothesis is not possible. B. G. Awty's study of the one extant set of forge accounts points to financial difficulties in the 1660s, which may reflect overproduction; and the difficulties of William Wright, the largest Cumbrian ironmaster, at the same time may arise from that also. Two other aspects of the industry can, however, be examined in detail, and the remainder of this essay is devoted, first, to the mining of, and trade in, iron ore; and, second, to some of the entrepreneurs of the Cumbrian iron industry in the seventeenth century.

The abundance of easily mined iron ore, in excess of local smelting demand, meant that ore owners were anxious to promote sales of ore outside Cumbria. Mining costs were low and, combined with the attractiveness of the high grade haematite ore, offset the high cost of transporting a bulk commodity. The three stages of this operation – mining the ore; transporting it to the coast for shipment; and, in less detail, shipment from the Cumbrian coast to the smelter – can be examined using the accounts of the Langaron (Egremont) iron mine, supplemented by evidence of mining operations and transport at Stainton (Furness) and in the Harrington–Workington area.

The accounts of the Langaron mine are preserved among the estate papers of the Honour of Cockermouth, which belonged to the Earl of Northumberland.[30] The mine was situated in the tenement of Richard Nicholson, in the manor of Egremont. The Earl of Northumberland first leased the newly discovered mine to William Pennington of Muncaster, esquire, in March 1635. The earl renewed the lease for twenty-one years from October 1638, sharing the costs and profits of the venture with Pennington under this second lease but allowing Pennington a bonus of 140 tons of ore per year for ten years, to be mined at Pennington's own cost.[31] The accounts for 1635–38, drawn up when the earl negotiated the second lease in 1638, and the accounts presented by Pennington at the earl's half-yearly audits between 1638 and 1658 show that the capital costs of setting up and maintaining the mine, of repairing the tools and gear, together with other commitments necessary to work the mine, were not great. These costs are summarised in table 1.1, which expresses them as a cost per ton of ore raised.

From March 1635 to Michaelmas 1638 Pennington set up the mine with a capital outlay of £43 17s 10d; unfortunately we are not told on

Table 1.1   Summary of capital expenditure, etc

Date[a]	Tons mined	Capital expenditure			Cost per ton d	Repair of tools, etc			Cost per ton d	Rent of store: Clerk's salary, etc			Cost per ton s d	Total s d
		£	s	d	d	£	s	d	d	£	s	d	s d	s d
March 1635/38	2,680	44	5	0	4	4	15	7	$\frac{1}{2}$	88	0	7	8	1 0$\frac{1}{2}$
1638/49	1,097	—		—		2	4	8	$\frac{1}{2}$	66	8	4	7	1 3
1649/53	1,242	29	6	5	5$\frac{1}{2}$	6	15	4	1$\frac{1}{4}$	38	5	10	7$\frac{1}{3}$	1 2$\frac{1}{4}$
April 1654– October 1658	715	18	11	0	6$\frac{1}{4}$	2	19	9	1	50	3	4	1 4$\frac{3}{4}$	2 0

[a] Except where specified, accounting periods ran from October to October, i.e. from Michaelmas audit to Michaelmas audit.

what the major portion of this money (£30 16s 5d, accounted for by one of the workmen) was spent. A further 8s was spent on repairs to a warehouse at Whitehaven. This initial capital outlay was apparently sufficient to keep the mines going for the next twelve years. Not until the accounting year ending Michaelmas 1650 is there evidence that a new pit was sunk, and therefore that Pennington incurred further capital costs. Repairs and renewals of tools from 1635 to 1650 cost £7 0s 3d.

In the spring and summer of 1650 a new pit was sunk, which took fifteen weeks' work, and cost in labour alone £3 1s 3d to dig. Water became a problem, and the pit was pumped, although £2 still had to be paid to the workmen for drawing out water by hand. More than one winder was provided to raise ore, and since the construction of these required four trees and special skills they were evidently quite massive. However, there is no indication that a horse gin was employed. Altogether the capital charge came to £7 6s 5d. This pit lasted only until October 1650, and no ore was mined in the following twelve months to October 1651. In the year after that another new pit was dug. Capital costs for this pit, completed by October 1652, amounted to £22, including £6 spent on a pump. In 1654, and again in 1655, new pits were dug, at a capital cost of £18 11s 0d. These were the last pits to be sunk under the 1638 lease, which was terminated in 1658. Repairs and provision of such necessities as ore bags between 1650 and 1658 amounted to £9 15s 11d.[32] From 1655 to the end of the 1658 lease ore stocks were run down, but probably in the summer of 1658 mining began again under a new lease to Sir Roger Bradshaigh of Haigh in Lancashire. The form of the ore accounts changes at Michaelmas 1658 according to the terms of the new lease; they are subsequently less informative and also fragmentary.[33]

Apart from the capital costs Pennington was committed to some current expenditure. Under the terms of the first lease (1635 to 1638) he paid the earl a rent of £6 13s 4d per annum. For the duration of the first lease rents totalling £8 8s 5d were paid to Sir Christopher Lowther of Whitehaven for a storehouse there. Pennington's third obligation was a salary of £13 6 s 8d per annum to the clerk of the works. These charges were reduced under the second lease, which operated from Michaelmas 1638, and the costs were shared between Pennington and the earl. No rent was therefore due to the earl. There was a standing charge on the partnership of £5 per annum rent for the storehouse at Whitehaven. The lease on the store was not renewed after 1652, and instead stears were leased at a variable rent which never exceeded £2 13s 4d per annum. However, from 1652 recurrent costs were increased because of an agreement to compensate the tenant of the ground on which the mine was situated, apparently for the flooding of his land by water from the mines. A lump sum of £14 11s was paid in 1652 and thereafter an annual payment of £1. The only other expenditure was that incurred by the clerk, who under the new lease was not paid a salary but was allowed his expenses; in the years after 1653 these became a significant charge, in some years as much as £10.

Throughout the period of these accounts Robert Copley was clerk of the works. Although he worked hard – his duties took him to Ireland in 1641 – it is clear from the accounts that he was not always on hand when needed. For example, in 1653 a messenger was sent to his home to bring him to Whitehaven to cinduct business. Copley was also clerk to William Pennington's Muncaster Head bloomsmithy, and he had other interests outside the iron trade. He was an estate officer of the Honour of Cockermouth, while for his own part he leased property from that Honour; in 1654 he purchased an estate at Gosforth on which he built Gosforth Hall.[34] The mine did not get his full attention, a sharp contrast with the management of the Keswick copper works.[35]

The labour cost of digging a ton of ore was soon reduced from 2s a ton in 1635 to 10d per ton in 1638, where it remained. There is a suggestion in one of Pennington's letters that the high rate paid initially was a recompense to the workmen against the possibility of losing their jobs if the mine proved unprofitable.[36] The labour charge for measuring ore was 1d per ton, and the ore was measured on sale at the pit head or on movement to Whitehaven.

Thus the cost of raising a ton of ore comprised capital outlay, the cost of tools and repairs, the clerk's expenses, and the storage facilities at Whitehaven (which had to be paid for whether or not ore was stored there), as well as the labour charges for digging and measuring the ore. Between 1635 and 1658 these costs varied between about 2s 1d and about 2s 11d per ton. It cost less to produce a ton of ore at the pit head than it cost to move that ton to Whitehaven, the port through which Langaron ore was exported. The expensive transport to the coast was the second prime control on the price of ore for export.

Only pack-horses could travel from the pits at Egremont to Whitehaven, according to Robert Copley, and they only in summer time. Copley reckoned that no more than 400 tons of ore could be moved in any one summer. Whitehaven was a new port of seventeenth-century creation; it was not served by ancient roadways. John Ogilvy's map of 1675 shows two routes from Whitehaven to Egremont, one passing near the mines in the Clintz area; neither is shown in its entirety on the map.[37] The descent down to the shore at Whitehaven was the likely cause of most difficulty, and in the eighteenth century a special way was constructed for pack-horses.[38] The organisation of the transport of ore from the pits at Egremont to Whitehaven is not made clear in the accounts. In 1635 and 1636 William Pennington and Robert Copley seem to have tried to organise the transport from Egremont themselves, and the accounts contain payments for horses, saddles and associated items totalling £13 17s 6d in these two years. Thereafter a flat rate of 4s a ton from Egremont to Whitehaven was charged.[39] This figure was entered in the accounts, but there are no further entries for horses and pack saddles. The likely presumption must be that the work was contracted out to local men at a fixed rate, a system similar to that at other mines. The records of ore mining at Harrington–Workington suggest that local farmers were employed, part-time at least, in moving ore to ships. This was apparently the case at another pit in the Egremont area later in the century. At Stainton in 1665 most of the transport was apparently done by men employed in the mining operation, and only when they were unable to cope were local men brought in.[40] The vendors at Whitehaven and in Furness seem also to have been responsible for paying for the loading of the ships, and the customs fees for the shipping of the ore. The records of the Workington trade would not, by their nature, include such items. Between 1638 and 1658 transport to Whitehaven, measuring, loading, harbour fees and customs there added between 4s 8½d and 5s 0½d to the cost of a ton of ore, the figure varying from year to year, as table 1.2 shows.

Table 1.2   Cost of transport from Egremont to Whitehaven, and clearing the port

	Cost			Cost per ton	
	£	s	d	s	d
October 1638–49					
Measuring 596 tons, and leading to Whitehaven	119	7	9	4	0
Measuring, loading, customs and[a] harbour fees for 333 tons sold	11	11	4		8½
	130	19	1		
October 1649–53					
Measuring 221 tons and leading to Whitehaven	45	2	5	4	1
Measuring, loading, customs and harbour fees for 281 tons sold	9	3	5		8
	54	5	10		
April 1654–October 1658					
Measuring 1,324 tons and leading to Whitehaven	271	10	0	4	1
Measuring, loading, customs and harbour fees for 1,492 tons sold[b]	74	3	6		11¾
	345	13	6		

[a] Not all these stage are separately recorded in the accounts on every occasion.
[b] There are discrepancies between the amounts of ore sent to Whitehaven and the amounts sold.

The third control on the price of ore for export was transport from the Cumbrian ports to the smelter. This was not the responsibility of the vendors, although by again as much as doubling the cost of ore it would affect demand from outside Cumbria. The boats employed were usually small. At Workington loads of iron ore varied between five tons and forty-eight tons; however, it is not certain that the entire cargo of the boats comprised iron ore.[41] At Whitehaven the amount of ore carried by each boat is not always stated, but when it is it compares with the Workington range. In Furness in 1665 boats carrying ore destined for Holmes Chapel in Cheshire loaded between twelve and twenty-six tons; boats for Ireland loaded twenty, forty and fifty-two tons.[42] The number of skippers involved at Workington was considerable; over the years 1626–41 nearly fifty men are named in the accounts. The number of ships involved at Whitehaven cannot be determined. From Furness in 1665 one man, Isaac Thompson, took all but one of five loads of ore sent from Stainton to Ireland; six other skippers besides him are named in the accounts. Only one note of the cost of shipping a load of ore from Workington has survived: twenty-one tons to, probably, Coleraine in Ulster, cost 6s a ton in 1630. In 1696/97 it cost an average of 15s 4½d per ton to transport ore from Cumbria to Vale Royal in Cheshire; this doubled the purchase price of the ore in Cumbria from 16s to near £1 10s a ton. The sea journey cost 6s 4d or 7s a ton; the remainder was incurred in fees and in land carriage from Frodsham.[43]

The ore trade represented welcome business for Workington and Whitehaven, but it was not the most important element of their trade. Workington had a long history as a fishing town, going back beyond John Leyland's time, and by 1605 coal was shipped from there to Ireland. The export of coal to Ireland, and the import of Irish livestock and foodstuffs, were the major occupations of the port, and iron ore was only one of a number of less important cargo commodities. The Curwen family, lords of the manor of Workington, dominated the port, through which they shipped their own coal, salt and salted fish in their own ships, as well as their own iron ore. Whitehaven, to the south of Workington, is not noticed as a port before the 1630s, when it was developed by Sir Christopher Lowther of Whitehaven, who built the first pier there. Well connected in the Irish administration of Strafford, Lowther clearly determined to use Whitehaven as a base for exporting coal and salt from his mines and pans there to the Irish market, represented especially by Dublin. As with Workington, coal was the major cargo, and iron ore only one of a number of less important commodities, although the trade through Whitehaven was much more varied than that of Workington. Both Sir Christopher Lowther and Sir Patricius Curwen benefited from the improving status of ports in the north and east of Ireland, and from the support given to trade by Irish administrations after the farm of the Irish customs in 1613.[44]

The low cost of ore mining reduced the impact of high transport costs on the ore trade, while the high quality and relative ease of access helped to ensure continued demand for Cumbrian ore. Profits were therefore not insignificant. At the pit head at Langaron ore was usually sold at 9s per ton c. 1640 but fell to 8s from 1649.[45] Between 1635 and 1658 the sale price of Langaron ore at Whitehaven varied between 12s 6d and 15s per ton, the whole cost of transport to the coast being passed to the purchaser. All three mining sites sold substantial quantities of ore outside Cumbria, but they also sold ore in the region, and the two trades are not easily separated. The paragraphs which follow look at the commercial operation of the three mining sites at (in chronological order) Harrington–Workington, Langaron (Egremont) and Stainton (Furness) and emphasise connections and sales outside Cumbria.[46]

The ore mines at Harrington were owned by the Curwen family, of Workington. The account book of Sir Patricius Curwen's steward for the years 1626–46 contains many items relating to iron ore, although, regrettably, the steward was often not very explicit when making his entries.[47] Curwen received 2s a ton on ore sold from the beginning of the book in 1626 to August 1631. Thereafter the sum was 2s 6d per ton until 1641. There are no receipts for ore after October 1641, although the accounts continue until 1646. There is no mention of the mine in Curwen's particular of estate submitted to the Committee for Compounding in 1646, or in the estate rental of 1660, suggesting that production ceased.[48] It is likely that the receipts represent a royalty to Curwen on each ton of ore sold, for the sums are too small to represent the actual sale price of the ore.

Curwen's steward does not always explain the position of the men from whom he received money for ore royalties. On a few occasions the purchaser personally paid the steward; in most such examples the purchaser was Thomas Curwen (either uncle or brother of Sir Patricius Curwen). Most of the men who paid were probably captains of ships or purchasers' agents. Informative entries, such as 'Rec[eived] of William Ronold [Raynold] aboard the Grace of God', probably refer to the ships' captains. Rarely is the name of the captain or agent and his principal given: 'Rec[eived] of Alex Boyd for Sir Moyses Hill'. John Rodgers, captain of Curwen's own barque, also paid for ore on behalf of Sir Moyses Hill. On another occasion 'Rec[eived] of Robert Miller taken by Alex Boyd' suggests that Miller paid the steward on behalf of Boyd, who was probably shipping ore for Hill. Robert Miller was also lessee of part of Curwen's demesne, and it is tempting to conjecture him as a farmer who supplemented his income by carrying ore from the pit to the ships. Sir Moyses Hill appears by name in the accounts in 1626 and 1627, and at least one of his agents in these two years continued to ship ore after that. Hill was dead by March 1630/31; in April 1632 Curwen's steward recorded a payment of £10 5s 0d, for eighty-two tons of ore, from Lady Hill.

There is a problem in determining the whereabouts of Hill's works, a problem which is made more difficult by the absence of port books for the west Cumberland ports at this time. Sir Patricius Curwen traded with Carrickfergus, in County Antrim, Ulster, and Sir Moyses Hill owned land there. But there is no evidence of an ironworks on that land. However, Hill was the joint exploiter of woodland in County Down, Ulster, with Sir Fulk Conway, who did own an ironworks at Carrickfergus, working in 1620. Another member of the Conway family, Dame Amy Conway, owned an ironworks at Hill Hall in County Down, working in 1625. Hill also owned land at Stranmillis (Belfast) where, later, there were ironworks. Hill may have been buying ore for any of these works.[49] Curwen also sold ore to Coleraine, in Ulster, certainly in August 1632 and probably on other occasions. It was perhaps carried from there up the river Bann, and then overland to Sir Thomas Phillips's works at Lissan, the route by which iron from this works was exported.[50] It does not follow that all Curwen's ore was sold to Ireland, but in the late 1620s and 1630s Curwen had two agents in Ireland, so that Ireland is not an unlikely destination. It is probable that one of Curwen's major customers, Thomas Curwen, smelted his ore in Cumberland, but there is no evidence of the whereabouts of such a works, nor is there evidence that Sir Patricius Curwen himself had an ironworks. However, the great majority of Curwen's ore was sold outside Cumbria, most of it to Ireland. The receipts from ore royalties at their best in 1635 perhaps amounted to a tenth of Curwen's annual income. Over the sixteen years receipts totalled £442 18s 5½d, an annual average of £24; some of the minor gentry families in the area had incomes of this level.[51] Table 1.3 summarises Curwen's receipts from ore.

William Pennington's ore trade from his mine at Langaron, Egremont, depended both on overland and seaborne transport for success. When Pennington began mining in 1635 he started a new venture, the potential obstacles to which he seems fully to have appreciated. For a start, his was not the only mine at Egremont, and he also had to face competition from Curwen at Workington, and from the Furness mines.[52] Pennington had gained some knowledge of the iron trade from William Wright, to whom he had leased lands and woods for ironworks in the previous decade.[53] No doubt this information helped him to secure the very low rent of £6 13s 4d a year for the mine. From the start Pennington must have expected to sell ore via the new port of Whitehaven, but he also intended to build up a trade with the local ironmasters if he could. On 31 March 1636 he contracted to supply William Wright with 300 tons of ore a year for a term of seven years, at a fixed price of £111 13s 4d per annum (fractionally under 7s 6d per ton). Following this, Wright contracted to build a bloomsmithy at Muncaster Head on Pennington's

Table 1.3   Sir Patricius Curwen's iron ore receipts, 1626–41

Year (Jan.–Jan.)	Tons sold	£	s	d
1626	117½	8	16	2[b]
1627	357[a]	35	15	0[c]
1628	188½	18	17	0
1629	110	11	1	0
1630	203	19	7	0½
1631	361	38	1	4
1632	420½	53	11	5
1633	214½	26	11	0
1634	190	24	10	0
1635	560	73	10	0
1636	453	56	13	9
1637	100[a]	12	10	0
1638	103	12	17	6
1639	(No receipts)			
1640	64	8	0	0
1641	355	44	7	6

[a] Tonnage not given in accounts, calculated from amount of receipts.
Does not include £40 from 'this year's ironstone' from a Mr Rutter or £14 17s
1d arrears for 1625 from the same man. These two sums have been omitted,
as there is no indication of the tonnage involved, or upon what basis Rutter
was supplied with ore.
[c] Does not include £31 10s 'for this year's ironstone' from the said Mr Rutter.

estates, in partnership with Pennington. After a short period the sole use
of this bloomsmithy would revert to Pennington, who was already
negotiating for wood to fuel the works once it was in his possession.
Pennington protected his interest in these two agreements by covenants
which prevented Wright from searching for ore in Cumberland, except
around Penrith, from smelting ore bought from Pennington at any works
in the Wasdale–Eskdale area in which Pennington was not a partner, and
from buying wood in west Cumberland.[54] The contract with Wright, and
the Muncaster Head bloomsmithy, should have ensured the profitable
operation of Pennington's mine. But apart from these outlets Pennington
can have expected to sell little ore at the pit head, for there were few
smelters, but a number of mines, in west Cumberland.

Under the first lease of the mine, 1635 to 1638, operations went
smoothly (see table 1.4 for a summary). Two-thirds of the ore mined was
sold, and the excess of receipts over expenditure amounted to £194 7s 2d.
Sales at the pit head totalled 940 tons, of which, as might be expected, all
but forty tons went to William Wright. Sales at Whitehaven totalled 492
tons. These years were marked by such success that in 1638 the Earl of
Northumberland renegotiated Pennington's lease in order to enjoy for
himself more of the profit. Ironically, the boom ended at this point. In a
letter of 12 April 1639 to the Earl's steward, Pennington recounts his

Table 1.4 Summary of transactions at William Pennington's Langaron mine, 1635–58

Period	Tons Produced	Tons sold Whitehaven	Tons sold Pit Head	Total^a	Receipts (£ s d)	Expenditure (£ s d)	Profits (£ s d)
March 1635–October 1638	2680	492	940 / 186^b / 1126 — ore in hand / 1062^c	1618	698 8 0	504 0 10	194 7 2
Pennington							
October 1638–39	400	–	–	–	33 7 0^d	17 3 4	
1639–40	–	26	105	131	–	14 18 6	
1640–41	300	268	23	291	219 0 4	147 8 4	73 7 2
1641–49	980^e	39	281	320	138 8 0	64 5 2	74 2 10
1649–50	442	–	140	140	56 0 0	31 18 5	
1650–51	–	36	–	36	24 0 0	6 16 10	
1651–52	800	92	90	182	91 8 0	66 8 1	
1652–53	–	153	36	189	110 5 0	72 6 8	104 3 0
April 1654–October 1654	460	282	20	302	186 3 0	125 7 8	60 15 4
October 1654–55	255	307	187	494	274 14 0	104 4 5	170 9 7
1655–56	–	322	112	434	251 9 0	91 1 1	160 7 6
1656–57	–	363	80	443	274 8 9	115 1 3^f	159 7 6
1657–58	–	218	–	218	145 13 6	15 7 10	130 5 8
							£1,127 5 9

^{a} There are discrepancies between the figures for the production and sale of ore.

^{b} At least 14 tons were sent to ironworks for trials, besides 126 tons sent to Pennington's works; 46 tons sold became desperate debts.

^{c} 140 tons of this 'disappeared' from the accounts; 922 tons valued at 2s per ton cost price gives Pennington a further £92 4s; sold at 8s per ton it would be worth £368 16s.

^{d} A further £30 due on bond and paid later is included below.

^{e} 1,214 tons valued at pit-head sale price less cost of miner's wages and measuring at 11d per ton gives Pennington £433 15s 0½d.

^{f} Th...

difficulties in selling the unsold ore mined in the 1635–38 period.[55] Competition from the Prestons of Holker was biting, whilst the uncertainty created by the Scottish war, especially rumours about Scottish warships, was damaging trade. More to blame was William Wright, who had not purchased any ore since the previous year. Also Pennington was, no doubt, anxious to sell first the ore mined under his own lease. The situation improved slightly in 1640 and 1641 with the sale of 422 tons, of which 294 were sold at Whitehaven; in these years the venture made a profit of £73 7s 2d to be shared by the two partners. At least some of the ore sold at Whitehaven went to Ireland via a Mr Thomas Dawson. Pennington certainly tried to promote Irish sales: Robert Copley, the clerk, was paid £5 for a trip to Ireland in 1641. Nevertheless disaster soon followed: from October 1641 to October 1649 only 362 tons of ore were sold; William Wright purchased 200 of these, and only thirty-nine were sold from Whitehaven. The works remained profitable, but made only £74 2s 10d over eight years. The interruption was probably caused largely by the Civil War, although in the accounts the war is explicitly blamed only for the complete cessation of work between April 1648 and October 1649.

From October 1649 there was a gradual improvement. Sales at Whitehaven between then and October 1653 reached 281 tons: Pennington bought 266 tons from the pit head for use at his own bloomsmithy. No doubt the pacification of Ireland helped, for after 1653 sales to Ireland grew as the Irish works, largely shut down in 1641, were reopened. The connections with Thomas Dawson established by Robert Copley in 1641 were renewed and sales from Whitehaven to Ireland became the chief source of revenue. Two of the great Irish ironmasters, Major (later Sir George) Rawdon and Sir Charles Coote, later Earl of Mountrath, became regular customers.[56] Between April 1654 and October 1658 Rawdon took 820 tons, Coote and Dawson 519; ninety-six tons went to Scotland, and the remaining fifty-seven tons sold at Whitehaven went to a variety of buyers, not all of whom can be identified. All 399 tons sold at the pit head went to Pennington's bloomsmithy.

The restarting of Coote's very profitable works at Mountrath, in 1654, fits well with his first appearance in the accounts, and offers a clue as to the destination of the ore he purchased, although a contemporary description of the works at Mountrath and elsewhere in central Ireland does not mention the use of English ore. Ore from Whitehaven for Coote was, according to the mine accounts, to be shipped to Dublin. Coote sold his iron in Dublin, after shipping it from Mountrath via the river Nore to Waterford and then around the coast; from the Coote works farther west in Ireland iron went downriver to Limerick and then via the coast to Dublin. The ore probably made the reverse trip.[57] When the port books for Whitehaven begin in 1688 we get a closer picture of this trade, with exports of ore being sent explicitly to Dublin, and also to other Coote centres via Wicklow and Wexford.[58] Some of these 1688 shipments were the responsibility of Thomas Addison, who was joint lessee of the Langaron mines from 1682 but who also leased other mines in the area.[59] The works supplied in the 1650s for Sir George Rawdon were probably those at Lambeg and Stranmillis, close to Belfast, but the destination of the ore is not stated in the accounts.[60] Again, in 1688 Thomas Addison was sending ore to Belfast.[61]

William Pennington died in 1651, but the iron ore venture he started was clearly a success which, in the untroubled years between 1635 and 1638, made a welcome profit. Between April 1654 and October 1658 the total profit was £681 5s 7d, or an average of £76 per annum for each partner. A major proportion of this profit came from Irish sales, while sales to local establishments amounted to 21 per cent of the tonnage sold. Over the period 1635–58 as a whole, just over half the ore sold was shipped from Whitehaven. The new lease taken by Sir Roger Bradshaigh from 1655 came into operation in 1658.[62] As it only required Bradshaigh to pay a royalty of 4s 6d per ton, the auditors' accounts record only tonnage mined and royalty payments, and are in any case fragmentary after 1658.[63] This makes it impossible to follow the fortunes of the mining venture in detail, although new leases were taken in 1675 and in 1692; the 4s 6d royalty remained in force until 1696, when it changed under the terms of the 1692 lease.[64] However, a summary of royalty receipts between 1667 and 1691, written probably in 1692, shows that 17,479 tons were produced, an average of 698 tons a year. Although it is not possible to calculate figures for annual ore production from the summary, in general the amount mined increased as the century advanced.[65] Irish works which were supplied in the 1650s remained customers. Ore from Whitehaven was also sent to Carlingford, Coleraine and Kilmore in Ulster, and to the Forest of Dean and Vale Royal, Cheshire, in England.[66] It is just possible that Pennington supplied the haematite ore found at the seventeenth-century smelting sites at Loch Maree in Wester Ross, which the nineteenth-century Scottish antiquarian W. I. Macadam described as similar to ores of the Ulverston area.[67] Certainly Pennington sold ore to some Scotsmen, but no names are given in the accounts, and the quantities sold were small. Both English and Scottish customs records are silent on this point, except to note a shipment from Whitehaven to Lochaber in 1688.[68]

The third and last ore trading venture at which it is proposed to look was that conducted by Sir Thomas Preston of the Manor, Furness. Only one year's accounts survive for his mine at Stainton: 514 tons were sold between May and November 1665.[69] It is not possible, of course, to say how typical 1665 was for the sale of ore, but certainly demand for Stainton ore was maintained, and the mines were supplying ore to Force Forge in 1685.[70] In 1665 one-third of the tonnage sold was shipped to

Ireland for the use of a Mr Kensham.[71] A mere twenty tons was sold to Sir George Rawdon for use in Ireland.[72] Fourteen per cent of the ore sold went to Holmes Chapel in Cheshire, and 53 per cent was sold to smelters in Furness and south Westmorland. Even here, where there was a concentration of smelting sites, so that local demand was at its greatest, almost half the ore mined was shipped away for smelting.

The industry's ironmasters and entrepreneurs were drawn from at least fifteen families, and doubtless there were others whom I have not identified; in some families more than one member or one generation were involved. This figure does not include a group centred about a Salford linen draper, Henry Wrigley, who were lessees of mines at Adgardley about 1640; so far as I know they were the only non-Cumbrians involved in the iron industry.[73] Only one family, that of William Wright, appears to have had more than one smelting site in hand at once, although another three families at least operated both mines and smelters.[74] Most of these families were from the peerage or gentry, but William Wright and Thomas Addison rose into the ranks of the gentry by their efforts in the industry, and William Coates of Egremont, a yeoman, laid claim to the title even if no one else recognised him as a gentleman. Eight of these families leased or purchased additional premises to participate in the industry, signalling some positive intention to profit; only one of them leased the premises so acquired to a third party. Except for the Earl of Cumberland, those who developed iron interests on their own lands first leased them to others, and then, when profitability was demonstrated, sometimes took over the working themselves. The Earl of Cumberland waited until he had lost money on his works at Brougham before leasing them to William Wright. The most successful of the gentlemen entrepreneurs was William Pennington, esquire, who, as we have seen, leased iron ore and timber from the Earl of Northumberland, developed a trade in selling ore, and built a bloomsmithy on his own estates. But this was done after leasing woods and premises to another ironmaster, William Wright, and so gaining some insight into the trade. Perhaps the most adventurous entrepreneurs were Richard Patrickson, of Calder Abbey, esquire, and Thomas Addison, of Whitehaven. Patrickson built and operated the first known blast furnace in the area, at Cleator.[75] Perhaps Patrickson, and certainly Addison, experimented with coal for smelting; neither achieved commercial success.[76]

The most important ironmaster of the area in the early seventeenth century was William Wright. Wright, as indicated in the appendix, was definitely associated with seven smelting sites. Despite this he has received scant notice from the historians of the industry. Fell, who gave extensive coverage to William Rawlinson, the major ironmaster at the beginning of the eighteenth century, barely noticed Wright. Wright and family were mentioned in a footnote to a paper on a smelting site published by the Cumberland and Westmorland Antiquarian and Archaeological Society in 1914, and incidentally in another of the Society's papers about the excavation of Muncaster Head, published in 1970.[77] The latest of these peripheral notices is in B. G. Awty's excellent paper on the working of Force Forge between 1658 and 1663. So relatively little is known about William Wright. He was born in circumstances so obscure that one must infer the date of his birth from the date of his marriage in 1608; he died some time after 1667. On the strength of his career in the iron industry he rose into the ranks of the gentry and purchased the manor of Brougham. But he died in relative poverty, only just recovered from bankruptcy.

His career in the iron industry had definitely begun by 1611, when he was living at Burnbarrow as a 'hammerman' or 'forgeman'; four years later he was lessee of that works, which he was forced to abandon in 1622.[78] He built a bloomsmithy at Cunsey in 1618, and remained as lessee of this until 1659. In 1621 he acquired a half share in Force Forge, which he sold in 1658. In 1630 he built a bloomsmithy at Hacket, in Little Langdale. By 1633 he had left Furness and lived at Brougham, where he was lessee of an ironworks owned by the Clifford family, until 1643 Earls of Cumberland. While there he built the bloomsmithy at Muncaster Head, in west Cumberland, and bought the manor of Brougham.[79] He sold this in 1650 and moved to Milnthorpe, where he probably built the bloomsmithy. After he left Milnthorpe his movements become less clear, but between 1658 and 1664 he was at Snab, on a tributary of the Lune, and in 1667, at the age of eighty or so, at Blencarn, near Penrith.[80]

We know something in detail of the construction and operation of two of the bloomsmithies with which Wright was associated, and these give us a valuable insight into his competence as a builder, and into his smelting technology. The Muncaster Head works, which he contracted to build in 1636, was modified, after Wright had finished with it, by the introduction of cast iron hearth plates, but was otherwise much as he had built it when it was finally abandoned at the end of the century. Dr Tylecote's recent excavation has shown that the site was a well designed, well built example of a seventeenth-century bloomsmithy. Analysis of the slag and blooms found there suggests that it was an efficient smelter. When Wright sold his moiety of Force Forge in 1658 the new owners had to put the works into operating condition. The accounts for these repairs, and for the maintenance of the works between then and 1663, give a good idea of the works as operated by William Wright. As with Muncaster Head, Force Forge was well designed, comparing favourably with other works of its type. From the evidence of these two works it is clear that Wright was a competent exponent of known, established construction and smelting techniques.[81]

When one looks at Wright as the proprietor of ironworks it is possible to point to some deficiencies in his career. The problems facing the owner or operator of an ironworks were numerous: the variety of property rights affecting the works; the need to secure supplies of charcoal and iron ore, and the marketing of the finished product – these three involving also the expensive difficulties of transport. It was necessary to recruit and supervise labour, and to secure financial backing. Finally, there was the problem of competition. Wright may have been the most important ironmaster in Lakeland in his time, but he was not the only one, and compared to some of his competitors he was at a disadvantage. As an obscure man of low social status, he was at best a *parvenu* gentleman, and lacked influence in the area. He was also illiterate, which raised problems of management, especially in connection with his accounts. It is not possible to discuss his handling of all these problems, but he certainly had difficulties with property rights and competitors, while he seems to have been relatively successful in financing his works, at least until 1664.

The property rights involved in Wright's ironworks were complicated. Wright owned a freehold estate in only one of his works, Force Forge, of which he was but joint owner. He was the lessee or customary tenant or sub-tenant of the others, in the two latter circumstances subject to the customary jurisdiction of the manorial court. There were two further complications: water-powered bloomsmithies involved water rights; and all iron works required rights of access to bring in raw materials and bring out iron. A dispute over such complicated property rights, inflamed, no doubt, by an element of competition, forced Wright to abandon Burnbarrow works. The powerful George Preston, of Holker, esquire, claimed Wright was infringing his rights as lord of the water, and pulled down the dam and otherwise interfered with Wright's work there on at least three occasions.[82] Thus when he built the Hacket works in Little Langdale Wright was careful to take a lease of the river Brathay (as far as the lord of the manor owned it) in order to protect his water supply.[83] He may have had trouble over water at Cunsey, where he had to pay a tenant of the manor compensation for flooding his ground with the dam. In 1654, five years before Wright's lease of Cunsey was due to expire, this tenant transferred a piece of property affected by the dam to a third party with effect from the end of Wright's lease, a move which would have further complicated the water rights connected with Cunsey.[84] At Milnthorpe Wright and his successors were repeatedly in trouble with the manorial court for taking sods from the common wastes to use on the 'forge'. The leases for Cunsey works and the articles for the building of Muncaster Head specifically permit the graving of sods for building and maintaining the dam. This probably indicates their use at Milnthorpe, although it is just possible that the issue centred on the burning of peat taken from the waste in the forge.[85]

The financial problem facing the operator of an ironworks was, basically, that he had to pay for his raw materials before he had sold the

iron that would pay for the raw materials. He also had to find the capital
to build his works and keep them in repair, and he had to rent the
necessary premises. The sums involved were not insignificant. In 1623
Wright purchased wood for £250 to use over a period of time. In 1633 he
was offering the Earl of Northumberland £800 for wood. In 1636 he
entered contract to pay £111 per annum for the supply of ore.[86] To some
extent these burdens could be eased by payment in instalments, and there
is evidence that this was permitted. Wright also had to pay an annual
rent for some of his sites: £10 for Cunsey, £30 for Brougham. There is no
direct evidence as to how he financed payments such as these, but there is
evidence pointing to loans from the local gentry and merchants, and that
such people were perhaps partners with him. Certainly in a dispute
lasting from about 1618 to 1623 between Wright and the lessor of the
Cunsey site Gawen Braithwaite of Ambleside and Christopher Philipson
of Calgarth, esquires, arbitrated. At his death in 1634 Philipson had an
unspecified legal interest in Cunsey, and as his probate inventory includes
wood, charcoal and iron, as well as monies due in payment for iron sold,
it looks as though he was an active participant in the works, perhaps
Wright's partner. Philipson also had an interest in the Hacket works,
which three years before Wright had built and leased from the
Penningtons. Philipson had sub-let his interest in Hacket the previous
year to one of his servants, and in the year of his death had sub-let it to
Gawen Braithwaite, who claimed to hold it at his death in 1653.[87] Wright
probably had a similar connection with Roland Dawson, a prominent
Kendal mercer, who witnessed some of his Cunsey leases and
agreements, and was for a time joint owner with him of Force Forge.[88]
Among the witnesses to one of Wright's documents relating to Cunsey,
dated 1639, was Thomas Sleddall, mercer, of Penrith. When he died in
1647 Wright owed him £52, and when William Wright sold the manor of
Brougham in 1650 Roger Sleddall, son of Thomas, was amongst those
who quit-claimed the purchasers of any interest in the manor, suggesting
some financial connection with Wright.[89]

If Wright successfully channelled the surplus finance of landowners
and men of commerce towards his ironworks he was not always
successful in his dealings with them. Lacking social status and the
connections and influence that came with it, he sometimes suffered, and
his attempts to exploit resources in west Cumberland are a good example
of this difficulty. To him is perhaps due the credit for starting the
exploitation of haematite iron ore on the Earl of Northumberland's
estates at Egremont, administratively part of the Honour of
Cockermouth. As early as August 1633 Wright planned to lease a mine
there, and also to buy the earl's timber in Wastdale and Mitredale with
which to smelt the ore.[90] Wright's old associate, William Pennington,
lieutenant of the Honour, took over these negotiations and leased the
mine and woods for himself.[91] Wright found himself in a situation where

he was buying from Pennington 300 tons of ore a year between 1635 and 1638, only half of which could be smelted in a year by Wright and Pennington in partnership at Muncaster. The other half was carried the long and costly distance to Brougham, Force Forge or Cunsey. Such a journey would at least double the cost of the ore to about 14s per ton. Wright found himself expensively outmanoeuvred by Pennington, whose influence with the administrative officers of the Honour was much greater than his.[92]

So we have a picture of William Wright involved in the construction and operation of a number of iron-smelting sites. He was an efficient builder of efficient plant. Despite the complex problems involved in running an ironworks he managed, financed and operated as many as five at once, although he was occasionally overwhelmed by better placed competitors. What benefit did he derive from this career? He started from obscurity, with probably little or no personal wealth. The first sign of an improvement in his social status came with the marriage of his eldest son, Edward, with Anne, daughter of Thomas Middleton of Leighton Hall, esquire, before December 1628.[93] From 1630 onwards Wright refers to himself as 'gent'. His entry into the ranks of the gentry was confirmed in 1638 with the purchase of two-thirds of the manor of Brougham; this purchase was completed in 1640, when the final third was acquired. Brougham cost Wright £1,000, a measure of the sums at his disposal. It is possible to suggest the level of his income in 1640. In 1649, as a compounding Royalist, he claimed that Brougham was worth £26 per annum.[94] Doubtless this was an underestimate. In 1642 an annuity in lieu of dower of £16 per annum was agreed for the widow of the ex-owner of the two-thirds of the manor. Assuming a purchase rate of eighteen years, the sale price of £1,000 for the whole manor indicates an annual value of about £55. In 1640 Wright was working Cunsey, Brougham and probably Muncaster, and either working or letting out Force Forge and perhaps Hackett. Without knowing details one can only speculate, but in a lawsuit Wright claimed a clear yearly revenue of £40 from Burnbarrow[95] This is an optimistic claim when compared with the cash account losses of Force Forge between 1658 and 1663 to which B. G. Awty has pointed. If we accept this figure of £40 as a maximum income, and multiply by three for the three works in his possession, Wright had an income of £120, with more in some form from Force Forge and, perhaps, Hackett. At the high point of his career, then, a figure of £175 is possible as a speculative estimate of his income.

Wright sold the manor of Brougham, for £1,000, in 1650, and from there on his career was in decline. The Civil War had interrupted his work by interfering with supplies of ore and charcoal, although he did obtain these and did work. A possible Royalist in the first Civil War, and a sequestered one in the second, he must have lost money, although there is evidence only of the sequestration of the manor of Brougham. The composition fine for this, at £76, cannot, alone, have been responsible for forcing the sale of Brougham. Although various people associated with Wright quit-claimed the purchasers of the manor, there is no evidence in the deed of sale of payment of monies to creditors, as was often the case when an indebted man sold land. It may be that the sale of Brougham marks not financial crisis but merely the abandonment of the ironworks there. Nevertheless in the 1650s Wright was only certainly working Cunsey until 1659. He may have worked Force Forge until he sold that in 1658. The nature of his connection with Milnthorpe is unclear, but by 1664 he was not, if he ever had been, a proprietor of that works. Because Wright was buying ore in the early 1660s one can assume he was operating somewhere, perhaps at Snab. The description of him in the Stainton iron mine accounts as 'broke' in 1665 must indicate problems. However, there is some evidence of overproduction of iron in the area at this time, and Wright's difficulties may have been general. His emergence at about the age of eighty as the lessee of the iron mine at Woodend, near Egremont, while living at Blencarn in 1667, at best can have marked only a very brief recovery. In the end, then, he appears to have returned to the obscurity from which he came. Yet this is not the only judgement we must make of William Wright. In his heyday he was the major figure in the iron industry of the area, commanding an income comparable with that of many of the substantial gentry. It is the magnitude of his rise up the social scale, the breadth of his initiative and enterprise, and the long span of his successful career, from 1611 until 1664, which give us the measure of William Wright.

Despite the efforts of Wright and others in building up the Cumbrian iron industry, the absence of blast furnaces meant that the amount of iron produced was, roughly, only one-hundreth of national production in 1660. Nevertheless the increase in the number of permanent bloomsmithy smelting sites throughout the seventeenth century represents a massive expansion of smelting capacity which must have been significant for the economy of Cumbria. From the admittedly limited evidence of sales from Force Forge and Coniston, most of this expansion was directed to supplying the local market, partly at the expense of imported Spanish, Irish and even English iron, but also to meet an increase in demand. There were fourteen sites in operation in the first half of the century, and a situation may have come about in which competition between ironworks for the available market increased – and even in which production saturated the local market. Either difficulty is a possible explanation of the cash account losses of Force Forge between 1658 and 1663, and of Wright's bankruptcy in 1665. Nevertheless the building of new smelting sites from the 1670s (if my chronology in appendix 1.2 is correct) suggests a recovery and an increase in demand. In the Cumbrian iron industry the role of iron ore mining was perhaps more important than in other regions. Ore mining for export was virtually a separate industry: a result, primarily, of the proximity of high-grade ore to the coast, which made transport in bulk an economic proposition. Certainly the detailed accounts of the Langaron iron mine give an unusual insight into iron ore mining. The export of large quantities of Cumbrian ore in the seventeenth century was only a start. In the eighteenth century and especially in the nineteenth, when ore mining was at its peak, most of the ore was sent outside Cumbria.[96]

The trade in iron ore was one way in which the expanding iron industry of the seventeenth century helped to diversify the Cumbrian economy. The sales of ore from Workington, and especially Whitehaven, helped to establish the commercial life of those ports, at an earlier date than the formal customs records indicate.[97] Landowners who owned or worked iron ore mines were able to benefit from sales not only to the local industry but also to distant smelting sites. Without these shipments the demand for ore would have been financially insignificant for them. Not only the gentry and peerage but also the lower orders of society benefited from participation in the ore trade. In the home smelting industry a number of gentry owned one works, but there was only a single important ironmaster who was almost exclusively engaged in smelting: William Wright.

The iron industry was only one of a number of stimuli to the Cumbrian economy in this period. The economic backwardness of the north-west at the time has probably been exaggerated. Tenurial change, enclosure, agricultural improvement through fertilisers and experimentation were all under way in the early seventeenth century. Indeed, one of the leaders in this field was the iron ore entrepreneur Sir Patricius Curwen. Curwen was also involved in other industries in which expansion contributed to the growth of the Cumbrian economy: coal and lead mining, and salt making.[98] The expanding west Cumberland coalfield was the leading sector of this diversification, more especially in the second half of the century, but by that time Cumbria was already famous in the iron interest in midland England, Ireland, and even Scotland, for its iron ore if not its iron.

Appendix 1.1

List of smelting sites referred to

This is not a complete list of smelting sites in seventeenth-century Cumbria, merely an alphabetical list of those mentioned in the text; space prevents full details being given, but enough references are provided to support the statements in the text. I am grateful to Mr B. G. Awty, Mr M. Davies-Shiel and Dr R. T. Spence for information, acknowledged below, on some of the sites; any imperfections there may be in the list are my responsibility. Unless otherwise indicated, the works are bloomsmithies.

Backbarrow. Built 1685, blast furnace commenced 1711, working 1712 (Fell, *Early Iron Industry*, p. 200). Does the presence of William Wright in 1608–11 indicate an earlier works?

Bardsea. Cannot be accurately dated (Davies-Shiel, letter to present writer).

Beckermet, Branthwaite. No accurate dates; probably seventeenth-century (Davies-Shiel, letter).

Brigham. Working 1624–1801 (Davies-Shiel, letter). Working 1660.

Brougham. Worked for Earl of Cumberland 1619–23; rented to William Wright in 1641. (Chatsworth House, Duke of Devonshire's MSS, Londesborough MS Accounts of Receipts and Disbursements, Westmorland, 1619–23; Bolton MS book No. 272, Brougham and Whinfell Demesne rents. I owe these references to Dr R. T. Spence.) William Wright was at Brougham from 1633 until 1650; in 1647 Sir John Lowther of Lowther supplied wood to the 'forge' at Whinfell (C.R.O., D/Lons/L.A1/4, f. 105r). Probably a bloomsmithy.

Burblethwaite. In existence by 1682 (G. P. Jones, "The deeds of Burblethwaite Hall", *Trans. C.W.A.A.S.*, LXII (1962), pp. 177–78; *cf.* Fell, *op. cit.*, p. 199, who gives a date of 1711), but Awty (forthcoming article) suggests that it was in existence in the early 1670s.

Burnbarrow. In existence 1609; leased to William Wright in 1615 and closed by about 1622 (Fell, *op. cit.*, pp. 200–1; P.R.O., DL.4/77/45).

Cark-Shaws, in Cartmel. Owned by Thomas Preston of Holker in 1685, but his family had a 'forge' in 1636 and probably in the 1620s. (*Ibid.*; C.R.O., D/Lec., box 240, Langaron ore accounts, 1635–38; Fell, *op. cit.*, pp. 199–200.) Working 1660.

Cleator. Caine, *Cleator and Cleator Moor*, pp. 216–21: blast furnace in 1690s (Schubert, *History of British Iron and Steel Industry*, p. 371). William Stout, writing in 1689 and 1709, makes no mention of this furnace. However, Patrickson died in 1705, and the furnace may have ceased working then; and Stout refers only to Furness. (J. D. Marshall, ed., *The Autobiography of William Stout* (Chetham Soc., 3rd ser., XIV, p. 294.) I owe this reference to Dr. W. H. Chaloner.

Coniston. Starting date uncertain, first quarter of seventeenth century. Iron from it sold in 1653, wood sold to it 1658–59; 1653–59 worked by Kirkby family of Kirkby Ireleth Hall. 1674 in hands of Sir Daniel Fleming, lord of the manor of Coniston, and mentioned in his will in 1701. Working 1713. (Fell, *op. cit.*, pp. 195–6; Kendall, *Iron Ores of Great Britain*, p. 17; C.R.O.K., D/Ry. HMC. 338, 339; D/Ry. box 56, charcoal papers; D/Ry. [original] MS k; J. R. Magrath, ed., *The Flemings in Oxford*, vol. III (Oxford Historical Society, LXXIX, 1924), p. 468). Working 1660.

Cunsey. Supposedly the sixteenth-century bloomsmithy; rebuilt by William Wright about 1618, having leased the land from the Sandys family of Graythwaite Hall. Lease renewed in 1638 to Wright's youngest son, Alexander. William Wright working this in 1657. Perhaps reverted to the Sandys family after 1659. (L.R.O., DDSa. Cunsey deeds; Davies-Shiel, *Trans. C.W.A.A.S.*, LXXI, p. 281; Fell, *op. cit.*, pp. 191–2; P.R.O., PL.6/22/144.) Working 1660.

Cunswick. A works, probably a bloomsmithy, here in 1674, from which Charles Russell was recruited to Coniston by Sir Daniel Fleming. Fleming's original MS refers to 'Conswick', not Cunsey as Fell, *op. cit.*, pp. 192, 195, suggests.

Fell Foot. Information by letter from Davies-Shiel. Working 1660.

Force Forge. Built by 1616; half freehold interest purchased by William Wright in 1621, which he sold in 1658. Worked by Thomas Rawlinson for the Fell Family: 1658–63 accounts survive. This site owned by Rawlinson in 1685. (L.R.O., DDSa. Force Forge papers; L.R.O., DDHj. Force Forge papers; *I.A. Lake Counties*, p. 242; Fell, *op. cit.*, pp. 193–5; Norman Penney, ed., *The Household Account Book of Sarah Fell of Swarthmoor Hall* (Cambridge, 1920); B. G. Awty is about to publish an article on Force Forge in the seventeenth century.) Working 1660.

Hacket. Built in 1630 by William Wright; land and water rights leased from the Pennington family of Muncaster. (Fell, *op. cit.*, pp. 196–9.) Working 1660.

Hornby. References to Hornby 'forge' between 1635 and 1640, *Melling Parish Register* (L.P.R.S., XL) pp. 9, 13, 16. (I owe this reference to Mr B. G. Awty.) Nature of works unclear.

Irton family, 'forge'. Referred to in Langaron mine accounts, 1635–38 (C.R.O., D/Lec. box 240). Davies-Shiel's map (*I.A. Lake Counties*, p. 122) indicates a number of possible sites close to the family's home at Irton, near Egremont. Nature of works unclear.

Kendal. Reference to a 'forge' 1606 in *Kendal Parish Register,* vol. IV (C.W.A.A.S., Parish Register section, XXXIX, 1960) p. 262. I owe this reference to Mr B. G. Awty. Nature of works unclear.

Millom. J. Nicholson and R. Burn, *The History and Antiquities of the Counties of Westmorland and Cumberland* (2 vols; London, 1777), II, p. 13. Nature of works unclear.

Milnthorpe. Probably built by William Wright 1650–53, and operated by him perhaps until the mid-1650s. His son, Balthazar Wright, was bloomer there until his death in 1688. In 1664 the works were jointly owned by Sir George Middleton of Leighton Hall and the Leybourne family of Cunswick. Reported in 1692 as having lately become a paper mill. (Fell, *op. cit.*, pp. 203–5; L.R.O., DDTo. H/13 [the two agreements besides that of 1664, referred to in the *Guide to the Lancashire Record Office* (2nd. edn, Preston, 1962), p. 181, could not be found when I visited the office]; Thomas Machell, *An Antiquary on Horseback,* ed. Jane M. Ewbank (C.W.A.A.S., extra series, XIX, 1963), p. 54; Levens Hall MSS, Milnthorpe court rolls.) Working 1660.

Muncaster Head. See Tylecote and Cherry, *Trans. C.W.A.A.S.,* LXX. Built by William Wright 1636–37. Working 1660.

Ulpha. Davies-Shiel (letter) says built 1625 and working 1671. Probably the 'Mr. Hudleston's forge' referred to in Langaron mine accounts, 1635–38 (C.R.O., D/Lec. box 240); 1640 reference is C.R.O.K., D/Ry. [original] MS R, f. 120. Working 1660.

Appendix 1.2

Chronological list of smelting sites, giving earliest known date for each site

1606	Kendal	1635	Hornby
1609	Burnbarrow	1636	Muncaster Head
1616	Force Forge	1636	Irton family's 'forge'
?1616	Coniston	1653	Milnthorpe
1618	Cunsey (rebuilt)	1670s	Burblethwaite
1619	Brougham	1674	Cunswick
1624	Brigham	1675	Fell Foot (certainly)
?1624	Fell Foot	1670s–1680s	Cleator
1625	Ulpha	1685	Backbarrow
1620s	Cartmel	1690s	Millom
1630	Hacket	1690s	Cleator (blast furnace)

Notes

1   The terminology of smelting sites used in this essay is that proposed by the Historical Metallurgy Group and set out by M. Davies-Shiel, 'The terminology of early iron smelting in Lakeland', *Transactions of the Cumberland and Westmorland Antiquarian and Archaeological Society,* new series [hereafter *Trans. C.W.A.A.S.*], LXXI (1971), pp. 280–4. Where there is any doubt about the nature of a works the general term 'ironworks' is used; the word 'forge' is used only as a contemporary quotation to describe a works. Cumbria in this essay comprises the old counties of Cumberland and Westmorland and the Furness district of Lancashire, not quite coterminous with the present-day Cumbria.

2   M. W. Flinn, 'The growth of the English iron industry, 1660–1760', *Econ. Hist. Rev.,* 2nd ser., XI (1959), p. 144, reviews the 'decline thesis', and (p. 146) lists new blast furnaces built. G. Hammersley, 'The Crown woods and their exploitation in the sixteenth and seventeenth centuries', *Bull. Inst. Hist. Research,* XXX (1957), pp. 136–61; and *id.,* 'The charcoal iron industry and its fuel, 1540–1750', *Econ. Hist. Rev.,* 2nd ser., XXVI (1973), pp. 593, 595, 597, 606, revises views on charcoal consumption and availability.

3   H. A. Fletcher, 'The archaeology of the west Cumberland iron trade', *Trans. C.W.A.A.S.* [old series], V (1880); J. D. Kendall, *The Iron Ores of Great Britain and Ireland* (London, 1893) and A. Fell, *The Early Iron Industry of Furness and District* (Ulverston, 1908; repr., London, 1968).

4   J. D. Marshall and M. Davies-Shiel, *The Industrial Archaeology of the Lake Counties* (Newton Abbot, 1969) [hereafter *I.A. Lake Counties*]; Davies-Shiel, *Trans. C.W.A.A.S.,* LXXI, pp. 280–4.

5   Detailed references to these and other smelting sites are given in appendix 1.1; for their location see fig. 1.1.

6   This figure is based on B. G. Awty's calculations of production at Force Forge between 1658 and 1663 (in his forthcoming article in *Trans. C.W.A.A.S.*) and on contemporary statements of production at Burnbarrow (Public Record Office, London [hereafter P.R.O.], Duchy of Lancaster, depositions, DL. 4/77/45) and at Muncaster (*Calendar of the Proceedings of the Committee for Compounding, etc, 1643–60,* ed. M. A. E. Green (5 vols; London, 1889–92), p. 384). I am grateful to Mr B. G. Awty for allowing me to read his work on Force Forge; the records of the

works are Lancashire County Record Office [hereafter L.R.O.], Harte-Jackson MSS, DDHj.

7 Hammersley, *Econ. Hist. Rev.,* 2nd ser., XXVI, p. 602, estimates that 24,000 tons of pig iron were produced in 1650; Flinn, *Econ. Hist. Rev.,* 2nd ser., XI, p. 147, n. 2, states that 27 cwt of pig made one ton of bar iron.

8 Hammersley, *Bull. Inst. Hist. Res.,* XXX, pp. 144, 154, 160–1; 'Technique or economy? The rise and decline of the early English copper industry, *c.* 1550–1660', *Business History,* XV (1973), pp. 19–20.

9 *I.A. Lake Counties,* p. 165.

10 Charlotte Kipling, 'Some documentary evidence on woodlands in the vicinity of Windermere', *Trans. C.W.A.A.S.,* LXXIV (1974), pp. 86–7.

11 Cumbria County Record Office, Kendal [hereafter C.R.O.K.], Fleming of Rydal MSS, D/Ry. [original] MS R, f. 145.

12 Cumbria County Record Office, Carlisle [hereafter C.R.O.], Pennington of Muncaster MSS, D/Pen. 185/17, articles of agreement, 24 September 1636; C.R.O., Leconfield MSS, D/Lec., box 240, memorandum dated 19 April 1639.

13 C.R.O.K., D/Ry. box 56.

14 Their wills are L.R.O., Kendal deanery wills and inventories.

15 G. R. Morton, 'The use of peat in the reduction of iron ore', *Iron and Steel,* XXXVIII, No. 9 (August 1965), pp. 421–4.

16 *Calendar of State Papers, Domestic, 1691–92,* pp. 137, 518, 523; *ibid., 1693,* p. 114. Addison had interests in iron-ore mines by this time.

17 Fell, *Early Iron Industry,* chapters I–IV, p. 88; O. Wood, 'The development of the coal, iron and shipbuilding industries of west Cumberland, 1750–1914' (London University unpublished Ph.D. thesis, 1952), p. 8.

18 L.R.O., DDHj, Force Forge papers; L.R.O., Sandes of Graythwaite MSS, DDSa 2/5.

19 For Wright's purchases from Langaron see below, p. 00; for his lease of the Woodend iron ore mine see L.R.O., Townley–O'Hagan MSS, DDTo. H/13. The ore used at Muncaster Head was analysed by R. F. Tylecote and J. Cherry, 'The seventeenth-century bloomery at Muncaster Head', *Trans. C.W.A.A.S.,* LXXI (1970), pp. 88, 96.

20 E. Straker, *Wealden Iron* (London, 1931), pp. 218, 238, 248, 278, 293, 308, 378, 413, 425; at Snape ore was, exceptionally, carted to the furnace (p. 289), while at Goseen (p. 417) the distance from ore supplies is suggested as a reason for closure.

21 R. A. Pelham, 'The establishment of the Willoughby ironworks in north Warwickshire in the sixteenth century', *University of Birmingham Historical Journal,* IV (1953–54), p. 28; R. S. Smith, 'Sir Frances Willoughby's ironworks, 1570–1610', *Renaissance and Modern Studies,* XI (1967), pp. 92, 98, 102, 103, 115, 134–5.

22 A. Raistrick and E. Allen, 'The south Yorkshire ironmasters, 1690–1750', *Econ. Hist. Rev.,* IX (1939), p. 173.

23 For Muncaster see below, pp. 00–00; for Force Forge, L.R.O., DDHj, Force Forge papers.

24 One instance of a new venture is the scythe mill at Prior Hall, built in 1614 (H. R. Schubert, *History of the British Iron and Steel Industry* (London, 1957), p. 191).

25 C.R.O.K., D/Ry. [original] MS k. I owe the identification of Richard Harrison as the writer of this manuscript to the archivist-in-charge at Kendal, Miss S. J. Macpherson.

26 C.R.O., Earl of Lonsdale's MSS, D/Lons/W, Sir Patricius Curwen's steward's account book, 1626–46 (no foliation).

27   L.R.O., DDSa. 16/5.
28   C.R.O., D/Lec. Lead mining papers, account dated 17 April 1647.
29   Such entries are to be found in the port books for the ports of Carlisle and
     Lancaster, P.R.O., Exchequer, King's Remembrancer, Port Books, E. 190.
     The information on Force Forge is the work of Mr Awty.
30   The accounts for the mine from March 1635 to Michaelmas 1638 are
     C.R.O., D/Lec., box 240; from 1638 to 1658 the accounts are Alnwick
     Castle, Duke of Northumberland's MSS [hereafter Alnwick Castle MSS]
     X.II.3(8a), 3(10). I am grateful to his Grace the Duke of Northumberland
     for permission to consult his papers, and to his agent, Mr D. P. Graham,
     and to the Northumberland County Record Office for facilitating my visit.
     Further reference to both sets of accounts will only be given for purposes of
     clarity.
31   No copy of the 1635 lease survives; the 1638 lease is C.R.O., D/Lec.
     16/133.
32   Nothing in the accounts of the iron mine adds to the descriptions of iron ore
     mining given by Fell, *Early Iron Industry,* pp. 74–87, or by Raistrick and
     Allen, *Econ. Hist. Rev.,* IX, p. 173, or by Schubert, *History of the British
     Iron and Steel Industry,* pp. 209–18, except that Pennington's pits seem to
     have had a longer productive life.
33   The lease is C.R.O., D/Lec. 16/134. From 1658 the surviving fragmentary
     accounts are D/Lec., box 240.
34   *Cal. Committee for Compounding,* I, p. 384; C. A. Parker, *The Gosforth
     District* (Kendal, 1904), pp. 48–52.
35   Hammersley, *Business History,* XV, pp. 25–7.
36   Alnwick Castle MSS, X.II. 3(10), Pennington to Hugh Potter, 25 January
     1634/35.
37   John Ogilby, *Britannia, or an Illustration of The Kingdom of England*
     (London, 1675), ed. A. Duckham (London, 1939), plate 96.
38   Wood, thesis (1952), pp. 8, 70–71.
39   This fell to 3*s* 4*d* in 1640 but rose to 4*s* again in 1641.
40   L.R.O., Cavendish of Holker MSS, DDCa.1/106; for Workington see
     below, p. 00; J. D. Marshall, 'The domestic economy of the Lakeland
     yeoman, 1660–1749', *Trans. C.W.A.A.S.,* LXXIII (1973), p. 209.
41   C.R.O., D/Lons/W, Sir Patricius Curwen's steward's account book (no
     foliation).
42   L.R.O., DDCa.1/106.
43   B. L. C. Johnson, 'The iron industry of Cheshire and north Staffordshire',
     Trans. North Staffs. Field Club (1953–54), pp. 36–7.
44   This paragraph is based on my 'The gentry in Cumberland and
     Westmorland, 1600–65' (University of Lancaster unpublished Ph.D. thesis,
     1973), pp. 195–8.
45   This price, which did not include the cost of transporting ore from the mine,
     compares with 4*s* 6*d* per ton for the ore bought by Force Forge between
     1658 and 1663, and 8*s* per ton for ore sold at Stainton in 1665. (L.R.O.,
     DDHj, Force Forge papers; L.R.O., DDCa.1/106.)
46   Trade in iron ore between southern England and Ireland is noted in H. F.
     Kearney, 'Richard Boyle – ironmaster', *Jnl. Roy. Soc. Antiquaries of
     Ireland,* LXXXIII (1953), and J. H. Andrews, 'Notes on the historical
     geography of the Irish iron industry', *Irish Geography,* III, No. 3 (1956).
     Andrews, and Schubert, *History of the British Iron and Steel Industry,* p.
     191, briefly notice the Cumbrian trade. A sixteenth-century trade in ore
     from Furness to Rossendale was suggested by J. Kerr, 'On the remains of
     some old bloomeries formerly existing in Lancashire', *Trans. Hist. Soc.
     Lancs. and Ches.,* XII (1872), pp. 65–70.

47   C. R. O., D/Lons/W, Sir Patricius Curwen's steward's account book (no foliation), 1626–46. There is nothing to suggest that this trade started in 1626, as the Curwen mines were worked before that date (C.R.O., D/Lons/L. A1/4, f. 8v.) But the port books for some Ulster ports, 1612–15 (Leeds City Library, Temple Newsham MSS, TN/PO/7/I/1, 3, 4) and Workington (P.R.O., E. 190/1448/1) make no reference to it.
48   P.R.O., State Papers, Domestic, Committee for Compounding, S.P. 23/179/580; C.R.O., D/Lons/W, Curwen rental, 1660. In the eighteenth century iron ore from Harrington was again mined (Edward Hughes, *North Country Life in the Eighteenth Century*, II, *Cumberland and Westmorland*, 1700–1800 (London, 1965), p. 205.
49   For Hill see *D.N.B.*, *sub* Arthur Hill; *Calendar of the Patent and Close Rolls of Chancery in Ireland, of the reign of Charles I, first to eighth year inclusive*, ed. J. Morrin (Dublin, 1863) p. 569. For the works see Sir William Brereton, *Travels in Holland, The United Provinces, England, Scotland and Ireland, 1634–35*, ed. Edward Hawkins (Chetham Society publications, I, 1844) p. 128; E. McCracken, 'Charcoal-burning ironworks in seventeenth and eighteenth century Ireland', *Ulster Journal of Archaeology*, XX (1957), pp. 127, 129; Morrin, *op. cit.*, p. 65; J. O'Laverty, *An Historical Account of the Diocese of Down and Connor* (2 vols; Dublin, 1878–80), II, pp. 241, 367.
50   T. W. Moody, *The Londonderry Plantation, 1609–41* (Belfast, 1939), p. 344.
51   For gentry incomes see my thesis, appendix II.
52   Alnwick Castle MSS, X.II.3(10), Pennington to Potter, 25 January 1634/35.
53   Fell, *Early Iron Industry*, pp. 191, 196–7.
54   Pennington's arrangements are detailed in Alnwick Castle MSS, X.II.3(8a), articles of agreement, 31 March 1636; C.R.O., D/Pen. 185/17, articles of agreement, 24 September 1636. See below, p. 00.
55   Alnwick Castle MSS, X.II.3(8a), Pennington to Potter, 12 April 1639.
56   For Coote and Rawdon see *D.N.B.*; I have not been able to identify Thomas Dawson, but he and Coote are bracketed together in the accounts, which may indicate a connection.
57   For Coote's works and shipping arrangements see McCracken, *Ulster Jnl. Arch.*, XX, p. 131; *ibid.*, XXVIII (1965), pp. 133, 135, and sources there cited.
58   P.R.O., E. 190/1448/8.
59   For Addison's ore interests see Marshall, *Trans. C.W.A.A.S.*, LXXIII, p. 209; C. Caine, *Cleator and Cleator Moor: Past and Present* (Kendal, 1916) pp. 203–4; as early as 1686 he was probably a partner in the Langaron mine, and was joint lessee under the 1692 lease (C.r.o., d-lec., box 240, summary of accounts; D/Lec. 17/125). See also Johnson, *Trans. North Staffs. Field Club*, p. 36.
60   McCracken, *Ulster Jnl. Arch.*, XX, p. 127.
61   P.R.O. E. 190/1448/8.
62   Bradshaigh may have taken this lease in his own interest, or in that of his wife, Pennington's daughter. There is nothing in his surviving papers to link the lease of the mine with the ironworks at his home, Haigh, in Lancashire, established by 1662 (B. G. Awty, 'Charcoal ironmasters of Lancashire and Cheshire, 1600–1785', *Trans. Hist. Soc. Lancs. and Ches.*, CIX (1957), p. 83. I am grateful to the Earl of Crawford and Balcarres for permission to consult his muniments in the John Rylands University Library of Manchester.)
63   The lease is C.R.O., D/Lec. 16/134.

64 C.R.O., D/Lec. 17/127, 128.

65 The few auditor's accounts which survive for these years (C.R.O., D/Lec., box 240) with the summary show that the royalty payments recorded on the summary were sometimes delayed. Thus for October 1670 the summary records payment of £50; in fact the auditor's vouchers show that 445 tons were mined in the year ending October 1670. £50 of the royalty was paid then, and the balance of £50 2s 6d secured by bond due Lady Day 1671; this was paid, but the receipt is included in the summary under 1671. Without a complete set of vouchers it is, therefore, impossible to calculate annual production figures.

66 Neither the copy Irish customs accounts 1683–86, nor the Customs and Excise accounts for 1698–1700 referred to by Andrews, *Irish Geographer,* III, p. 146, record ports of origin of Irish ore imports. P.R.O. E. 190/1448/8; Awty, *Trans. Hist. Soc. Lancs. and Ches.,* CIx, p. 87; G. Benn, *A History of the Town of Belfast* (2 vols; London, 1887, 1880), I, p. 335; Fell, *Early Iron Industry,* p. 88, and Kendall, *Iron Ores of Great Britain,* p. 8, refer to some destinations of Whitehaven ore.

67 W. I. Macadam, 'The ancient iron industry of Scotland', *Proc. Soc. Antiquaries of Scotland,* XXI (1886–87), pp. 109–15. The Scottish Record Office has no customs accounts for this area.

68 I have searched Scottish customs records of west coast ports known to have trading links with Cumbria, to no avail. Lochaber, referred to in P.R.O., E. 190/1448/8, could be in Kirkcudbrightshire or Inverness.

69 L.R.O., DDCa.1/106.

70 L.R.O., DDHj, Force Forge papers, 1685.

71 I have not been able to identify Mr Kensham.

72 Sir George Rawdon's name is variously spelt in the accounts; his agent was in Lancashire at this time (*Calendar of State Papers, Ireland, 1663–65,* p. 602).

73 L.R.O., Hopwood of Hopwood MSS, DDHp.34/1–5.

74 The Earl of Cumberland, the Pennington family of Muncaster, and Thomas Addison.

75 Schubert, *History of the British Iron and Steel Industry,* p. 371.

76 R. P. Littledale, 'Some notes on the Patricksons of Ennerdale', *Trans. C.W.A.A.S.,* XXV (1925), p. 165.

77 Fell, *Early Iron Industry,* pp. 191, 192, 194, 196, 200–1; J. W. Jackson, 'On the discovery of a bloomery at Lindale Church', *Trans. C.W.A.A.S.,* XIV (1914), p. 261; Tylecote and Cherry, *ibid.,* LXX, pp. 71–2.

78 Wright's movements in Furness until about 1625 can be followed in *Cartmel Parish Register, 1559–1661* (Lancashire Parish Register Society [hereafter L.P.R.S.], XXVIII) and H.S. Cowper, ed., *The Oldest Register Book of the Parish of Hawkshead in Lancashire, 1568–1704* (London, 1897). Detailed references to Wright's involvement with the works named in the following paragraphs are to be found in the appendix.

79 The deeds relating to Wright's purchase and sale of Brougham manor are C.R.O.K., Hothfield MSS, D/Ho., box 12: Brougham bundle.

80 Fell, *Early Iron Industry,* p. 194; P.R.O., Chancery proceedings, C. 10/72/165; P.R.O., Palatinate of Lancaster, proceedings: bills, PL.6/22/84, PL.6/22/94, PL.6/22/144; L.R.O., DDTo.H/13.

81 Tylecote and Cherry, *Trans. C.W.A.A.S.,* LXX, pp. 69–109 (*cf. Post-medieval Archaeology,* II (1968), p. 192); for Force Forge see B. G. Awty's paper.

82 P.R.O., DL.4/77/45.

83 C.R.O., D/Pen. bundle 46, No. 3.

84 The compensation was deducted from Wright's rent for the site, L.R.O., DDSa.2/6, 2/13.
85 Milnthorpe court rolls (Levens Hall, near Kendal, MSS of Mr and Mrs O. R. Bagot, to whom I am grateful for permission to consult them), October 1654, 1656, 1657, 1664. The October 1666 roll contains a paine against the burning of sods from the commons, which included mosses, in the tenants' houses. G. R. Morton (n. 15 above) suggests that peat was not used at Milnthorpe.
86 C.R.O., D/Pen., bundle 46, No. 58; C.R.O., D/Lec., letters, 1633; Alnwick Castle MSS, X.II.3(8a), articles of agreement, 31 March, 1636.
87 L.R.O., DDSa.2/5, 2/6; L.R.O., Kendal deanery wills and inventories. Philipson's interest in Hacket must have been a sub-tenancy under, or an assignment of, the 1631 lease to William Wright. The 1631 lease would have expired in 1652, but Gawen Braithwaite's heir engaged in a lawsuit to retain the premises (C.R.O., D/Pen., bundle 46, No. 60).
88 L.R.O., DDSa.2/6, 2/8, 2/11; 16/2.
89 L.R.O., DDSa.2/11; C.R.O., MSS of the Dean and Chapter of Carlisle, Machell family papers, vol. IV, No. 97 (I am grateful to the Dean and Chapter for permission to consult their archives); C.R.O.K., D/Ho., box 12; Brougham bundle.
90 C.R.O., D/Lec., letters, 1633.
91 For these negotiations see above, p. 00; Pennington's purchase of the woods is C.R.O., D/Lec., box 240, memorandum dated 19 April 1639.
92 There are a number of well informed petitions and complaints against Pennington in the archives of the Earl of Northumberland, for some of which the information may have come from Wright. C.R.O., D/Lec. 265/155, petition of John Salkeld; Alnwick Castle MSS, X.II.3(10), accounts and notes of Langaron iron mine to Michaelmas 1636; C.R.O., D/Lec., box 240, document endorsed 'Information of Mr. Pennington Intreiques in taking the iron mines and to buy Mosdale woods cheap'.
93 For the marriage see William Hutton, *The Beetham Repository, 1770*, ed. J. R. Ford (C.W.A.A.S. Tract Series, VII, 1906), p. 152. (I owe this reference to Mr. C. R. Hudleston.)
94 P.R.O., S.P.23/227/937.
95 P.R.O., DL.4/77/45.
96 Wood, thesis, p. 71; chapter IX, *passim*.
97 See T. S. Willan, *The English Coasting Trade 1600–1750* (Manchester, 1938), pp. 183–8; id., *Studies in Elizabethan Foreign Trade* (Manchester, 1959), p. 89. The records of the Lowther of Whitehaven and Curwen of Workington families are the main sources for the early seventeenth-century trade of these ports.
98 Phillips, thesis, pp. 344–6, 350, summarises these arguments. For the coal industry see J. U. Nef, *The Rise of the British Coal Industry* (2 vols; London, reprinted 1966), I, pp. 69–72; *I.A. Lake Counties*, pp. 105–10.

Bibliographical note

B. G. Awty's paper on Force Forge, referred to in the text as forthcoming, has appeared in *Trans. C.W.A.A.S.*, n.s., LXXVII (1977), entitled 'Force Forge in the Seventeenth Century'.

I have dealt more extensively with William Wright and his family in 'William Wright: Cumbrian ironmaster', *Transactions of the Lancashire and Cheshire Antiquarian Society*, LXXIX, and interest in Wright's presence at Blencarn (above, p. 20) is intensified by evidence of iron mining in nearby Milburn Fell in D. Welch, 'Three Elizabethan documents concerning Milburn Fell', *Trans. C.W.A.A.S.*, LXXV (1975).

M. J. Galgano's claim, in 'Iron-mining in Restoration Furness: the case of Sir Thomas Preston', *Recusant History*, XIII, No. 2 (1976), that about 1664 Sir Thomas Preston of the Manor built a blast furnace is not substantiated by the evidence Galgano cites, some of which relates to lime kilns and not to the iron industry (see *Recusant History*, May 1977).

Acknowledgements

I am grateful to Professor Owen Ashmore, of the Department of Extra-mural Studies at Manchester University, who read the essay in typescript, and to the staff of the Cumbria Archives Service for help and advice. The responsibility for any errors is mine.

Cattle droving in the seventeenth century

A Yorkshire example[1]

... the inland trade, of which the coasting trade was a part, needs much fuller investigation if we are to understand the economy of England in the seventeenth and eighteenth centuries.[2]

I

When the second edition of his classic study *The English Coasting Trade, 1600–1750* appeared in 1967 Professor Willan suggested that if he were to rewrite the book 'it would be a different book ... but I do not think it would tell a very different story'. His review of the literature that had appeared on the coasting trade since the first edition of 1938 left him disappointed that so little had been done to follow his lead.[3] However, the failure of others to follow is largely a tribute to the success of the original study. Similarly, Professor Willan's study of the development of the river network, which appeared in 1936,[4] has not been superseded. Both books remain essential reading for scholars of the pre-industrial period.

Most years see the appearance of a new batch of specialised monographs dealing with English overseas trade,[5] but the development of inland trade remains sadly neglected. A major cause of this imbalance in historical enquiry is the inadequacy of the sources relating to inland trade, and especially to overland trade. The absence of internal customs barriers may have been conducive to economic development, but it is a deficiency to be lamented by the economic historian. For the historian of overland trade there are no great quarries of information such as the port books and other customs records which can be plundered by the historian of overseas trade. A study of overland trade must proceed by the piecing together of scattered references or by the reconstruction of trading patterns from business records.[6]

The relative difficulty of studying overland trade can be illustrated
briefly by the early history of the Anglo-Irish livestock trade.[7] During the
seventeenth century Ireland, like Scotland, was considered a foreign
country for customs purposes, so the details of Anglo-Irish trade can be
obtained from the English port books. By collating the information thus
obtained with contemporary estimates of the scale of the livestock trade
it is possible to establish the broad lines of its development. Few Irish
beasts were sent to English markets at the start of the seventeenth
century, but numbers grew considerably down to the Civil War, when
there was a sharp break in the trade. Recovery set in at some point
during the 1650s, and in the 1660s, before the trade was ended by the
Act of 1667, some 60,000 Irish cattle and 100,000 Irish sheep were
shipped each year to English ports. How many Irish beasts entered
England between 1600 and 1667 will never be known but the number
was certainly greater than a million and perhaps amounted to several
millions in total.

Few traces have been discovered of the progress of these sizable flocks
and herds across England. Some Irish stock was sold to farmers or
butchers in the immediate neighbourhood of the port of entry; at his
death in 1601 Robert Brerewood, a wealthy Chester glover, owned
twenty-eight 'Irish Kine'.[8] In 1664–65 Edward Backwell, the great
Restoration financier, in partnership with Colonel Charles Wheeler,
bought ninety-six cattle in Ireland, of which ninety-three arrived safely in
Chester, where they were promptly sold.[9] However, it is not certain
whether Backwell was selling to local butchers and farmers or to English
drovers. Sometimes Irish drovers kept control of the stock in England; in
1665 some Irish drovers, failing to sell their cattle at Carlisle, proceeded
to Norwich in the hope of selling them there.[10] No doubt the majority of
Irish beasts were destined for the rapidly expanding metropolitan market,
but the evidence to support this suggestion is scanty.[11] The accounts of
the Toke family, who farmed in Kent and specialised in fattening beasts
for the London market, contain only a single reference to Irish stock; in
1661 twenty-one Irish steers were purchased at Charing fair.[12] Similarly
Edward Backwell occasionally bought Irish stock for fattening on his
estate at Creslow in Buckinghamshire, but the bulk of his purchases were
of English stock most of which he sold not at Smithfield but on contract
to the victuallers of the navy.[13]

The paucity of references to the movement of cattle and sheep in
England is not unique to the Irish branch of the trade. The standard
accounts of English, Scottish and Welsh droving provide little detailed
information about the seventeenth century.[14] In particular the economics
of seventeenth-century cattle droving are almost completely unexplored.
In this situation the discovery of detailed accounts relating to the
movement of no more than 107 cattle, belonging to Michael Warton of

Beverley, from the East Riding of Yorkshire to Smithfield assumes considerable importance.

II

Michael Warton, Member of Parliament for Beverley, died in London in 1688, aged sixty-five.[15] He had arrived in London from Beverley on 2 July and seems to have been taken ill early in August. On 5 August a 'bottle of spirit of salt' was acquired for him, and on the following day Dr Lister received £1 1s 6d, 'his first fee for coming to Mr Warton'. On 7 August 5s was paid to 'a surgeon for letting Mr Warton's blood', and on the following day a 'glister', or enema, was acquired for him. Despite the attentions of two more doctors, Dr Needham and Dr Lower, Michael Warton died on 9 August.[16] His corpse was carried back to Yorkshire with great pomp and ceremoniously buried in Beverley Minster on 23 August 1688.[17]

The bulk of Michael Warton's estate passed to his eldest son, Sir Michael Warton, although his younger sons, Charles and Ralph, received legacies and were appointed executors. In their roles as executors Charles and Ralph kept careful accounts, two volumes of which have survived.[18] These volumes provide a great deal of information relating to the estate, including the details of driving cattle to London which form the central subject of this essay. In addition a rental of Michael Warton's Yorkshire estate has survived for 1684–85 and provides useful additional information.[19]

Michael Warton came from a well established gentry family. His grandfather, also called Michael, had been knighted in 1617 during his year as Sheriff of Yorkshire and he is classified as a member of the upper gentry of Yorkshire in J. T. Cliffe's recent book.[20] This first Sir Michael Warton was prominent among the disaffected gentry of Yorkshire during the 1630s but he pledged his support to the Crown on the outbreak of the Civil War and reputedly lent £20,000 to Charles I.[21] Sir Michael Warton's son – another Michael and the father of our Michael Warton – was Member of Parliament for Beverley in 1640. He took up arms in the Royalist cause and died in 1645 at the siege of Scarborough Castle. Thus, as a result of his father's early death, our Michael Warton became his grandfather's heir and enjoyed the estates from the old man's death in 1655[22] until his own death in 1688. Both the first Sir Michael and his grandson were fined for their delinquency during the Civil War,[23] although the subsequent history of the estate makes it certain that Sir Michael Warton did not experience 'the total ruin of his fortune' caused by 'the unrelenting severity of fanatic intolerance, and revolutionary hate' as one historian of Beverley suggested.[24]

The exact size of the estate during Michael Warton's tenure (1655–88) cannot be established, although there is no doubt that it was extensive.

Michael Warton's son and heir, the second Sir Michael Warton, died in
1725 and the estate then passed to his three married sisters.[25] However,
the estate was not formally divided until 1775, when a private Act of
Parliament was obtained.[26] A schedule, drawn up in 1774, was attached
to the Act and reveals that in 1725 the Warton estate amounted to
12,540 acres valued at nearly £240,000 in 1774. In addition standing
timber on the estate was valued at nearly £11,500. The bulk of the estate
was in the East Riding, although there was a considerable area owned in
north Lincolnshire, together with some land in the West Riding and some
land and property in and around London.[27]

It seems likely that the Warton estate, amounting to 12,540 acres in
1725, had not been added to substantially since the death of Michael
Warton in 1688. A search at the Registry of Deeds in Beverley has
revealed that the second Sir Michael Warton did not add to the estate
between 1708 and 1725.[28] Moreover the two account books and rental
mentioned previously contain references to land or property holdings in
every place listed in the schedule of 1774. This suggests that although Sir
Michael Warton may have made small additions to the estate between
1688 and 1708, the Warton estate as revealed by the schedule of 1774
was substantially the same as that enjoyed by Michael Warton between
1655 and 1688.

Unfortunately neither a will nor probate inventory of the possessions
of Michael Warton has survived, although there is an inventory without
values in his executors' accounts which gives a vivid impression of his
high standard of living.[29] His large town house, at the North Bar in
Beverley, was sumptuously furnished and the coach house contained a
'velvet chariot' and a 'new coach made at Beverley'. His personal
possessions included a gold tobacco box and a 'gold striking watch',
while his 'clothes' included nine fancy swords and a number of rings set
with emeralds and diamonds. The cellar was stocked with no less than
thirty-eight dozen and two bottles of claret.

III

Like other members of the Yorkshire gentry[30] Michael Warton was not
merely a rentier; he also farmed on a scale that went far beyond the
needs of his own table. He had interests in both arable and pastoral
agriculture. The inventory lists the 'utensils for husbandry', including
seven harrows with iron teeth, two toothless harrows and two ploughs.[31]
In October 1688 his crops 'on the ground' at Killingwoldgraves near
Beverley — comprising twenty-two acres of barley, ten acres of wheat and
one-and-a-half acres of beans — were sold for £55.[32] But Michael
Warton's main interests were in animal husbandry. At his death in
August 1688 he owned 170 oxen, fifty-two steers, two oxen or steers,
three milch cows, a young heifer, fifty horses, twenty-two wethers, ten

asses 'old and young', twenty geese and an undisclosed number of deer.[33]

The bulk of the land which Michael Warton kept in hand was at his seat, Beverley Park, just to the south of Beverley, and at near by places in the Hull valley such as Thearne, Weel and Woodmansey.[34] During the seventeenth century much of the Hull valley was unimproved and liable to inundation during the winter months.[35] Despite this the low-lying carrs and ings, so characteristic of the area, provided good summer pasture, and at various points the Warton accounts refer to these pastures being 'summer eaten with oxen'.[36] In August 1688 the pastures at Thearne were supporting eighty head of cattle, although numbers were gradually reduced as winter approached and the stock was either sold off or moved to more suitable feeding grounds. Michael Warton also kept in hand other pastures near Beverley — at Cottingham, Wolfreton and Newland — which may have been carr land, and some land farther afield, at Dunnington and Marton in Holderness, and at Muston, near Filey.

Michael Warton's main farming activity was fattening cattle for the market. The composition of his stock and references in the accounts to buying in cattle make it plain that he did little, if any, breeding. It seems that he played no part in developing the Holderness breed of cattle for which the area was to be famous in the following century.[37] The 1684–85 rental refers to pasture in various places which was to be 'summer eaten' by cattle 'from South Cave to be bought',[38] but the only detailed reference to buying in stock is for July 1688, when twenty-two steers and four oxen were bought at Hedon fair, near Hull.[39] On this occasion the vendors were from various East Riding villages mostly close to Hedon, although it is possible that some of the stock came from farther afield.

Little can be said about the type and quality of the animals fattened on the Warton estate, although details of cattle purchases in July 1688 make it seem likely that the stock was mixed; twenty-one oxen were purchased, and they comprised one brown ox, nine red oxen and eleven black oxen.[40] The age of the cattle is similarly obscure. In the absence of information it must be presumed that Michael Warton conformed to normal practice and prepared mature beasts for the market. It may be that the oxen he fattened had been used for draught by their previous owners, as was customary in the seventeenth century.[41] Unfortunately the Warton accounts say nothing about the weight of the animals or the meat they yielded. However, the six oxen killed for the Warton household between September and December 1688 yielded an average 6 st. $6\frac{1}{2}$ lb of tallow, although the yield varied considerably from beast to beast; one beast yielded 10 stone of tallow while one yielded no more than 4 stone.[42] This may be compared with the tallow yield of the oxen delivered to the victuallers of the navy from Edward Backwell's Creslow estate between 1664 and 1671; the tallow yield varied from an average of 4 st. 2 lb to 6 st. 6 lb, while the meat yield varied from an average of 4 cwt 2 st. 3 lb to 5 cwt 4 st. 12 lb per beast. The larger beasts produced a greater quantity of both meat and tallow.[43] But both the Warton and Backwell cattle were much smaller than two huge Yorkshire beasts recorded for the late seventeenth century. At Newby Hall, near Ripon, Celia Fiennes saw the picture of an ox that had yielded 19 st. of tallow, and the live weight of a beast which was slaughtered in 1692 was computed at 20 cwt 3 st.[44]

Running the Warton household and estate in the East Riding necessitated a full-time staff of twenty-three men and women, together with a varying number of day labourers. The permanent staff included John Dooker, 'Mr Warton's overlooker of oxen', paid £10 a year, John Coates, annually paid a £10 'salary for buying and selling oxen', and Ralph Thurnam, the 'steward of the stock', paid £14 a year plus an additional £2 a year 'riding charges'.[45]

John Dooker features rarely in the Warton accounts, but John Thurnam appears many times and it is evident that he played a crucial part in the cattle fattening business. His activities in the early days of September 1688 give a good indication of his role. On 3 and 4 September he was busy organising the dispatch of eighteen cattle to London; on 5 September he was at Marton marking thirty beasts prior to their sale; on 7 September he supervised the removal of some cattle from Thearne to Wolfreton and Cottingham; and on the following day he concluded the sale of the Marton cattle.[46] As his high salary suggests, Ralph Thurnam was a valued workman, and he was given a substantial amount of responsibility. Thus on 14 November 1688 he was in charge of leasing a close at Seaton, in Holderness, which was needed for hay. A week later, aided by a labourer, he took twenty steers to Seaton. He checked on their progress on 29 December and finally supervised their return to Beverley on 5 January 1689.[47] In addition to his salary and 'riding charges' Ralph Thurnham frequently received extra allowances. Thus he received 1s for going to see the stock at Marton and Dunnington on 17 August 1688; on that trip he 'blooded' twelve steers at Dunnington and prepared drinks for sick oxen.[48]

It seems likely that John Coates was not a full-time employee but was employed on a part-time basis for the specialist tasks of choosing stock to be bought and organising local sales. He appears in the accounts on a number of occasions in connection with such transactions; for example, in March 1689 he was paid 2s 6d in recompense 'for the like he spent on Beverley butchers ... on selling them oxen'.[49] John Coates seems to have been a substantial farmer in his own right; according to the 1684–85 rental he was leasing a farm and other pieces of land at an annual rent of more than £52.[50] Like Ralph Thurnam, John Coates was a valued employee, and he was still in the service of the Wartons in 1694.[51]

Running the Warton estate also necessitated the employment of numerous day labourers. They were employed for many different tasks such as haymaking, hedging, moving stock, 'fothering' the stock during winter,[52] leading hay or straw. Boys were paid 6d a day for such work and the men normally received 10*d* a day. Building craftsmen were paid at higher rates; carpenters received 1*s* 4*d* or 1*s* 6*d* a day and their labourers 1*s* a day.[53]

IV

The stock which Michael Warton owned at his death was disposed of in a number of different ways. The horses, deer and asses passed immediately to Sir Michael Warton, the eldest son and heir, and were not accounted for by the executors. The bulk of the remainder of the stock was sold off locally or in London, although some beasts were eaten by the Warton household and some were killed by accident or died from natural causes. This information is summarised in table 2.1. In addition

Table 2.1   Disposal of the stock of Michael Warton, 1688–89

	Sold at Smithfield	Sold locally	Died or killed	Eaten by Warton household	Total
Oxen	53	111	–	6	170
Oxen or steers	–	–	2	–	2
Steers	–	51	1	–	52
Young heifer	–	1	–	–	1
Cows	–	1	2	–	3
Wethers	–	–	–	22	22
Geese	–	12	2[a]	6	20

a These geese were 'got by the fox'.
Source. Brynmor Jones Library, University of Hull, DP/81, Account Book, Warton accounts, 1688.

two calves that were born after Michael Warton's death were sold off, one of them to John Dooker, the 'overlooker of Oxen'.[54] Also eight swine were sold in March 1689 for £4 10*s* 0*d*; they had been bought for £3 after Michael Warton's death 'to eat the bean offal in the barn yard'.[55]

Nearly all the stock disposed of locally was sold at Beverley. This 'fair market town'[56] had two weekly markets – Wednesday and Saturday – and when only a few animals were to be sold by the Wartons the sale usually took place on market day. Some of the larger sales also took place on a market day, although such transactions were normally finalised outside the market. However, Thursday was a popular day for these transactions and it may be that the bargain had been struck at the market of the previous day. The only stock sold locally but not at Beverley were four beasts sold at South Cave in May 1689.[57]

Much more detailed information is available concerning the cattle that were sent to the great Smithfield market in London. Three droves, each of eighteen head, were dispatched to London during the last months of

Michael Warton's life and a further three droves – two each of eighteen
head and one of seventeen head – were sent during the following six
months.[58] This was not a new trade for the Wartons. During the mid-
1670s Michael Warton had employed a man called Thomas Wilson, but
he had 'run into Ireland', leaving substantial debts behind him which
were 'esteemed desperate'. Part of the debt related to the movement of
cattle to London organised by Thomas Wilson during 1678; he sold fifty-
eight oxen in February, thirty in May and a further forty in August.
Thomas Wilson was eventually tracked down, but he 'died very poor' in
York Castle in 1695 and the debt was not recovered.[59]

From the accounts of the six droves of cattle sent to Smithfield
between May 1688 and February 1689 it is possible to reconstruct the
details of the trade.[60] The first task, after selecting those animals that
were ready for the market and strong enough for the march, was to equip
the beasts with shoes. This was commonly done when cattle were driven
long distances, but it was a difficult task. Cattle cannot be shod like
horses; they have to be thrown on to their backs and their feet tied
together. For a complete job each beast needed eight shoes, although
sometimes only the outer hoof of each foot, which took most of the wear,
was shod.[61] Only the account of February 1689 refers to shoeing,
although it seems likely that all the Warton cattle were shod for the long
journey.

Ralph Thurnam was in charge of the operation at this early stage, and
he supervised the movement of the cattle to Hull and their shipment
across the Humber on the Barton ferry. On other drove routes cattle
were expected to swim across substantial rivers[62] or even, according to
Aikin's famous account, across the Menai Straits.[63] However, the
Humber, with its fast currents and shifting sands, was always to be
respected. As Celia Fiennes suggested:

... This great River Humber ... rolls and tosses just like the sea only the soil
being clay turns the water and waves yellow and so it differs from the sea in
colour, not else; it's a hazardous water by reason of many shores the tides meet,
I was on it a pretty way and it seems more turbulent than the Thames at
Gravesend.

Having seen the cattle safely to the Lincolnshire shore – that is, all except
the beast which in February 1689 'would not take boat' – Ralph
Thurnam returned to Beverley Park and left the drove in the charge of a
single drover.

Only the account of the final drive of February 1689 mentions all the
places at which the cattle were rested overnight, although sufficient
details are given for the two previous drives to allow us to suggest that a
similar route was followed on each occasion. The journey south began on
Tuesday 12 February 1689, when the cattle crossed the Humber and
were driven about eleven miles to Brigg.[65] On Wednesday 13 February

the cattle were driven about twelve miles to Spital and a similar distance
to Lincoln on the Thursday. Two longer days followed – on Friday the
cattle marched some seventeen and a half miles to Ancaster and a little
farther on the Saturday to Stretton. On the following day the cattle were
rested; this may have been simply due to the need to rest the cattle after
six days on the move (including the short walk to Hull on 11 February)
or because of the reluctance to drive cattle on a Sunday. Perhaps the
latter suggestion is correct, for an Act of Charles I prohibited Sunday
droving.[66]

On Monday 18 February the march got under way again, and the
night was spent at 'Brookes', probably after passing through Stamford.
The exact location of 'Brookes' is not certain, although it is probably
represented on a contemporary map as 'Bruck Castle' and as Bruce's
Castle Farm on modern maps.[67] Bruce's Castle Farm is just off the line
of Ermine Street, which the drive had followed since shortly after
crossing the Humber, and no alternative place has been located which
could possibly be identified as 'Brookes'.[68] If this identification is correct
the cattle had their longest march on 18 February, covering some
twenty-six miles. Tuesday 19 February saw them arrive at Buckden for
the night, eleven and a half miles south of 'Brookes', and on the
following day they covered fifteen and a half miles to reach Biggleswade.
A march of thirteen and a half miles took the cattle to Stevenage on
Thursday 21 February; on Friday they covered a mile more, to reach
Bell Bar, just south of Hatfield; and on Saturday 23 February, after
walking some fifteen miles, they reached the Islington grazing grounds.
The cattle were rested at Islington on the Sunday and were probably
driven the two or three miles to Smithfield at first light or earlier on
Monday 25 February, ready for that day's market.

Thus the whole journey from Barton to Islington took eleven days on
the road, together with rest days at Stretton and Islington. It was
important not to over-drive cattle, especially in the early days of a drive,
and the Warton cattle covered an average of fifteen miles a day.[69] One
historian has suggested that it was more difficult to move cattle in winter
than summer,[70] but it seems that the Warton cattle made as good time in
February 1689 as during the previous summer.

The men employed by the Wartons as drovers during 1688–89 – John
Wardell, William Jennison and John Shearwood – were not employed on
a permanent basis. Nor do they appear elsewhere in the accounts as day
labourers. In fact only John Shearwood features in the accounts in
another context. In 1688 he owed 'farm arrears' amounting to £9 5s
which were due on Lady Day, and some months later he bought small
amounts of hay from the executors.[71] These references suggest that John
Shearwood was a farmer who earned some extra cash by conducting the
Warton cattle to Smithfield.

Despite the responsibility of their task the drovers were not well paid;

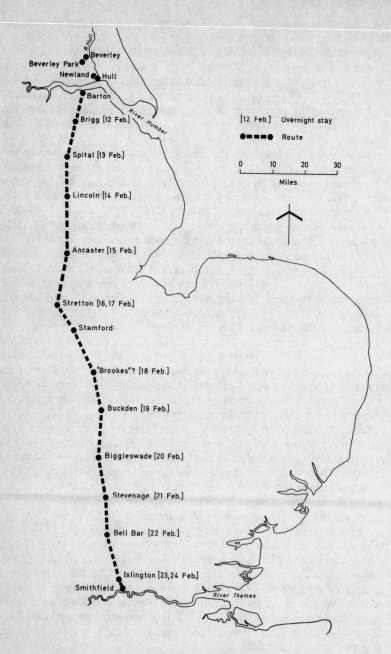

Fig. 2.1   The route taken by Michael Warton's cattle, February 1689.

they received 1s a day, compared with 10d a day normally received by the day labourers in Yorkshire. The absence of any reference to allowances for food suggests that, apart from the 'Smithfield dinner' they received after the sale of the cattle, they were expected to pay for their own food. Similarly the absence of allowances for lodging makes it seem likely that the drovers slept out with their charges, although they did hire a night watchman on occasion in order to get a good night's sleep. Similarly they needed help to drive the cattle through Lincoln and Stamford, plus undisclosed aid from pinders at various places *en route*. The lack of any reference to horses suggests that the drovers travelled on foot. For the return journey they were allowed 5s, which suggests that they were expected to walk the 170 or so miles back to Beverley in five days.

On arrival at Smithfield John Birch[72] took over from the drover, although the latter stayed on to help with the beasts in the market and sometimes stayed on for a few more days to look after the cattle that remained unsold after the first market. Thus William Jennison stayed in London with some unsold cattle between the market of Monday 17 September 1688 and the following Friday market. For his pains he was treated to a second 'Smithfield dinner', but it seems that he then left London rather than wait with the five oxen that were not sold until the next Monday market.

Selling a small batch of Warton cattle could involve John Birch in attending up to three separate markets. He sold the beasts mostly in ones and twos, although occasionally a purchaser took three or four. During the sale he had to meet a number of incidental expenses; these included 'abatements', that is, a small sum given back to the purchaser out of the selling price, the cost of extra help in the market, and the cost of feeding the animals if they were unsold at the end of the day. He also received 1s 6d a head 'for selling', which may refer to his commission for organising the sale. Once the sales were completed the money was handed over to Mr Robert Fotherby, and it was his task to remit the money to the north or else pay debts for the Wartons in London.

V

Michael Warton ran an extensive cattle fattening business in the East Riding of Yorkshire, but his final transactions and those of his executors proved to be unprofitable. The English harvests of 1687 and 1688 were good,[73] and livestock farmers could well have expected a buoyant market for their meat, but it seems that special circumstances were operating against them during 1688. According to Michael Warton's executors, 'the year 1688 was a very bad year to sell goods, etc, the Prince of Orange then landing in England, and there being no public settlement for some time, so that nothing gave reasonable prices'.[74] Later they

returned to the same theme and explained that Michael Warton bought
the cattle 'at near the prices they sold for . . . so that they brought in little
or nothing for their keeping'. Moreover it was alleged that 'that year
1688 all things were at so low a rate by the invasion, etc, that it was a
great damage to the sale of them, besides forcing us to winter so many of
them at hay'.[75] Price and cost data given in the executors' accounts
suggest that their assessment of the situation was correct. In July 1688
Michael Warton bought twenty-one oxen at an average price of £6 2s 3d
and twenty-two steers at an average price of £2 4s 3d. But during the
year beginning June 1688 the receipts for 217 oxen sold at Beverley and
London averaged only £7 0s 4d a head, while the receipts for forty-eight
steers sold at Beverley averaged £3 7s 3½d a head.[76] Thus the margin
between the purchase price and selling price was narrow, especially for
oxen, and if the costs incurred in fattening the beasts and moving them to
market are added the cattle account moves into deficit.

It is impossible to account for all the costs of fattening the cattle,
although there is sufficient evidence to corroborate the executors' gloomy
findings. The cost of summer grazing was computed at 6d a head per
week, but as summer drew to a close costs began to mount. In this
situation it was natural, as the executors implied, to sell off much of the
stock, but by 13 November 1688 only 112 oxen had been sold; on that
day 'fothering began' and 113 oxen and three cows 'were at hay'.
During the following months these cattle ate 330 wainloads of hay,
'which at 18s 0d per load was worth £297 but reckoning forty loads of it
worth only 13s 4d per load £9 6s 8d must be deducted for it and then the
remainder is only £287 13s 4d'. The beasts also 'ate grass of Sir Michael
Warton to the value of £83 6s 0d'.[77] Thus the cost of wintering 116 head
of cattle averaged more than £3 a head for hay and grass alone. In
addition there were incidental charges to be met – payments to labourers
for tending the cattle, payments to Ralph Thurnam and others for out-of-
pocket expenses – together with the salaries paid to John Coates, John
Dooker and Ralph Thurnam.

Finally there was the cost of getting the beasts to market and selling
them. The cost of marketing the beasts at Beverley amounted to no more
than a few pence a head, but the overall cost of moving cattle from
Beverley Park to Smithfield amounted to over 10s a head.[78] This narrows
substantially the differential between Beverley and London prices; the
107 oxen sold at Smithfield averaged £7 9s 4½d a head, whereas the 109
oxen sold at Beverley averaged £6 11s 5½d a head.

VI

It has been suggested recently that cattle 'can be regarded as the
backbone of seventeenth-century Yorkshire farming, almost irrespective
of district'.[79] This was especially true of Holderness; in the late

seventeenth century Holderness farms carried an average of 16.5 cattle, rather more than in other districts.[80] But Michael Warton was not a typical East Riding farmer. His cattle ranching business was on a more extensive scale than that of any other grazier of the district about whom we have information; at his death in 1693 John Townson, a wealthy Keyingham farmer and the largest Holderness grazier previously identified, possessed a mixed herd of seventy-six cattle.[81]

As Member of Parliament for Beverley from 1660 and as an owner of London property Michael Warton was a frequent visitor to the capital, and it seems only natural that he should have despatched some of his stock to feed the growing metropolitan market. The fragmentary data for the 1670s suggest that the arrival of Warton cattle at Smithfield was a well established trade by the late 1680s. If so it must be presumed that the trade was usually profitable, although losses could be expected from time to time in even the best regulated business.[82] However, it seems that losses were kept to a minimum by careful management. Only a few beasts were lost during 1688–89 through accident or death from disease, and all the Warton cattle that crossed the Humber arrived safely at Smithfield. This contrasts with a number of references in the Backwell accounts to the sale of 'tired sheep' by the roadside during a drive.[83] However, it is possible that the low selling price of some of the Warton beasts at Smithfield reflected the toll taken by a long and tiring journey.

During the seventeenth century the growing demands of the metropolitan market necessitated an increasing flow of foodstuffs from the provinces. Where practicable, produce was carried down the rivers or along the coast,[84] although livestock – especially sheep and cattle but also turkeys and geese – were driven to market. The movement of a few score cattle from the East Riding estate of Michael Warton played a minute part in feeding London, but his enterprise has considerable value for historians. Michael Warton's death in 1688 engendered a unique record of cattle droving to illuminate this obscure aspect of English economic history.

Appendix 2.1 The accounts of the movement of the cattle of Michael Warton to London, 1688–89[85]

£   s   d

Transactions 1–3

[B, p. 40] *Mr Robert Fotherby's receipts for Michael Warton Esq.*
9 June 1688: paid Mr Fotherby by Mr John Birch being the price clear of eighteen oxen Mr Warton sent to London [Monday] 21 May 1688 and sold [Monday] 4 June 1688 by Mr Birch [*Margin:* By acquittance and Fotherby's paper is £9 4s 4d a piece and 6d over]   165 18 6

10 July 1688: paid Mr Fotherby by Mr John Birch being the
price clear of eighteen oxen Mr Warton sent to London [Saturday]
23 June 1688 and sold by Mr Birch [Friday] 6 July 1688
[*Margin:* By acquittance and Birch's bill at £8 4s 7d a piece]   148   2   6
9 August 1688: paid Mr Fotherby by Mr John Birch being the
price clear of eighteen oxen Mr Warton sent to London [Saturday]
21 July 1688 and sold by Mr Birch [Friday] 3 and [Monday] 6
August 1688 [*Margin:* By acquittance and Mr Birch's bill at
£6 19s 0d a piece and 18d over]   125   3   6

[Total]	439	4	6

Note. Mr John Birch's account of the sale of the fifty-four oxen
above in this page was, *viz*:

		£	s	d
[Monday] 4 June 1688: eighteen oxen sold as in particulars in Mr Birch's paper for		167	10	0
To be deducted	for selling	1	7	0
	abatements		4	6
	Clear	165	18	6

		£	s	d
[Friday] 6 July 1688: eighteen oxen sold as in particulars in Mr Birch's paper for		149	12	6
To be deducted	for selling	1	7	0
	abatements		3	0
	Clear	148	2	6

		£	s	d
[Friday] 3 and [Monday] 6 August 1688: eighteen oxen sold as in particulars in Mr Birch's paper for		126	15	0
To be deducted	for selling	1	7	0
	for abatements		4	6
	Clear	125	3	6

[B, p. 41] *Mr Robert Fotherby's payments in discount of his receipts for Michael
Warton, Esq.*

8 June 1688: charged on him by Mr Warton by bill to pay Charles Warton or
order (who assigned it to Sir Michael Warton) within four days, for value
received of Charles Warton [*Margin:* As by Fotherby's paper]   100   0   0
27 June 1688: charged on him by Mr Warton by bill to pay Mrs
Elizabeth Carlile for like value then received of Mr William Forge
[*Margin:* As by Fotherby's paper]   40   0   0
7 August 1688: paid to Charles Warton for Mr Warton by Mr
John Fotherby [*Margin:* This is accounted for in Charles Warton's
account in page 24]   150   0   0
So the balance due from Mr Robert Fotherby to Michael
Warton, Esq., at the death of the said Mr Warton was   149   4   6

[Total]	439	4	6

Mr Robert Fotherby paid in discharge of the above balance due from him to Michael Warton, Esq., unto the executors of the said Michael Warton, *viz*:

27 September 1688: paid to Charles Warton by Mr John Fotherby in part	59	4	6
4 October 1688: paid to Charles Warton by Mr John Fotherby by Mr Edward Chapellow in full of the said balance	90	0	0
[Total]	149	4	6

[B, p. 24] [Charles Warton's receipts and payments for Michael Warton include] 7 August 1688: received of Mr Robert Fotherby by Mr John Fotherby on account of money received by him for Mr Warton's oxen sold at London [*Margin*: Ox money at London etc, see the account in page 41]	150	0	0
[B, p. 21] 11 August 1688: paid John Wardell's bill of charges for driving eighteen oxen sent up to London 21 July 1688 and sold 3 and 6 August	5	18	0
[A, p. 81] 1 September 1688: paid by Charles Warton to John Coates for postage of an acquittance from Mr Fotherby for ox money			4
18 September 1688: paid Mr Coates for a letter from Mr Robert Fotherby with an acquittance for ox money			4

Transaction 4

[A, p. 58] *Paid Ralph Thurnam's disbursements about boating eighteen oxen sent to London.*

[Tuesday] 28 August 1688. Ralph Thurnam's charges at Hull

[Monday] 27 August 1688 to hire the boat		6
For straw to put in the boat		6
For help to boat eighteen oxen		7
For boat hire for eighteen oxen at 6*d* each	9	0
Given the boatmen in money 2*s* 6*d*, in ale 6*d*	3	0
Ralph Thurnam and his horse's charges two days and one night	4	7
[Total]	18	2

[A, p. 60] 24 September 1688: paid by Charles Warton to John Wardell for charges of driving up eighteen oxen sent to London [Tuesday] 28 August 1688, *viz*:

For thirteen nights' grass for eighteen oxen at 6*s* 0*d* per night being 4*d* per ox	3	18	0
Paid the pinders in several places		2	6
For help through Lincoln and Stamford			4
For watching at Ancaster 6*d*, *ditto* at Bell Bar 4*d*, *ditto* at Islington 8*d*		1	6
For help in Smithfield		3	0
For a link [86]			3
For John Wardell's dinner in Smithfield			6
Paid at 'Wrope' (?)			6
For John Wardell's wages fourteen days at 1*s* 0*d*		14	0
For John Wardell's journey coming down		5	0
[Total]	5	5	7

[B, p. 42] *Mr John Birch's account of oxen sold by him for Ralph Warton and Charles Warton as executors to Michael Warton, Esq., and to whom the clear proceed thereof was paid.*

Eighteen oxen sent up [Tuesday] 28 August 1688 and sold 10 and 14 September, sent up by John Wardell.

[Monday] 10 September: two to Mr Birch for		18	10	0
one to Mr Norman for		8	5	0
one to Mr Mann for		7	0	0
one to Mr Sigerd for		7	6	8
two to Mr Collier for		13	15	0
one to Mr Birdeys for		7	5	0
two to Mr Smith for		13	10	0
two to Mr Dalby for		15	0	0
one to Mr Webb for		6	17	6
two to Mr Cowell for		16	0	0
[Friday] 14 September: one to Mr Joff for		6	10	0
one to Mr Alsop for		6	5	0
one to Mr Miller for		5	15	0

[Total]	131	19	2

Deductions			
	for selling	1	7	0
	abatements		3	0
	help			6
	three beasts four nights		4	6

[Total]	1	15	0

Declare paid to Mr Robert Fotherby charged in his account	130	4	2

Transaction 5

[A, p. 59] *Paid Ralph Thurnam's disbursement about sending eighteen oxen to London [Tuesday] 4 September 1688, viz:*

Spent by Thurnam [Monday] 3 September on removing them		6
Paid to William Paulin to help to drive eighteen oxen from Newland to Hull		6
Paid for litter to put in the boat		6
Paid for help to boat eighteen oxen		8
Paid for help to get an ox out that fell overboard	1	4
Paid for boat hire for eighteen oxen at 6d each	9	0
Given the boatmen in money 2s 6d, in ale 6d	3	0
Ralph Thurnam's charges one night at Newland 1s 4d and his horse charge 1s 2d	2	6
Given to the house at Newland where he lay		4
Ralph Thurnam's charges at Barton and Hull	1	6

[Total]	19	10

[A, p. 60] 29 September 1688: paid William Jennison for driving charges of eighteen oxen sent to London [Tuesday] 4 September 1688, *viz:*

	£	s	d
For thirteen nights' grass for eighteen oxen at 6s 0d per night being 4d per ox	3	18	0
For four nights' grass at Islington for fifteen oxen unsold the first market day at 4d per night per ox	1	0	0
For watching at Ancaster 6d, at Lincoln 6d, at Bell Bar 4d, at Islington six nights 2s 0d		3	4
Paid to the pinders in several places		2	6
For help at Lincoln and Stamford 4d, and ditto two market days in Smithfield 3s 0d		3	4
For William Jennison's two dinners in Smithfield		1	0
For William Jennison's wages eighteen days at 1s 0d		18	0
For William Jennison's journey coming down		5	0
[Total]	6	11	2

Note. Charles Warton paid William Jennison only £6 1s 2d for this last bill, Mr John Birch having paid him 10s 0d at London, but his acquittance is for the whole £6 11s 2d.
Note. Mr Birch deducts [sic] that 10s 0d when he paid Mr Fotherby the money third cow was sold for, so it is not here charged as paid.

[B, p. 42] [Mr John Birch's account] eighteen oxen sent up to London [Tuesday] 4 September 1688, sold 17, 21 and 24 September, sent up by William Jennison, *viz*:

	£	s	d
[Monday] 17 September: one to Mr Wood for	8	10	0
two to Mr Walton for	11	10	0
one to Mr Halfondon for	6	0	0
[Friday] 21 September: four to Mr Workman for	23	10	0
two to Mr Birch for	11	10	0
two to Mr Holmes for	11	0	0
one to Mr Tune for	6	0	0
[Monday] 24 September: two to Mr Tring for	10	10	0
one to Mr Wood for	5	6	8
one to Mr Tune for	5	0	0
one to Mr Hawkins for	5	6	8
[Total]	104	3	4

		£	s	d
	For selling	1	7	0
Deductions	Abatements		3	0
	Paid William Jennison the driver on account of charges		10	0
	[Total]	2	0	0

Declare paid to Mr Fotherby charged in his account   102   3   4
Note. 8 October 1688: Mr Birch wrote that the charge for three nights for five of these last eighteen beasts was owing.

Transaction 6

[A, p. 63] *9 February 1689: Ralph Thurnam's bill [includes the following items].*

	£	s	d
John Kilpin part of one day in the fair with beasts to sell[87] and one day helping to shoe eighteen oxen to go to London		1	2
Robert Dring part of one day, and one day *ditto*		1	2
Fran. Greenop part of one day, and one day *ditto*		1	2
Paid John Reachay for shoeing eighteen oxen to go to London at 8d per ox for shoes		12	0
Ralph Thurnam's charges at Hull to take the boat for eighteen oxen to go for London			6
Spent by Ralph Thurnam with the smith at the shoeing the eighteen oxen			6

[A, p. 64] 16 February 1689: Ralph Thurnam's bill paid by Charles Warton *viz*:

	£	s	d
[Tuesday] 12 February 1689: for boat hire of seventeen oxen from Hull to Barton then sent to London by John Shearwood at 6d		8	6
Given to the boatmen 2s 6d and spent on them in ale 7d [*Margin: gift to boatmen*]		3	1
Paid for litter for the oxen in the boat			6
Paid for help to drive those oxen from the pasture and to boat them		1	0
Paid the turn key for opening Hull gates by four o'clock to let in those oxen		1	0
Paid for help to the skiffmen to get four oxen that leapt out of the boat		1	0
Paid Mrs Kitchen for one night's hay for eighteen oxen and for one night's hay for the ox that would not boat at 4d		6	4
Ralph Thurnam's and John Shearwood's charges that night and next morning at Hull		4	4
Ralph Thurnam's charges at Barton			4
Ralph Thurnam's charges at Hull coming back			6
John Robinson half a day driving eighteen oxen from the Park to Hull and half a day bringing an ox back from Hull to the Park that would not take boat			8
[Total]	1	7	3

2 March 1689: paid by Charles Warton to John Shearwood for charges of driving up seventeen oxen sent to London [Monday] 11 February 1689, *viz*:

	£	s	d
For four trusses of hay at Brigg 8s 0d and for five trusses of hay at Spital 10s 0d		18	0
For five trusses of hay at Lincoln 10s 0d, and five trusses of hay at Ancaster 10s 0d	1	0	0
For ten trusses of hay at Stretton	1	0	0
For five trusses of hay at 'Brookes' 10s 0d, and five trusses of hay at Buckden 10s 0d	1	0	0
For five trusses of hay at Biggleswade 10s 0d, and five trusses of hay at Stevenage 10s 0d	1	0	0
For five trusses of hay at Bell Bar 10s 10d, and twelve trusses of hay at Islington £1	1	10	10
Paid to the pinders 2s 6d and for watching 2s 6d		5	0
Paid for help and toll 7d, and for help in Smithfield 3s 0d		3	7
Paid for John Shearwood's dinner at Smithfield			6
John Shearwood, fifteen days' wages		15	0
John Shearwood's journey coming down		5	0
[Total]	7	17	11

Note. Mr Birch paid John Shearwood £2 10s 0d on account for charges which is deducted in Mr Birch's account of the sale of the said seventeen oxen, so the remainder of the above bill is only here charged being £5 7s 11d

[B, p. 42] [Mr John Birch's account] seventeen oxen sent up to London by John Shearwood [Monday] 11 February 1689 and sold by Mr John Birch [Monday] 25 February 1689, *viz*:

one to Mr Hawkins for	7	10	0
one to Mr Hatton for	7	10	0
three to Mr Weng for	21	10	0
one to Mr Hamon for	7	0	0
one to Mr Oliver for	7	0	0
one to Mr Gladston for	6	15	0
one to Mr Holmes for	6	5	0
one to Mr Hall for	6	10	0
three to Mr Johnson for	22	10	0
one to Mr Ruff for	7	0	0
one to Mr Reed for	7	0	0
one to Mr Mossack for	6	15	0
one to Mr Harris for	6	10	0
[Total]	119	15	0

	For selling	1	5	6
Deductions	abatements		2	10
	Paid to John Shearwood the driver on account of charges	2	10	0
	[Total]	3	18	4

Paid to Mr Robert Fotherby which is charged in his account	115	16	8

[A, p. 82] 1 March 1689: paid by Charles Warton to John Coates for like he paid for postage of an acquittance from Mr Fotherby for the money paid him for seventeen oxen sent up to London 12 February, 1689   4

Transactions 4–6

[B, p. 46] *Mr Robert Fotherby's receipts for Mr Ralph Warton and Charles Warton executors of Michael Warton, Esq.*

15 September 1688: paid him by his servant John Izard by Mr John Birch being the price clear of eighteen oxen sent up to London by the executors 28 August 1688 and sold 10 and 14 September [*Margin:* sent by John Wardell – eighteen oxen]   130 4 2

27 September 1688: paid him by his servant John Izard by Mr John Birch being the price clear of eighteen oxen sent up to London by the executors 4 September 1688 and sold 17, 21 and 24 September [*Margin:* sent up by William Jennison – eighteen oxen]   102 3 4

8 December 1688: paid him by Mr Nathaniel Adams (which Mr Adams had in his hand of the executors, as by his account in page 52) as by Adam's letter then dated [*Margin:* this was for ox money see in Mr Adam's said account][88]   160 0 0

[Total] 392 7 6

26 February 1689: paid Mr Fotherby by Mr John Birch by acquittance being the price clear of seventeen oxen sent by the executors to London 11 February 1689 by John Shearwood and sold 25 February

115 16   8

[B, p. 47] *Mr Robert Fotherby's payments for Mr Ralph and Charles Warton*

30 November 1688: paid by order to Mr William Russell in full of a bill for funeral of Michael Warton, Esq., which is entered paid at the other end in page 29 [i.e. A., p. 29] and by acquittance; so is here entered as received

237   0   0

16 January 1689: paid on Charles Warton's bill dated 18 December 1688 to Sir Michael Warton by R Cook and which Sir Michael Warton owns receipt of in his of 26 January and 14 February 1689 in which last he orders Charles Warton to repay himself: so 18 February 1689 Charles Warton took out of Sir Michael's iron chest (being part of the two bags told by Charles Warton) the like sum being

155   7   6

[Total] 392   7   6

[*In the margin*] Copy of bill, *viz.*, Beverley 18 December 1688. Mr Fotherby, you are hereby desired on sight hereof to pay unto my brother Sir Michael Warton or his order one hundred fifty-five pounds seven shillings and six pence, and place the same to the account of Mr Ralph Warton and myself – your friend Charles Warton.

13 March 1689: Mr Robert Fotherby by Mr John Fotherby paid Charles Warton in part of the £115 16*s* 8*d* charged on the other side [i.e. B, p. 46]

100   0   0

22 April 1689: Mr Robert Fotherby by Mr John Fotherby paid Charles Warton in full of the £115 16*s* 8*d* charged on the other side, £100 of it being paid as before

15 16   8

[Total] 115 16   8

[Grand] Total 508   4   2

Vide p. 82 at 't'other end' [i.e. A, p. 82], where 1*s* 6*d* was paid Mr Fotherby for letters sent him, etc.
[A, p. 82] 22 April 1689: paid by Charles Warton to Mr Robert Fotherby by Mr John Fotherby for letters sent him about ordering the payment of moneys of the executors he had in his hand 1*s* 6*d*

Notes

1 I should like to acknowledge the debt I owe to Professor Willan, who first aroused my interest in the economic history of Tudor and Stuart England. I am also indebted to Dr A. Harris for his helpful comments on an earlier draft of this article and to Dr K. J. Allison and Mr D. R. J. Neave for their advice. Thanks are also due to Mr D. Waite, who drew the map, and the various archivists and librarians who have rendered assistance.

2   T. S. Willan, *The English coasting trade 1600–1750* (2nd edn., Manchester, 1967), p. ix.

3   *Ibid.*

4   T. S. Willan, *River navigation in England, 1600–1750* (1936).
5   Professor Willan has also made a substantial contribution to this field of study; see 'A chronological list of the writings of T. S. Willan' at the beginning of this volume.
6   See, for example, T. S. Willan, *An eighteenth century shopkeeper: Abraham Dent of Kirkby Stephen* (Manchester, 1970). Since this article was completed Professor Willan has added another valuable study on inland trade: T. S. Willan, *The inland trade: studies in English internal trade in the sixteenth and seventeenth centuries* (Manchester, 1976).
7   Based on D. Woodward, 'The Anglo-Irish livestock trade in the seventeenth century', *Irish Historical Studies*, XVIII (1973), pp. 489–523.
8   Cheshire C.R.O., WS Robert Brerewood 1602.
9   Williams and Glyn's Bank Ltd, Backwell ledgers, M, f. 588. I am grateful to Dr J. Broad for introducing me to this source.
10 L. M. Cullen, *Anglo-Irish trade, 1660–1800* (Manchester, 1968), p. 33.
11 See P. V. McGrath, 'The marketing of food, fodder and livestock in the London area in the seventeenth century' (M.A. thesis, University of London, 1948) which does not contain a single reference to the sale of Irish cattle.
12 E. C. Lodge (ed.), *The account book of a Kentish estate, 1616–1704* (1927), p. 265.
13 Backwell ledgers, *op. cit.*, L, ff. 14, 57–8, 403, 422; M, ff. 128, 324, 383–4, 405, 506, 588, etc.
14 C. Skeel, 'The cattle trade between Wales and England', *Transactions of the Royal Historical Society*, 4th ser., IX (1926), pp. 135–58; K. J. Bonser, *The drovers* (1970); A. R. B. Haldane, *The drove roads of Scotland* (1952). Dr R. J. Colyer is about to produce a book on Welsh droving which will contain some discussion of the period before 1700.
15 He was baptised on 27 April 1623: see his monument in Beverley Minster.
16 Brynmor Jones Library, University of Hull, DP/81, Warton Account Book, B, p. 29. This account book, known hereafter as 'Hull Acct.', has entries at both ends – one end is headed 'Funeral Charges of Michael Warton 1688' and is subsequently referred to as 'A', the other end is headed 'Warton Accounts 1688' and is subsequently referred to as 'B'. All quotations are rendered in modern spelling.
17 Hull Acct., A, pp. 17–29.
18 Hull Acct., *op. cit.*, and Beverley Public Library, Local History section, Y–B/War/Bev., Warton Account Book. The latter volume, subsequently referred to as 'Bev. Acct.', also has entries at both ends. The end which begins with an inventory of Michael Warton's Beverley houses is referred to as 'A' and the other as 'B'.
19 Yorkshire Archaeological Society, MS 661, Rental of Michael Warton's Yorkshire estate, 1684–85, hereafter referred to as 'Rental'.
20 J. T. Cliffe, *The Yorkshire gentry from the Reformation to the Civil War* (1969), pp. 29, 244.
21 *Ibid.*, pp. 305–6, 335, 343.
22 Sir Michael Warton died in his eighty-second year: see his monument in Beverley Minster.
23 P.R.O., Committee for Compounding, S.P. 23/187/283–328. J. W. Clay (ed.), *Yorkshire Royalist Composition Papers*, vol. 2, Yorkshire Archaeological Society Record Series, 18 (1895), pp. 55–7, 93–4.
24 G. Oliver, *The history and antiquities of the town and minster of Beverley* (Beverley, 1829), p. 226.
25 Sir Michael, Charles and Ralph all died childless.
26 Humberside C.R.O., Beverley, CSR 26/12.

27   *Ibid.*, schedule 1; 200 acres at Adlingfleet and Ousefleet in the West Riding,
     105 acres in Chelsea, 3,163 acres in north Lincolnshire, of which 2,330
     acres were at Saxby and 833 at South Ferriby. The rest of the land was in
     the East Riding, including the 2,509 acres of Beverley Park.
28   Records at the registry begin in 1708.
29   Bev. Acct., A, pp. 4–39.
30   Cliffe, *op. cit.*, pp. 49–50.
31   Bev. Acct., A, p. 36.
32   Hull Acct., B, p. 209.
33   *Ibid.*, p. 207; Bev. Acct., A, p. 37.
34   Rental, pp. 385–7, 393–4.
35   A. Harris, 'The agriculture of the East Riding of Yorkshire before the
     parliamentary enclosures', *Yorkshire Archaeological Journal*, 40 (1962), p.
     121; A. Harris, *The rural landscape of the East Riding of Yorkshire,
     1700–1850* (1961), pp. 35–9; J. Sheppard, *The draining of the Hull valley*,
     East Yorkshire Local History series, 8 (1958), pp. 1–13.
36   For example, Rental, pp. 385–7.
37   R. Trow-Smith, *A history of British livestock husbandry, 1700–1900*
     (1959), pp. 28–9, 90.
38   Rental, p. 385.
39   Hull Acct., B, p. 25.
40   *Ibid.*
41   Trow-Smith, *op. cit.*, pp. 166–8.
42   Hull Acct., B, pp. 215–16. The five beasts that yielded under 10 st. of
     tallow produced an average of 5 st. 10½ lb. An ox killed in an accident
     yielded 3 st. 5 lb of tallow, while one that died from disease yielded 3 st. 7
     lb.
43   Backwell Ledgers, *op. cit.*, L, ff. 84, 421–2; M, f. 128; P, f. 30; Q, f. 619; R,
     f. 503; S, f. 252. The average weights of tallow and meat relate to ten
     batches of cattle ranging from forty to 684 cattle in a batch, totalling 2,659
     cattle altogether.
44   C. Morris (ed), *The journeys of Celia Fiennes* (1949), p. 84; R. Trow-
     Smith, *A history of British livestock husbandry to 1700* (1957), p. 240.
45   Hull Acct., A, p. 101. The other staff with their annual salaries were:
     chaplain, £20; male cook, £15; 'Mr Warton's own man', £12; butler, £10;
     park-keeper, £10; head groom, £10; male 'clerk of the kitchen', £10; female
     housekeeper, £8; groom, £7; gardener, £7; coachman, £6 10s; male brewer,
     £4 10s; undergroom, £3 10s; footboy, £3; washmaid, £2 10s;
     chambermaid, £2 10s; postilion, £2 10s; dairymaid, £2; kitchen maid, £2;
     female 'servant at Answorth's house', £2.
46   Hull Acct., A, p. 59.
47   *Ibid.*, A, pp. 62–3.
48   There are a number of references to medicines for stock, and the ingredients
     included ale, milk, buttermilk, saffron, bayberries, turmeric and diapente.
     Hull Acct., A, pp. 57, 61, 66.
49   *Ibid.*, A, p. 82.
50   Rental, pp. 195, 197, 225, 227. Altogether he leased fourteen closes, two of
     which amounted to 20 acres 2 roods 2 perches. The rent of one close is not
     given.
51   Bev. Acct., B, p. 10.
52   'Fothering' or foddering means to feed stock on fodder.
53   Hull Acct., A, pp. 57–69. Agricultural labourers occasionally received 1s a
     day.

54 Hull Acct., B, p. 207. John Dooker may have had a smallholding; the accounts refer to the four cow gates which he held in Beverley Park, and in 1688 he had six cows grazing there. (*Ibid.*, B, pp. 118, 124.)

55 *Ibid.*, B, p. 221.

56 R. Davies (ed.), *The life of Marmaduke Rawdon of York*, Camden Soc., 85 (1863), p. 149. Celia Fiennes was also impressed by Beverley; C. Morris, *op. cit.*, p. 86.

57 Hull Acct., B, p. 207.

58 See appendix 2.1 for the detailed accounts of these transactions.

59 Bev. Acct., B, p. 10.

60 The following section is based on the data presented in appendix 2.1.

61 Skeel, *op. cit.*, pp. 143–4; Bonser, *op. cit.*, pp. 58–63; Haldane, *op. cit.*, pp. 33–5. For illustrations see Haldane, plate 1; Bonser, plate 2.

62 Haldane, *op. cit.*, pp. 38–40.

63 A. Aikin, *Journal of a tour through North Wales and part of Shropshire* (1797), pp. 153–5. Haldane, *op. cit.*, pp. 75–6, refers to Scottish cattle being forced to swim in the sea.

64 C. Morris, *op. cit.*, p. 88. Cattle were also taken across the Severn by boat; T. S. Willan, *Coasting trade, op. cit.*, p. 170.

65 The mileages given in this account are approximate because the exact route of the cattle cannot be established. However, it seems that for much of the way the cattle moved down the ancient line of Ermine Street.

66 3 Car. I, cap. 1(2). Enforced by 29 Car. II, cap. 7 (1676): Michael Warton was an MP in this Parliament.

67 J. B. Harley (ed.), *The county maps from William Camden's Britannia, 1695 by Robert Norden* (1972); 'Bruck Castle' appears on the map of Huntingdonshire. Bruce's Castle Farm: grid ref. TL 184846.

68 A. Mawer and F. M. Stenton, *The place-names of Bedfordshire and Huntingdonshire*, English Place Name Society, 3 (Cambridge, 1926).

69 This was in line with contemporary practice; Bonser, *op. cit.*, p. 45, says that cattle travelled about fourteen to sixteen miles a day.

70 McGrath, *op. cit.*, p. 152.

71 Hull Acct., B, pp. 22, 123, 209.

72 Unfortunately I have not been able to find any information about John Birch apart from that presented here: the same is true of Robert Fotherby, whose role is discussed below.

73 W. G. Hoskins, 'Harvest fluctuations and English economic history, 1620–1759', *Agricultural History Review*, 16 (1968), pp. 24, 30.

74 Hull Acct., B, p. 17.

75 *Ibid.*, B, p. 207.

76 *Ibid.* For variations in the London prices see appendix 2.1.

77 *Ibid.*, B, pp. 117, 119, 207.

78 See appendix 2.1. It is impossible to give an exact figure because the various accounts do not give the same details; however, the total cost of selling the cattle in London rather than in Beverley was about 11s a head. Costs were greater in winter because of the need to buy hay.

79 W. Harwood Long, 'Regional farming in seventeenth-century Yorkshire', *Agricultural History Review*, 8 (1960), p. 113.

80 *Ibid.*, p. 106; this judgement is based on seventy-nine Holderness inventories.

81 Harris, 'The agriculture of the East Riding', *op. cit.*, p. 126.

82 During 1664–65 Edward Backwell bought ninety-six oxen and 570 sheep in Ireland for sale in England, but he had to record a small 'loss upon this affair', Backwell Ledgers, M, f. 588.

83 *Ibid.*, Q, ff. 62, 503; T, ff. 93, 607.

84 T. S. Willan, *River navigation, op. cit.*; *Coasting trade, op. cit.*
85 Based on Hull Acct. The spelling, except for names, has been modernised.
86 *I.e.* a light.
87 Beverley fair took place on the Thursday before St Valentine's day; in 1689 St Valentine's day (14 February) fell on a Thursday, so that the fair was on 7 February.
88 Hull Acct., B, p. 52. Mr Nathaniel Adams's receipts for Mr Ralph and Charles Warton:

	£	s	d
29 September 1688: paid him by Christopher King by acquittance being part of the price of twenty-nine oxen and one young heifer sold to him [at Beverley] 6 September 1688	60	0	0
8 October 1688: paid him by William Wardman and George Whitfield by John Birch by acquittance being part of the price of twenty oxen sold to them 20 September 1688	100	0	0
	160	0	0

The Lancashire bill system and its Liverpool practitioners

The case of a slave merchant

I

By the eighteenth century bills of exchange had become the established means of payment between trading parties and the most convenient store of value amongst merchants and bankers. Their relative safety in use, their wide circulation, as well as their self-liquidating properties, had made them indispensable to the functioning of the money markets of Europe. Much has been written on the early use of these credit instruments, their subsequent development in the form of foreign and inland bills, as well as the ultimate decline of the latter in the last quarter of the nineteenth century.[1] The detailed working of the bill system in its heyday has attracted some attention since the late Professor Ashton first gave it prominence as a crucial factor in enabling eighteenth-century businessmen to overcome the difficulty and expense of making credit transfers. In particular it has now been well established that it was the South Atlantic trade network, which presaged the multilateral character of English trade more than any other branch, that brought the bill system to the peak of its development.[2] By contrast with the payments problems involved in commerce to the East, which for so long was essentially a bullion trade, long-distance traffic on the Atlantic brought several diverse interest groups together in a pattern of trade which achieved overall balance by means of indirect settlements between its constituent parts. The bulk growing and marketing of raw materials to exchange for manufactures produced under regimes of considerable specialisation, together with the purchase and resale of supplies of slave labour, could not have been carried on with any facility without an efficient clearing system. Not only were merchants called upon to display all their traditional functions in these trades and to exploit them more intensively, but some came to act as trader and banker as well. Those who did so

were the key figures in a system of mutual accommodation in which
personal liability was unlimited.

Such a system was at once flexible and frail, for, while it enabled
traders to remit the bills they received of others, rather than invariably
drawing up their own obligations, it also required those who received
them to reciprocate by trusting that in due time the bill would be satisfied.
While the trader could thus come to expect the convenience of a paper
settlement to the approximate amount of his credit or debit, normally
payable in his own locality, there was always the fear that one or more
links in the chain of endorsements might be found wanting at the
appointed time. Against the eventuality that a whole series of settlements
might be thrown into doubt in this way the system had evolved two
safeguards during the eighteenth century. One was a product of the very
fact that wealth and credit standing were not evenly distributed among
merchants themselves, irrespective of the soundness of individual
transactions, so that it was possible and profitable for some to act as
intermediaries or bankers for the rest. The other was the interval of time
to maturity which attached to a bill and which, though it normally varied
according to the time taken to complete a given trade round, did allow
the trader to order his settlements more closely to his own convenience.
In few trades were these safeguards so important as in the slave trade,
where, even compared with the lengthy transaction periods of other
foreign trades, the customary currency of bills was so long that the
existence of reliable acceptance specialists was crucial to its development
after the Seven Years war.

The importance of the bill system in the slave trade was to some
degree an outgrowth of the consolidation of the commission system in
the West Indies, from where the sugar trade was largely organised and
directed by London agents. As a result it was the outport merchants who
increasingly came to specialise in the slave-carrying branch of the West
India trade. For the merchants of Liverpool this meant exploiting their
comparative advantage in the Guinea trade, so as to increase still further
the dominant position they had gained by the middle of the century. At
the same time it also entailed a reduction of direct sales of slaves to the
West India planters in favour of selling through slave factors in the
Islands and receiving payment in bills of exchange or, to a decreasing
extent, in produce.[3] In Liverpool especially, these changes in the financial
organisation of the South Atlantic trades appear to have been primarily
responsible for the emergence of a relatively small number of slaving
entrepreneurs whose function was to oversee the complex web of trade
relations that made up the African trade.

This study is based on the bill of exchange register of William
Davenport & Co., a Liverpool merchant house that was closely involved
with developing the slave trade of the port from the 1740s onwards.
Davenport's bill transactions are complete for the period 1769 to 1787

and cover two contrasting periods in the fortunes of the slaving community, the latter years of what the late Professor Pares designated 'the silver age of sugar' and the period of the American war and its aftermath. In conjunction with the rest of Davenport's papers, the bill register shows him to have been a member of the inner circle of men who, by locating themselves at the focal point which linked the various and far-flung domestic suppliers to the markets of the Islands via West Africa, can indeed be called the princes of the slave trade. His long involvement in the traffic, together with the extent of his connections with other key figures in London, the West Indies and elsewhere, suggests that the role of outport merchants such as Davenport was largely complementary to that of the London West India houses. Just as the latter found themselves accommodating the growing indebtedness of the planters from the Seven Years War on, and controlling both sugar marketing and slave factorage in the process, so groups of slave merchants were increasing their influence over the procurement of supplies and manufactures as well as over the slave-carrying operations.

The great wealth and numerous connections of the West India houses made it difficult to enter this branch of the trade, which ensured a degree of continuity in the financial arrangements made between an Islands proprietor and a London merchant and facilitated the growing dependence of the proprietor. At the same time the consequent increase in the acceptance business of the London agencies obviated the need to develop banking facilities in the Caribbean.[4] A close relationship between shipper and cargo owner had always been an important, even unique, feature of the slave trade voyage. Not only were many of the ships purpose-built, but the high value of the cargo carried demanded maximum co-operation by the participants if profits commensurate with the heavy capital outlay were to be secured. Continuity of operations in the slave trade normally required, therefore, that a substantial merchant of experience take on the function of 'ship's husband' to oversee the detailed organisation of the venture and attend to the interests of all those involved.[5] From the point of view of these slave merchants an efficient remittance system, involving a relatively small number of reputable West India houses in London who accepted final responsibility for payment, was crucial for spreading the high risks inherent in their operations.

II

An important stimulus to the expansion of Liverpool's share of the slave trade in the first half of the eighteenth century came from an infusion of new men. Over this period a number of Liverpool West India merchants had been instrumental in fostering a considerable market for Lancashire textiles with Spanish contraband traders centred on Jamaica. When, in 1747, this trade was prohibited many of these merchants turned to the

African trade, where their commercial connections at home and in the Islands continued to serve them well. It is probable that this was how William Davenport entered the slave trade. In the mid-'60s, when Liverpool's advantage in the trade was already established, the growth of the Irish market for Lancashire textiles, together with the utility of Irish ports as victualling points for slavers, reinforced the position of Liverpool merchants in the slave trade as it did their import trade in Irish linen to Britain. Finally, the growth of Liverpool's share of the slave traffic at the expense of other ports was partly attributable to the circumstances of war. Throughout the eighteenth century the shipping activity of the port showed a rather perverse tendency to increase noticeably in time of war, frequently to the detriment of London, whose ships attracted most attention from enemy privateers. It was in the midst of just such a re-routing of trade, during the War of the Austrian Succession, that the Davenport brothers appear to have settled in Liverpool. William (1725–97) and Christopher (1730–93) were both born in London, though the main branch of the family, the Davenports of Woodford, where of a long line of Cheshire gentry. As the younger sons of an ancient county family it was not, of course, remarkable that the Davenport brothers were apprenticed to trade; indeed, in the first half of the century there were many who spent some time on the Continent for that purpose.[6] But the Davenport brothers appear to have been apprenticed in Liverpool and to have pursued their entire trading careers in the town; certainly both died there unmarried towards the close of the slave trade era.[7]

The record of the firm's bill receipts opens at the start of the second quarter of 1769 with trading activity at a high level and still growing rapidly on the basis of a sustained growth of produce imports. Over the next few years the details relating to the source, destination, currency and discount of Davenport's bills provide ample illustration for Wadsworth and Mann's observation that, for a short but crucial period, the slave trade was an important route along which British, and especially Lancashire, manufactures tested their competitive strength in the expanding markets served by the Atlantic trades.[8] The period before 1773 was the most prosperous of Davenport's career, and the bill register for these years shows the pattern of his transactions to have been more complete than at any other time. In describing this pattern it is necessary to begin with the domestic transactions, for they were of great importance in the overall context of his business.

While the value of inland bills was invariably lower, on average, than the value of foreign bills, the former were much more numerous in most years, and in only one year, 1786, did the average number of inland bills fall below 60 per cent. In 1787 there were no foreign bills registered at all, and in most years inland bills accounted for upwards of three-quarters of all bills registered. It is not possible to draw any firm conclusions as to the velocity of the bill circulation from the register, because the number of endorsements on a bill at the time Davenport received it is not given. But it is clear from the entries, however, that the proportion of small bills rose with marked regularity during periods of slack trade, as did inland bills as a whole. There were exceptional years, of course, and in the wake of a real crisis of confidence the bill circulation would in any case have been an inadequate guide to the level of economic activity as traders became wary of accepting them. This insistence on cash payments which was a characteristic of such times probably had most effect on the domestic bill circulation. Among foreign traders, however, the impact could take a precisely opposite course and produce longer payment intervals for bills.[9] In interpreting the figures presented in appendix 3.1 it is necessary to bear these qualifications in mind, even though no attempt is made to measure them. The Davenport register comes to an end just before the imposition of stamp duty on bills of exchange; this means that it covers the last years before notes and coin began to be substituted for bills for tax avoidance reasons to any noticeable extent, and before marked interest-rate changes also began to influence the relative position of bills of exchange as a means of payment.[10]

Davenport's business career spanned more than half a century in Liverpool, from his apprenticeship in 1741 and subsequent partnership as a grocer with William Whalley, a pioneer slave trader, up till 1792, when he sold what appears to have been his last remaining share in the ship *Perseverance* of 300 tons to the Earle family.[11] Approximately two-thirds of the entries recorded in the bill register cover the latter half of the most prosperous period of his trading activities between the end of the Seven Years War and the outbreak of the War of American Independence. The record it provides of his transactions within Liverpool itself cannot be regarded as a complete illustration of the growth of slave trading in the port, but rather as one example, not entirely typical, of the pattern of transactions of a specialist slave merchant in the peak years of his involvement with the trade. The years of greatest activity extend from 1769, and presumably some years earlier, to 1773, and by focusing on this short period it is possible to give some indication of the variety of his local trade links in time of boom. The names of those Liverpool merchants and tradesmen who drew bills on more than one occasion in Liverpool and its environs, and which Davenport received at some stage in their circulation, totalled around 130. Many of these names do not appear in the town's directories of the period, but in any case it is clear that the larger and regular payments were with a fairly small group of no more than twenty merchant associates. In addition the entries for each year always show a number of bills received which were drawn in Liverpool by non-residents, generally from Manchester and London, but these always came to Davenport from a Liverpool resident and appear to be unexceptional. The bulk of the smaller payments were undoubtedly

made in connection with domestic affairs and voyage provisions of the
type represented in appendix 3.3.[12]

Davenport's larger local payments and receipts show that he was
dealing regularly with the most prominent slave traders of the period, and
it is known from his voyage accounts that he joined with them in both
ship and venture investment. Nevertheless his closest ties appear to have
been with the Earle family, William Earle and the related concern of
Earle & Hodgson. The names of William James, John Knight, Richard
Middleton and W. A. & R. Lightbody, who were related to the cotton
spinner Samuel Greg of Styal, also occurred frequently. Davenport also
dealt regularly with Felix Doran, Gill Slater and William Boats. All these
men were active in the slave trade in the early 1770s, but a complete list
even of Davenport's immediate associates would be considerably longer.
Furthermore not all his large transactions were with the slaving
fraternity, and some prominent names that recur in the entries for these
years are known to have been mainly occupied in other trades. For
example, Crosbies & Trafford and John Sparling were American
merchants, Edward Grayson was a shipbuilder, John Wyke was a
watchmaker, and George Campbell was a sugar merchant and refiner,
yet all had some connection with the slave trade. Indeed, as the bill
entries for this prosperous period reveal, few members of the Liverpool
mercantile community could have avoided being involved in a trade of
such wide ramifications.

Outside Liverpool the largest number of bills which Davenport
received were drawn in Manchester, typically by a well known merchant
at forty-five days, on average. Among the more important Manchester
drawers a number of different groups are recognisable. One consists of
substantial smallware manufacturers and includes names such as
Thomas Slack, Thomas Bancroft, Cheshyre & Ashworth, and N. & J.
Phillips, the greatest of all those who were bringing this branch of the
textile trade into the factory by the 1760s and were employing some of
the largest capitals in the industry. There were a small number of country
woollen manufacturers, including Thomas Smith of Ellenbrook and J. &
T. Kinder of Breightmet Hall. Most numerous, however, were the
fustian makers: smaller men such as J. Barton, J. Booth, J. & T.
Lawrence, who no doubt were representative of many in the growing
fustian branch that was thriving on new export markets at this time. In
Manchester and Salford their number rose from eighty-one in 1773 to
184 in 1788 and included men who were linking fustian to other branches
of the trade, such as J. Hadfield, Edward Kenyon, R. Hyde and James
Touchet (check and fustian). There were also representatives from other
branches such as the silk manufacture, with bills drawn by J. Harmar
and Caleb Clough, and from cotton by Charles Chadwick and William
Brocklehurst (manufacturers) and Charnbill & Clegg (merchants).
Among the rest there was J. Wilson, calico printer; T. Partington, malt

dealer; J. Allen, hatter; and not least S. Jones & Sons, tea dealers and bankers. Bills drawn by more than thirty Manchester names came into Davenport's hands with more or less regularity over the period.[13]

From elsewhere in the Lancashire textile area bills were drawn most frequently in Rochdale, mainly by fustian makers such as J. Teasdale, J. & R. Holt, Abraham Fletcher & Son, R. Chadwick, J. & B. Smith and T. Law & Co. Next came Stockport, with J. Scott, J. Palmer, R. Ellison and James Brown, the last being a check and cotton manufacturer. Preston bills were drawn by Edward Bolton, Adam Sanderson and Phibian Browne & Co. Those from Bolton came drawn by J. Ridgeway and Philip Bury, fustian makers and dyers, and from Bacup by James Maden. Warrington, Wigan and Prescot produced more variety. The first town was represented by ironmongers (Chorley & Harrison and Isaac Turner), sailcloth manufacturers (Samuel Gaskell and R. Rogerson, the patentee of the laundry machine for washing linen), J. Woodcock, an attorney, and E. Rimmer, a corn factor.[14] Similarly in Wigan bills were drawn by J. Lathom, a founder, J. Greenough and J. Scott, check manufacturers, and J. & J. Hodson, a merchant–manufacturer. Finally, from Prescot, there were bills drawn by the major coal proprietors, Edward Mollineux and Charles Dagnall, and by Hamlet Bell, a woollen and linen draper.

Occasionally these Lancashire bills went directly to Davenport, having been drawn on him personally, but most of them he received from other Liverpool merchants, many of whom were also involved in the slave trade. Most, though not all, of these Lancashire bills were ultimately paid to the credit of those involved in the supply of slave trade cargoes. But whereas Davenport received very few bills from the hinterland direct, he did send the majority direct to the London agents. This suggests that the Liverpool merchant community, and particularly the slave traders, cleared most of their debts to one another locally, and sent only their residual obligations to London. In the provision of textiles for Guinea cargoes Liverpool had always been well placed. Earlier in the century the port's efforts to break into the trade were aided by its ability to offer cheap Manchester goods to the West Indies markets, from where profit margins could be increased as a result of the opportunities for subsequently smuggling them into Spanish America. By the late 1760s the American colonies, the West Indies and Africa were the port's principal export markets for textiles.[15] Textiles were usually the most valuable part of a slave ship's cargo, and African demand for the lighter cotton and linen checks and stripes remained buoyant throughout this period. A considerable proportion of these cloths were re-exported Indian cottons, which were generally preferred by the exacting African buyer, but the falling off of Indian supplies in the 1750s with the break-up of the Mogul empire had given the Lancashire manufacturers an opportunity to improve their market share. At the end of the 1760s, however, re-exports of Indian cottons rose strongly once more, and, in the face of increasing raw cotton prices, Lancashire cotton checks were increasingly unable to maintain their tenuous hold on the African market.[16]

In the supply of light metal goods to the slave trade Liverpool appears to have reaped the greatest advantage from the decisive technical superiority gained by the English copper and brass manufacturers during the 1730s.[17] Copper and brass goods were valuable items in slave cargoes, and the development of the Lancashire industry was instrumental in enabling Liverpool to gain a competitive edge in the African trade. Here the port's proximity to copper ores from Anglesey and Ireland was an important advantage and enabled the Cheadle, Warrington and Macclesfield companies, all of which manufactured African goods such as neptunes and manillas, to carry on a growing export trade in the 1760s. According to Enfield, by 1770 the African market was by far the most important for wrought brass, copper and pewter wares exported from Liverpool.[18] In addition, Africa was second only to the American colonies for wrought iron exports at this time; indeed, both the Carron and Coalbrookdale companies had warehouses in Liverpool, the latter since 1745, largely for the purpose of supplying the slave trade.[19] The Carron gun warehouse was set up in 1780 to cater to the requirements of slave traders, privateers and the African market directly.[20] Following on the establishment by Charles Craven of a warehouse for Coalbrookdale goods in 1745, the company's interests in Liverpool were further increased in 1758 when George Perry, a Scots draughtsman employed by the company, came to Liverpool and set up the Phoenix foundry. This concern produced iron pots and kettles, as well as sugar-boiling pans, but Perry was also involved with experiments in boring cannon as well as carrying on a substantial gun trade.[21]

It is likely that Davenport obtained his trade firearms locally, since the relatively small number of Birmingham-drawn bills contain no obvious reference to arms suppliers there.[22] The most notable names were those of Humphreys & Lee and R. Walker, both linen and woollen drapers. In fact the only clear Birmingham connection with the trade was bills drawn by J. Lightwood, a buckle maker. Outside Lancashire, indeed, bills drawn in Yorkshire were much the most important group. From Leeds bills came drawn by Wormald & Fountaine, Greene & Ridsdale, Close & Carter, and Homer & Turner, all well known cloth exporters. From Halifax, they carried the names of Cooke & Kershaw, D. & D. Dyson, Pollard & Fenton, J. Woolner, J. Royds and W. Walker & Sons. Many Yorkshire firms were regular suppliers of cloth to Liverpool exporters for several overseas markets, most notably America, and since few appear to have been drawn for or against Davenport directly, or received from other Liverpool slave traders, it seems probable that few of the underlying transactions were concerned with the slave trade.[23] Three Sheffield firms were also regularly drawing bills received in Liverpool.

They were J. & J. Kenyon, the slitting-mill proprietors who produced files, bolts and hoops; Watson Raynor & Turner, merchants; and J. & B. Broomhead, later Broomhead Wilkinson & Brittain, from which firm all Davenport's Sheffield bills came.

Although bills drawn in a considerable number of other towns pass through Davenport's hands from time to time, it is impossible to be certain of the nature of the transactions they represent. These include Hull (Field & Alder), Bradford, (W. Butt and Thomas Wood), Bristol (Joseph Vaughan and Gillam & Edge), and Chester (Smith & Co. and J. Chamberlaine, both Irish factors). Irish-drawn bills came chiefly from Dublin (Richard Blood, Wm. Fuller and J. Allanson) and from Waterford (Edward Bill and Newport & Hobbs).[24] Scots-drawn bills came almost invariably from Glasgow, in particular from W. & W. Tait, Young Auchencloss Lang & Co., David Elliot and Adam Walker. Scots influence was, of course, considerable in the Islands, especially in Antigua and St Kitts.[25] Very few of Davenport's bills were drawn in London, but a large number were paid there. Since, however, these were virtually all foreign bills, it is convenient to consider them under that heading.

III

Firstly, there were those foreign bills which were drawn outside the West Indies and were not slave sales remittances. European bills were drawn mainly from Leghorn, Rotterdam, Bremen and Amsterdam, though a few also came from Danzig, Genoa and Ostend. The Leghorn bills are of some interest, for while they come in for payment quite frequently up to the early months of 1773 Davenport receives no more thereafter. Leghorn's free port had come to be the fulcrum of British trading activity in the Mediterranean by the eighteenth century. Earle & Hodgson were the premier Liverpool house in the Levant trade and by the 1770s had developed a direct trade with Leghorn, where they had a well established agency.[26] Davenport's Leghorn bills were invariably drawn against him by Earle & Hodgson, and he paid them direct to one or other of the firm's partners in Liverpool, or else to Peter Thelluson in London. These bills were drawn in favour of various Italian firms, including Franco Bros., Uzielli Bros. and David Archivotti, and a few English merchants, principally G. Oates & Son and Joseph White. We cannot be certain what these goods from Leghorn consisted of, beyond the fact that Liverpool's main inward trade with Italy covered a variety of drugs, such as aloes, aniseeds and liquorice, as well as cowries and beads of the Venetian type used in the slave trade, but they were always for Davenport's personal account. His other bills drawn in Continental ports were too few in number to have played a significant part in the pattern of his transactions, and their only interest is in showing that, in the case of

Rotterdam, they were almost always paid to W. & J. Anderson of Tower Hill, London, up to 1772, and thereafter to Sargent Chambers & Co.[27]

The main body of Davenport's bills were drawn in the West Indies and were remittances for the sales of slaves in the Islands to the credit of himself and his partners in their various ventures. Accordingly the chief interest of appendix 3.2, showing the sources of overseas trade bills registered by Davenport, lies in the picture it provides of the markets to which his slave cargoes were carried. In order of importance, Dominica was by far the most lucrative for the Davenport partnerships, followed by Jamaica, Grenada and Barbados. In addition, both the Leeward Islands and the Virgin Islands were of small significance compared with the Windward group, except in years of poor sales elsewhere. Among the principal markets Dominica and Grenada stand in sharp contrast with the older colonies of Jamaica and Barbados. The former were the most important of the ceded islands of 1763, and the rapidity with which they were subsequently developed for monoculture was a reflection of the acute scarcity of suitable unexploited land in the older British possessions in the Caribbean. The development of St Vincent was retarded by large privilege land grants covering more than a quarter of the island, together with the presence of a sizable Carib population which obstructed surveying work until it was effectively put down in 1772. The last Windward Island, St Lucia, was acquired only at the end of 1778 and was restored to France at the peace in 1783; it served as a naval base during the American war, its harbour being the main attraction for the British; indeed, its cultivation for sugar had only begun in 1765, and the war disrupted its progress for the remainder of the '80s.[28]

The Leeward and Virgin Islands as a whole were much less significant in the pattern of slave receipts, but Antigua, St Kitts and Tortola were important in certain years. By the third quarter of the eighteenth century Antigua had developed the most advanced plantation economy in the British Caribbean. By virtue of its low proportion of absentee proprietors, a somewhat more diverse agriculture, and a larger number of locally born slaves among its population, it had no appreciable need for imported labour for twenty years before 1775. Davenport had a large remittance from Antigua in 1778, the year in which France entered the American war, and another one in 1782, when the French were again in the ascendant. This was the period of marked reduction in the supply of sugars from the British islands, followed by sharp price increases, and this stimulus, together with the fact that in 1782 Antigua alone among the Leeward Islands remained in British hands, probably accounts for its importance in that year. The bulk of Davenport's returns from St Kitts came in 1774–75 and may well have been the result of precautionary slave purchases on the outbreak of war. Similarly, in the case of Tortola, the chaotic condition of administration and tenure rights long after the Virgins were granted a separate legislature in 1774 discouraged settlement and trade, and this almost certainly accounts for Davenport's unwillingness to venture there except in the bleak years of 1783–84.

The Davenport venturers' gross returns from the islands amounted to £216,844 between 1769 and 1786, of which more than 80 per cent came from Dominica, Jamaica, Grenada and Barbados. The dominance of Dominica, which alone accounted for more than 40 per cent of total receipts, cannot be explained in terms of its later development alone, for in addition it was a free port after 1766 and continued as such until 1780. The rapid growth of Davenport & Co.'s slave sales to this island during the late '60s and early '70s is not surprising in view of its rapid planting at this time, but the free status of its port, Roseau, also enabled slave traders to exploit its entrepot facilities in order to carry on a re-export trade to other islands and to South America. This no doubt explains Davenport's recurring interest in Dominica in 1770–73, 1775–78 and 1784–86. When it fell to the French in 1778 the major prop to slave trading was removed, and Davenport was forced to turn his attention to Jamaica. After the close of the American war, apart from a brief but lucrative spasm of sales in St Vincent, it was again Dominica which provided a market for Davenport's last ventures in the slave trade. These last returns were made between the end of hostilities early in 1783 and the upturn of trade in the last year of the decade, and it seems that the Dominican market alone was capable of any sustained expansion once the brief post-war activity of 1784 had extinguished itself. Even here individual sales were for relatively small sums, a reflection of how badly the island had suffered during the war and of the continued closure of the free ports until 1787.

Returns from Grenada were of most importance during the boom years of 1771–72, when the island was being actively settled by British planters, and again in 1774–75, but thereafter it became a negligible source of returns. Similarly in the case of Barbados, whose highest returns were registered in 1769–71 and 1774–75; its contribution was greatest during the general buoyancy of the slave markets in the first half of the '70s, albeit rather better sustained than in the case of most of the smaller islands. The other older colony of Jamaica, however, which had developed into the wealthiest slave entrepot even before the British had taken it from Spain in the previous century, appears to have held the greatest attraction for the Davenport venturers when demand in other important markets had already peaked or was at a low ebb. During the first half of the '70s, for example, the market was supported in turn by the demands of Barbados, Dominica and, in 1774, Jamaica. It contributed almost nothing in the period 1775–78 and then, in the years 1779–82, when demand was poor in almost all markets, including Dominica, there was a strong resurgence in Jamaican receipts, especially in 1779–80. The entry of the French into the American war in 1778 immediately re-emphasised the importance of Jamaica's position for

British merchants in the Caribbean. This was borne out in September of the same year when Dominica fell and, in 1779, when Grenada and St Vincent also capitulated to the French. Natural disasters in the British islands followed, and in 1781 only meagre returns came from St Lucia and St Kitts.

The loss of Dominica was naturally a severe blow to Davenport's trade, and it is clear that, apart from redirecting his attention to Jamaica, there was little he could do elsewhere to recompense himself. Antigua had made a useful contribution in 1778 by way of mitigating the fall-off in Domincan returns, and it was again to the fore in 1782 as the Jamaica receipts lost impetus. In 1783–84 Davenport registered receipts from Tortola, which suggests that in a final bid to wring some profit from the trade he had turned to the Virgin Islands, hitherto virtually ignored. In common with many merchants the year prior to Rodney's victory in April 1782 saw Davenport's fortunes at their lowest point. It was the year in which St Kitts, Montserrat and Nevis were taken, with the result that all the Leeward group, apart from Antigua, together with St Vincent and Grenada, were in French hands. The bill register cannot reveal how far produce returns were substituted for the operation of the bill system in these years but it seems unlikely to have been very significant. An estimate from the voyage accounts shows that in virtually every year in which voyages were undertaken, and for which accounts are reasonably complete, proceeds were remitted in the form of postdated bills in all but 8–10 per cent of cases. If, as seems likely, the condition of trade had little effect on the trader's willingness to accept produce or specie by way of remittance, then the bill register fairly accurately reflects the much reduced state of the slave trade in the last years of the war.[29]

Despite the fact that hostilities ceased early in 1783 and the last years of the Davenport bill transactions are a period of peace, the continuance of American exclusion from the West India trade ensured that planters' costs were kept high notwithstanding some reduction of freight and insurance rates to Britain. At the same time sugar prices fell during the post-war period so that profits were squeezed and sterling indebtedness lengthened. A series of hurricane disasters in 1784–86 completed a gloomy prognosis for planter and slave trader alike. The last bill entries were made in December 1788 and, though direct evidence is lacking, the failure of Davenport's slave trade activities to recover in the period 1784–86, when slave bills were still being entered in the register, can be attributed to three main factors. Davenport was sixty years of age in 1785, and this fact alone must have been something of an inducement to reduce the level of his involvement in trade. Furthermore, although the parliamentary campaign for abolition of 1787–89 failed to secure its object, the evidence of considerable abolitionist support which it revealed was sufficient to shake confidence in the future of the trade. It is difficult to gauge the immediate impact of the passage of Dolben's Bill on the firmness of merchants' commitments to the slave trade, but the terms of the Act, though they failed to prove as ruinous as the counter-propaganda of the slave interest had predicted, were nonetheless sufficiently onerous to affect Liverpool's competitive position. Thus even the limited success of political efforts to regulate the trade cannot be seen as a victory for the African merchants in the longer term.[30]

These considerations, taken together with the current state of the trade in the mid-'80s, must have merited a downward adjustment of profit expectations. The Liverpool merchants had gained a supremacy in the slave trade largely because of the peculiar suspectibility they had shown to changes in its profit opportunities. Those like Davenport, who had coped for so many years with the vagaries of the trade, could be expected to read the signs earlier and more clearly than most. Throughout his career he seems to have eschewed the political lobbying and the in-fighting for public offices that figured so largely in the rise of most of the prominent merchants of Liverpool. He was not even a member of the Company of Merchants Trading to Africa from Liverpool at its foundation in 1750.[31] It could be argued that this was an optimal position to adopt for a specialist in a trade that increasingly became a cause for humanitarian concern. But whatever the factors which encouraged Davenport to maintain a low public profile, his overseas trade links offered greater scope for a flexible response to changes in trading conditions. Even here, however, it would seem in retrospect that the generation of Liverpool merchants to which he belonged, and the pattern of the port's commercial relationships which he had helped to foster, had exerted their most pervasive influence in the decade or so before the American war. During the 1780s a series of changes in the direction and personnel of Liverpool's trade were coming to fruition, and these had the effect of seriously constraining the efforts of specialist slave merchants like Davenport to widen their trading interests.

Unlike others involved in the slave trade Davenport does not appear to have had direct trade links with the American mainland on his own account, and, as the few small American bills which came into his hands reveal, mainland transactions had little to do with the slave trade in his case. At the same time his relations with the trades to the Continental ports were few, and clearly incidental to his main business interests. He had, of course, developed some specialities which appear to have been an important source of profit from time to time, but these activities were, with one possible exception, closely related to his prime function as the ship's husband of slave-trading partnerships. His trading accounts and the reference to him in appendix 3.3 are evidence that Davenport was a major supplier of beads to the slave trade. It seems likely that his early ventures to the Gambia, where beads had always been an important trade good, had given him a certain expertise in this branch of West African commerce. As with so many currency and luxury items in demand there, such as cowries, copper and brass articles, fabrics and salt, an indigenous trade in beads predated by many centuries the first European contacts with the area and was certainly highly developed by the time of English pre-eminence in the slave trade. Indeed, as in the case of the slave traffic itself, Europeans diverted an existing trade as much as they created a new one. Glass beads or 'corals' were imported for the slave trade from Venice in the seventeenth century, and English manufacturers could certainly have emulated them by the eighteenth, besides adding porcelain beads and other glassware as well. Large quantities of beads, flint and green glass, and looking glasses were exported from Liverpool to Africa from the 1760s and some *emigré* traders in the port, most notably Solomon D'Aguilar, operated as specialist bead merchants at this period.[32] In Davenport's case his main interest in the bead trade was during the period 1766–70, when bead sales were accounted in a separate book kept for the purpose. The reason for this can almost certainly be attributed to the success in these years of Davenport's pioneering efforts in the late '50s to open up the Cameroons trade, in which beads were the most important item in demand, and when his receipts from bead sales alone were averaging around £10,000 per annum.

Davenport's ventures to West Africa were principally to Old Calabar, where textiles and copper goods were popular, and to the Cameroons, where beads, iron and brass wares were wanted.[33] It is not clear, on the other hand, how far he was also involved in the import trade from West Africa to Liverpool. This was principally concerned with dyewoods, such as barwood, camwood and orchella, but he does not appear to have had any agency arrangements on the West African coast similar to those of Edward Grace, the London merchant who was active in the direct trade to Senegambia at the same time. In the trade to Old Calabar, a collection of settlements on the Cross river which served as the main slave distribution centre for the area east of the Niger delta, African produce was less important as a supplementary cargo. But at the Cameroons, where slave traders usually dealt directly with the Dualas on their ships in Ambas bay, there appears to have been rather more produce trading. However, since this was a barter trade, the few bills drawn in Old Calabar which Davenport received, usually drawn on him by the master of his vessel in favour of another ship's master, can tell very little about the import trade apart from the fact that it was integral to the slaving venture as a whole.

Davenport's other activities can also be interpreted as being ancillary to his chief function as a manager of slaving ventures. He was, for example, the principal partner in a firm of wine merchants during the late '60s and '70s, possibly involving his brothers, Christopher and Richard, who also resided in Liverpool and were concerned in some of his ventures. The bill register shows that he was also transacting business with Peter Holme, a Liverpool brandy merchant, as well as with a firm styled Davenport Gaskell & Co., which suggests a link between him and the Liverpool brewers, Gaskell & Co. Although the precise nature of his connection with the wine trade is not known, it was a well established practice for wines imported from Portugal, Spain and Madeira to be taken aboard by slave ships *en route*. Davenport's marketing contacts were virtually all in the West Indies, so that he does not appear to have been well placed to break into the corn trade as some slave traders to Virginia and Maryland were doing at this time. His connection with the Leghorn trade and his early experience in the grocery business, however, were an ideal background for wine merchanting and, indeed, for his bead business. Another facet of the Liverpool slave merchant's activities was the part ownership of vessels and privateering and insurance speculations. Ownership of shares in the vessel and control of the partnership venture it undertook were normal practice in the slave trade, and in addition, of course, Davenport owned shares in ships which he did not manage; apart from the reduction of risk to the individual merchant this two-tier partnership organisation gave such merchants an extremely wide interest in ship owning. Such a pronounced tendency to risk aversion was a necessity forced on the slave trader by the variable profits of his trade. It showed itself not only in the broad spread and high turnover of his shipping investments but also in his willingness to speculate in privateering, marine insurance and sometimes banking. Being related activities, they required similar aptitudes, and slave merchants such as Davenport moved naturally from one to another or combined several of them together. During the American war, when the number and profitability of his slaving voyages fell away, Davenport took a share in the privateer *Sturdy Beggar*, which brought home three prizes in 1779, and he was also involved in the underwriting partnership for the notorious slaver *Zong* in 1781.[34] These activities, however, need to be seen in the overall context of his career in the slave trade through the entire period covered by the record of his bill receipts; these enable us to trace the broad lines of his fluctuating fortunes from the time of his greatest influence in the trade to his exit from it.

IV

The expansion phase which came to an end in mid-1771 had been very broad-based and was characterised by a rapid increase in foreign trade. Davenport's foreign bill receipts reflect these favourable trading conditions, which particularly affected the West India trade. In 1769 there were large receipts in May and to a lesser extent in July; they were high-value bills drawn in Barbados by firms such as Comberbach & Walker, J. Hamilton & Co. and Stevenson & Went on their parent houses in Britain. Usance was from three to nine months, and usually

Davenport masters had received them from the slave factors who directed the sales, in these instances John Haslon and Lake & Prettijohn. When discounted these credit balances must have helped to finance his Leghorn expenditures in July, when he was drawn on directly by Earle & Hodgson. The following year saw another upsurge in foreign bills, again drawn in Barbados and amounting to more than £4,000: their receipt coincided with the entry of debit bills drawn in Rotterdam and Leghorn. All the Rotterdam bills on Davenport were drawn by W. & J. Manson in favour of W. & J. Anderson, and it would appear that, as with Earle & Hodgson in the Leghorn trade, Davenport invariably conducted whatever Rotterdam business he had through Manson & Co. Another batch of high-value bills arrived in July 1770, on this occasion from Dominica, and were drawn to Davenport's credit by Lovell Morson & Co. on Kinder Mason & Co. in London. In turn these were followed by a series of Leghorn bills which, as usual, were paid to or through Earle & Hodgson by means of Davenport's credit with Peter Thelluson in London.

During the winter further batches of slave bills arrived from the islands. Those from Barbados were drawn by Stevenson & Went on Lascelles & Co., and those from Dominica by W. & W. Dickinson on Soccothick & Apthorpe. In March 1771 a very large set of Grenada bills at twelve months arrived, to be followed by others from Dominica, Antigua and one from St Eustatius. Although several of the Grenada bills were drawn in Davenport's favour, most of them were to the credit of Clarmont & Pache, from whom he had received the entire set. Most of these were drawn on Lewis Chauvet and paid immediately to Tennant & Co. Foreign bill receipts remained at a high level through April and May, with three Barbados bills for large sums coming from Stevenson & Went. Davenport paid these to Joseph Wimpey eventually, though one he held for almost a year. A set of Jamaica bills were entered in the register for November; these were drawn for only ninety days in favour of Charles White, and received from him, against various Liverpool traders, including Peter Holme and Sorocold & Jackson. These completed Davenport's slave receipts for 1771 and, again, they coincided with the entry of a series of Leghorn bills drawn against him and others. Leghorn debits continued to come in during the opening months of 1772 as well, with Earle & Hodgson drawing against him on behalf of various suppliers and being paid through Thelluson & Co. Then in March and April there came a stream of bills from the Islands, first from Dominica, with Lovell & Morson drawing on Kinder Mason & Co., then from Jamaica, with Charles White drawing on Peter Holme, and lastly from Grenada, with Threlfall & Anderson drawing on William Snell. In May and June came a group of Leghorn bills conforming to the usual pattern of groups of debit bills of low value being paid after the receipt of a batch of high-value slave bills.

The decline in trading activity during 1773 is reflected in Davenport's bill transactions for the year. The returns from Barbados in April were at a much lower level than previously; in fact his best month was June, when he received just under £4,000 in two bills from St Vincent. They were drawn by R. Cunningham on William Snell and were eventually paid to Joseph Denison. The returns from Dominica in August were of small consequence; those which arrived in October were little better, and the last months of the year showed no foreign returns at all. The situation improved in 1774, but while transactions were at a higher level the foreign entries in particular were heavily concentrated in January, March, June and July. The Barbados bills again came in January and those from Jamaica and Grenada in March. In Jamaica slaves had been sold to Ford Clarke & Co., who drew on Samuel Delpratt in London. More came from Jamaica in June, and in July the first significant returns from St Kitts arrived, drawn by Baillies Fraser & Co. on Maitland & Boddington. But the second half of the year saw very few foreign returns and none of any great value.

In 1775 the slave remittances were again highly concentrated, with a large parcel from Dominica and some from Barbados. April brought a set from St Kitts, then there was a long gap through the summer before three Grenada bills were entered in September. These were drawn by Thomas Willis on Richard Willis & Co., the parent house, at between fifteen and twenty-four months. These bills were noticeably longer-dated than previously, but if credit was getting easier sales were still falling. Over the next two years Davenport's dependence on the Dominican market, always considerable, now became complete. Bills from this island arrived in February 1776 drawn by Robert Vance on Kinder Mason & Co. and ranged from nine to twenty-four months. More came from the same source in June and August, but then came a bleak year for both domestic and foreign transactions. At length, in August 1777, the Dominica returns arrived, this time drawn by the reconstituted partnership of Morson Vance Caldwell & Vance. They were not strictly bills of exchange but personal promissory notes ranging from eighteen to thirty months, but they were all apparently paid. Either Davenport must have been confident of payment or, more likely, the rapid contraction of the market and the exhaustion of credit in the other islands had left him no choice. Certainly in October he took another parcel of notes ranging from six to thirty-six months. The evidence of the register entries at this time indicates that some time during the latter half of 1776 and the first half of 1777 the slave factor had refused to cover the planter's slave purchases with his own bills and instead was selling them at the slave trader's own risk, then transmitting the buyer's notes direct. In such a poor market situation, when the bill system no longer operated, the only defence of the agency factor may have been to vacate the ground between planter and slaver, apart from acting merely as an intermediary.

If this was the case, then it provides an answer to the question what happened to the slave merchant when the financial support of the planter by the London West India house, via its Island agent, broke down.[35] For Davenport the answer was a Dominican debt of almost £15,000 at the end of 1777 which, even in the short term, must have severely strained his resources.

During 1778 Davenport appears to have allowed Vance Caldwell & Vance to draw on him in favour of a large number of people at forty days' sight, apparently to ensure that his slave remittances came through in August. But sales in Dominica were half the level of the previous year and the remittance was again made in notes of hand. Three Antigua receipts were entered in July, but credit appears to have been so bad there that Davenport took produce to the value of his sales. From September 1778 to September 1779 foreign bills received were barely more than £1,000, then in October three high-value Jamaica bills came drawn in his favour by W. Thompson on J. Thompson & Co. Another lean period followed, until in July 1780 a sudden upswing in receipts gave him his second highest monthly returns for the whole period. These too were Jamaica bills, a parcel of fifteen for £660 each, drawn in favour of Thomas Earle, John Copeland, Parke & Heywood and Davenport himself. Yet they proved to be no more than a sharp fluctuation in a trend that continued to move down to the low point of 1781, when foreign bills accounted for only 6 per cent of the total received and 10 per cent of their value. The final quarter saw the beginnings of a modest rise in the level of bill transactions, extending through to the autumn of 1784, but lack of support from activity elsewhere brought a sharp retraction in 1785, and during 1787 Davenport's business was virtually at a stand.

The cyclical behaviour of the number and value of the bill transactions, together with changes in their currency or usance, provide a useful guide to the course of Davenport's business, and when allowance is made for a lag of some months, in the case of foreign bills especially, they show how slave trading responded to the economic and political vicissitudes of the period. The dominant feature of these transactions was the relatively high value, small number and long currency of bills drawn outside Britain, and specifically those emanating from the West Indies. Two peaks can be identified in the level of foreign transactions. One coincided with the crisis of 1772, following which the recovery was fairly rapid, and the other was attained in 1776 on a very narrow base. It was only from this second peak, marking the outbreak of the American war, that the decline in the number of foreign bills which had begun during 1772–73 had a significant effect on their values. The trough in foreign transactions came in 1781 but, though the proportion of foreign to total bills quickly recovered, the overall level of transactions continued to fall. Thus domestic influences appear to have been partly responsible for the fact that the ending of the American war failed to restore Davenport's trading position. The onset of the trade depression in Lancashire, culminating in the crisis of 1788, has been characterised as "largely, though not exclusively, a matter of the cotton industry".[36] Yet domestic conditions unquestionably had an important impact on the slave trade, not only during the war years when the progressive reduction in Davenport's overseas activities did not drastically depress the overall level of his transactions until 1782, but also during the post-war period when domestic activity fell in line with total transactions.

The key figures in the remittance system linking Davenport to his suppliers and partners on the one hand, and to his customers in Africa and the Islands on the other, were the payees of the slave bills sent to him. Examination of these shows that the slave trader was ultimately dependent on a fairly small group of major acceptance merchants in London for his payments. This was also the case with most bills drawn overseas and, indeed, for a considerable proportion of inland bills as well. In the case of some American-drawn bills Davenport found it more convenient to pay them to local merchants in the Virginia trade, such as Crosbie & Co. or John Sparling; and similarly with bills drawn in Bremen and Danzig, which he paid to Baltic traders such as Lace & Co. or Thomas Lickbarrow. But the large remittances from the Islands were almost invariably sent to London. The names of these payees changed from time to time, but those which appear consistently through the period numbered no more than a dozen. Some, such as Thelluson, Sanderson and Alexander, were the forerunners of the specialised bill-broking firms of the nineteenth century. These were the discount bankers – literally merchants' bankers – whose assets largely consisted of commercial bills. Others were still active in trade and not yet completely specialised discounters, such as Joseph Wimpey, merchant; Morson & Stevenson, goldsmiths; Tennant Cust & Co. and Clarmont & Pache, merchants. Some were respected City merchants, such as George Mason of Kinder Mason & Co., who was a Sun Fire Office director, and Richard Maitland of Maitland & Co., who was a Royal Exchange Assurance director. Yet others were connected with specific trades, such as Pigou Andrews & Co., the gunpowder merchants, and A. & C. Lindegren, an important name in London's trade with the Low Countries.[37]

There is no evidence in the bill register that discounts were calculated on bills in order to adjust for usance at this period, and it seems safe to assume that the time to maturity was normally compensated for in the price of the goods which the bill was used to purchase. This cannot have been the case invariably, for houses of high standing must always have been able to insist on an allowance, while bills of very long currency often had to be treated with some leniency, as in the case of some of those accepted by Davenport from the West Indies. In Henry Thornton's words, "If any bill given in payment has a longer time than usual to run,

he who received it is considered as so far favouring the person from
whom he takes it; and the favoured person has to compensate for this
advantage, not, perhaps by a recompense of the same kind accurately
calculated, but in the general adjustment of the pecuniary affairs of the
two parties."[38] Forbearance and co-operation between merchants was
essential to the working of the bill system at times of commercial
pressure. In general, Davenport appears to have retained quite long-
dated bills to maturity even when trade was poor, and only when his own
financial position became pressing did he have them discounted. It is
noteworthy that at such times more of his bills appear to have been paid
away locally to discharge the mounting obligations which he owed to
other Liverpool merchants.[39]

V

Davenport's voyage accounts begin in 1757 and end in 1785, while the
bill register contains no entries of slave remittances, or indeed of foreign
bills at all, after 1786. His apparent retirement between the two periods
of rapid trade expansion in the early '70s and the early '90s meant that he
failed to participate in the last great West India boom of the eighteenth
century when slave trading, having recovered in 1789, reached
unprecedented heights after the uprising in Saint Domingue sent sugar
prices soaring and transformed the prospects for the British islands. In
addition to this new lease of life for the slave trade, the wine and spirits
trade in which Davenport had also been involved expanded enormously
down to 1793 after the commercial treaty with France.[40] After the
outbreak of war with France many Liverpool slave traders reverted once
more to privateering, where success could bring vast profits.

On the other hand it can be argued that Davenport had quit the trade
at the most opportune time. Profitability was falling for many European
slave traders during the 1770s, and some attempts were even made to
subsidise the trade on grounds of national importance.[41] The American
war had disrupted the mechanism of interrelated payments in
the Atlantic trades, and slave prices fell. Moreover during
the 1780s the African and West Indian trades, though they continued to
be the most important of Liverpool's trades, were no longer the dynamic
force in the growth of the port's economy. Between the mid-'60s and the
early '90s the African trade was the slowest-growing branch of
Liverpool's trade in terms of additional shipping employed. Arrivals and
sailings from Africa and the American colonies accounted for more than
a quarter of total entries and clearances at Liverpool in 1764. In the
depression year of 1786 they accounted for only one-sixth and even in
the boom year of 1792 for less than one-fifth of the total. Since these
figures included the American trade, the African and West Indian trades
were even less important than they suggest. Liverpool's extra-colonial

trade, on the other hand, was already responding to the push and pull of industrialisation. The port's trade with America and Europe grew remarkably: in the case of the latter the number of entries and clearances had all but doubled between 1764 and 1792.[42] But as Davenport's experience shows, the rapid regeneration of Transatlantic trade after the American war yielded few easy profit opportunities for slave traders in general.[43] In addition to having seen their profits squeezed between rising costs and falling prices during the war, English merchants in the West Indian and African trades had also had to contend with the incursion of foreign ships that occurred at the same time. One estimate puts the growth of foreign tonnage entering British ports at 13 per cent in 1775, rising to 36 per cent in 1782.[44] Furthermore after 1783 the United States could no longer trade directly with the British plantations, and the West Indies continued to be depressed as a result. The fact that United States exports could now enter Britain on equal terms with those of British possessions was, on the other hand, one of the key elements in bringing about a major structural change during the trade revival in favour of Anglo-American commerce. The American trade was the most important of the new import trades which took shape in the 1780s and, notwithstanding continued political difficulties, it grew at a faster rate than any other branch of Liverpool's commerce. In the next decade Liverpool was to displace London as the chief port in American trade. Moreover after 1787 the relaxation of the navigation laws enabled Spanish colonial ships to enter the 'free' West Indian ports, and this opened up a potentially large trade with South America to Liverpool merchants. These new trading opportunities exerted considerable attraction on the younger merchants, who often lacked the wide contacts and strong credit of those who were reared on sugar and slaves. They also began to emerge just when the traditional role and privileges of the British West Indies in the supply of tropical produce to the mother country were being seriously questioned.[45]

Thus at the time of Davenport's retirement the Liverpool mercantile community was already in process of making itself much less dependent on the slave trade. For the African–West Indian connection of Liverpool the 1790s was a decade punctuated by severe setbacks, and failures and near-failures figured prominently in the crises of 1793, 1795 and 1799. These branches of the port's trade remained the most valuable, nonetheless; indeed, Liverpool continued to increase her share of the slave trade from under 70 per cent in 1785–87 to just less than 85 per cent in 1795–97, and to virtually 90 per cent in 1802–04.[46] Such an achievement, in a trade that was no longer growing rapidly, has yet to be fully explained. It seems unlikely, however, that the alleged superiority of Liverpool's expertise in the fitting out of slave ships and in the time taken to complete the voyage can be regarded as entirely adequate. Initial fitting out costs and the number of slaves purchased on the African coast were, of course, the most important factors determining the profitability of a slaving venture.[47] It may be that Liverpool managed to maintain its efficiency in these respects during the 1790s by enlarging the partnership organisation of its trade, thus facilitating limited participation by individuals in a trade whose capital requirements had risen after the war. Too little is known of the size, structure and constitution of the Liverpool slaving interest at this period to be certain, but there does appear to have been a considerable concentration of control in the decade after 1783. An anonymous account of the trade in 1795 held that it was "... clearly affianced to about ten capital houses who by making regular and annual returns from that commerce, may be supposed to considerably increase their fortunes ...". The real significance of this comment may not be the number of specialist houses involved but the emphasis laid by the author on "regular and annual returns".[48] There is a growing body of evidence to suggest that the ultimate yardstick of success or failure in the slave trade was not so much the achievement of a healthy internal rate of return to the individual expedition but the ability of the trader to realise his net profit quickly and easily on a regular basis. Here the role of British merchants, and those of Liverpool in particular, in fashioning the bill remittance system to the requirements of the slave trade was arguably the crucial factor behind their success. By comparison with their French and Dutch counterparts the Liverpool slave traders appear to have been much more independent of colonial credit and relatively unencumbered with the heavy indebtedness of the plantation economy. The case of William Davenport shows that the secret of success in the slave traffic lay with those who vigorously pursued a limited commitment to the triangular trade, and who had access to the financial arrangements necessary to extricate their profits from it.

Appendix 3.1 Abstract of the bill register of Messrs. Davenport & Co., 1769–87.

	(1)	(2)	(3)	(4)	(5)	(6)	(7)
Month and year	No. of bills received	Value of bills received (£)	(2)–(1)	Average usance (days)	No. of foreign bills received	Value of foreign bills received (£)	(6)–(5)
April	12	1,313	109	49	1	100	100
May	42	4,996	119	66	11	3,220	293
June	38	1,997	52	55	2	267	133
July	36	2,716	75	50	7	1,136	162
August	18	2,359	131	48	1	463	463
September	15	1,218	81	76	3	505	168
October	27	2,458	91	47	1	650	650

November	27	2,371	88	51	1	300	300
December	26	2,072	80	55	0	0	0
1769	241	21,500	89	55	27 (11%)	6,641 (31%)	252
January	31	7,616	246	74	12	6,135	511
February	7	1,388	198	55	3	1,184	395
March	25	2,650	106	56	6	1,232	205
April	19	1,155	61	47	0	0	0
May	34	3,097	91	66	3	479	160
June	8	1,335	167	54	3	1,048	349
July	25	5,925	237	83	8	3,081	385
August	27	3,388	125	60	11	1,447	131
September	21	4,983	237	57	3	502	167
October	20	3,099	155	67	5	941	188
November	14	1,979	141	54	4	778	194
December	23	3,319	144	69	7	2,578	368
1770	254	39,934	155	62	65 (26%)	19,405 (49%)	254
January	21	5,621	268	94	5	4,628	926
February	12	1,405	117	98	3	1,060	353
March	33	9,641	292	216	20	8,506	425
April	27	5,732	212	75	8	3,747	468
May	28	7,635	273	77	8	5,811	726
June	32	3,834	120	60	1	709	709
July	27	1,146	42	45	4	311	78
August	30	2,128	71	65	0	0	0
September	30	4,561	152	74	4	648	162
October	9	508	56	46	1	187	187
November	32	3,150	98	70	15	2,065	138
December	26	3,058	118	62	5	1,415	283
1771	307	48,419	158	82	74 (24%)	29,087 (60%)	371
January	16	2,859	179	122	4	403	101
February	23	3,857	168	57	13	2,312	178
March	31	8,105	261	142	18	7,369	409
April	27	6,644	246	220	14	5,546	396
May	26	2,430	93	64	11	1,422	129
June	22	1,979	90	58	8	1,049	131
July	16	6,286	393	109	5	4,732	946
August	18	1,737	96	76	3	874	291
September	21	6,678	318	88	4	5,372	1,343
October	13	748	57	51	0	0	0
November	33	5,384	163	71	13	4,356	335
December	32	3,646	114	62	17	2,369	139
1772	278	50,353	181	93 (40%)	110 (71%)	35,804	367

January	32	3,108	97	63	7	1,456	208
February	18	1,933	107	56	4	368	92
March	11	625	57	54	0	0	0
April	22	2,423	110	97	9	1,546	172
May	15	2,137	142	76	1	100	100
June	9	4,534	504	126	3	4,208	1,403
July	12	1,174	98	67	1	50	50
August	10	1,938	194	204	5	1,382	276
September	10	839	84	50	1	269	269
October	25	1,295	52	164	6	1,592	265
November	17	1,243	73	66	0	0	0
December	11	580	53	51	0	0	0
1773	192	21,829	114	89 (19%)	37 (50%)	10,971	236
January	14	5,195	371	139	8	4,781	598
February	3	704	235	47	0	0	0
March	39	12,472	320	297	28	11,914	426
April	18	1,523	85	56	1	39	39
May	15	1,257	84	60	0	0	0
June	22	4,335	197	180	10	3,948	395
July	24	5,411	225	280	7	3,867	552
August	11	324	29	24	0	0	0
September	30	3,118	104	71	2	373	187
October	7	152	22	37	0	0	0
November	11	462	42	59	0	0	0
December	14	1,096	78	62	2	171	86
1774	208	36,049	173	109 (28%)	58 (69%)	25,054	190
January	14	986	71	46	1	82	82
February	25	10,380	415	201	19	10,079	530
March	9	1,562	173	56	2	131	66
April	18	2,833	157	118	5	1,846	369
May	3	264	88	80	0	0	0
June	12	699	58	44	0	0	0
July	6	262	44	51	0	0	0
August	3	138	46	58	0	0	0
September	19	4,584	241	152	4	2,256	564
October	12	786	65	51	2	120	60
November	6	423	70	49	0	0	0
December	5	184	37	36	1	17	17
1775	132	23,101	175	78	34 (26%)	14,531 (63%)	141
January	7	824	118	49	0	0	0
February	16	6,544	409	363	12	6,250	521
March	7	686	98	69	1	240	240
April	22	1,874	85	45	0	0	0
May	6	429	71	67	0	0	0
June	19	5,156	271	277	8	4,696	587
July	4	210	52	56	1	135	135
August	17	6,402	376	235	6	5,654	942

September	7	486	69	49	0	0	0
October	7	284	40	64	0	0	0
November	10	1,127	113	172	3	678	226
December	3	137	46	54	0	0	0
1776	125	24,159	193	125	31 (25%)	17,653 (73%)	221
January	7	715	102	84	1	310	310
February	10	807	81	68	1	33	33
March	10	739	74	53	0	0	0
April	18	1,964	109	50	0	0	0
May	22	2,345	106	130	0	0	0
June	6	1,121	187	160	2	504	252
July	15	5,551	370	337	7	4,305	615
August	15	778	52	67	1	103	103
September	17	2,417	142	86	3	1,556	519
October	22	9,411	428	291	7	8,324	1,189
November	10	1,095	109	42	1	100	100
December	18	3,230	179	116	0	0	0
1777	170	30,173	177	124	23 (14%)	15,235 (50%)	260
January	7	500	71	0	0	0	0
February	8	718	89	48	1	110	110
March	20	2,467	123	76	14	1,801	129
April	10	616	62	62	1	300	300
May	31	1,408	45	146	1	123	123
June	34	2,719	80	57	0	0	0
July	15	6,929	462	130	8	6,369	796
August	9	5,290	588	314	5	5,038	1,008
September	32	2,957	92	55	0	0	0
October	12	623	52	39	0	0	0
November	2	138	69	60	1	100	100
December	9	431	48	58	2	194	97
1778	189	24,796	131	92	33 (17%)	14,035 (57%)	222
January	19	1,994	105	61	0	0	0
February	12	685	57	61	0	0	0
March	20	1,482	74	63	1	100	100
April	49	2,441	50	60	0	0	0
May	11	1,027	93	63	1	400	400
June	9	1,212	135	66	3	369	123
July	14	590	42	55	0	0	0
August	7	387	55	49	0	0	0
September	7	249	35	40	1	100	100
October	23	9,440	410	108	3	6,480	2,160
November	16	1,364	85	55	0	0	0
December	7	396	56	46	0	0	0
1779	194	21,267	110	61	9 (5%)	7,449 (35%)	240

January	3	440	147	64	0	0	0
February	18	3,698	205	47	0	0	0
March	29	2,431	84	64	4	992	248
April	12	2,197	183	49	0	0	0
May	12	2,358	196	53	1	60	60
June	5	385	77	65	0	0	0
July	40	11,816	295	375	15	9,915	661
August	33	1,566	47	53	2	208	104
September	17	1,387	81	65	1	83	83
October	12	795	66	73	0	0	0
November	12	1,637	136	115	4	1,048	262
December	27	2,482	92	53	2	738	369
1780	220	31,192	142	90	29 (13%)	13,044 (42%)	149
January	48	3,699	77	57	1	16	16
February	26	1,270	49	56	0	0	0
March	19	1,866	98	47	2	279	140
April	52	8,230	158	63	3	357	119
May	7	885	126	71	0	0	0
June	7	197	28	55	0	0	0
July	12	2,475	206	36	0	0	0
August	8	350	44	48	0	0	0
September	4	915	229	34	0	0	0
October	26	5,527	212	72	4	1,136	284
November	27	3,129	116	58	1	305	305
December	21	3,165	151	92	4	1,077	269
1781	257	31,708	123	57	15 (6%)	3,170 (10%)	94
January	18	4,987	277	199	3	1,848	616
February	8	1,151	144	61	2	324	162
March	3	267	89	45	1	228	228
April	5	739	148	66	1	150	150
May	21	598	28	58	0	0	0
June	11	477	43	55	0	0	0
July	12	2,943	245	152	3	2,172	724
August	1	114	114	10	1	114	114
September	14	2,334	167	56	1	1,293	1,293
October	17	2,214	130	51	5	1,029	206
November	10	504	50	57	0	0	0
December	13	420	32	52	0	0	0
1782	133	16,748	126	72	17 (13%)	7,158 (43%)	291
January	8	1,214	152	62	2	200	100
February	11	860	78	76	0	0	0
March	24	2,668	111	63	0	0	0
April	10	943	94	47	0	0	0
May	13	3,276	252	116	6	2,889	482
June	4	486	121	43	0	0	0
July	10	3,577	358	189	6	2,985	498
August	1	37	21	0	0	0	0

September	6	918	153	44	1	264	264
October	4	439	110	36	0	0	0
November	2	43	21	60	0	0	0
December	4	1,293	323	468	3	1,242	414
1783	97	15,754	162	102	18 (19%)	7,580 (48%)	147
January	3	209	70	60	0	0	0
February	11	969	88	63	0	0	0
March	5	249	50	41	0	0	0
April	11	1,918	174	189	4	1,428	357
May	11	2,897	263	256	10	2,835	284
June	3	310	103	64	0	0	0
July	4	704	176	53	0	0	0
August	7	506	72	46	1	209	209
September	23	8,017	348	327	14	7,634	545
October	5	324	65	48	1	14	14
November	3	51	17	60	0	0	0
December	1	44	44	40	0	0	0
1784	87	16,198	186	104	30 (34%)	12,120 (75%)	117
January	1	62	62	70	0	0	0
February	2	21	10	75	0	0	0
March	1	125	125	285	0	0	0
April	6	1,871	312	365	4	1,461	365
May	6	2,195	366	287	4	2,012	503
June	4	522	130	71	0	0	0
July	1	55	55	10	0	0	0
August	1	32	32	60	0	0	0
September	3	885	295	455	3	885	295
October	0	0	0	0	0	0	0
November	5	917	183	61	0	0	0
December	1	43	43	40	0	0	0
1785	31	6,728	217	162	11 (35%)	4,358 (65%)	97
January	1	204	204	10	1	204	204
February	0	0	0	0	0	0	0
March	6	1,500	250	199	2	194	457
April	26	4,329	166	380	25	4,244	170
May		0	0	0	0	0	0
June	0	0	0	0	0	0	0
July	8	315	39	54	1	35	35
August	31	4,457	144	331	24	3,792	158
September	6	196	33	61	0	0	0
October	1	84	84	30	0	0	0
November	7	585	84	57	0	0	0
December	0	0	0	0	0	0	0
1786	86	11,670	136	140	53 (62%)	9,189 (79%)	85

concluded on p. 88

APPENDIX 3.2 Sources of foreign bills, 1769–86

Year of receipt	1769	1770	1771	1772	1773	1774	1775	1776	1777	1778	1779
Barbados	2,348(6)	7,091(13)	4,959(3)	221(1)	1,380(8)	4,137(7)	1,959(8)		130(2)	50(1)	6,635(4)
Jamaica	230(2)	183(3)	1,310(9)	3,127(15)	469(3)	10,478(30)	40(1)				
Windward Islands											
Dominica	493(2)	7,312(8)	5,638(5)	14,072(12)	2,391(9)		8,060(10)	17,313(28)	15,195(2)	8,392(23)	
Grenada		184(1)	7,894(19)	4,946(10)		6,387(13)	2,273(5)				
St Vincent			2,001(1)		4,177(3)						
St Lucia											
Leeward Islands											
Antigua	300(1)		80(1)								
Montserrat										5,241(3)	400(1)
Nevis											
St Eustatius			682(1)								
St Kitts			786(2)			3,817(6)	3,210(4)	55(1)			
Virgin Islands											
St Croix	357(2)										
Tortola									310(1)		
Old Calabar					264(1)						
America											
Virginia	126(2)	272(4)	456(4)	2,919(4)							
South Carolina		118(1)	200(1)				2(1)				
Maryland			434(2)	50(1)							
New York			100(1)	200(1)							
Rotterdam, Amsterdam and Antwerp	1,628(7)	220(1)	700(3)	391(2)	1,066(5)	319(3)	271(4)	285(2)	100(1)	458(4)	414(4)
Bremen and Danzig			260(3)	279(4)							
Leghorn and Genoa	1,599(8)	7,489(33)	4,398(19)	9,340(60)	1,224(8)		40(1)				

Year of receipt	1780	1781	1782	1783	1784	1785	1786	1787	1788	Total (£)
Barbados	10,097(17)	105(2)	2,098(5)		18(1)					22,225(48)
Jamaica										34,840(93)
Windward Islands										
Dominica	2,527(6)				1,463(5)	2,897(7)	8,894(50)			94,154(183)
Grenada				264(1)		1,221(3)				23,662(54)
St Vincent		1,233(4)			7,634(14)					12,011(18)
St Lucia					1,242(3)					2,703(8)
Leeward Islands										
Antigua	60(1)		2,567(4)		1,372(5)	240(1)				9,860(16)
Montserrat										400(1)
Nevis					209(1)					209(1)
St Eustatius										682(1)
St Kitts		1,186(5)	70(1)							9,124(19)
Virgin Islands										
St Croix										685(3)
Tortola				4,879(10)	1,410(3)					6,289(13)
Old Calabar	50(1)		114(1)				260(6)			688(5)
America										
Virginia										3,773(14)
South Carolina										400(3)
Maryland										484(3)
New York			1,293(1)							1,593(3)
Rotterdam, Amsterdam and Antwerp	309(4)	584(3)	788(4)							7,533(47)
Bremen and Danzig										574(8)
Leghorn and Genoa							35(1)			24,090(129)

January	0	0	0	0	0	0	0
February	2	299	149	60	0	0	0
March	0	0	0	0	0	0	0
April	2	204	102	30	0	0	0
May	0	0	0	0	0	0	0
June	0	0	0	0	0	0	0
July	0	0	0	0	0	0	0
August	0	0	0	0	0	0	0
September	2	15	7	40	0	0	0
October	5	570	114	42	0	0	0
November	0	0	0	0	0	0	0
December	1	337	337	90	0	0	0
1787	12	1,425	119	52	0	0	0

Appendix 3.3 Invoice of Sundry Merchandize shipt on board the Snow Aston for the River Gambia on the proper account and risque of Messrs. John Knight & Co., Owners of Said Vessell, and goes consign'd to Capt. John Clifton for Negroes, Bees Wax & Ivory viz.

Liverpool, 25 June 1771

		£	s	d	£	s	d
148 p.s. 7/8 Chelloes, 7 yards,	6/4,	46	17	4			
112 p.s. yd. wide, 8 yards,	7/-,	39	4				
30 p.s. Checkorees, 10 yards,	9/-,	13	10				
30 p.s. mixt Checkorees, 10 yards,	10/6,	15	15				
20 p.s. Erminetts, 8 yards,	9/4,	9	6	8			
10 p.s. yd. wide Carrideries, 10 yards,	17/-,	8	10				
10 p.s. mixt. Photaes, 14 yards,	15/-,	7	10				
40 p.s. Tearing Basts, 18 yards,	24/-,	48					
20 p.s. All Cotton Basts, 18 yards,	28/-,	28					
210 p.s. St. Iago Cloths,	9/-,	94	10				
10 p.s. Superfine Cloths,	12/-,	6					
Cartage to the quay and freight to Liverpool		6					

317 9

Negroe Fringe

		£	s	d	£	s	d
200 p.s. Blue Basts, India dye,	42/-	420					
200 p.s. Blue Basts, English dye,	35/-,	350					
30 p.s. Cushtaes,	14/6,	21	15				
10 p.s. Bandanoes Spotted,	27/-,	13	10				
10 p.s. Bandanoes Flowered,	20/6,	10	5				
4 p.s. Persians, Narrow Stripe,	58/-,	11	12				
30 p.s. Chintz, 18 yards, Sattin stripe,	34/-,	658					
10 p.s. Chintz, 18 yards, Guinea Hen,	32/-	16					
Charges of Entry, etc.		3	12				

914 14

		£	s	d
4 doz. Men's bound Hatts,	15/-		3	
4 doz. Men's worsted Caps,	5/6		1	2
4 p.s. Scarlett Cloth, 133¾ yards,	6/3	41	15	11¼
Wrapper etc.		4		

41 19 11¼

Description	Rate	£	s	d	£	s	d
80 rheams writing paper,	6/-				24		
151 p.s. Sillesias,	8/-,				60		4
7 punch.s cont.g 764 gall.s Brandy,	22d.	70	8				
7 punch.s @ 16/- & cartage	4/8	5	16	8			
					75	17	4
2 punch.s Jamaica Rum, q.ty. 215 gall.s,	3/6				37	12	6
3 Hog.hds. qt.y. 3183 lb. Tobacco,	3½d.				46	8	4½
1,600 Spread Eagle Dollars,	2/9,				211	13	4
1,000 barrs Iron, q.ty 161.2.16,	18/10				152	4	3
					1,886	1	0
250 Fuzes to the Short pattern,	13/-	162	10	4			
100 Fuzes to the Long pattern,	13/6	67	10				
100 French Soldiers' Musketts,	13/6	67	10				
20 Neat Fowling pieces,	15/-	15					
140 Catch Trading Guns,	6/8	46	13	4			
10 Beech Jamaicas,	9/6	4	15				
30 pairs Neat Iron Mount'd pistols	15/-	22	10				
25 chests. 1 box 500 List Cases		21	5	6			
					407	13	10
300 Crook'd Cutlasses, red handles etc.	1/6	22	10				
50 Crook'd AR blades, etc.	2/2	5	8	4			
4 Boxes		17					
					28	15	4
800 Bunches, white Bruzed No. 6	13d.	43	6	8			
250 Bunches, small round red]							
150 Bunches, small round black]							
150 Bunches, small round white]							
40 Bunches, small round purple] q.ty. 1762	9d.	66	1	6			
60 Bunches, small round yellow]							
6 Bunches, Munghi Munghi]							
50 Bunches, large white Bruzed] q.ty. 63¼	3/6	11	1	4			
7 Bunches, oval and 7 large blue egg beads, 197 lb.	13d.	10	13	5			
70 Bunches, gilt Muffatees	18d.	5	5				
					136	7	11
250 Bunches, red Counterburdo, 114 lb.	2/9	15	13	6			
200 Bunches, pipe, Mock Coral, 115 lb.	3/6	27	2	6			
21 Bunches, pipe, White Piccado, 147 lb.	7½d.	4	11	10			
151 Bunches, Crack my Callabash,	7d.	4	8	1			
110 Bunches, Harlequins,	1/10	10	1	8			
18,000 Stones, very fine dark Cowberry, 52¼ lb.,	10/6	27	8	7½			
8,000 Arrangoes,	£4	32					
300 Bar Arrangoes,	8d.	10					
80 Bunches red Piccado]							
19 Bunches white Piccado] 866 lb.	7½d.	27	1	3			
15 Bunches yellow Piccado]							
20 p.s. mock Cowberry, 13 lb.	5/6	3	11	6			
30 p.s. large blue & black Margaretta	5/6	8	5				
114 p.s. Crack my Callabash,	7d.	3	6	6			
75 Bunches, Harlequins,	1/10	6	17	6			
					213	14	8
51½ oz.s pipe Coral	15/-	38	12	6			
8¼ oz.s round Coral	10/-	4	2	6			
					42	15	
		140					
		11	10	5			
					151	10	5

		£	s	d	£	s	d
11 Gross wood Guinea Knives & Sheaths,	18/-	9	18				
6 doz. Snuff boxes,	2/-		12				
4 doz. fine Steels,	8/6	1	8	4			
10,000 Gunflints,	23/-	2	6				
					14	4	4
6 cwt. Muskett Balls,	21/-	6	6	2			
2 cwt. drop Shot,	18/6	1	17				
					8	3	
250 Brasspans, q.ty 3 cwt. 1 lb.-6 oz.	148/-	24	9				
Cask for ditto			4	6			
					24	13	6
36 two pound]							
12 one pound] 82 cwt.	8½d.				2	18	1
Charges viz.							
Carriage of goods from London & Manchester		10	4	1			
Entry bonds etc. at Custom house		3	9	11			
					13	14	
					£2,930	11	1
Deduct discount allow.'d J. Parr on Arms		71	7				
Deduct discount allow.'d W. Davenport on Beads		17	1				
Deduct discount allow.'d R. Vigne			3				
Net deductions		55	5	1¼			
					143	16	1¼
Amount of Aston's Net Cargoe					£2,786	15	0¼

A List of Tradesmen's Notes for the Aston's Cargoe & Voyage to Gambia, 1771

		£	s.	d.	£	s.	d.
1. T. & J. Tipping	Manchester Goods ..	317	9				
2. Sargent, Chambers & Co.	India Goods	914	14				
3. James Hargreaves	Hatts	3					
4. John Kay	Caps	1	2				
5. John Berwick	Scarlet Cloth	41	19	11			
6. Peter Broster	Paper	24					
7. W. & R. Lightbody	Linnen	60		4½			
8. John Parr	Pans & Cutlasses	53	8	10			
9. Richard Wicksted	Brandy	75	17	4			
10. Dobson, Daltera & Walker	Tobacco	46	8	4			
					1537	19	9½
11. Joseph Leay & Co.	Gunpowder	140					
12. Thomas Pickop	Kegs	3		9			
13. Thomas Gill	Kegs	2	17	2			
14. Edward Bate	Knives & Flints	14	4	4			
15. James Aspinal	Shott	8	3				
16. John Rhodes	Pewter	2	18	1			
17. Thomas Ratcliffe	Pipes	—					
18. William Penketh	Boat Gunpowder	—					
19. Holme & Holden	Kegs	5	12	6			
					176	15	10
John Knight's Disbursements		1071	19	4½			
					2786	15	0

A List of Tradesmen's Notes for the Snow Aston's Outfitt, 1771.

1. William Farrar & Co.	Ropery	117	17	1				
2. George Kendall	Smith	41	0	4				
3. John Galley	Sailmaker	68	17	6				
4. Peter Baxter	Blockmaker	14	12	11				
5. Edward Grayson	Carpenter	26	13	2				
6. Holme & Holden	Coopers	19	5	4				
7. Thomas Pickop	Coopers	3	6					
8. Baker & Crossland	Tar, Pitch & Oil	10	6	11				
9. John Clarke	Groceries	5	11					
10. John Nunes	Iron Hoops...........	8	18	9				
					316	9		
11. Andrew Harold	Sawyer	1	18	8				
12. James Aspinall..................	Plumber	2	9	2				
13. Edward Alcock	Painter	3	16	8				
14. Peter Bradley	Gunsmith	3	8					
15. Samuel Kirks	Beads	3	3					
16. John Rhodes	Brazier	2	17	7				
17. Oliver Martin	Bread	41	1	8				
18. Thomas Appleton	Shill'd Barley........	8	8					
19. Joseph Rider	Iron Potts		11	3				
20. William Bonney.................	Chandler	3	8	3				
					71	2	3	
21. J. & R. Mercer	Boatbuilder	39	8	7				
22. Benson & Postlethwaite	Butter.................	2	16	8				
23. Thomas Houlston	Vinegar...............	1	17					
24. Robert Thwaites	Earthenware		17					
25. Josiah Perrin	Glass		4	7				
26. John Wright	Boatbuilder	2	19	9				
27. Thomas Richmond	Apothecary	2	5					
28. Old Comp.s Carters	Cartage...............	2	19	6				
29. Edgar Corrie & Co.	Beer	4	5					
30. Knight, Woods & Co.	Sugar	4	18					
					62	11	1	
31. Earle & Grayson	Smiths		9					
32. William Penketh	Boat Gunpowder	1	16	10				
33. William Stanton	White Cooper........		15	2				
34. John Fearon	Slops	7	0	6				
35. Naylor & Jenkinson	Tar & Oil.............		5	10				
John Knight's Disbursements		289	15	3				
					300	2	7	
					£750	4	11	
John Knight	Wine.................				9	10	4	
					£759	15	3	

Notes

1 In particular see T. S. Ashton, *An Eighteenth Century Industrialist* (Manchester, 1939), chapter 8, and 'The bill of exchange and private banks in Lancashire, 1790–1830', *Economic History Review*, XV, (1945), reprinted in T. S. Ashton and R. S. Sayers (ed.), *Papers in English Monetary History* (Oxford, 1954); S. G. Checkland, 'The Lancashire bill system and its Liverpool protagonists, 1810–27', *Economica*, XXI (1954); S. Nishimura, *The Decline of Inland Bills of Exchange in the London Money Market, 1855–1913* (Cambridge, 1971).

2   On the use of West India and African bills in financing these trades from
    the late seventeenth century see L. J. Ragatz, *The Fall of the Planter Class
    in the British Caribbean, 1763–1833* (New York, 1928, repr. 1963),
    chapter 3; R. Pares, *A West India Fortune* (1950) and 'Merchants and
    planters', *Economic History Review*, supplement No. 4 (1960); K. G.
    Davies, 'The origins of the commission system in the West India trade',
    Trans. Royal Historical Society, 52 (1952), and *The Royal African
    Company* (1957), chapter 2; R. B. Sheridan, 'The commercial and financial
    organisation of the British slave trade, 1750–1807', *Economic History
    Review*, XI (1958), 'The wealth of Jamaica in the eighteenth century',
    Economic History Review, XVIII (1965), and *Sugar and Slavery. An
    Economic History of the British West Indies, 1623–1775* (1974), chapters
    12 and 13; S. G. Checkland, 'American versus West Indian traders in
    Liverpool, 1793–1815', *Journal of Economic History*, XVIII (1958), and
    'Finance for the West Indies, 1780–1815', *Economic History Review*, X
    (1958).

3   Although initially slaves were sold direct to the West Indian proprietors, by
    the 1750s growing specialisation in the negro-carrying trade had made it
    more convenient to sell through commission agents and to purchase
    produce in the same way; see R. B. Sheridan, 'The commercial and
    financial organisation of the British slave trade, 1750–1807', *loc. cit.* Much
    closer links existed between planter and sugar merchant; see the
    correspondence cited in T. S. Ashton, *Letters of a West African Trader,
    Edward Grace, 1767–70* (1950), pp. ii, 34, and P.R.O., Board of Trade
    papers, B.T. 6/7, 1788, Evidence of John Tarleton.

4   The chronic shortage of specie in the Islands was always a serious obstacle
    to the growth of banking and loan facilities there. For early banking
    projects see R. B. Sheridan, *Sugar and Slavery, loc. cit.*, pp. 278–81. A
    West India Loan Company was formed in 1825, but the first West Indies
    bank, the Colonial Bank, was chartered as late as 1836; see L. J. Ragatz,
    loc. cit., pp. 106 n. 3, 381.

5   For details of ship-owning partnerships see R. Davis, *The Rise of the
    English Shipping Industry in the Seventeenth and Eighteenth Centuries*
    (1962), pp. 94–6.

6   See, for example, W. H. Chaloner, 'The Egertons in Italy and the
    Netherlands, 1729–34', *Bull. John Rylands Library*, 32, pp. 157–70.

7   There were two other brothers, Richard and Thomas, but they appear to
    have been involved in the business to only a small extent. The main branch
    of the family lived at Capesthorne Hall, in Macclesfield hundred, where in
    1795 its head was William's nephew, Davis Davenport, an improving
    landowner; see C. S. Davies, *The Agricultural History of Cheshire*
    (Manchester: Chetham Society, 1960), p. 28. For the genealogy of the
    Davenport family see Ormerod's *History of Cheshire* (1819 edn), III, pp.
    346–7, and *Burke's Landed Gentry* (18th edn, 1965–72), I, pp. 188–90.
    The Davenport slave trade accounts and papers are contained in the
    Davies–Davenport papers, Raymond Richards collection, University of
    Keele Library, Staffs. They consist of sixteen volumes of trading accounts,
    RR 57/1–16, including a bill of exchange register, RR 57/15, upon which
    this study is primarily based. I wish to acknowledge Mr I. H. C. Fraser for
    making these records available and for answering enquiries concerning the
    Davenport family, and to thank David Richardson of the University of
    Hull for helpful discussion in the course of his research on the voyage
    accounts.

8   A. P. Wadsworth and Julia de L. Mann, *The Cotton Trade and Industrial
    Lancashire, 1600–1780* (Manchester, 1931) pp. 227 ff.

9   On the difficulties involved in the compilation and interpretation of statistics of bill circulation see S. Nishimura, *loc. cit.*, chapters 2, 3 and 5. An early discussion of the data problems can be found in W. Newmarch, 'An attempt to ascertain the magnitude and fluctuations of the amount of bills of exchange (inland and foreign) in circulation at one time in Great Britain ... 1828–47 ...', *Journal of the Statistical Society*, May 1851.

10 In fact inland bills of exchange were first assessed for stamp duty in 1782 at 3*d* for bills under £50 and 6*d* for those above. Rates were rapidly increased after 1815, and over time these impositions brought about a marked reduction in the number of small bills in circulation, and their replacement by bank post bills and notes. Foreign bills were not assessed for duty before 1854; see S. Nishmura, *loc. cit.*, pp. 11–17.

11 Davenport became a freeman of Liverpool in 1749, when he was described as a 'grocer, now merchant', and in that year he was already investing in ships, being the part owner, with William Whalley, Robert Hallhead and George Clowes, of the brig *Orrell* of fifty tons; see Freemen's Register, 352 CLE/REG 2/2, Fines Book, 1746–90, 352 CLE/REG 1/7, Liverpool Record Office. For ship-owning partnerships see A. C. Wardle, 'The early Liverpool privateers', *Trans. Lancs. and Ches. Historic Society*, 93 (1941), p. 94, and R. Craig and R. Jarvis, *Liverpool Registry of Merchant Ships* (Manchester: Chetham Society, 1967), pp. 105–6. The earlier experience of William Stout of Lancaster suggests that the grocery trade, with its emphasis on the supply of a wide variety of goods, including tropical produce, was a convenient route to slave trading and often involved knowledge of the provision and contraband trades in the West Indies; see J. Harland (ed.), *Autobiography of William Stout of Lancaster, Wholesale and Retail Grocer and Ironmonger ... 1665–1752* (Manchester, 1851), pp. 45–60.

12 This outfitting invoice and attached list of tradesmen's notes relates to a venture undertaken by John Knight, an associate of William Davenport. It shows the range of goods and suppliers involved in the preparations for a slaving venture of the type organised by a specialist slave merchant in the early '70s.

13 A. P. Wadsworth and Julia de L. Mann, *loc. cit.*, pp. 148–61. Davenport may have concerned himself with cotton imports from the Levant, following the opening up of a direct trade between Liverpool and Leghorn in the early 1770s. But his transactions during the next decade, when Levant cotton came in regularly as part of the rapid expansion in cotton imports, do not suggest that he took part in this new trade of the 1780s. (*Ibid.*, pp. 187–9, 233.)

14 Large quantities of sailcloth were exported from Liverpool to Africa at this time; see W. Enfield, *An Essay towards the history of Leverpool* (2nd edn, 1774), pp. 80–8.

15 See tables in B.P.P., *House of Commons Accounts and Papers*, vol. XXIII, 1789, Nos. 573–6, Port of Liverpool, An Account of ... goods exported ... to the Coast of Africa, 1772–87.

16 A. P. Wadsworth and Julia de L. Mann, *loc. cit.*, p. 160, table IV. It is from this time that the fustian branch of the textile trade began to seek compensation in Europe for its declining markets in America, Africa and the West Indies, and from 1780 Europe became the most important overseas market for the cotton industry; see M. M. Edwards, *The Growth of the British Cotton Trade, 1780–1815* (Manchester, 1967), p. 243.

17 J. R. Harris, *The Copper King* (Liverpool, 1964), pp. 8–11.

18 *Ibid.*, p. 8 n. 8. See also W. H. Chaloner, 'Charles Roe of Macclesfield (1715–81), an eighteenth-century industrialist', I, *Trans. Lancs. and Ches.*

Antiq. Soc., LXII (1950–51), and J. R. Harris, 'Michael Hughes of Sutton: the influence of Welsh copper on Lancashire business, 1780–1815', *Trans. Lancs. and Ches. Hist. Soc.*, 101 (1949).

19 Earlier still, in the late 1730s, plans were being advanced for the building of a new warehouse specifically intended to house the large quantities of Indian goods which were brought up from London to supply '. . . a very considerable trade to the coast of Guinea . . .'. (R. C. Jarvis (ed.), *Customs Letter Books of the Port of Liverpool, 1711–1813* (Manchester: Chetham Society, 1954), 18 April, 1738, 150, p. 50.)

20 R. H. Campbell, *Carron Company* (Edinburgh, 1961), pp. 89–93. Also Wakefield MSS, 43/983, Liverpool Record Office.

21 A. Raistrick, *A Dynasty of Ironfounders: the Darbys and Coalbrookdale* (1953) pp. 10, 207; R. Dickinson, 'James Nasmyth and the Liverpool iron trade', *Trans. Lancs. and Ches. Hist. Soc.*, 108 (1956). In 1771 Joseph Rathbone succeeded Perry at the Phoenix foundry. His father, William Rathbone II, had purchased iron supplies from the Darbys, who became indebted on mortgage to him in due course. The alliance was cemented by the marriage of Joseph Rathbone and Mary, the sister of Abraham Darby II. In 1784 Joseph Rathbone took his son-in-law, William Fawcett, into partnership, and on his death bequeathed him £2,500 and his five shares in the iron bridge across the Severn. The Rathbone interest in Coalbrookdale must have been considerable at this time, for the will instructs his wife to 'be particularly carefull in looking over my Papers both here and at Coalbrookdale' (see will of Joseph Rathbone of Liverpool, gentleman, 1790, Lancashire Record office). The Darbys subsequently granted Fawcett a seven-year lease of the Phoenix foundry, and in 1794 he purchased it and other premises from them for £2,300. After profiting immensely from the wartime boom he and his successor went on to develop an important engineering business. H. White, *'Fossetts' (Fawcett, Preston & Co. Ltd): a record of two centuries of engineering* (Liverpool, 1958).

22 Trade guns have always been regarded as denoting the extreme inhumanity of the slave trade, yet it appears that their limited effectiveness in killing men can be attributed to the fact that their primary use was in hunting and crop protection. It has even been suggested that the 'musket' may have made agriculture possible for the first time in dense game areas of the West African hinterland, and that the Birmingham-type musket rather than a proper military arm was purposely manufactured on simple handicraft lines for the African trade because it was more easily hand-repaired. See B. M. D. Smith, 'The Galtons of Birmingham: Quaker gun merchants and bankers', *Business History*, IX (1967), and G. White, 'Firearms in Africa: an introduction', *Journal of African History*, XII (1971).

23 For examples of Yorkshire manufacturers exporting to other markets through Liverpool at this time see M. M. Schofield, 'The Virginia trade of the firm of Sparling & Bolden, 1788–99', *Trans. Hist. Soc. Lancs. and Ches.*, 116 (1964). The Leeds merchants George and Walter Beaumont and Francis Ridsdale were part owners in at least one ship by the early 1790s, with George and Thomas Booth one of the leading firms of corn merchants in the port; see A. H. John, *A Liverpool Merchant House, being the history of Alfred Booth and Company, 1863–1958* (1959), p. 16, and D. J. Pope, 'Shipping and trade in the port of Liverpool, 1783–93', unpublished Ph.D. thesis, University of Liverpool (1970), p. 371. Similarly the Heywood family, who were active in the slave trade at this time, also had interests in sugar refining and banking in Liverpool as well as in the woollen

manufacture at Wakefield; see F. E. Hyde, B. B. Parkinson and Sheila Marriner, 'The nature and profitability of the Liverpool slave trade', *Economic History Review*, V (1952–53).

24 It is likely that most of these Irish bills, as well as a number drawn in Chester, were for provisioning. In this connection there was also a reciprocal trade in salt from Liverpool for pork salting; see L. M. Cullen, 'The overseas trade of Waterford as seen from a ledger of Courtenay and Ridgway', *Journal of the Royal Society of Antiquaries of Ireland*, LXXXVIII (1958).

25 See R. B. Sheridan, *Sugar and Slavery*, loc. cit., pp. 368–70.

26 The Earles appear to have been Davenport's closest business associates at the height of his career in the slave trade. The notorious Liverpool privateer Fortunatus Wright had sailed for this firm on his series of successful Mediterranean cruises during the 1740s. In 1772 Earle and Hodgson commenced a regular packet service between Liverpool and Leghorn and subsequently imported Levant cotton; they were also part owners of a considerable number of Liverpool ships with Davenport and others. An alternative explanation of Davenport's trade connection through this firm with Leghorn may be found initially in the import of currants and oil for the grocery trade; see C. N. Parkinson, *The Rise of the Port of Liverpool* (Liverpool, 1952), p. 107, and Gomer Williams, *History of the Liverpool Privateers and Letters of Marque, with an account of the Liverpool slave trade* (Liverpool, 1897, repr. 1966), *passim*.

27 Most of these bills, indeed all before 1775, were drawn in Rotterdam, usually by W. & J. Manson & Co. on Davenport direct. Manson & Co. appear to have been the London agents for a number of firms involved in trade with Holland, and the bills are drawn in favour of such names as Oswald Denistoun & Co., Dunlop & Crope, W. de Drusina & Co. and W. & J. Anderson. The number of Scots names suggests a link with the tobacco re-export trade, but this is not certain; see, for example, H. Hamilton, 'Scotland's balance of payments problem in 1762', *Economic History Review*, V (1953), and C. Wilson, *Anglo-Dutch Commerce and Finance in the Eighteenth Century* (Cambridge, 1941), p. 178.

28 For developments in the ceded and other islands at this period I have drawn heavily on L. J. Ragatz, *loc. cit.*, chapters IV and V, and R. B. Sheridan, *Sugar and Slavery*, loc. cit., chapter 19.

29 The extent to which the slave merchant became involved in the produce trade could, of course, change according to the circumstances of war, sugar harvest and the availability of good bills. There seems little doubt, however, that by the 1760s the specialists who prosecuted the trade for its own sake preferred the convenience of the shortest bills they could obtain on the best London agents; see, for example, S. G. Checkland, 'Two Scottish West Indian liquidations after 1793', *Scottish Journal of Political Economy*, IV (1957).

30 See Jean Trepp, 'The Liverpool movement for abolition', *Journal of Negro History*, XIII (1928), and F. E. Sanderson, 'The Liverpool delegates and Sir Wm. Dolben's bill', *Trans. Lancs. and Ches. Historic Society*, 124 (1972).

31 Committee Book of the African Company of Merchants Trading from Liverpool, 1750–1820, 352 MD 1, Liverpool Record Office.

32 D. J. Pope, *loc. cit.*, pp. 477 ff.

33 See J. D. Fage, 'Some remarks on beads and trade in lower Guinea in the sixteenth and seventeenth centuries', *Journal of African History*, III (1962). Cowrie shells were another important item in these trades and represent an

interesting link between the African merchant and the East India trade. The main source of supply was the Maldive Islands, and an extensive Indian Ocean trade with Bengal and West Africa can be traced back to the fourteenth century. Most of the cowries which entered into the European slave trade came via Calcutta and Chittagong, and Davenport could have obtained them from an East India connection in London, or from Holland or Hamburg; see Marion Johnson, 'The cowrie currencies of West Africa', I, *Journal of African History*, XI (1970).

34   Gomer Williams, *loc. cit.*, pp. 253–4, 547, 669, and R. Weisbord, 'The case of the slave ship *Zong*, 1783', *History Today*, XIX (1969). See also Elizabeth Donnan (ed.), *Documents Illustrative of the History of the Slave Trade to America* (Washington, D.C., 1930–35), II, p. 555 n. Windfall gains resulting from prize money were sometimes an important factor in building up the personal wealth of merchants, but the really substantial fortunes were made in the navy; see, for example, J. Gwyn, *The Enterprising Admiral. The Personal Fortune of Admiral Sir Peter Warren* (Montreal, 1974).

35   R. B. Sheridan, 'The commercial and financial organisation of the British slave trade, 1750–1807', *loc. cit.*

36   T. S. Ashton, *Economic Fluctuations in England, 1700–1800* (Oxford, 1959) p. 132.

37   Sir J. H. Clapham, *The Bank of England. A History* (Cambridge, 1966), II, pp. 142–3, and the London directories of Kent and Lowndes for the 1780s.

38   F. A. Hayek (ed.), H. Thornton, *The Paper Credit of Great Britain* (1939) p. 93.

39   For example, when, in 1786, Davenport was in serious need of remittances from the Islands he paid away a large number of low-value Dominican bills, drawn at between nine and eighteen months, within a few days of their arrival. At such times the names of well known local slave traders and discounters occur among the payees; for example, Denison, Heywood, Galley, Parker and Copeland; see J. Hughes, *Liverpool Banks and Bankers, 1760–1837* (1906), and Gore's Liverpool directories for the 1780s.

40   D. J. Pope, *loc. cit.*, pp. 231–6.

41   P. Viles, 'The slaving interest of the Atlantic ports, 1763–92', *French Historical Studies*, VII (1972).

42   D. J. Pope, *loc. cit.*, pp. 477–8.

43   The ensuing Anglo-Dutch war brought Holland's small and declining participation in the trade to a virtual halt; see J. Postma, 'The dimension of the Dutch slave trade from West Africa', *Journal of African History*, XIII (1972), and W. S. Unger, 'Bijdragen tot de geschiedenis van de Nederlandse slavenhandel: de slavenhandel der Middelburgsche Commercie Compagnie, 1732–1808', *Economisch-Historisch Jaarboek*, 28 (1958). On the profitability of the French trade see P. Viles, *loc. cit.*; D. Rinchon, *Les Armements négriers an XVIIIe siècle* (Brussels, 1956); J. Meyer, *L'Armement nantais dans la deuxième moitié du XVIIIe siècle* (Paris, 1969); R. Stein, 'The profitability of the Nantes slave trade, 1783–92', *Journal of Economic History*, XXXV (1975). For the Danish trade see G. Nørregard, *Danish Settlements in West Africa, 1658–1850* (Boston, Mass., 1966).

44   T. S. Ashton, *An Economic History of England: the Eighteenth Century* (1955), p. 147.

45   See S. G. Checkland, 'American versus West Indian traders in Liverpool, 1793–1815', *loc. cit.*, and 'Corn for south Lancashire and beyond,

1780–1800: the firm of Corrie Gladstone and Bradshaw', *Business History*, 2 (1959).

46 P. D. Curtin, *The Atlantic Slave Trade: a census* (Madison, Wis., 1969), pp. 135–6.

47 It is important to remember that the supply of slaves to the traders depended largely on the efficiency of indigenous marketing arrangements. These were often highly developed, as in south-eastern Nigeria, as distinct from the Delta area, which had become one of the fastest-growing sources of slaves in the eighteenth century. The internal supply organisation here was controlled by the Arochuku traders. The basis of this elite group's power was military and religious as well as entrepreneurial, and they appear to have conducted their slave trade on a scale and with an efficiency quite the equal of the Europeans. Significantly, the Arochuku trading grid accommodated the internal trades in produce as well as slaves, which, because they were interdependent, expanded together during the eighteenth century. These indigenous traders most resented the abolition of the trade; D. Northrup, 'The growth of trade among the Igbo before 1800', *Journal of African History*, XIII (1972).

48 *Liverpool and Slavery. An historical account of the Liverpool–African slave trade. Was it the cause of the prosperity of the town?* Compiled by a Genuine 'Dicky Sam' (Liverpool, 1884), chapter XIII, pp. 100, 117, quoted in Elizabeth Donnan, *loc. cit.*, p. 628.

Great Britain and tariff reform in France
1831–36

I

Historians have usually seen the tariff reform campaign of the July
Monarchy as the child of the upswing of the trade cycle of the early
1840s, and of Britain's liberalisation of her tariff, particularly by the Peel
administration of 1841–46. Previous agitation had thus been but the
gestation of the brilliant, if butterfly, campaign that emerged with
Bastiat's arrival in Paris and the foundation of the Association pour la
liberté des échanges in 1846. In truth the July Monarchy witnessed not
one but two campaigns to reform the tariff, and it is at least arguable that
the importance of that of the 1840s has been exaggerated while that of
the 1830s has been unduly overlooked.

The two campaigns had a number of traits in common. Both
coincided with upturns in the trade cycle. In each, similar economic
interests pressed for a moderation of the tariff, and economists and the
press played a prominent role. Both owed some of their inspiration to
British example in the shape of tariff reforms and the promptings of
British representatives. Both evoked a powerful response from
protectionist interests: in the 1830s the response was demonstrated in
evidence given before the Duchâtel inquiry of 1834–35 and in debates in
the Chambers; in the 1840s the massive response came in the form of the
vociferous opposition to the proposed tariff union with Belgium and the
formation of the Comité pour la défense du travail national and *le
Moniteur industriel*. There were also dissimilarities. At first blush the
1840s campaign appears more extensive, more significant, more
successful. This, however, is the semblance rather than the reality, for the
campaign achieved scant success and it is quite evident that it did not
need a depression or a political revolution to end it. Its journal had but a
small circulation among the converted, its meetings were staid gatherings
of the faithful and its propaganda was a pale imitation of the Anti-Corn

Law League's ceaseless outpourings. No organisers or orators of the calibre of a Wilson or a Cobden emerged.[1] The 1830s campaign was less doctrinaire and produced no Bastiat, but it did achieve some modest results: the extensive debates in the Chambers in April and May and the tariff laws of 2 and 5 July 1836 were, in large part, the result of the reform agitation.

The tariff reform movement of the 1830s was marked by moderation and realism. Reformers recognised the intricacy of the problems involved, the need to safeguard interests created behind prohibitions and the political strength of protectionists. The way to bring about reforms was thus to change the tariff gradually. Some argued that France should undertake a reform programme that other countries would emulate, others that she should seek reciprocity. All argued that the prohibitions and high duties on raw materials and semi-manufactured goods should be removed as a matter of urgency. Only a minority argued that the British and French economies were complementary rather than competitive and that France could therefore safely move towards free trade.

The emphasis on abolishing prohibitions and reductions in imposts on raw materials and semi-manufactures was understandable in that one of the weakness of the tariff was that imposts were levied on all imports. It was in such areas that Britain had already begun to make reforms and that the Maassen tariff, introduced in Prussia in 1818 and extended to the Zollverein in 1834, was most liberal. It was there that the greatest support could be expected from business groups. Reformers therefore sought not some distant and beatific goal of absolute free trade but a cosmetic surgery that would remove the inconsequences and excesses in the customs list. Even such changes – like reductions on high-count cotton yarns – threatened vocal interests and occasioned acrimonious debates. Nowhere was this more true, or more important perhaps, than in the case of coal and iron, the vital sinews of the new industrialism of the paleotechnic age.

The reform movement had four important elements. One was the economists and economic journalists who were at the forefront in both campaigns of the July Monarchy. They had the tribune offered by the Chairs of political economy at the Conservatoire des arts et métiers and at the Collège de France. They enjoyed a prominent position in the reconstituted Académie des sciences morales et politiques. All of them – Say, Blanqui and Rossi – assumed a moderate stance on the question of reform, as did a number of lesser lights, like Théodore Fix, Emile Berès and Léon Faucher.

A more important element was made up of economic interest groups who, for differing reasons and with varying devotion, also pressed for tariff changes. The protectionist front was not monolithic: a number of industrialists wanted to be able to import raw materials, semi-

manufactured goods or machinery, and their support for some
moderation of the tariff on such items was demonstrated at the iron
inquiry of 1828 and at the coal inquiry of 1833. It would also be proper
to ascribe some of the impetus to reform to a growing confidence, fuelled
by the gradual recovery from the recent depression, among those
merchants and industrialist who had little to fear from foreign
competition and much to gain from increasing international exchange,
like the silk manufacturers of Lyons or wine interests in the Gironde. It is
important to note, however, that the spur was more likely to be doubt
and uncertainty; the spur could be fear of foreign competition or
retaliation; the spur could be recession. This was certainly true in Britain,
where reform was advocated and instituted not in a mood of gay
abandon as outmoded clothes were cast aside but rather in a mood of
sobriety and in the face of the evident failure of previous commercial
policies. The same was true of the greatest supporters of tariff reform in
France. The silk manufacturers of Lyons appear, *prima facie*, to be a
clear instance of a group whose support for tariff reform was a function
of their ability to sell abroad. In fact Lyonnais concern over the tariff
system was also the result of fears, which were certainly exaggerated,
that competitors in Crefeld, Zurich, Elberfeld and Spitalfields were taking
an ever larger share of foreign and domestic markets. Such fears grew
during the commercial crisis of the late 1820s and intensified in the early
years of the July Monarchy, marked as they were by continuing crisis,
two insurrections of Lyons silk weavers and further emigration of skilled
workers. Doubts and fears also subtended the reform campaign of
Bordeaux. In Bordeaux's case, however, the fears were better founded.
Bordeaux faced economic problems that were partly structural and
partly the result of the late 1820s depression, whose effects on Bordelais
trade lingered on throughout the following decade. The first three years
of the July Monarchy were particularly harsh, for the crisis the port faced
was deeper than any other in the entire century. Because of its long-
standing devotion to change in the tariff and because of the very tenor of
its campaign Bordeaux was the most vital element in the reform
movement.

The press constituted a third element in the reform campaign. The
tariff was debated in chambers of commerce, in *conseils-généraux*, in the
Chambers, in missives sent to the Minister of Commerce and to
Parliament, in submissions to inquiries, in rival pamphlets, but above all
it was discussed in the columns of the press, and not merely the Parisian
but also in the provincial press, which enjoyed its golden age in this
period. Newspapers enjoyed more prestige, and possibly more power, in
France at this time than they did elsewhere or were to again in France.
Journalists basked in the prestige that resulted from the excitement
among newspaper readers that had been generated by the remorseless
opposition campaign undertaken by journalists in the last years of the

Restoration. The French press was much more a commentator on and critic of current affairs than its counterpart in Britain or Germany, and to contemporaries it seemed a mighty political weapon that could make or break governments. In the 1830s the press was strongly in favour of tariff reform, and support for reform cut across political affiliations. This was true in Paris, where espousal of reform was in part a function of opposition to the Ministry in power or to the regime in general and in part a reflection of the strength of opposition newspapers and the relative weakness of conservative organs. It was especially true in the provinces, where the press was more a defender of local interests than a spokesman of a particular shade of political opinion.

The tariff campaign had a final element. The tariff issue involved other countries, for tariffs were also a matter of foreign policy. Preference treaties, for example, offered one solution to the closing of foreign markets, and even unilateral reductions could lead to closer diplomatic relations. Concern about the tariff both in the country at large and among members of the government was prompted by three important developments outside France. One was the success of Prussian commercial diplomacy: the founding of the Zollverein and the gradual absorption into it of the Rhenish and south German states. This frightened the French departments that bordered Germany and alarmed other export interests, especially when there appeared a danger that Belgium would reach some kind of accord with the new customs union. Reformers suggested a number of ripostes to the German customs union. The best known of these was Léon Faucher's Union du Midi, which he first put forward in 1837, but both journalists and deputies – and particularly, of course, deputies from Alsace – pointed out that the British were already following an active policy of encouraging parts of northern Germany to remain outside the Zollverein and suggested that France take advantage of the difficulties the Prussian government was encountering in persuading south German states to join the customs union. The second development was the establishment of an independent Belgium. Fitful negotiation between the two countries took place in the early '30s.[2] Though Belgian representatives failed to persuade the French to abolish prohibitions on cotton and woollen manufactures and to effect significant changes in the iron tariff, the second Bill that became the 5 July tariff law was prompted by the French desire to offer concessions to their neighbour, which was already threatening to reach a commercial agreement with the Zollverein.[3] Indeed, in September 1835 Duchâtel, the French Minister of Commerce, revived earlier plans for a customs union between the two countries and in November 1836 the French sent Brussels an official proposal to this effect.[4] The third and most important stimulus to reform agitation and to reform itself was Great Britain. British commercial policy offered an example. The political *rapprochement* that followed the Convention of London in 1831 helped pave the way to the commercial negotiations that lasted from November 1831 until the end of 1834.[5] If these discussions did not yield a commercial treaty they did encourage the reform campaign and helped to nudge the French government into making modest tariff reductions.

II

That the British example should be cited may well appear surprising, given the long-standing anglophobia and given the stereotype of national character and nature of society that had been developed during the Restoration: the myth of an Albion that was perfidious, hypocritical and materialistic, a myth that was all the more powerful in conservative eyes because of Britain's Protestantism, capitalism, industrialism and emerging liberalism.[6] There were long-standing, and not unfounded, fears of British commerce and suspicions of the British government, 'un gouvernement identifié et presque incorporé avec le commerce', as Chaptal wrote in 1819. These fears lived on: after Bastiat published his history of the Anti-Corn Law League in 1845 he complained bitterly to Cobden that nobody was buying it, that the press was ignoring it, that the public had no knowledge of British affairs.[7] He claimed that anglophobia was rampant[8] and that British tariff reductions were viewed as a Machiavellian plot to bamboozle France into similar reforms.

Worse, the advocates of even the most limited form of commercial treaty or tariff reform found they had to combat not only the familiar arguments of protectionists but the constant citation of the reputedly evil consequences of the 1786 Eden–Vergennes commercial treaty. Thiers frequently referred to the 1786 treaty,[9] while in its written submission to the Duchâtel inquiry the Rouen chamber of commerce reproduced the petition that the Normandy chamber of commerce had sent to the king in 1787 complaining of the nefarious effects of the treaty.[10] Small wonder, then, that Stéphane Flachat lamented that when the 1786 treaty was mentioned it appeared that 'on réveille le souvenir d'*une Saint-Barthélemy industrielle*, et que la France tout entière se soit alors révoltée contre un acte arbitraire et insensé d'une administration ignorante'.[11] Reformers like Bowring and Flachat tried to demonstrate that the market had not been flooded with cheap British goods and that far from being a catastrophe the treaty had actually benefited the French economy.[12] Defenders of the tariff also pointed out – long before List did so eloquently in his *National System* – that prohibitions, protection and export bounties had been a powerful element in British industrial and commercial success and that if Britain now sought to temper her system it was because she no longer feared foreign competition and was seeking new markets to conquer.

Tariff reformers used two principal arguments. They argued that Anglo-French trade was unnecessarily restricted, that it was low compared with the level of exchanges reached in the 1780s and that it had not grown at the same pace as the total foreign trade of either country. Horace Say pointed out in 1835 that France's trade with Britain had remained at the same level for the previous ten years, and this despite the fact that Britain was the richest and one of the closest of her neighbours. [13] In their parliamentary report on commercial relations between the two countries Bowring and Villiers produced statistics showing that British imports from France had increased fivefold between the 1780s and 1830, while British exports to France had not grown at all, and that as a result France was Britain's most important supplier after Russia but ranked only ninth in Europe as an export market. [14] Secondly, reformers held British reforms as worthy of emulation. The report of the 1828 select committee and Sir Henry Parnell's *On Financial Reform*, published in 1830 and in French translation in 1832, the tariff reforms begun by Huskisson and continued, if falteringly, by the Whig administrations of the 1830s were all examples France might follow. J.-B. Say saw these reforms as a way of increasing consumption, customs revenue and international exchange. [15] Stéphane Flachat pointed out that Britain had not only reduced duties on raw materials and semi-manufactured goods but had carried out these reductions unilaterally and had made reductions on goods, like silks, which threatened domestic producer interests. [16]

Reformers were obliged to recognise, however, that there were limitations to the British example, that Huskisson's tariff reforms had been moderate, [17] that the British government still drew over 40 per cent of its revenues from customs [18] and that the *soi-disant* Whig reforming Ministries of the 1830s were Whiggish before they were reforming. Indeed, Huskisson's tariff reforms were under some attack in the early 1830s and the Commons silk committee of 1832 was established following complaints from British manufacturers about the effects of recent tariff changes. British industrialists were still divided as to the desirability of abandoning the prohibition on the export of machinery, [19] and it was by no means clear to contemporaries in Britain or elsewhere as to whether, and if so by what means, Britain would move towards an even more liberal policy: if some advocated unilateral reforms others, like Robert Torrens, whose *Letters on Commercial Policy* was published in 1833, argued that Britain should advance only through the signing of reciprocity treaties.

The British example, then, was flawed and could be – and was – dismissed by protectionists as a policy of economic nationalism. A more significant part in the tariff campaign was played by British commercial diplomacy: the tariff negotiations that took place between 1831 and 1834 were the first, the most extended and the most influential of four different attempts by the two governments during the period of the July Monarchy to reach a commercial agreement. [20]

There was a vital political dimension to these commercial negotiations which goes a long way to explain why the negotiations were begun and why, despite the poor progress, they were persevered with. Following the July revolution in France and the advent to power of the Whigs in Britain, circumstances – partly political, partly a matter of personalities – were peculiarly favourable to closer relations between the two countries. If the *rapprochement* that resulted was sometimes fraught by disagreements, as over the Belgian question, and if in the end no real alliance was formed, there was nevertheless a closer collaboration and a better understanding during this period than at any time before the Crimean war. In Britain the Foxite Whigs – Althorp, Holland, Landsdowne and Russell – had long been critical of Tory foreign policy, which since the 1790s had opposed France and collaborated with the absolutist powers. They believed that Britain's true interest lay in more amicable relations with France, which, as the July revolution seemed to show, was now moving towards a liberal constitutional government. Foxite Whigs like Holland already had close ties of friendship with members of the new French government, and particularly with de Broglie. Although Palmerston, the new Foreign Secretary and a recent Tory recruit to Whig ranks, did not share this francophile outlook, he was led to co-operate even more closely with the French following France's acceptance of an independent Belgium under Leopold and a deterioration in Britain's relations with the Eastern powers. This *rapprochement* was further prompted by growing British fears of Russian intentions in the Near East, fears fuelled by the defensive treaty of Unkiar Skelessi that the Russians and Turks signed in July 1833 and by the Münchengrätz convention signed by Russia and Austria in September of the same year.[21] On the French side the new regime was anxious to escape its diplomatic isolation, to overthrow the system established by the Congress of Vienna, and, in its early years, regarded Britain as its most likely supporter. A number of leading politicians worked for closer ties. Talleyrand, ambassador to the Court of St James's from 1830 to 1834, was a strong advocate of closer collaboration.[22] Indeed, late in 1833 he pressed Louis-Philippe and his government to conclude a formal written alliance.[23] Equally fervent in his advocacy of Anglo-French understanding was the Duc de Broglie, who was Foreign Minister in the 11 October administration, and held the post with one break until early 1836.[24] De Broglie made a number of visits to Britain – the one he made in April 1831 in particular convinced him that the fall of the Tories and the promised electoral reform would radically alter the character of the British government and its foreign policy.[25] Palmerston thought highly of him and worked better with him than with any other French Foreign Minister in the 1830s.[26]

It was this Anglo-French diplomatic *rapprochement*, together with the British Board of Trade's cherished policy of seeking reciprocity, a policy

Board officials had already pursued, and were to continue to pursue, with determination and striking lack of success, that ushered in the commercial negotiations which contined spasmodically from December 1831 until December 1834. One of the principal levers applied by the British was political. The British ambassador, Lord Granville, British representatives in the negotiations, Bowring and Villiers, and the British Foreign Secretary in London stressed to French colleagues that a commercial agreement would cement closer relations. As early as 1830, before negotiations began, Bowring told Louis-Philippe and Baron Louis, then Minister of Finance, that a political alliance would be secured only if France's tariff barriers were lowered.[27] De Broglie, for his part, was more an economic liberal than he was to prove a political liberal,[28] and he too was aware that some tariff reforms on France's part would strengthen political relations with Britain.[29]

III

The negotiations that began in December 1831 were the result of an initiative of Baron Louis, Minister of Finance, who suggested to Bowring that a mixed commission be established to examine what tariff reductions each country could make for their mutual advantage.[30] In view of the opposition to tariff reform, not only in the French Chambers but in the Cabinet itself, it was deemed inadvisable either to attempt to negotiate a commercial agreement or to attempt to introduce immediate major reforms in the French tariff. Instead a commission composed of two commissioners appointed by each country was set up, whose purpose was to inquire into the state of trade between Britain and France and the extent and deleterious effects of smuggling, and to indicate what reductions could be made in the French tariff that would improve Anglo-French commerce and reduce smuggling.[31] It was decided to examine the French tariff not only because Britain had already undertaken some tariff reform but because she had also made reductions that were of particular benefit to France: the lowering of import duties on silk goods and the tariff equalisation on French wines introduced earlier in the year by Lord Althorp.[32] The British hoped to persuade the French to allow the export of raw silk, but they hoped above all to secure some moderation in French prohibitions and high protection on import items on their export list, like cotton yarn and piece goods, coal and iron products. As the official letter of instruction to the British commissioners shows, however, their immediate aims were much more modest. The Commissioners were not to attempt a frontal attack on tariffs that protected powerful interests but to concern themselves with duties on items of relatively minor importance where vested interests would not be antagonised but whose reduction or abolition would increase trade and pave the way for more important changes.[33] Indeed, the first recommendations of the Anglo-French commission were the ending of prohibitions on the export of raw silk, on the import of cotton yarns above No. 180 (French) and the reduction of duties on coal and tin.[34]

The negotiations benefited from having enthusiastic British representatives. C. E. Poulett Thomson, vice-president of the Board of Trade from 1830 and president from 1834, visited Paris on two separate occasions – in November 1831 and in October 1834 – to sound out the possibility of a reciprocity treaty with the French. Thomson was not only a firm believer in the desirability of tariff reform[35] but had spent two summers in Paris in 1829 and 1830 and already enjoyed good relations with a number of French politicians, including Baron Louis, de Broglie and Anisson-Duperron. The real labour, however, was undertaken by his two lieutenants in Paris. The first of these was George Villiers, brother of the free-trader C. P. Villiers and a professional diplomat who, as Lord Clarendon, was destined to be a distinguished Foreign Secretary. Until his appointment as special British plenipotentiary at Madrid in August 1833 Villiers brought his special qualities of industriousness, tact and charm to the Paris discussions.[36] John Bowring, Thomson's second representative in Paris, was to play a major role in the French tariff reform campaign. He had long had close ties with French liberals, had been arrested in 1822 on suspicion of complicity in the affair of the four sergeants of la Rochelle,[37] and had already been warmly received by Louis Philippe.[38] Both Villiers and Bowring brought enthusiasm, energy[39] and some expertise.[40] On the French side, some lowering of the tariff and an improvement in Anglo-French trade were held to be important, chiefly for reasons of diplomacy. The principal advocates of this policy were de Broglie and the king.[41]

Despite these advantages there were difficulties. There was an initial problem over the appointment of the French commissioners. The British refused to accept David, chief permanent official at the Ministry of Finance, because of his protectionist views, while Baron Fréville, who was appointed in his stead, aroused little enthusiasm.[42] The other French commissioner, Comte Tanneguy Duchâtel, had liberal antecedents, and both Villiers and Bowring felt that from their point of view his was a good appointment. They soon found him wary of committing himself and, with some reason, believed him to be dominated by Adolphe Thiers.[43] Moreover the British commissioners themselves had weaknesses. They talked of their task as a crusading mission to bring the light to their benighted brethren across the Channel. 'You and I,' Bowring wrote to Villiers, 'have sworn to each other upon the altar that the Baal of monopoly should be overthrown by these blessed hands of ours – and overthrown he shall be.'[44] They – and particularly Bowring, whose utilitarian zeal aroused considerable antipathy, and not just among defenders of the status quo[45] – moved in a world where their plans were constantly being endangered by the machinations of anglophobic, prohibitionist or similarly prejudiced enemies. Three redoutable enemies were toiling to thwart their plans. One of these was Charles Dupin, who, thanks to his visits to and writings on Britain,[46] passed for something of an expert on British affairs. Dupin was reporter for d'Argout's ill fated corn Bill, sat on the commission on the December 1831 tariff Bill, tried unsuccessfully to secure a place on the commission on the 1833 Bill, spoke eloquently against tariff reform in the Chamber, and was reputed to want to be Minister of Commerce. Bowring and Villiers saw him constantly intriguing against them.[47] The second was the Comte de Saint-Cricq, who had played an important part in the foundation of the French tariff during the Restoration.[48] On three occasions this respected protectionist injured the British cause. The first was in the Conseil du Commerce in 1832 when the recommendations of the Anglo-French commission were being discussed. The second was when he acted as reporter for the Chamber's commission on the 1833 tariff Bill, and the third was when he was absent from the Chamber when he was meant to move a motion to enable the government to lower duties between sessions. He too became an arch-enemy for the British representatives.[49] The third was Adolphe Thiers, who, as successor to d'Argout at the Ministry of Commerce from December 1832 until April 1834 and as President of the Council during the passing of the 1836 tariff Bills, was to play an important part in the Anglo-French negotiations. If Thiers respected the diplomatic importance of some tariff reforms he was a reluctant reformer and a defender of the existing system.[50] Worse, he disliked Bowring's hectoring and schoolmasterish manner, and the two never had amicable relations. He outmanoeuvered Bowring by refusing to see him, keeping him waiting and alternately promising him reforms and berating his and British intentions in general.[51]

There was, however, a more fundamental problem: the political power and powerful arguments of protectionists in France. They were powerful in the Cabinet, and when negotiations began the President of the Council, Casimir Périer, had long directed the Anzin Mining Company, which benefited from the coal tariff.[52] The strength of protectionist sentiment in parliament seemed to be proved by the treatment accorded to d'Argout's corn law amendment, which was mauled by the Chamber in April 1832.[53] Protectionist feelings among important business interests had been demonstrated at both the 1828 iron inquiry and at the coal inquiry of 1833, and it was to be shown again in meetings of the conseils-généraux, which had advisory functions on tariff matters. Worse, the British were anxious to secure the ending of prohibitions and reductions in duties on cotton twist and piece goods, on iron and on coal – in other words, in the sectors where the French were least willing to effect important changes. It seemed to the French that neither the tariff concessions the British could offer as a quid pro quo[54] nor the promise of closer political collaboration was a weighty enough compensation. This explains not

merely why the British failed to secure all the changes they would have
liked but also why French Ministries prevaricated and placated, why they
were reluctant to put through changes but never actually refused to do
so. George Villiers, lamenting Casimir Périer's failure to bring the tariff
Bill before the Chamber, reported that the President of the Council had
promised Granville 'qu'il s'en est occupé, qu'il s'en occupe, qu'il s'en
occupera – in short declines the verb but doesn't do the thing'.[55]

Bowring and Villiers adopted two tactics to coax tariff reforms from
the French government: they themselves put pressure on king and
Ministers, and they sought to encourage reform agitation in the press,
among deputies in the provinces. As for the first, they used promises and
threats. They promised further tariff reductions on French exports and
they used the most powerful weapon at their command: tariff reforms
were the best way of ensuring a lasting diplomatic *rapprochement*
between the two countries. They threatened that France's failure to
reciprocate British tariff reductions was a source of hostile popular
feeling in Britain. [56] They threatened that the Select Committee on Silk
might recommend raising duties on French silks. [57] They threatened an
across-the-board increase on duties on French goods. [58] They also sought
to persuade David at the Ministry of Finance and Théodore Gréterin,
chief permanent official at the Commerce Ministry, that government
revenue – the budget was in deficit until 1834 – would benefit from a
removal of prohibitions and a reduction of duties. One of the tasks of the
Anglo-French commission was to study the extent and cost of smuggling,
but even when the commission had ended Bowring continued to
emphasise reform as a way to increase revenue. [59] Deputies with whom
Bowring was in close contact also took up this argument, [60] and it was to
be one of the central arguments of the *First Report on the Commercial
Relations between France and Great Britain*, [61] a report whose
publication was widely noted in the French press. [62]

The second tactic the British representatives – and Bowring especially
– adopted was to encourage the reform movement. Bowring arrived in
France armed with copies of Perronet Thompson's incisive *Catechism on
the Corn Laws*, which had had enormous success in Britain. [63] Within
weeks of arriving in France Villiers was in contact with Johnston, the
Bordeaux merchant, providing him with advice on how to conduct a
tariff reform campaign and providing him with a copy of the 1820
London merchants' petition to the House of Commons as a model of
clarity and economy of words. [64] At the same time Bowring and Villiers
wrote to Thomson requesting that the Treasury provide them with a
special fund to enable them to translate and circulate some of Thomson's
and Althorp's speeches on the broad principles of tariff reform. [65]

Their attempts to stimulate a reform campaign took three forms.
Bowring addressed himself to the press and formed close ties with Rodet
of *le Temps*, Stéphane Flachat of *le Courrier français* and *le*

Constitutionnel, and Emile Pereire of *le National*. Early in 1833 he could write that 'no day now passes in which some article in a liberal sense fails to appear'. [66] By June of the same year he announced, 'I have got with us the Constitutionnel, National, Courrier, Messager, Tribune, Bon Sens, Moniteur du Commerce, Journal du Commerce, Temps, Revue encyclopédique, and many allies, with *the whole* of the departmental press of Southern and Western France.' [67] Of course, Bowring exaggerated his own part but it may be some indication of his success that in February 1834 he was accused in the Chamber of Deputies of having lavished large sums of money buying the allegiance of Parisian newspapers. [68]

Bowring addressed himself, secondly, to deputies. Until the lengthy debates on the 1836 tariff Bills the Chamber resolutely failed to discuss the tariff Bills presented to it from December 1831 onwards. It therefore constituted a less useful platform of the reform campaign. It was still important, however, for Bowing to gain allies among deputies, for they could lobby Ministers, ask questions in reply to the speech from the throne, intercalate questions on the tariff in discussions on the budget and on other Bills. More, even if Parliament itself did not debate tariff Bills they were discussed in the commissions, and the reports of these committees were subsequently published. [69] He therefore worked to extend the group of deputies who supported tariff reform – in the event a group that covered a wide spectrum of political colourings – and to get them to act in concert. [70] He also worked to persuade electors and chambers of commerce to ensure that their deputies were aware of their views on the tariff and acted accordingly.

Some of the deputies with whom Bowring had to work were of little vocal help in the Chamber: Fulchiron, the Lyons deputy, was a figure of fun, [71] while Roul, one of the Gironde delegation, gave such excruciatingly boring speeches that he once spoke to an entirely empty Chamber. Others, though, proved devoted advocates of commercial reform. Three deputies in particular – Amédée Desjobert (Seine-Inférieure), A.-J. Lherbette (Aisne) and A.-J.-L. Anisson-Duperron (Seine-Inférieure) collaborated with Bowring and raised the issue of tariff reform on every possible occasion. Desjobert, who represented his constituency for nearly twenty years, had two issues closest to heart: one was a lonely but determined opposition to the French presence in North Africa and the other was reform of the tariff, especially the duties on iron and coal. [72] Lherbette, a lawyer and an active deputy, not merely supported Desjobert in interventions and amendments but in 1835 published a book advocating reform of the tariff. [73] Anisson-Duperron, who had early believed that France should follow the example of Huskisson's reforms, published a number of pamphlets arguing the case for lower tariffs and made numerous reform speeches in the Chamber. [74] Other deputies also gave valuable support to the reform cause. Théodore

Ducos (Gironde), a Bordeaux ship owner and opposition deputy, first elected in 1834, was not only an outstanding speaker [75] but, as reporter of the commission of the Chamber, played an important part in the debates on the 1836 tariff Bill. Other deputies with whom Bowring established contacts were the Comte de Laborde (Seine), who spoke in favour of reform, that adept parliamentarian Duvergier de Hauranne (Cher), the poet Lamartine (Nord), who made a fervently idealistic speech in the debates on the 1836 tariff Bill and was to collaborate with Bastiat in the 1840s.

It may be partly an indication of increasing reform agitation that the 1834 elections returned a greater number of deputies who were explicitly committed to tariff reform – like Toussin (Seine-Inférieure), Roger (Nord), Ducos, Guestier Jr. and Martell (Gironde), Hennessy (Charente), Maès and Robinson de Bougon (Loire-Inférieure). Immediately after the elections the Girondin delegation went in a body to the Minister of Commerce to ascertain his intentions in the new session. [76] In August 1834 Bowring told Thomson that his 'own personal relations extend to about *sixty deputies* of all colors and parties', [77] and his allies included both government supporters and opponents and politicians as different as Odilon Barrot and Passy, Janvier and Vatout, Roul and Ducos.

More important, perhaps, were the three provincial tours Bowring undertook in 1832, 1833 and 1834. There can be no question that these journeys, if they were not the instigator of the reform agitation, were at least a stimulus to it. Two things prompted his first trip, which took him to Lyons, Grenoble and Saint-Etienne in April and May 1832. One was the need to gather information on the French silk industry – Bowring went armed with a questionnaire sent to him by Thomson – with a view to his presenting evidence to the 1832 Select Committee on the Silk Industry. The other was the desire to foster agitation in favour of allowing the export of silk, which the Anglo-French commission had recently recommended. Indeed, Bowring went with the blessing of d'Argout, who asked him to encourage the Lyonnais and the Bordelais to press for tariff reform so as to strengthen the government's hand. [78] In Lyons Bowring was warmly received by Laurent Dugas, president of the chamber of commerce, and by one of the most dynamic silk merchants, Arlès-Dufour. [79] Meeting members of the chamber both individually and collectively, he argued that the best way to safeguard the British market – about whose importance no silk merchant needed to be convinced – was for France to abolish prohibitions on imports of cotton yarn and on the export of raw silk. Though some, already afraid of burgeoning foreign competition, were against allowing the export of indigenous raw silk, the majority were in favour, and when the chamber of commerce met in plenary session on 27 April it passed a series of resolutions on commercial relations with England, and agreed to send a letter to the Minister of Commerce asking the government to allow the admission of cotton twist and raw wool and to abrogate that part of the Anglo-French agreement of 1826 which prevented them buying colonial produce in British markets. The chamber also decided to send letters to other chambers asking for their co-operation in the campaign. [80] The Grenoble chamber of commerce, which hitherto had not made representations on tariff reform, promised to send a similar letter to the Minister of Commerce. [81] After his visit Bowring kept in touch with the Lyons chamber, and the chamber instructed local deputies to support raw silk export. [82] He later claimed that 'we should have carried nothing without Lyon at our back'. [83]

Bowring's second provincial trip was longer and more wide-ranging than the first: it took him to Bordeaux and to other ports in western and northern France. Again he went armed with letters of introduction to the prefects from d'Argout and Soult as well as with letters to their constituents from local deputies. [84] Once more the purpose was to 'lay grains of gunpowder', to foster some concerted reform agitation. Bordeaux, long a vocal opponent of the tariff system of the Restoration, was his principal target, and for some months previously Bowring had contemplated raising a protest there akin to the opposition of South Carolina to federal tariff policy in the United States. He spent a month in the port early in 1833. [85] Warned about the danger of making tariff reform an issue between rival political factions and of antagonising different sections of the business community, he tried to tread as carefully as a John Bowring could by first meeting a delegation of Republicans, by dining with leading merchants, by meeting the chamber of commerce and the wine growers separately. Warmly received by the merchant R. F. Guestier, already a leading figure in Bordelais tariff agitation, he not surprisingly received promises of support not only from representative bodies but also from local journalists, several of whom 'spontaneously offered their services', and above all from Henri Fonfrède. [86] In April and May he visited Angoulême, Rochefort, la Rochelle, [87] Nantes, Angers, Morlaix, St-Brieuc, Brest, Caen, Rouen and le Hâvre. Even where he found little interest in tariff reform among the merchant community he had some success with the local press – as at Brest, where the editors of the two local newspapers promised their support, and at Rouen, where the principal paper published articles advocating some moderation of the tariff. [88] Indeed, Bowring regarded his second propaganda tour as an enormous success, and even when allowance is made for his hyperbole and Panglossian optimism there can be little doubt that his trip helped fan the flames of agitation. [89]

The third provincial tour – from late August until late October 1834 and the most extensive of all – was chiefly undertaken to encourage representations against differential duties. [90] But it had other aims: Bowring wanted to complete his statistics of the French wine trade for his *Second Report* and he wanted to visit Marseilles, of all the major ports the least active in reform agitation. [91] This time, however, he went without official blessing.[92] He went first to Champagne and Burgundy. He met members of the chamber of commerce at both Rheims and Troyes but failed to convince. After a two-hour session with him the Marseilles chamber agreed to press the government for a gradual abandonment of prohibitions and for a major reduction in iron duties. *En route* to Bordeaux he met the chambers of commerce of Montpellier, Carcassonne and Toulouse and called on most of the deputies there. In Bordeaux itself he found the various pressure groups and the newspapers, including the Carlist one, extremely active, preparing a vigorous response to the proposed inquiry on prohibitions. [93] Throughout his journey Bowring sought not merely to canvass merchants but to have electors exert pressure on their representatives, to lobby deputies, to meet newspaper editors and to put tariff reformers in touch with one another – a measure of the way in which his propaganda tours had become more sophisticated.

IV

For Bowring, raising the standard of reform in the provinces and gaining allies in the press and in Parliament were secondary to the primary task of ensuring advantageous recommendations from the Anglo-French commission and exerting pressure on the French government to reform the tariff. To achieve these ends he undertook four separate campaigns in Paris, on the first two of which he was accompanied by Villiers.

    The first resulted in a series of recommendations from the commission, the most important of which the government submitted to the Conseil supérieur du commerce for consideration. In the commission Bowring and Villiers successfully argued in favour of ending the prohibition on the export of raw silk on the grounds that the British had already allowed the import of silk manufactures and recently permitted the free exportation of long wool, of which France was the largest importer. They also persuaded the French commissioners that, in the light of extensive smuggling into France and the consequent higher cost to manufacturers of tulle and muslins and loss to the Treasury, high numbers of cotton twist should be admitted. Less important, the commission recommended a reduction in the duty on tin imports. These recommendations were submitted to the government early in February 1832,[94] but already d'Argout was expressing doubts that the government would be able to put through even such modest reforms. [95] Early in March the question of ending the prohibition on raw silk exports was submitted to the Conseil supérieur du commerce, where, though there seemed to be a majority in favour of abolition, Saint-Cricq successfully delayed a final decision. When it discussed the matter again later in the month the opposition of Saint-Cricq delayed a vote until after midnight, when the Conseil

Supérieur voted in favour by a nine-to-three majority.[96] It was evenly divided on the issue of allowing the import of cotton twist above French No. 180 (or 162 English), which it debated a couple of days later. Again Saint-Cricq spoke strongly against proposed change, which he saw as the thin end of the wedge that would eventually lead to wider reforms.[97] Throughout these meetings Bowring, Villiers and Granville in Paris and Palmerston in London put pressure on the French government to bring the recommendations before the Chambers.[98] Casimir Périer reassured and hesitated, and the arrival of the cholera effectively ended the session.[99] However, Périer was persuaded to give a written undertaking to the British ambassador whereby he promised to introduce the recommended changes as soon as practicable.[100] This was to be used as a lever by Bowring and Villiers in the second round of negotiations.[101]

The second campaign in Paris – from November 1832 until June 1833 – involved the final recommendations of the Anglo-French commission and the question of a final joint report. More important, it involved the tariff Bill which d'Argout presented in December 1832 and which contained the February recommendations of the commission.[102] Most of Bowring's and Villier's efforts were directed, first, at securing a favourable report from the commission which the Chamber set up to examine the Bill and, second, at ensuring the report was presented and the Bill discussed and passed. Both the Bill and the commission of the Chamber raised difficulties. D'Argout's Bill contained a clause proposing a reduction in the duty levied on imported livestock[103] which roused concerned agriculturists, and at least one member of the commission – Falguerolles (Tarn) – was appointed by his *bureau* to defend existing livestock legislation. The other contentious clause in the Bill was that which proposed the ending of prohibitions on imports of cotton twist of No. 180 and above. This caused spinners to send strong representations to the government and a delegation to Paris to lobby the Minister of Commerce. Besides, in contrast with later tariff Bill commissions, which were rather more liberal in their recommendations than the Bills they examined, this commission had Saint-Cricq as reporter and included Dupin among its members.[104] In the meantime d'Argout changed posts with Thiers. Adolphe Thiers arrived at the Ministry with little knowledge of commercial problems but with a willingness to learn, protectionist feelings and a desire to make his mark. Once more, then, the government found itself in the difficult position of being pulled one way by the diplomatic desirability of some tariff changes and the other by the danger posed by an unco-operative commission and a refractory Chamber already buzzing with commentaries on the Bill.

Although the Anglo-French commission went on to discuss other duties which occasioned considerable smuggling[105] it floundered on the hesitancy and finally on the refusal of the French representatives to sign a final joint report.[106] In the event only Bowring and Villiers published their report as a parliamentary paper, and Bowring added a second report a year later.

The lengthy discussions in the commission of the Chamber indicate some of the strength of protectionist feelings, as well as the determination or at least the loquacity of Dupin and Saint-Cricq, the most fervent critics of the Bill. On the issue of raw silk exports the commission held thirteen meetings, each lasting six hours, before it gave its support. [107] When cotton twist was discussed Dupin assured his colleagues that French spinners would surely be ruined by the proposed measure, since, once English yarns were admitted, the British government would immediately allow the Speenhamland system to be applied to factory workers, and manufacturers would thus be able to flood the French market with extremely cheap yarns. His assurance carried all the more weight since he was reputed to have unrivalled knowledge of Great Britain. Though the commission did vote to allow the import of cotton twist it accorded two years' grace before the clause was to become effective along the lines adopted – in different circumstances, as Bowring protested – when Britain ended prohibitions on imports of silk goods. [108] Bowring and Villiers used their political argument to persuade Ministers and king to put pressure on members of the commission. [109] Both the king and de Broglie were asked – and both complied – to influence Saint-Cricq by pointing out the political import of the recommended changes. [110] When the commission had ended its deliberations the British representatives protested to all and sundry that not enough had been achieved, but they did so only in the hope of getting the Bill accepted and perhaps getting the government to agree to allow the import of tulle. [111]

Learning of rumours that Saint-Cricq intended to delay submitting his report and that the Bill would not therefore be discussed during the 1833 session, Bowring, Villiers and Granville remonstrated with Thiers. [112] Once the report was presented – 'a series of lies and frauds', according to Bowring [113] – they again tried to nudge Thiers into bringing on the discussion of the Bill by reminding him of the political aspects and of the written pledge given by the French government, [114] and by organising a pressure campaign in favour of reform. [115] When he returned from his second provincial tour Bowring secured interviews with Louis-Philippe, Humann, and then with Thiers, who accused him of fomenting insurrection in the south of France, treating French Ministers like schoolboys and quoting political economy at them. [116] When he saw him again a few days later Bowring found Thiers conciliatory and anxious to do something. [117] What he did agree to do was to propose an amendment in the discussion of the budget to allow the government, between the 1833 and 1834 parliamentary sessions, to put into effect some of the measures proposed in the tariff Bill by means of royal decree. In this way Thiers believed he could placate the British and still avoid bringing the tariff Bill before the Chamber. [118] Unfortunately there was an outcry in the Chamber as soon as the amendment was printed. Not only were protectionists against it but so were many of the opposition groups, who objected to the powers the amendment conferred. Bowring, who attended the 19 June session, when the amendment was to be moved by Saint-Cricq, began to be suspicious when he noted that as the time approached for the amendment to be proposed a number of Ministers, including Thiers and de Broglie, began to drift out of the Chamber. He became alarmed when Saint-Cricq left and dismayed when Dupin, president of the Chamber, moved the amendment from the chair, nobody spoke in its favour and it was rejected by an overwhelming majority. Saint-Cricq later claimed that he had left the Chamber only for an instant and that it was all the fault of the president, who had maliciously raised the question earlier than had been agreed. The fact was, however, that the proposed amendment had raised such a furore that when it came to the crunch no one had the courage to defend it. [119] Something, however, was rescued from the debris, for de Broglie was already busy persuading his Cabinet colleagues that a gesture should and could be made to placate the British. The gesture was the issue of a royal decree ending the prohibition on the export of raw silk. [120]

The third round of negotiations began with a further setback. On his return from a private trip to the Rhineland at the end of September 1833 Thomson held a series of meetings with Adolphe Thiers in Paris. [121] Their purpose was once more to test the ground for a commercial treaty, but again the French Minister claimed that any treaty would have to be submitted to the Chambers, where, given their temper, it was likely to be mutilated. Both Thiers and Thomson agreed, however, that for the benefit of Anglo-French commerce and diplomatic concord each government should continue mutually advantageous tariff reductions. Thiers was unwilling to touch iron – still, he maintained, in a convalescent state following recent crises – and Thomson therefore refused to touch the duty on French wines. They did agree on certain less important reforms that each side could make. Thiers promised that the French would abolish prohibitions and replace them with 30 per cent duties. Failing this – and Thiers was very doubtful that the Conseils généraux or the Chambers would accept such a sweeping revision – he undertook to end prohibitions on a number of items, the most important of which was that on cotton twist of Nos. 180 (French) and above, as previously proposed in the 1833 tariff Bill. He also promised to attempt to lower the import duty on raw wool and to abolish the prohibition on foreign woollen cloths, provided French manufacturers could be persuaded to accept, and he agreed to end prohibitions on carriages, Cornish tinware, cutlery, copperware and plated ware. All these reforms were to be introduced in a tariff Bill to be presented to the 1834 session, which was to open in December. [122]

Since the Anglo-French commission had ended its deliberations, and following the not unexpected failure to conclude a commercial treaty, Thomson regarded Bowring's mission as ended. Indeed, though the latter had been present in Paris during the negotiations, he had been scrupulously excluded from the discussions. Granville suggested, however, that Bowring might be well employed in watching over the progress of the tariff Bill, which Thiers promised would be presented in January 1834. [123] Giving his written instructions to Bowring, Thomson warned him that Thiers's oratory in the Chamber had further strengthened his position and that Bowring should not resume his hectoring tactics. Bowring directed his attention to pressing Thiers into presenting the promised Bill, [124] even though the latter assured him that he would be able to accomplish more by royal decree than by Bill. [125] Once the Bill had been presented, and despite Thiers's highly protectionist preamble, Bowring hoped to be able to influence the liberal members of the commission [126] and worked to persuade the government to have the Bill discussed before the end of the session, a tactic some tariff reformers believed misguided, since a new Chamber was to be elected which, in view of the campaign of petitions and newspaper articles, might well be more liberal in its composition. [127] Throughout he exploited his links with the press to encourage discussion of the issues. Thiers's preamble, with its passionate defence of the existing system as not merely the consecration of time and experience but as having an internal logic superior to that of the political economists advocating free trade, certainly helped because it provoked a strong reaction in the press and among reform interests. Le Hâvre merchants sent a petition to the Chambers, and so did wine growers from the Gironde. [128] Bordeaux merchants had already sent their most famous petition, in which they spoke of the possibility of two tariff areas for France, and this was widely discussed and, in general, sympathetically received. [129]

In April the government fell and Thiers was replaced at the Ministry of Commerce by Duchâtel. Duchâtel came to office with the best of credentials: he was a typical representative of the Orleanist elite and a rising star in the political firmament, occupying his first Ministerial post at the age of thirty-four [130] He had also long shown an interest in political economy [131] and had helped draw up a wine growers' petition to the Chambers in 1829. [132] His arrival therefore raised hopes among colleagues like de Broglie [133] and among reformers. Bowring, however, knew some of his failings. He knew him to be timorous, and he knew that Thiers, the old incumbent and now once more Minister of the Interior, with his stronger position and continuing 'intrigues', [134] would ensure that Duchâtel was even more afraid of taking an independent line. Duchâtel was also a dull speaker in the Chamber. As Minister of Commerce he proved conscientious rather than innovating. The tactics of Bowring and his allies consisted of reminding Duchâtel of the 1829 wine growers' petition [135] and trying to force a statement of intent from him in the

Chamber.[136]

Already by the end of April Duchâtel had told Bowring that he intended to bring in important changes by decree in the interval between sessions. He did so partly because the report of the commission on the tariff Bill, published on 29 April, made some more liberal amendments to the Bill and, most important, recommended a reduction of one-third in the duties on coal and a 15 per cent reduction in iron duties, neither of which had featured in the original Bill.[137] He did so, too, partly because the Commission on the Budget of Receipts, which reported the same day, also recommended a more liberal tariff policy, declared that customs would thus yield greater revenue for the government and, with the approval of both Minister of Commerce and the commission on the tariff Bill, added an article to the budget which allowed the government to raise prohibitions on a series of semi-manufactured and manufactured articles included in Thiers's Bill.[138] In consequence Duchâtel issued two decrees in June and July, the first of which abolished prohibitions on cotton yarns of No. 143 (French) and above, on cashmere shawls, marine cables, clocks, lace and pure silk cloths,[139] and the second of which reduced the duty on raw wool and on a number of raw materials of secondary importance.[140]

Bowring's final spell in Paris lasted from the end of July until late November 1834. He returned there armed with new weapons. Since his last visit Thomson had submitted a proposal to Parliament to reduce duties on several items of some – if minor – interest to French exporters: the duty on dried fruit was to be lowered by two-thirds, while that on foreign books was reduced by a half.[141] These were modest changes because France was still not felt to have reciprocated earlier tariff changes affecting French goods and because the funds available to the careful Whig administration were limited. They were, however, to be treated as proof of the British government's desire further to improve commercial relations with her neighbour, which since they were revenue rather than protecting duties they could hardly do. Second, Bowring was empowered to threaten that, unless differential duties were removed, or at least a statement of intent issued, an order-in-council raising duties on French goods by 20 per cent would result. He was instructed to seek support on the differential duties question from the US ambassador. Third, he was empowered to offer a significant reduction on duties on French wines in return for a minimum of a one-third reduction in the French iron tariff.[142]

Once in Paris, Bowring resumed his familiar tactics of putting what pressure he was able on the French government, feeding the press, contacting deputies in the new Chamber and chambers of commerce in the provinces, particularly on the question of differential duties.[143] To his regret he found Duchâtel an unwilling collaborator who complained that his Ministry had been inundated with complaints from exporters about the illegally high duties imposed on silk manufactures by British customs officials,[144] who complained, again like his predecessor, about Bowring's propaganda activities and his recent provincial tour.[145] What was more, Duchâtel responded to Bowring's talk of differential tariffs by declaring them an internal affair of no concern to Britain, adding, more significantly, that France needed to placate Belgium. The fact was that Belgium was talking of a treaty with the Zollverein and threatening retaliation if France did not moderate her tariff.[146] The king and his government were therefore more anxious than ever to draw Belgium away from Prussia by means of some commercial agreement or tariff reductions,[147] and Belgian negotiators made several journeys between the two capitals during the course of the year.[148]

Duchâtel's intention to hold an inquiry into prohibitions also threatened Bowring's plans. At first he suspected that the planned inquiry was a protectionist plot to delay tariff reform, for he recognised that it would be a platform for protectionist manufacturers who, whatever the cogency of their arguments, would pass for practical men.[149] Once the inquiry was under weigh, however, he sought to make the best of it by providing reformers with statistics and arguments to combat the protectionists. His most ambitious plan was to collaborate with his friend Perronet Thompson, owner-editor of the *Westminster Review*, in the publication of a pamphlet, on the lines of the *Catechism on the Corn Laws*, as an antidote to the protectionist arguments paraded before the inquiry. This was the *Contre-enquête, par l'homme aux quarante écus* – a title borrowed from Voltaire – which consisted of a refutation of forty-two quotations from protectionists in written or verbal submissions. Unfortunately Thompson and Bowring were let down by their Paris printer, and Thompson's pamphlet did not appear.[150] Bowring did not stay long enough to see the inquiry through, for he left Paris at the end of November and did not return.

V

British commercial diplomacy, and in particular Bowring's promptings, peregrinations and propaganda, did not result in any commercial agreement. Further discussions from 1839 until 1843 were to meet a similar fate. The British had, however, helped to nudge the French government into bringing forward tariff Bills, and if the government had never been pushed as far as actually putting the proposed legislation to the vote it had been persuaded to issue royal decrees abolishing some prohibitions and reducing some protective duties.

Bowring and Villiers did not initiate the tariff campaign of the 1830s, and one needs to be chary about accepting at their face value Bowring's claims about his success in fostering agitation, as disgruntlement with the tariff in some areas and among some groups had been evident throughout the 1820s and this disaffection had increased in the harsher times of the later 1820s. However, he undoubtedly encouraged and channelled agitation at important moments. More, he often complained that the reform movement lacked co-ordination, that different areas had contacts with Paris but not with each other. In part it was Bowring himself who acted as the orchestrator of the reform campaign.[151] A measure of his success can be ascertained from the opprobrium heaped upon him by opponents of reform,[152] from the reproaches of Thiers and Duchâtel for agitation that was too successful, from the weight of petitions, memoranda and articles in the daily and periodical press.[153]

In 1836 the government braved the Chambers and the Chambers themselves finally deigned to debate and, in the event, to pass two tariff Bills. The first and most important of these abolished prohibitions and made reductions in duties on 120 articles and this gave sanction to changes which in large part had already been put into effect by royal decree. The second made tariff reductions on various items of less importance. Together they constituted the major tariff amendment effected during the July Monarchy period. They were, indeed, the only significant tariff reform before Napoleon III signed the 1860 commercial treaty with Britain and the only tariff reductions of any import voted by a French parliamentary body in the nineteenth century. As does the 1860 treaty,[154] they demonstrate the importance of foreign policy considerations in French tariff reforms. The amendments of 1836 were partly aimed at improving commercial, but above all political, relations with both Britain and Belgium.

A number of the changes that received parliamentary approval in 1836 were of interest to British exporters: the export of raw and thrown silk was permitted; cotton yarns above metric No. 143 (170 English) were now legally admitted; iron goods were allowed in at a slightly lower rate and the levy on sea coal was considerably reduced. Neither the Belgians nor the British had been able to persuade the French to make major reductions in their iron duties or to relinquish prohibitions on cotton and woollen textiles. The changes that were made, however, were not without effect on Anglo-French commerce. British cotton twist exports proved disappointing,[155] but for a variety of reasons exports of linen and coal greatly increased. Coal exports, to take the most spectacular instance, increased markedly, partly because the British themselves abolished their export levy, partly because demand for particular types of coal was increasing, partly because transport difficulties meant that the lower Loire, Gironde and Seine regions found it easier to import sea coal than to use supplies from the interior, but chiefly because the tariff was considerably reduced. Although reductions in duties on coal imported across the land frontier ensured that Belgian coal continued to benefit from even lower tariffs and to provide over three-quarters of imports, British imports also rose; by 1838 they had reached

300,000 tons,[156] by 1845 1 million and by 1913 12 millions.[157] Total Anglo-French commerce, which had stagnated between 1832 and 1836, more than doubled over the next quinquennium.[158] Bowring's and Villiers's toil was thus not entirely in vain.

Notes

1   Bastiat to Cobden, 20 March and 15 October 1847, Cobden papers, West Sussex Record Office, Chichester.

2   The Belgian representative, le Hon, was in Paris in 1832 preparing the ground for negotiations. These began only in 1833, following a formal proposal from the Belgian government. They continued spasmodically until 1836. (Le Hon to Broglie, n.d., de Broglie to Thiers, 24 April, Thiers to de Broglie, 23 May 1833, 'Arrangements commerciaux. Correspondance ministérielle, 1833–37' Archives nationales, F. 12 2660.)

3   The Comte de Latour Maubourg to de Broglie, 14 January, Duchâtel to Latour Maubourg, 8 February, de Broglie to Duchâtel, 22 January, Duchâtel to de Broglie, 15 February, Thiers to Passy, 9 March and 15 April 1836, Archives nationales, F. 12 6241.

4   Copy of a note from Duchâtel to de Broglie, 30 September 1835, *ibid.*, F. 12 2660.

5   For a general discussion of British commercial diplomacy in the first half of the nineteenth century see Lucy Brown, *The Board of Trade and the Free Trade Movement, 1830–42*, Oxford, 1958; Judith B. Williams, *British Commercial Policy and Trade Expansion, 1750–1850*, 1973. For the problems posed by commercial negotiations see Karl F. Helleiner, *Free Trade and Frustration. Anglo-Austrian Negotiations, 1860–70*, Toronto, 1973.

6   See Pierre Reboul, *Le Mythe anglais dans la littérature française sous la Restauration*, Lille, 1962. For a general sketch of Anglo-French misunderstanding in the nineteenth and twentieth centuries see François Crouzet, 'Problèmes de la communication franco-britannique aux XIXe et XXe siècles', *Revue historique*, vol. CCLIV, 1975, pp. 105–34.

7   'Parler de la Ligue en France c'est comme si l'on parlait d'une chose qui se passerait dans le Spitzberg.' (Bastiat to Cobden, 8 April 1845, Cobden papers, West Sussex Record Office.)

8   Bastiat to Cobden, 28 March 1846, *ibid.* At the end of 1846, when the Association pour la liberté des echanges was at the height of its propaganda activities, Bastiat could still lament that *'The cry* contre l'Angleterre nous étouffe. On a soulevé contre nous de formidables préventions. Si cette haine contre la perfide Albion n'était qu'une mode j'attendrais patiemment qu'elle passât. Mais elle a de profondes racines dans les coeurs. Elle est universelle, et je vous ai dit, je crois, que ma vieille tante m'ecrit que dans mon village elle n'ose plus parler de moi qu'en famille.' (Bastiat to Cobden, 25 December 1846, *ibid.*)

9   As, for example, in his speech on the tariff Bill on 3 May 1836 (*Archives parlementaires*, vol. CIII).

10   Ministère du Commerce, *Enquête relative à diverses prohibitions établies à l'entrée des produits étrangers*, Paris, 1835, vol. I, pp. 84–98.

11   *L'Indusrie. Exposition de 1834*, n.d., pp. 10–11.

12   The best exposition of the arguments and (suspect) statistics is in an article entitled 'Du Traité de Commerce de 1786', in the *Journal du Commerce*, 4 November 1834.

13 'Des Relations commerciales entre la France et l'Angleterre' (a report to
    the Paris chamber of commerce), *Moniteur universel*, 10 March 1835.

14 *Parliamentary Papers*, 1834, XIX, First Report of Bowring and Villiers
    on the Commercial Relations between France and Great Britain, appendix
    I, pp. 80–94, and appendix XV, p. 149. As an export market in Europe
    France ranked after Germany, Italy, the Netherlands, Russia, Turkey,
    Portugal, Spain and Gibraltar. As an export market for France, Britain
    ranked first but came fourth, after the USA, Sardinia and Belgium, as a
    supplier of imports. These figures, of course, do not take account of the
    considerable smuggling between Britain and France.

15 *Cours complet d'économie politique pratique*, Paris, 1828, vol. III, pp.
    362–3.

16 Flachat also quoted approvingly Poulett Thomson's declaration in the
    House of Commons on 14 April 1829 that he was of the same opinion as
    Huskisson in that if France did not realise that it was in her interest to
    lower her tariff, Britain should not follow her bad example but should
    undertake unilateral reductions to encourage others to follow. ('De la
    réforme commerciale', *Revue des deux mondes*, November 1834, pp.
    245–91 and particularly 245–57.)

17 For example, the Dunkirk chamber of commerce, in its written submission
    to the Duchâtel inquiry, pointed out that the British had not attempted to
    put the theories of her political economists to the test. 'Ce serait donc le
    système commercial de la Grande-Bretagne et non les doctrines de ses
    économistes que nous proposerions pour modèle à tout gouvernement
    sage, faisant application de ce système dans ses différentes phases, selon
    les circonstances particulières à chaque peuple.' (Ministère du Commerce,
    Enquête relative à diverses prohibitions . . ., vol. I, pp. 74–7.

18 Albert H. Imlah, *Economic Elements in the Pax Britannica*, Cambridge,
    Mass., 1958, p. 147.

19 For the debate on machinery exports see A. E. Musson, 'The Mancheser
    school' and exportation of machinery', *Business History*, vol. XIV, 1972,
    pp. 17–50. The Lille chamber of commerce argued that so long as Britain
    banned the export of machinery France should retain her tariff system;
    only when the British allowed others to use their weapons should the
    French agree to join combat with them. (Ministère du Commerce,
    Enquête relative à diverses prohibitions . . ., vol. I, pp. 141–7.)

20 The other three occasions were in 1837, 1838–39 and 1839–41. In 1839
    the French government complained that prohibitive duties were levied on
    French brandies and in response the British suggested it would reduce
    duties in return for a *quid pro quo* in the form of either an abolition of
    prohibitions on cotton manufactures or a reduction of duties on British
    iron goods. In the following year the French government planned to raise
    duties on imported flax and linens but in the face of threats of reprisals
    proposed that British flax and linens be admitted at a preferential rate in
    return for a reduction of duties on French brandy. Though the British
    refused this offer, the two governments did agree to resume the tariff
    negotiations of 1831–34, and a new commission was appointed.
    Discussions took place from 2 January until 14 February 1839 but
    nothing came of them. At the end of 1839 negotiations were resumed on
    France's initiative and in fact an agreement was reached whereby France
    was to reduce duties on ten articles and in return the British were to lower
    imposts on twenty-one, but the discussions were brought to a sudden halt
    by the treaty of 15 July 1840; and in May 1841 the British ambassador
    informed Guizot that his government considered the negotiations at an
    end. Early in 1843 there was an attempt to revive the tentative agreement

of 1840 but no agreement could be reached and negotiations were again broken off. ('Résumé analytique des négotiations commerciales survies entre la France et l'Angleterre de 1826 à 1859', dated 15 December 1859, Papiers Baroche, 1184, Bibliothèque Thiers. These negotiations are also discussed in the Correspondance consulaire et commerciale (Londres), 28 (1838–40), Archives des Affaires étrangères, in 'notes échangées entre les commissaires anglais et français', Archives nationales, F. 12 6219, and 'rapport au ministère sur le projet de traité de commerce avec l'Angleterre', March 1841, and 'rapport à l'Empereur sur le traité de commerce franco-anglais', 24 January 1860, ibid., F. 12 6220.)

21   For British foreign policy see C. K. Webster, *The Foreign Policy of Palmerston, 1830–41*, London, 1969 (edition), two vols, and Roger Bullen, *Palmerston, Guizot and the Collapse of the Entente Cordiale*, London, 1974, pp. 1–14. For Anglo-French relations in this period see Raymond Guyot, *La Première Entente cordiale*, Paris, 1926.

22   Talleyrand declared in his *Mémoires* that an alliance between Britain and France was the goal he worked for. He was well suited, despite his age, to carry out this task, for he was well received in London society. (See letters from the Duchesse de Dino to Thiers, 1, 4, 6 and 7 October 1830, Papiers Thiers, N.a.f. 20601, Bibliothèque nationale.) Talleyrand's successor in London, General Sébastiani, who had been Foreign Minister in the first three years of the July Monarchy, was also anxious to foster good relations. (Sébastiani to Thiers, 24 February and 25 June 1836, Papiers Thiers, N.a.f. 20606, Bibliothèque nationale.)

23   *Correspondance diplomatique de Talleyrand. Ambassade de Talleyrand à Londres, 1830–34*, Paris, 1891, vol. V, pp. 278–9, and letter from de Broglie to Talleyrand, 16 December 1833, *ibid.*, 279–91; Paul Thureau–Dangin, *Histoire de la Monarchie de Juillet*, Paris, 1884, vol. II, pp. 386–7; C. K. Webster, *op. cit.*

24   He was Minister of Foreign Affairs from 11 October 1833 until 3 April 1834 and President of the Council and Minister of Foreign Affairs from 12 March 1835 until 22 February 1836.

25   *Souvenirs du feu duc de Broglie, 1785–1870, publiés par son fils le duc C.-J. V.-A. de Broglie*, Paris, 1886, vol. III, pp. 242–6; Raymond Guyot, *op. cit.*, pp. 103–4.

26   C. K. Webster, *op. cit.*, vol. I, p. 351, and Palmerston to William IV, 29 September 1833, cited *ibid.*, vol. II, pp. 802–4.

27   John Bowring, *Autobiographical Recollections, with a brief memoir by Lewin B. Bowring*, London, 1877, pp. 259–60. Raymond Guyot goes so far as to claim that Britain and France failed to conclude a formal alliance in the 1830s because they were unable to agree on a commercial treaty and because intellectual exchange between the two countries remained so restricted. This, of course, is an exaggeration.

28   Although he was later to join the Association pour la liberté des échanges, de Broglie's advocacy of tariff reform remained moderate and practical. In 1851 he wrote that whilst political economy is a science, applied political economy is an art, and that if both protection and absolute free trade were unacceptable extremes the countries that benefited most from free trade were those that had the best resource endowment and had reached a certain stage in their economic growth. ('Liberté commerciale', pp. 133, 169–71, 188, in *Le Libre Echange et l'impôt, études d'économie politique par le feu duc de Broglie, publiées par son fils*, Paris, 1879.)

29   *Souvenirs du feu duc de Broglie*, vol. IV, pp. 270–3.

30   Bowring and Villiers, *First Report on the Commercial Relations between France and Great Britain*, pp. 2–3. A very full, if biased account of

Anglo-French commercial negotiations in this period is given in the private papers of the Earl of Clarendon at the Bodleian Library, Oxford. These papers not only contain letters from Bowring to Villiers, who were the British commissioners, but two files belonging to the Board of Trade which contain the Board's correspondance relating to the negotiations, mainly letters to and from Poulett Thomson. The author is grateful to the present Earl of Clarendon for granting him permission to study and microfilm these papers. The French side of the negotiations is to be found in the Correspondance consulaire et commerciale (Londres), Archives du Ministère des Affaires étrangères, CC, 24–7, and in the Archives nationales, F. 12 6216–20 and 2647.

31 Bowring to Thomson, 8 and 12 December 1831, Clarendon papers, Bodleian Library.

32 Letters from the French consul-general in London to Sébastiani, 14 July, 12, 17 and 25 August, 10 and 19 September and 3 October 1831, Correspondance consulaire et commerciale (Londres), CC, 24, and Talleyrand to Sébastiani, 1 October 1834, Correspondance diplomatique, C.P. 635, Archives du Ministère des Affaires étrangères. The second note of the British commissioners to their French counterparts in 1840 indicates that French wine exports increased by 70 per cent between 1831 and 1838. Archives nationales, F. 12 6219.

33 Thomson to Bowring, 29 November 1831, Clarendon papers, Bodleian Library. A pencilled marginal note by Palmerston, dated 12 December 1831, read: 'Nothing can be more ably nor more perspicuously drawn up.' Bowring and Villiers, *op. cit.*, pp. 3–5, 8–9.

34 Bowring and Villiers to Lord Granville, 21 March 1832, Clarendon papers, Bodleian Library.

35 A friend of Bentham, Thomson effected a number of modest reforms whilst he was at the Board of Trade. In April 1829 he made a much-quoted speech advocating Britain's unilateral adoption of free trade: 'If we wait till they grant reciprocity, we are slaves of their will; if we give free admission to their produce, they become servants of ours'. (Cited, *Memoir of the Life of the right honourable Charles Lord Sydenham, with a narrative of his administration in Canada by his brother, G. Poulett Scrope*, London, 1843, p. 30.)

36 Walter Bagehot, *Biographical Studies*, London, 1881, pp. 346–7.

37 John Bowring, *Autobiographical Recollections*, p. 7.

38 Bowring had written the congratulatory address from the citizens of London to the French people after the July revolution, been part of the delegation that took the address to Paris and was the first Englishman to be received by Louis-Philippe after his recognition by the British government.

39 In March 1832 Bowring claimed, 'I give habitually sixteen hours a day to the labours of the Commission – I have not even been to a place of amusement since I have been in Paris.' (Bowring to Thomson, 3 March 1832, Clarendon papers, Bodleian Library.) A year later he was writing, 'I scarcely ever get to bed till three o'clock in the morning and never go to any place of amusement or to any place but to advance our objects, to which I am bound by flesh, blood, brains, and every thought and feeling.' (Bowring to Thomson, 10 January 1833, *ibid.*)

40 Villiers already had some expertise in tariff questions, having been a commissioner of customs, while Bowring had knowledge of government finance in various European countries, including France.

41 As Bowring wrote to Thomson early in 1833, 'The real and simple and substantial fact is that nobody but the King and de Broglie are *hearty* and

convinced and acting upon the true grounds — while the rest are all *French Toads* under the *English Harrow* — thinking only how they can wriggle out of these concessions extorted from their convictions.' (Letter of 11 February 1833, Clarendon papers, Bodleian Library.) In his often peevish *Autobiographical Recollections* Bowring roundly condemned what he regarded as Louis-Philippe's duplicity, claiming that the king had his secretary calculate what tariff reductions would cost him personally. It is clear, however, that Louis-Philippe was strongly in favour of the Anglo-French *rapprochement* and of tariff reductions in favour of Britain. At the time Bowring believed — at least until 1834 — that his ease of access to the king and the latter's liberal professions were of considerable import for Britain. Early in 1832 Louis-Philippe assured Bowring that he hoped the French would be able to emulate every liberalisation of the British tariff. (Bowring to Thomson, 9 and 16 January 1832, Clarendon papers, Bodleian Library.) The king told Granville in 1833 that he and de Broglie were the strong supporters of improved commercial relations and that the rest of his Ministers looked upon tariff reductions as 'the unavoidable price of English alliance'. (Villiers to Palmerston, 11 February 1833, *ibid.*) The importance the French government attached to the negotiations is evidenced in the enthusiastic assurances given to Bowring by Marshal Soult, hardly known for his anglophile sentiments, early in 1833. 'He employed the strongest language as to his wishes to lend assistance to our commission and to extend the mutual intercourse of the two countries. In fact he did this with remarkable earnest holding my hand all the time and squeezing it again and again while he repeated that he would do anything that could be suggested for the advancement of the object.' (Bowring to Thomson, 6 January 1833, *ibid.*)

42   Villiers and Bowring regarded Fréville as shallow and opinionated. (Villiers to Thomson and Bowring to Thomson, 16 December 1831, and Bowring to Thomson, 30 December 1831, Clarendon papers, Bodleian Library.)

43   Bowring to Villiers, 29 April 1833, *ibid.* Even when Duchâtel became Minister of Commerce Bowring still believed him under the spell of his more eloquent and more powerful colleague, who was also his predecessor at the Ministry. 'If Duchâtel had the eye of a lynx, or the ears of a fox, he would set up for himself, but Thiers has still his black thumb upon him and his eyes are dim and his ears dull.' (Bowring to Villiers, 23 May 1834, *ibid.*)

44   Bowring to Villiers, 8 April 1833, *ibid.*

45   Even Adolphe d'Eichthal, banker and ally of tariff reform in the 1830s and 1840s campaigns, could write in 1834, 'Bowring est de nouveau ici pour la loi de douane; maintenant son ton tranchant, charletan et menaçant fait plus de mal que de bon.' (Adolphe to Gustave d'Eichthal, 28 February 1834, Fonds d'Eichthal, 13748, f. 47, Bibliothèque de l'Arsenal.)

46   These writings were collected as *Voyages dans la Grande-Bretagne entrepris relativement aux services publics de la guerre, de la marine et des ponts et chaussées, en 1816, 1817, 1818, 1819 et 1820*, Paris 1821–24, several volumes.

47   To Bowring he was 'vain, shallow and spiteful'. Villiers called him 'that prince of jackasses', and even stooped to doggerel: 'To the meanest trickeries stooping / Ever lying — lurching Dupin.' (Bowring to Thomson, 4 January 1833; Villiers to Thomson, 6 and 25 January 1833, Clarendon papers, Bodleian Library.)

48 Saint-Cricq gave his views on an Anglo-French treaty in a speech in 1834
    in the Chamber of Peers. (He was elevated to the peerage in 1833.) He
    repeated the already familiar argument – but no less true for that – that
    Britain had reduced her tariffs only slightly and had done so only when
    British industries had nothing to fear from foreign competitors. He agreed
    that the admission of French silks was a different matter but pointed out
    that duties still remained high and that home production had expanded.
    France, he said, should emulate the British but should not try to go
    further. (Chambre des Pairs, séance du 11 mars 1834, *Archives
    parlementaires*, vol. LXXXVII.)

49 On Saint-Cricq's activities on the 1833 tariff Bill commission Villiers
    wrote, 'But the knave St-Cricq / Is concocting a plan / To play us a trick /
    If his knaveship can.' (Villiers to Thomson, 25 January 1833, Clarendon
    papers, Bodleian Library.)

50 Evidence of Thiers's protectionist sentiments is to be found in his
    preamble to his 1834 tariff Bill. (Projet de loi, 3 February 1834, *Archives
    parlementaires*, vol. LXXXVI.)

51 For Bowring Thiers was 'that little knave', (Bowring to Villiers, 25 March
    1833, Clarendon papers, Bodleian Library.) In 1834 he happily reported
    that *le Corsaire* had nicknamed Thiers 'l'atome babillard'. (Bowring to
    Thomson, 9 May 1834, *ibid.*) But even Bowring recognised Thiers's
    adroitness: 'I never saw a creature so slippery, vain, witty, ignorant,
    sportive, presumptuous, passionate, foolish and clever. Land your hand as
    you will, there is no catching the eel.' (Bowring to Thomson, 31 January
    1834, *ibid.*)

52 The *Revue indépendante* cited a conversation in 1831 between Périer and
    a general of the empire who was pressing for the Belgian provinces to be
    incorporated into France. Périer told him, 'Il me semble, mon cher, que
    vous voyez la question à travers la fumée de la gloire,' to which the
    general responded, 'Mais vous-même ne la voyez-vous pas à travers la
    fumée des mines d'Anzin.' (Cited, H.-T. Deschamps, *op. cit.*, p. 197.)

53 Léon Amé, *Etude économique sur les tarifs de douanes*, Paris, 1859, pp.
    168–72, and Emile Levasseur, *Histoire du commerce de la France*, Paris,
    1911–12, two vols., vol. II, p. 161.

54 Since the British had already removed prohibitions on silk imports, since
    the prospects for increased French wine sales in Britain seemed, to some
    at least, limited and since the Whigs did not have the budget surpluses or
    the reforming zeal to put through far-reaching tariff reductions, the
    concessions the British could offer appeared to be of minor import. This is
    why the threat of discriminatory duties on French goods was resorted to
    by the British representatives.

55 Villiers to Thomson, 2 April 1832, Clarendon papers, Bodleian Library.

56 Bowring and Villiers, in a joint letter to d'Argout, said that France's
    failure to reform its tariffs 'fournit un prétexte constant pour exciter des
    sentiments hostiles, et d'arrêter la sympathie que, heureusement, s'établit
    entre les deux pays.' (Letter of 21 March 1832, *ibid.*)

57 Bowring to Thomson, 3 March 1832, *ibid.*

58 There was polite talk of retaliations early in 1832. (Villiers to Thomson,
    24 February, and Bowring and Villiers to d'Argout, 21 March 1832, *ibid.*)
    But in July 1834 Thomson was using the threat of a 20 per cent increase
    in all duties on French goods. (Thomson to Bowring, 28 July 1834, *ibid.*)
    Such a threat lost some of its weight when, as in silk manufactures,
    smuggling remained as important as it did.

59 In April 1834 Bowring wrote, 'I have had a serious talk with Gréterin
    about the necessity of making the Douanes more productive. I think that

will be a great instrument of change. Their finances are dreadfully
embarrassed ... and even Duchâtel owned to me on Wednesday that
some measures must be taken to find funds.' (Bowring to Thomson, 24
April 1834, *ibid.*)

60 Thus in the May 1834 discussion of the budget Anisson-Duperron, a close
collaborator of Bowring's, claimed that the 48 million franc deficit that
was being forecast could be avoided if customs revenue were increased.
He pointed out that while the USA raised all federal revenue from customs
and Britain drew a third of its enormous revenue from the same source,
the French government drew only one tenth. The explanation of this was
the existence in France of prohibitions and high protection. (Chambre des
députés, séance du 19 mai 1834, *Archives parlementaires*, vol. XC.)
Another collaborator, the deputy Lherbette, also took up the issue of the
high cost and poor return of French customs – 20,000 customs officers,
25 millions in expenses. (A.-J. Lherbette, *De la liberté commerciale et de
la réforme de nos lois de douanes*, Paris, 1835, pp. 6–7.)

61 The report described the over 2 million kg of contraband annually carried
across the northern frontier by specially trained dogs, despite the 40,000
dogs killed between 1820 and 1830. It calculated that smuggling from the
Channel ports into Britain deprived the Treasury of about £300,000 a
year and estimated the annual loss to the government by smuggling of
French brandy alone to be more than £500,000. (*First Report* ..., pp.
46–8, 54, 57.)

62 Bowring exulted to Villiers in May 1834, 'Our Report *makes fortune*. The
papers are full of it and it will, I hope, have much influence on the question
which had marched nobly of late.' (Bowring to Villiers, 23 May 1834,
Clarendon papers, Bodleian Library.) The report was given wide publicity
not only in the newspapers but in the periodical press: the *Revue
britannique*, whose editor, Saulnier, was in favour of tariff reductions,
published a translation of MacCulloch's article on the report in the
Edinburgh Review ('Des rapports commerciaux entre l'Angleterre et la
France', May 1834, pp. 36–54). Horace Say published *Rapport sur le
commerce entre la France et l'Angleterre à l'occasion des documents
publiés à Londres par George Villiers et John Bowring*, Paris, 1835.

63 Perronet Thompson to Bowring, 5 December 1831, Perronet Thompson
papers, University of Hull. The author is grateful to the archivist of the
University of Hull for permission to consult these papers.

64 Villiers to Thomson, 23 December 1831, Clarendon papers, Bodleian
Library. Early in 1832 Sir Henry Parnell published a pamphlet entitled
Observations sur le commerce entre la France et la Grande-Bretagne,
which advocated mutual tariff reductions in preference to a commercial
treaty. (*The Times*, 21 January, *Journal du Commerce*, 29 January,
Parnell to the Baron Louis and to d'Argout, 26 January, 1834, Archives
nationales, F. 12 6216.)

65 Bowring to Thomson, 23 December 1831, *ibid.*

66 Bowring to Thomson, 15 February 1833, *ibid.* A few days earlier Bowring
had written to Villiers, 'I have made arrangements for a series of articles in
the Constitutionnel, Courrier, National, Temps, etc.' (Bowring to Villiers,
11 February 1833, *ibid.*)

67 Bowring to Villiers, 9 June 1833, *ibid.*

68 Séance du 13 février 1834, *Archives parlementaires*, vol. LXXXVI;
Bowring to Villiers, 14 February 1834, Clarendon papers, Bodleian
Library.

69 Parliament also discussed petitions sent to it, for, as in Britain at this time,
the right to petition and Parliament's duty to discuss the petitions that

were sent occupied a more important place in political procedures than they did later in the century.

70   As, for instance, he was already doing on the question of the d'Argout tariff Bill early in 1833. (Bowring to Thomson, 10 January 1833, *ibid.*)

71   As one biographical guide to parliamentarians put it, 'il se lève, on rit; il monte à la tribune, on rit; il ouvre la bouche, on rit; il a fini de parler, on rit encore. Quand on en est arrivé là, on devrait se rendre justice en quittant la scène politique.' (*Sessions 1838–39. Biographie politique et parlementaire des députés*, Paris, 1839.)

72   As might be expected of a deputy representing the Seine-Inférieure department. In June 1833, soon after becoming a deputy, he propsed an amendment to the budget for 1834 which would have lowered duties on iron by a quarter and on coal by a half. (Séance du 18 juin 1833, *Archives parlementaires*, vol. LXXXV.) Thereafter he spoke at every opportunity in favour of reform of the tariff. For a brief biographical summary see obituary notice in *Bulletin de la Société de l'histoire de France*, 1853, p. 101.

73   His *De la liberté commerciale et de la réforme de nos lois de douanes* was published in 1835. In the 1840s he joined Bastiat's free-trade pressure group.

74   *De l'affranchissement du commerce et de l'industrie* (Paris 1829), advocated that France follow the example of the Huskisson reforms, while his *De l'Enquête sur les fers, ou application des principes généraux à la question de la taxe sur les fers étrangers* (Paris 1829) sought to refute the arguments put forward by Saint-Cricq and Baron Pasquier. He also published a pamphlet on the sugar inquiry of 1829. In the 1840s he joined the Association pour la liberté des échanges, became vice-president and was the largest donor, with 2,000 francs, in the first year. (*le Libre-Echange*, 13 June 1847).

75   'C'est la poésie appliquée aux affaires,' said the *Biographie politique et parlementaire des députés*. He was the nephew of Roger Ducos.

76   They were accompanied by Anisson-Duperron. (Bowring to Thomson, 8 and 11 August 1834, Clarendon papers, Bodleian Library.)

77   Bowring to Thomson, 18 August 1834, *ibid.*

78   Bowring to Thomson, 16 April 1832, *ibid.* Copies of letters from d'Argout to Prunelle, mayor of Lyons, the Lyons chamber of commerce, the prefect of the Rhône, April 1832, Archives nationales, F. 12 2647.

79   Bowring to Thomson, 17 and 28 April 1832, *ibid.* He was later to claim that Arlès-Dufour had been 'worth a king's ransom to us'. (Bowring to Villiers, 25 March 1833, *ibid.*)

80   Bowring to Thomson, 28 April 1832, *ibid.* Early in May the Lyons chamber sent two further letters to the Minister urging the government to make tariff changes before the Chambers reassembled. (Bowring to Thomson, 2 and 5 May 1832, *ibid.*)

81   Bowring to Thomson, 29 April 1832, *ibid.*

82   Bowring to Villiers, 15 October, and Bowring to Thomson, 23 November 1832, *ibid.*

83   Bowring to Thomson, 15 February 1833, *ibid.*

84   Bowring to Thomson, 8 March 1833, *ibid.* Copies of letters from the Minister of Commerce, dated 9 March 1833, Archives nationales, F. 12 2647.

85   On arrival he was shocked to discover how much the port had declined since he had lived there twenty years previously. He confessed to Villiers that he was 'a little disgusted at finding my old Bordeaux – the ville joyeuse of my boyhood – anéanti. Strangely has it been overturned, sadly

bedevilled. There were two houses in which I passed delicious hours, occupied by two of the first families if Bordeaux – alas! that was a fifth of a century ago. I hurried to enquire of them. I found them both *à louer*, with that look of desolation upon them which contrast makes so terrible.' (Bowring to Villiers, 14 and 19 March 1833, *ibid.*)

86   Bowring to Villiers, 14, 19, 25 March and 7 April 1833, *ibid.*

87   The support given by the chamber of commerce of La Rochelle is shown in the letter to the Minister of Commerce of 18 June 1833 sent by the mayor of La Rochelle (Archives nationales, F. 12 2647).

88   Bowring to Thomson, 25 May 1833, *ibid.* In a letter to Villiers, written on May 23, he claimed, 'There are sixteen newspapers on the ground over which I have gone. There is *not one* of them that has not published *several* hearty articles in condemnation of the protecting system.'

89   See, for example, 'Mission du Docteur Bowring en France', *Revue mensuelle d'économie politique*, vol. I, 1833.

90   Bowring to Thomson, 8 August 1834, Clarendon papers, Bodleian Library.

91   Marseilles had failed to respond to the calls for support issued by Bordeaux. (Thomas to Thiers, 10 April 1834, Papiers Thiers, N.a.f. 20601, Bibliothèque nationale.) It was the only major French port to have expressed satisfaction at Thiers's tariff Bill. (Bowring to Thomson, 30 September 1834, Clarendon papers, Bodleian Library.)

92   De Rigny, the Foreign Minister, promised letters which never materialised, while Duchâtel, the Minister of Commerce, politely refused to provide any, saying Bowring no longer had need of them. (Bowring to Thomson, 18 August, and Bowring to Palmerston, 7 September 1834, *ibid.*)

93   Bowring to Thomson, 20 October 1834, *ibid.*

94   Bowring to Thomson, 16 February 1832, *ibid.* Bowring and Villiers, *First Report . . .*, pp. 8–9.

95   Although at his first meeting d'Argout had been confident that the tariff changes could be made (Bowring to Thomson, 13 January 1832, Clarendon papers, Bodleian Library), by the time the commission made its recommendations he was worried about the reactions of French cotton spinners. 'D'Argout was washy and timid and full of feeble phrases delivered with the pomp and circumstance of a second-rate actor at the Française,' wrote Villiers to Thomson. (17 February 1832, *ibid.*) Périer was gracious to the British representatives, but he too expressed worries about possible opposition. (Villiers to Thomson, 24 February 1832, *ibid.*)

96   Villiers to Thomson and Bowring to Thomson, 19 March 1832. After the first meeting Bowring called Saint-Cricq 'that vile mischief-maker' and prophesied, 'We shall throw the tricks / Of M. Saint-Cricq's / Into the Styx.' Saint-Cricq said after the vote that if the government had a political motive in the matter he would not oppose the abolition in the Chamber. (Bowring to Thomson, 26 March 1832, *ibid.*)

97   The vote was five to five, chiefly because Lefèvre, the deputy for the Seine who was generally in favour of reductions, was so frightened by Saint-Cricq's arguments that he voted against. (Bowring to Thomson, 29–30 March 1832, *ibid.*)

98   A meeting of the Anglo-French commission was held after it had made its first recommendations. Duchâtel and Fréville both agreed that the best way to influence the government was to stress the political rather than the commercial argument. (Villiers to Thomson, 20 February 1832, *ibid.*) Granville secured an interview with Périer, which Bowring also attended, to put pressure on Louis-Philippe. (Villiers to Thomson, 17 February and

23 March, and Bowring to Thomson, 23 March 1832, *ibid.*) See also the note submitted by Bowring to the Minister of Commerce (Archives nationales, F. 12 6216).

99   'People pretend it is more malignant here and that the infected die quicker and bluer than in any other town of Europe – which I believe is all vanity.' (Villiers to Thomson, 30 March 1832, *ibid.*)

100   Bowring to Thomson and Villiers to Thomson, 2 April 1832, *ibid.*; Bowring and Villiers, *First Report* ..., p. 9. Copies of letters from Sébastiani to Granville, 12 April, and Granville to Sébastiani, 13 May 1832, Correspondance commerciale (Londres), 25, Archives du Ministère des Affaires étrangères.

101   Already in October Granville was reminding de Broglie of the written promise of the previous April. (Copy of his letter of 17 October and of de Broglie's reply of 24 October 1832, Correspondance consulaire et commerciale (Londres), 25, Archives du Ministère des Affaires étrangères.)

102   Chambre des députés, séance du 3 décembre 1832, *Archives parlementaires*, vol. LXXVIII. The Bill proposed to end prohibitions on imports of cotton yarn above 180 (French) and on imports of less important items like cashmere shawls, some kinds of leather and clocks and watches and on exports of raw and thrown silk.

103   The 1816 duty on cattle had been essentially a revenue duty. In 1822, because of a large influx of cattle for accidental reasons the previous year, the government proposed to increase the duty tenfold and the Chamber of Deputies raised these duties even further. Retaliations abroad and representations from Alsace led d'Argout to propose a 50 per cent reduction of the duties imposed by the 1832 tariff. Villiers wrote to Thomson, 'Our affairs it must be owned have been somewhat embarrassed, unintentially I am quite sure for d'Argout never dreamt of the resistance which had been seen, by being made part of so extensive a change as this projet de loi – too many interests are threatened at once and they are making common cause against an innovating government.' (Letter of 21 January 1833, Clarendon papers, Bodleian Library.)

104   Its members were Cunin-Gridaine, Duvergier de Hauranne, Fulchiron, Meynard, Barbet, Boignes, Falguerolles, Dupin and Saint-Cricq. (*Archives parlementaires*, vol. LXXVIII.) Of these only Duvergier and Fulchiron could be relied upon to support the suggested reforms.

105   They discussed tulle – of which at least 12 million francs' worth were smuggled into France every year – as well as plated goods and cutlery. (Bowring to Thomson, 7 January 1833, Clarendon papers, Bodleian Library.)

106   Bowring to Thomson, 22 January 1833, *ibid.*

107   According to Bowring at least, Dupin spoke an average of three hours at each meeting. (Bowring to Thomson, 4 January, 1833, *ibid.*)

108   Bowring to Thomson, 22 January, Villiers to Thomson, 25 and 28 January 1833, *ibid.*

109   In January 1833 Villiers asked Auckland to suggest to Talleyrand that he write to de Broglie to impress upon him how 'utterly baseless and unreal any alliance between the two countries would be which was not one of extended commercial relations.' (Letter of 6 January 1833, *ibid.*) Talleyrand duly wrote to de Broglie stressing just this and pointing out that the position of the new Whig administration was not as strong in the House of Commons as it might be and that French tariff reforms might strengthen it. (Talleyrand to de Broglie, 20 January 1833, *Mémoires du Prince de Talleyrand*, vol. V, pp. 105–8.) Pressure was also put on Thiers

in informal meetings and a formal letter. Bowring to Thomson, 7 January, Villiers to Thiers, 21 February 1833, Clarendon papers, Bodleian Library.) Granville saw the king and Thiers. (Villiers to Palmerston, 11 February 1833, *ibid.*)

110   Bowring asked the king to speak to Saint-Cricq, which the king did. (Bowring to Thomson, 6 January 1833, *ibid.*) De Broglie assured Granville that he had personally convinced Saint-Cricq and that, as Villiers said, the latter had 'promised, *foi d'honnête homme* (which is making free with somebody else's foi, for it can't be his own) that he will do his utmost to support the project in the committee.' (Villiers to Thomson, 14 and 25 January 1833, *ibid.*)

111   Villiers to Thomson, 4 February 1833, *ibid.*

112   The first time Bowring and Villiers met Thiers in February 1833 he assured them that he was aware of the immense political importance of the Bill, which would be submitted during the current session. A couple of days later Thiers and Saint-Cricq assured them that procedural problems in the Chamber made it impossible to submit the report of the commission before the end of the session but that this meant a delay of only two or three weeks. (Villiers to Thomson and Bowring to Thomson, 22 February 1833, *ibid.*)

113   'What a volume of scoundrel perfidies.' (Bowring to Villiers, 7 April 1833, *ibid.*) The introduction to the report was an argument in favour of the existing tariff, and the commission itself opposed any reduction of duties on imported livestock. (Chambre des députés, séance du 3 avril 1833, *Archives parlementaires*, vol. LXXXII.)

114   Thomson wrote to de Broglie threatening that if nothing were done the British government would publish the written undertaking made by the French. (Letter of 28 May 1833, *ibid.*)

115   'I am come to a solemn league and covenant with Flachat and the Constitutionnel. The day after tomorrow they are to break out. I have settled with Perreire [*sic*] an article for the National, with Rodet for the Temps, with Guillemot for the Messager, with Darth for the Moniteur du Commerce, with the Journal du Commerce, and Comte for the Courrier. The Messager is at work for us. Fie! Every day you will have an article somewhere. Since I found the state of things here, I am become a boiling cauldron. I feel as if we – the honest – were pitted against the knaves – and shall not succeed? Aye! that we will.' (Bowring to Villiers, 3 June 1833, *ibid.*)

116   Thiers, according to Bowring, added, 'Vous avez une vingtaine de fous en Angleterre – qui ne savent rien – et vous venez débiter vos bêtises à une vingtaine de fous ici mais nous ne sommes pas si pauvres écoliers comme vous nous jugez. Vous êtes des charlatans qui parlez comme des médecins qui ont fait des livres, contre les médecins qui étudient les maladies.' Thiers also denounced British intentions. 'Vous voulez nous empêcher de faire des fers et des cotons – voilà tout. Vous parlez dans l'intérêt de votre pays et j'agirai dans l'intérêt du mien. Nous aurons une alliance politique, mais vous soignerez vos affaires commerciales et je soignerai les miennes . . .' Bowring's French has not been altered. (Bowring to Villiers, 5 June 1833, *ibid.*)

117   Bowring to Villiers, 12 June 1833, *ibid.*

118   Any royal decrees issued were, of course, to be submitted to the 1834 session of the Chambers. Parliament was to break up on the 26 June and reassemble for the 1834 session only in December.

119   Both Humann and Duchâtel were in the Chamber but 'Humann sat still as a stone, while Duchâtel looked round in amazement'. (Bowring to

Villiers, 19 June, 1833; de Broglie to Talleyrand, 29 June 1833, *Mémoires du Prince de Talleyrand*, vol. V, pp. 190–1; Chambre des députés, séance du 18 juin 1833, *Archives parlementaires*, vol. LXXXV.)

120   The government already had power to end prohibitions under article 34 of the law of 17 December 1814. Thiers and de Broglie refrained from touching the prohibitions on cotton yarns on the grounds that the commission of the Chamber had recommended that the ending of the prohibition on twist of 180 (French) and above come into effect two years after the passing of the tariff Bill. In this way it was argued that Britain was losing nothing, since the tariff Bill would be presented in the following session. (de Broglie to Talleyrand, 1 July 1833, *Mémoires du Prince de Talleyrand*, vol. V, pp. 191–7.)

121   G. Poulett Scrope, *Mémoir of the Life of the right honourable Charles Lord Sydenham*, p. 69; Thiers to Thomson, 29 October, Thomson to Thiers, 20 November, and Bowring to Villiers, 12 October 1833, Clarendon papers, Bodleian Library. Thomson's letter to Thiers is to be found in Archives nationales, F. 12 6216.

122   Thiers to Thomson, 20 October 1833, *ibid*. Though Thomson did not agree to further British reforms until the French had taken the first steps, Thiers listed the reforms his government would like to see put into effect. These included a reduction of the excise duty on wines to enable French *vins ordinaires* to reach the British market, the abolition of the prohibition on the export of machinery, and the reduction of duties on various French exports like wallpapers, artificial flowers, shoes, books, furniture and agricultural produce. Thiers also asked that the British ensure their customs officers did not impose a heavier duty on French silks than they should, a problem about which there had been loud complaints from French silk interests.

123   Lord Granville to Thomson, 10 January 1834, *ibid*.

124   'I do assure you that ever since I came I have laboured like a galley slave – I have had to move heaven and earth – King – Ministers – Deputies – Press – to get the projet de loi *presented*.' (Bowring to Thomson, 7 February 1834, *ibid*.)

125   Bowring to Thomson, 31 January 1834, *ibid*.

126   The 1834 commission was far more liberal in its composition than its predecessor. Anisson-Duperron beat one of the most energetic defenders of the *status quo*, Demarçay, in the first *bureau*, while Desjobert, Roul, Fulchiron and Gay-Lussac, all of whom could be expected to support a measure of reform, were also elected. Though Meynard and Cunin-Gridaine were more doubtful, only Berard, a forge master and Falguerolles were overtly protectionist. Duchâtel, who had earlier expressed a desire to sit on the commission, managed to wriggle out of it by getting elected to another commission, explaining to his friends that he did not want to compromise himself on the question. (Bowring to Thomson, 19 February, and Bowring to Villiers, 14 March 1834, *ibid*.)

127   Bowring to Thomson, 17 and 24 February 1834, *ibid*.

128   Dusserrier, who drew up the wine growers' petition, claimed, 'Jamais réunion n'avait été aussi considérable. L'opinion est ici à 28 degrés de Réaumur. Vous pourrez en juger par la pétition qui a été votée à l'unanimité et par acclamation.' (Dusserrier to Bowring, 24 February 1834, *ibid*.)

129   Bowring to Thomson, 7 February 1834. The Chamber of Peers also treated the petition seriously and on the whole warmly, and in the debate Baron Fréville took the opportunity to advocate tariff concessions to Britain. (Séance du 11 mars 1834, Rapport de M. Villemain, rapport sur

la pétition de 438 négociants de Bordeaux, par l'organe d'une commission de 15 membres, adressée à la Chambre des Pairs, *Archives parlementaires*, vol. LXXXVII.)

130   There are no modern studies of Duchâtel apart from Robert Koepke, 'Charles Tanneguy Duchâtel and the revolution of 1848', *French Historical Studies*, vol. VIII, 1973, pp. 235–54. His lifelong friend Ludovic Vitet published a biography in 1875. (*Le Comte Duchâtel*, Paris, 1875.) The Duchâtel papers at the Archives nationales (2 AP, Papiers Duchâtel) are disappointing.

131   According to Vitet, *op. cit.*, p. 22, his interest dated back to 1822. He published articles on political economy in *le Globe* and in 1829 published a work strongly influenced by Malthusian ideas: *La Charité dans ses rapports avec l'état moral et le bien-être des classes inférieures de la société*, Paris, 1829. This book was reprinted under a slightly different title in 1836.

132   This was reprinted in Bowring, *Second Report*, appendix LXI.

133   De Broglie wrote enthusiastically to Talleyrand that he had high hopes that the young Duchâtel, with his antecedents and ability, would achieve something positive. (De Broglie to Talleyrand, 6 April 1834, *Mémoires de Talleyrand*, vol. V, p. 351.)

134   In April 1834, for instance, Bowring questioned an influential Girondin elector on the reason for a certain lukewarmness for reform on the part of one or two Gironde deputies. He was told that Thiers had informed them confidentially that he had discovered during his recent visit to Britain – and he hinted that he had picked it up from Thomson himself – that the British quest to secure a reduction in the iron tariff was merely to enable them to ruin French ironmasters and that they did not intend to do anything for French wines in return. (Bowring to Thomson, 24 April 1834, Clarendon papers, Bodleian Library.)

135   Bowring to Thomson, 5 May 1834, *ibid.*

136   In the discussion of the 1835 budget Roul advocated tariff reform, while the Marquis de Bryas (Gironde) reminded Duchâtel of his old economic principles and asked whether he would be putting them into practice. Duchâtel replied that his principles would be seen in his acts. (Séance du 2 mai 1834, *Archives parlementaires*, vol. LXXXIX.) On 19 May Desjobert, seconded by Anisson-Duperron, asked what use the new Minister intended to make of article 34 of the law of 17 December 1814 that permitted the government to abolish prohibitions by decree between sessions. (Séance du 19 mai 1834, *ibid.*, vol. XC.) Nonetheless Duchâtel's first speech as Minister of Commerce was disappointing to reformers. (*Moniteur universel*, 14 May 1834; 'Premier discours de M. le Ministre du Commerce', *Journal du Commerce*, 16 May 1834.) The *Journal du Commerce* lamented that while Duchâtel had described the tariff system as disastrous in 1829 he found it necessary and in no need of change in 1834.

137   The commission also amended the proposed duties on cotton twist. (Report of Meynard, séance du 29 avril 1834, *Archives parlementaires*, vol. LXXXIX.)

138   Rapport fait au nom de la commission chargée de l'examen du projet du budget des recettes pour l'exercice 1835, par M. Alexandre Gouin (Indre-et-Loire), séance du 29 avril 1834, *ibid*. The government was given the right to determine the rate of duty to be imposed. The Budget of Receipts was adopted on 20 May 1834. (*ibid.*, vol. XC)

139   The June decree also renewed the abolition of the ban on the export of raw and thrown silk issued in the decree of the previous year. (*Moniteur universel*, 3 June 1834.)

140   *Moniteur universel*, 11 July 1834.

141   French Consul General in London to de Rigny, 7 July 1834, Correspondance consulaire et commerciale, 26, Archives du Ministère des Affaires étrangères. The change in duty had no visible effect on French raw, dried and preserved fruit exports. (Ministère du Commerce, *Annales du commerce entre la France et le Royaume-Uni*, Paris, 1908, table XIII and p. 42.)

142   Thomson's letter of instruction, dated 28 July; Bowring to Thomson, 1 and 4 August 1834, Clarendon papers, Bodleian Library. Bowring obtained the support of Livingstone, the American ambassador. The question of French duties on British coal and iron was not a new one. Granville had already protested to de Broglie about duties the British regarded as differential in February 1833. (Copy of a letter from Thiers to de Broglie, 12 February 1833, Archives nationales, F. 12. 6216.)

143   Bowring to Thomson, 11 and 15 August 1834, *ibid.* In a letter of 18 August he announced, 'I am in communication with the following for that purpose – Dunkirk, Calais, Boulogne, Havre, St-Brieuc, Bordeaux, Nantes.' Both Janvier and Vatout suggested tariff reforms in their critical replies to the address from the throne. (Chambre des députés, séance du 13 aout 1834, *Archives parlementaires*, vol. XCI.)

144   Such complaints were of long standing. See note drawn up in May 1840 by officials at the Ministry of Commerce, Archives nationales, F. 12 6216; letters from de Broglie to Talleyrand, 13 January and 17 February, and de Rigny to Talleyrand, 26 July 1834, Correspondance consulaire et commerciale (Londres), 26, Archives du Ministère des Affaires étrangères.

145   Lord Granville to Thomson, 27 October, and Bowring to Thomson, 31 October 1834, Clarendon papers, Bodleian Library.

146   Bowring had long been concerned about a possible Franco-Belgian treaty. In February 1834 he claimed that Louis-Philippe had made unfavourable changes in the Thiers Bill because he wanted to safeguard any future treaty with Belgium. (Bowring to Thomson, 12 February 1834, *ibid.*) In May he reported that Belgian commissioners had arrived to sound out the possibility of a commercial agreement.

147   Thus when, in an interview with Louis-Philippe, Bowring played what he thought to be one of his best cards – the threat of British reprisals – the king replied that he regarded keeping Belgium out of the Prussian commercial union as a matter of great priority. (Bowring to Thomson, 15 August 1834, *ibid.*)

148   Bowring to Thomson, 4, 15 August, 31 October and 4 November 1834, *ibid.* Bowring too had several meetings with the Belgian representatives. In October de Brouckère, one of the Belgian commisisoners, when warned of Britain's objections to any extension of differential duties, sounded out the possibility of a tripartite agreement.

149   'I understand nought of his strategy,' he wrote to Thomson. 'He mounts all his enemies on horseback in order that he may win the battle. He asks the wolf in what particular way he would like to have his throat cut.' (Letter of 27 October 1834, *ibid.*) He regretted that Duchâtel had not adopted the procedure he had hoped he would, namely to deal first with raw materials like coal and iron, then with semi-manufactures like cotton twist and finally with prohibitions on manufactures. To lump prohibitions together meant that reformers lost some support in areas where there were interests in favour of some relaxation for raw materials and semi-

manufactures but against foreign competition for their own products. (Bowring to Thomson, 31 October 1834, *ibid.*)

150 Perronet Thompson to Bowring, 3 November 1834, 1, 2, January and 26 March 1835, Perronet Thompson papers, University of Hull. Bowring suggested to Thomson that the cost of publication be borne by the British government. (Bowring to Thomson, 31 October 1834, Clarendon papers, Bodleian Library.) The pamphlet was published in the *Westminster Review* in both English and French. (*Westminster Review*, vol. XLIII, January 1835, pp. 226–59.) Thompson had the article made up into pamphlets and sent to Paris.

151 Bowring wrote to Thomson, 'You are aware how their cursed centralisation has cut away all means of intercommunication except through bureaucratic Paris.' (Letter of 17 September 1834, *ibid.*) He later wrote that 'the isolation of one part of France from another is incredible – nobody knows anything of the people of any other place than Paris – and at Paris all is absorbed in the monopoly of centralisation. But since I came among them the efficient people are proceeding with unity and purpose – association and organisation are gradually introducing themselves – and I expect we shall see some important results when the Chambers meet.' (Letter to Thomson, 30 September 1834, *ibid.*)

152 The Rouen chamber of commerce, which sent in a protectionist submission to the Duchâtel inquiry, wrote, 'L'Angleterre, si fortement intéressée dans cette grande question, entretient et soutient ces idées, les répand par des émissaires dont le talent ne peut être révoqué en doute, aui parcourent nos provinces, nos ports de mer, et parviennent à se faire des partisans jusque chez nos manufacturiers, en leur persuadant que la mode et le désir de la nouveauté doivent donner une grande vogue à nos tissus français dans tous les pays soumis à l'Angleterre.' (*Enquête relative à diverses prohibitions, établis à l'entrée des produits étrangers*, vol. I, pp. 84–94.) In fact, or course, Bowring did not venture into the lion's den of the industrial north. The nearest he came was Rheims and Rouen itself. In the debates on the 1836 tariff Bill protectionists attacked the role played by Bowring. (See, for example, the attacks made by Jaubert on 13 and 14 April: *Archives parlementaires*, vols. CI and CII.)

153 Bowring exulted in his *Second Report* (p. 181), 'At no period have commercial questions occupied so much of the attention of the community in that country, and certainly never has the progress of those convictions, which must ultimately lead to the emancipation of commerce from the fetters which have so long and so pernicioulsy bound it, been so salutary and strikling.'

154 Barrie M. Ratcliffe, 'Napoleon III and the Anglo-French treaty of 1860: a reconsideration', *Journal of European Economic History*, vol. II, 1973, pp. 582–613.

155 In the five years from 1833 to 1838 France took less than £200,000 worth of the £36 millions of cotton twist Britain exported. ('Second note from the British to the French commissioners', 1840, Archives nationales, F. 12 6219.)

156 'Compte rendu des travaux des ingénieurs des mines pendant l'année 1839, Du mouvement commercial des combustibles minéraux en France pendant l'année 1838', *Journal de l'industriel et du capitaliste*, vol. IX, 1840, pp. 65–93.

157 Though Britain furnished only a quarter of French coal imports in the 1840s, by 1913 she provided half. (François Crouzet, 'Le charbon anglais

en France au XIXe siécle', *Charbon et sciences humaines. Actes du collo-que organisé par la Faculté des lettres de l'Université de Lille*, Paris, 1966, pp. 173–206.

158 These figures are official values and should be regarded as indicative only of general trends. (Ministère du Commerce et de l'Industrie, *Annales du commerce extérieur: un siècle du commerce entre la France et le Royaume-Uni*, Paris, 1908, pp. 10–11, 26, and tables II and VII. The 1830s tariff campaign and its results are discussed at greater length in Barrie M. Ratcliffe, 'The tariff campaign in France, 1831–36', *Journal of European Economic History*, vol. VI, 1977.

Friedrich List
Railway pioneer

Friedrich List was a man of many parts. He was at various times a civil servant, a university professor, a politician, an entrepreneur and a journalist. He strongly advocated the industrialisation of Germany, and he mounted a series of propaganda campaigns to promote economic unity, improved communications, and import duties to protect infant industries. He was indefatigable in interviewing Ministers, officials and businessmen, and he bombarded them with letters, petitions and pamphlets.[1] One project for which he energetically campaigned was the establishment of a unified railway network for the whole of Germany. Although his advice was not taken,[2] the fact that Germany – divided into many states – built railways faster than many of her neighbours[3] was to some extent due to List's persistent advocacy of this form of transport.

List stated that he became interested in railways when he visited England in May 1824. Since he was in the country for only about a fortnight – and does not appear to have been in any town other than London – his opportunities for inspecting railways were very limited.[4] The only line that he could have seen was the one between Wandsworth and Croydon on which waggons were drawn by horses. On this visit List met Poulett Thompson and John Bowring.[5]

Soon afterwards, while serving a term of imprisonment at the fortress of Hohen Asperg for his political activities, List advocated the building of railways in Württemberg. He suggested that the timber trade of the Black Forest could be stimulated by laying wooden tracks on which waggons with iron wheels could carry logs to the sawmills. He argued that this would be cheaper and quicker than floating them down the river Enz.[6] But this was not an original idea, since such rails were already in use in various mines in Germany. In the Saar, for example, a coal tramway, running from the Gerhard colliery down the Frommersbach valley, had been built in 1821.

Nothing came of List's proposal, and by April 1825 – having been released from prison on condition that he left Württemberg – he was on his way to the United States. On sailing from Le Havre, he wrote in his diary that the traffic of this port could be greatly expanded by linking the Seine and the Rhine by a canal or a railway. German merchants would then be able to engage in overseas trade through Le Havre without having to pay the high tolls levied by the Dutch at the mouths of the Rhine.[7]

When he settled in Reading (Pennsylvania)[8] – where most of the inhabitants were of German origin – List found himself in a very different environment from his native Württemberg. From a relatively stagnant state in Germany he had come to a new country which was developing rapidly. New England, New York State and Pennsylvania were becoming industrialised and their towns were growing. Philadelphia, then the second largest city in the country, was no exception. List wrote that on returning there after an absence of only six months he saw 'completely new streets and completely new suburbs'. In the west new lands were being opened up by hunters, traders, prospectors and farmers. When he edited a German weekly (*Der Adler*)[10] in Reading, List advocated the construction of canals and railways to promote economic expansion.

He soon had an opportunity to put his theories into practice. In 1826 the Schuylkill Canal was opened, linking Philadelphia and Port Carbon, and in the following year anthracite deposits were discovered in the Pottsville district in the Blue Mountains. There was a rush to stake out mining claims. List joined the fortune hunters in the race for coal concessions. He found rich seams of anthracite – north of the Pottsville deposits – at Tamaqua, on the Little Schuylkill river, and he bought land containing coal measures as well as forest land before the coal boom forced up the price of land from $10 an acre to $100. List and his associates secured about 7,000 acres of land, of which 5,000 acres (adjoining the Mauch Chunk mines) contained deposits of anthracite. They also purchased 270 acres at the forks of the Little Schuylkill river as the site of a town.[11]

List soon realised that he had embarked upon a highly speculative enterprise. Although coal could be mined cheaply in Pennsylvania its conveyance to the nearest market was slow and costly, particularly in winter. 'Twenty-two miles of hills and a rock-filled river separated the List–Hiester properties from Port Clinton, the nearest point where the Schuylkill Canal could be reached.' List was not the only entrepreneur to realise that a coal railway might be the answer to the problem. Not far away the construction of a 'switchback railway', nine miles in length, had been begun in 1827 to link the Mauch Chunk collieries with the river Lehigh, on which coal could be conveyed to Easton.[12]

List approached the Schuylkill East Branch Navigation Company, which held a charter from the Pensylvania legislature (20 February 1826) authorising the construction of a canal from Tamaqua to Port Clinton. The directors had failed to raise the money to build the canal, and List suggested that investors might find a railway a more attractive proposition. The directors followed his advice and in April 1828 the company secured an amendment to its charter, authorising the construction of a railway.[13]

List and his partner, Dr Isaac Hiester, now had to raise the capital to mine their coal and build their railway. In fourteen months they travelled some 3,000 miles in search of financial backing,[14] keeping their heads above water by selling some of their timber. They negotiated with List's friend Stephen Girard for a substantial loan, but in the end they secured the money they needed from the firm of Thomas Biddle & Co. of Philadelphia. (Thomas Biddle described himself as a broker.)[15] A new undertaking – the Little Schuylkill Navigation, Railroad & Coal Company – was established, with a capital of $700,000. Isaac Hiester was the president of the company and Edward R. Biddle (Thomas's brother) its secretary and treasurer. The company took over the land owned by List and Hiester,[17] and it eventually owned coal mines, a railway and the land on which the townships of Tamaqua and Port Clinton were built.

Largely on List's initiative a single-line colliery railway – wooden rails strapped with iron – was constructed in the valley of the Little Schuylkill river to carry anthracite from Tamaqua to Port Clinton on the Schuylkill Canal, a distance of twenty-one and a half miles. The line had been authorised in 1828 but construction was not begun until June 1830. The railway was opened on 18 November 1831, but by that time List had been in Europe for a year trying to sell American coal on the Continent. At the inauguration ceremony Isaac Hiester paid a tribute to List. He acknowledged 'how much the successful result of our labours was indebted to his talents, ingenuity, and perseverance'.[18]

In 1833, in his pamphlet on railways in Saxony, List gave an account of the railway. On construction costs he remarked that land and timber were cheaper in the United States than in Germany but that wages were higher, since an American labourer could earn a dollar a day. List stated that at first horses had been used to pull the coal waggons, but by 1833 they had been replaced by two locomotives – the *Comet* and the *Catawissa*[19] – purchased in England. (In 1838, however, horse traction was temporarily restored.) It has been observed that List had played a leading role in building the railway. He had 'bought the land, raised the capital, founded the company, and traced the route for the railway'. 'It was his first practical achievement in the field of transport, and it was the one in which he was most directly involved.'[20]

Coal was conveyed by rail from the pit head to Port Clinton. There was a daily service of two trains, each consisting of sixteen waggons.

Some 50,000 tons of coal were transported annually to the Schuylkill Canal. The coal was then transported by barge to Reading (by canal) and to Philadelphia (by river). On the return journey the barges carried foodstuffs and manufactured goods. In 1828 List had complained that traffic on the Schuylkill Canal had been frequently interrupted owing to the need to undertake repairs.[21] But these teething troubles appear to have been overcome, for in 1837 he cited the Schuylkill Canal as an example of a successful transport undertaking. By that time Philadelphia was consuming so much coal that water transport was no longer adequate, and the company that List had helped to found was planning to extend its railway to Philadelphia.[22]

List's activities as an entrepreneur in Pennsylvania brought him little financial reward. He lost his capital when Thomas Biddle & Co. went bankrupt during the financial crisis of 1837, for which List blamed 'General Jackson's insane banking policy'.[23] To a certain extent, however, he had only himself to blame for his misfortunes. If he had retained control over his shares in the Little Schuylkill Navigation, Railroad & Coal Company he would have been a rich man. But he had long been in financial difficulties, and he had handed over his shares to Thomas Biddle & Co. as security for various loans.[24]

List later wrote that even while he was planning the construction of the colliery railway 'in the wilderness of the Blue Mountains' he was 'dreaming of a German railway system'.[25] In correspondence with Joseph von Baader he urged the building of railways in Bavaria. Baader, an eminent engineer and Director of Mines in Bavaria, was a leading authority on railways and canals. List wrote to him on 27 April 1827 giving him particulars of canals recently built in the United States and suggested that Bavaria should construct a railway or a canal linking the Main and the Danube.

Since Baader had made a similar suggestion in 1822,[26] he was favourably disposed towards his new correspondent and sent him a copy of his most recent pamphlet.[27] When List wrote further letters on transport problems in the United States and Bavaria Baader was so impressed that he sent them to the editor of the influential Augsburg *Allgemeine Zeitung*, who printed them. Shortly afterwards List's friends Ernst Weber and E. W. Arnoldi arranged for their publication as two pamphlets.[28]

In his *Letters from America* List argued that Bavaria needed improved transport facilities to promote the growth of her economy. Bavaria was a predominantly agricultural country and four fifths of the population lived and worked on the land. Owing to inadequate communications, foodstuffs and manufactured goods could only reach markets which were close to the place where they had been produced. With better transport facilities, Bavarian farmers and craftsmen could send their products farther afield to large towns where higher prices could be secured. List

showed how canals in the United States – particularly the Erie Canal[29] –
had stimulated rapid economic growth, and he suggested that a similar
expansion could be achieved in Bavaria.

In the earlier letters to Baader, List seemed undecided as to whether to
recommend canals or railways as the improved form of transport that
would propel Bavaria into the industrial age. On the one hand he argued
that railways could be built more quickly and would require less
maintenance than canals. Part of a railway could be opened and could
earn dividends for its shareholders long before the entire line was
completed. On the other hand, under favourable conditions, a canal
might be preferable to a railway. In a low-lying country such as Holland,
where few locks were needed, the construction of canals had undoubted
advantages.

In his second pamphlet, however, List firmly advocated the building of
railways rather than canals. He now stated that the great merit of
railways was that a complete network of lines for the whole of Bavaria
could be planned in advance. The planning of canals was a different
matter, since their routes were limited by geographical factors. Parts of
Bavaria, such as the Alpine regions, could not have canals but they could
have railways.[30] List's insistence upon the need to plan a network of
railways for the whole of Bavaria – indeed, for the whole of Germany –
was an important aspect of his thinking on railways. The same idea was
developed a few years later in his more famous pamphlet on the railways
of Saxony.

List considered that Augsburg, in the centre of the country, should be
the focal point for railways in Bavaria. From Augsburg lines could
radiate in all directions to Donauwörth, Lindau, Munich and Bamberg.
For Germany as a whole he thought that Gotha, in Thuringia, should be
a major railway centre. Here his proposed 'Hansa-Bavaria' line, running
south from the ports of Hamburg and Bremen to the Bavarian network
of railways at Bamberg, would cross a trunk line running from Frankfurt
am Main across Germany to Leipzig.

Next List discussed the economic benefits to be derived from railways.
He argued that Bavarian coal, peat, timber, grain, wine and beer would
reach more distant markets and would fetch better prices than before,
while imports such as raw cotton, coffee and sugar could be secured
more cheaply. He had little to say about passenger traffic. His arguments
were based almost entirely upon the advantages of moving freight by rail.
He considered that railways should normally be built by private
enterprise rather than by the State and suggested that the noble owners of
great estates – such as the Prince of Thurn and Taxis – and the wealthy
burghers in the cities might be expected to buy railway shares, while
private banks might be prepared to lend money to railway companies.
On the other hand if a line ran through several states the governments
concerned should purchase shares in the undertaking so as to secure a

measure of control over its administration. And List thought that troops might be used to build railways if contractors were unable to engage a sufficient number of navvies.

It may be doubted whether his pamphlets had much influence upon the development of railways in Bavaria. King Ludwig realised the need to improve communications in his dominions and he had sent Klenze to England to study railways there. But the king's imagination was fired by a plan to link the Main and the Danube by a canal. The resources devoted to carrying out this grandiose project would probably have been used to greater advantage had they been devoted to building railways. The first railway in Germany – the short line from Nuremberg to Fürth – was opened in Bavaria in December 1835, but the earliest longer lines, such as the Leipzig–Dresden and the Cologne–Minden railways, were built in Saxony and in Prussia.

On returning to Europe at the end of 1830, List – now an American citizen – lived in Paris for two years. Nothing came of his attempt to set up agencies on the Continent for the sale of American coal. His interest in railways was unabated, and he urged upon the French government the desirability of planning a railway network for the whole country. In 1831 he contributed three articles on this subject to a French review.[31] He argued that France had been slow to take advantage of the invention of the locomotive. He thought that railways had been ignored because of the political situation. After 1815 the struggle for political reforms had diverted attention from the need to foster economic expansion. But now that the Bourbons had fallen and Louis Philippe was in power the situation had changed, and the country might be expected to face the problem of improving France's system of communications.

List deprecated the planning of isolated lines – such as one linking a manufacturing district to a port – and urged the French to plan a complete railway system to serve the needs of the whole country. When discussing railways in Bavaria he had emphasised the importance of moving freight rapidly by rail, but when writing on future railways in France he declared that passenger traffic was also of vital importance. In his view the experience already gained on pioneer lines in England and the United States showed that railway companies could make substantial profits by carrying passengers.

No attempt was made in these articles to indicate the routes which the network of French railways should follow. But List was anxious to promote trade between France and the United States, and he suggested that a railway running from Le Havre to Paris and Strasbourg would stimulate French commerce with North and South America. He recommended that the State should guarantee 4 per cent interest on the shares of the company which built the line in return for a share in the profits. The Le Havre–Strasbourg line would carry manufactured goods from France, the Rhineland and southern Germany to Le Havre for shipment to the United States, while American products, such as cotton, could be distributed from Le Havre to many parts of the Continent. List argued that if France built a network of railways – linked with lines in Germany, Belgium, Switzerland, Italy and Spain – she would be the centre of a new sort of Continental System, very different to the one imposed upon States which she had conquered. 'Elle introduirait le seul véritable système continental propre à consolider son ascendant moral, politique, et commercial, sur les nations de l'Europe, sans avoir craindre l'opposition ou la puissance navale de l'Angleterre, la vengeance et la jalousie des autres nations.'[32]

Ludwig Börne, who was living in Paris at this time, wrote, 'List has published an excellent pamphlet in French, recommending the establishment of a company to build railways from Paris to Le Havre and to Strasbourg so that one could travel to Strasbourg from the French capital in twelve hours and on to Frankfurt am Main in eighteen hours. If I left Paris in the morning I could be drinking tea in Strasbourg in the evening, and I could be back in Paris by the following evening. But Heine says that it is an awful thought that one could be in Germany again in twelve hours! List and I are really keen on railways because of their immense political potentialities. Every despotism would have its neck broken and wars would be quite impossible in the future.'[33]

At the same time List criticised the existing arrangements in France for authorising major public works and for fixing the compensation due to those whose property was expropriated so that construction could take place.[34] The need to consult the Department of Highways and Bridges as well as local authorities – from the commune to the department – before a decision was taken by a Minister or by the Council of State consumed a great deal of time and added considerably to the initial cost of building a canal or a railway. List asserted that after ten years the claims for compensation in connection with the construction of the Loire lateral canal had still not been settled. France would never have a network of railways unless there was a radical reform of the methods by which public works were approved and the value of the property to be expropriated was assessed.

List thought that a draft law then under consideration would not improve matters, and he urged the French to consider adopting the relatively simple and efficient methods of authorising the construction of canals and railways that were employed in England and the United States. He was, of course, not alone in expressing such views. He was supporting the demands of a number of railway promoters, engineers, contractors and politicians who considered that existing arrangements concerning the compulsory purchase of property should be reformed so that France could go ahead quickly with the building of railways.[35]

After leaving France List went to Hamburg, where he stayed for twelve months. His efforts to arouse interest in his plan for a 'Hanseatic-

Hanoverian' railway fell upon deaf ears in a city where, in his view, 'the spirit of enterprise had expired'.[36] He moved to Leipzig, where he secured employment as American consul in the kingdom of Saxony. List arrived at a time when the building of railways was being discussed not only in Saxony but in other parts of Germany as well. A number of German states were on the point of adhering to the Prussian customs system, so forming a customs union with a common tariff. Customs barriers between members of the Zollverein were due to fall in 1834 and it was expected that this would be followed by a rapid expansion of Germany's internal trade. To handle this increased traffic railways would be needed. In 1833 Friedrich Harkort put forward a plan for a railway between Cologne and Minden,[37] while Ludolf Camphausen advocated the construction of a line from Cologne to Antwerp.[38]

In Saxony there was much speculation concerning the effect that adherence to the Zollverein would have upon the economy of the country – particularly upon Leipzig and its fair. Leipzig, Saxony's chief commercial city, had long been a great centre of international trade, since it was here that the 'Highway to Poland' (from Frankfurt am Main to Cracow) crossed several main roads running from the northern ports of Hamburg, Bremen and Danzig to Bavaria and Austria. It was feared that if passengers and goods were conveyed by rail instead of by road, Leipzig and its famous fair might decline in importance. Leipzig relied entirely upon roads, since no canals had been built to link the town with the Elbe or the Saale. And the chances of Leipzig becoming the focal point of a network of railways – as she had once been the centre of a network of roads – appeared to the threatened by Prussia's railway policy. There was reason to believe that Prussia might one day control railways crossing Germany from east to west and from north to south. And these lines might go through Halle an der Saale in the Prussian province of Saxony, rather than through Leipzig in the kingdom of Saxony. This posed a serious threat to the future prosperity not only of Leipzig but of Saxony as a whole.

In the circumstances it was hardly surprising that by 1833 the question of Saxony's railway policy had already been a subject of lively discussion in commercial circles and in the press. Before List arrived, J. W. Schmitz had been campaigning in Leipzig in favour of the building of railways in Saxony. List promptly attacked Schmitz's proposals. He denounced Schmitz's plan for the construction of a line from Leipzig to Frankfurt am Main, arguing that – in the existing state of technical knowledge – it would be folly to embark upon such a project. He considered that the engineers and contractors would find it difficult to build a line through so unpromising a terrain as the hills and forests of central Germany. List proposed that a railway should be built to join Dresden, the capital of Saxony, with Leipzig, the main commercial centre of the kingdom. This line would be constructed entirely in the territories of the kingdom of Saxony and would run through a plain and a valley. He claimed that soon after settling in Leipzig he had gained the support of 'a number of young enterprising merchants and bankers' for his plan.[39]

Only three months after coming to Leipzig, List wrote a pamphlet which established his reputation as a railway expert. It was a powerful plea for the construction of a network of railways in the kingdom of Saxony, with particular reference to a line from Leipzig to Dresden.[40] List summarised his previous activities as a promoter of railway projects such as the construction of the line from Tamaqua to Port Clinton. He declared that he 'could not observe in England and America the astonishing results of constructing railways without wishing that my German Fatherland should enjoy similar benefits'.

His pamphlet opened with a discussion of the economic position of Leipzig. He observed that Leipzig was a city of 40,000 inhabitants. It was famous for its commerce, transit trade and international fair. A hundred thousand travellers visited the city every year, including about 30,000 itinerant journeymen. But in List's view the potentialities of Leipzig as a centre of trade and domestic crafts were not being fully exploited. The failure to construct canals to the nearest rivers had forced traders to depend entirely upon road transport. The streets lacked pavements because it was too expensive to bring the stones that were required from Pirna. The cost of living was higher than in many other German towns because the expense of transporting goods by road raised the price of good and fuel. The Zwickau coalfield was not far away but the charges made by carters to carry coal to Leipzig by road were prohibitive. List considered that the city urgently needed improved communications and that this could be achieved by constructing a network of railways in Saxony.

Leipzig would be an excellent railway centre, since it lay in a plain and the surrounding countryside posed no problems to railway constructors such as those which had confronted English engineers when they had to cross Chat Moss to join Manchester and Liverpool by rail. List suggested that Saxony's first railway should link Leipzig and Dresden and that the second should run from Leipzig to the country's main mining and manufacturing districts at Freiberg, Chemnitz and Zwickau. Looking further ahead, he saw Saxony as the centre of a railway system covering the whole of Germany. In a map at the end of his pamphlet he indicated where Germany's main lines should run, and his forecast proved to be substantially correct.

Next List discussed the cost of building a line from Leipzig to Dresden, the traffic that it would carry and the revenues that it would earn. He thought that the railway would cost three or four million thalers, and that it would earn dividends of 15 or 20 per cent. A railway network in Saxony might be expected to carry 100,000 passengers a year. The construction of railways would stimulate the economy, provide employment for skilled and unskilled workers, and promote an expansion in the demand for local raw materials such as timber, coal and iron. And when her railways had been built – and linked with those of her neighbours – Saxony would enjoy a new era of prosperity. List wrote that 'population, buildings, and manufactures, commerce and property values will be doubled in a short time, and I am sure that the increase in the value of property will, in a few years, exceed the capital invested in the railways'. He added that the state would benefit from the construction of railways because economic expansion would produce increased revenues from taxation, and the royal domains would share in the general prosperity. Moreover the state could secure a new source of revenue by purchasing shares in railway companies, which might be expected to yield high dividends.

List dealt with the arguments advanced by the opponents of railways. To the complaint that railways would create unemployment he replied that the introduction of any new invention inevitably inconvenienced somebody. No doubt the invention of printing had thrown some scribes out of work, but by the 1830s the publishers of Leipzig were employing 5,000 printers. Similarly the losses likely to be suffered by carters, ostlers and innkeepers if railways were built would soon be offset by the new jobs created by the railways. To those who declared that railways were unsafe because Huskisson had been killed at the opening of the Manchester to Liverpool railway he replied that pedestrians should look where they were going when crossing a railway line. And List flatly rejected the view that Saxony was too poor to afford railways. He declared that landowners, mine owners, industrialists, merchants and private banks could easily raise the required capital. Any hesitancy on the part of investors could be overcome by the offer of a state guarantee of 4 per cent interest on railway shares. List stated that, from his own experience of railway finance, a railway network in Saxony would very soon lead to an increase of 10 per cent in the value of land and of the gross national product.

Five hundred copies of this pamphlet were sent to Ministers of State, officials in central and local government, merchants and bankers – in fact to anybody whose influence might count when the time came to set up a company to build a railway. Most of the pamphlets were distributed in Saxony, though some were sent to leading personalities in other German states. List's call for the construction of a line from Leipzig to Dresden brought him support from several leading figures in the commercial life of Leipzig, such as Wilhelm Seyfferth, Albert Dufour-Féronce, Gustav Harkort, Carl Lampe, Wilhelm Gross and August Olearius. For some months the project seemed to hang fire, though in December 1833 the government encouraged the supporters of the scheme to go ahead with their plans. In March 1834 List issued a powerful 'Appeal to the people of Saxony concerning a railway between Dresden and Leipzig'[41] which has been described as 'one of List's most powerful and successful propaganda tracts'.[42]

His appeal undoubtedly played a part in securing enthusiastic support for the proposed railway at a public meeting which was held shortly afterwards. It was attended by everybody who was of any consequence in Leipzig. In April 1834 a 'railway committee' was set up – with Gustav Harkort as chairman – to prepare for the promotion of a company to build the line. As List was not a burgher of Leipzig – indeed, he was now a naturalised American citizen – he was not elected a full member of the committee but was appointed an honorary member. Other honorary members were Friedrich Harkort (Gustav's brother), Reichenbach (a Berlin banker), Jenisch (a Hamburg senator), Cotta von Cottendorf (publisher of the Augsburg *Allgemeine Zeitung*) and Joseph von Baader (Director of Mines in Bavaria). Clearly every effort was made to establish a committee representative of the whole of Germany.

List was one of the most active members of the committee. He wrote, 'For years I worked day and night to overcome immense obstacles which threatened the success of the enterprise. I wrote twelve reports for the public on behalf of the committee.[43] I helped to draw up the draft of the Expropriation Law. I was in charge of the committee's correspondence and I influenced public opinion through the journals and newspapers.[44] The prospectus of the railway company appeared in May 1835, and within two days the initial capital of $1\frac{1}{2}$ million thalers had been fully subscribed. On 15 June 1835 the first general meeting of the shareholders was held and already there were signs of a rift between List and some of the leading supporters of the railway. List regarded the project simply as the first stage of an ambitious plan to construct a network of railways for the whole of Germany, but for Gustav Harkort and his friends the Leipzig–Dresden railway was a purely local enterprise which would benefit Saxony alone. They wanted to build the line quickly so as to reap their reward in handsome dividends. And List was also involved in other disputes, such as one concerning the route that the line should take.

Having seen the first section of the railway – Leipzig to Althen – opened on 24 April 1837,[45] List left Saxony in the following August for France. He complained bitterly that he had been very shabbily treated in Leipzig. He considered that but for his efforts there would have been no Leipzig–Dresden railway at that time. He had hoped to become the manager of the railway but his only reward had been a gilded silver goblet from the merchants of Leipzig and a mere 4,000 thalers from the railway company. He declared that after four years of hard work on behalf of the project he was out of pocket to the tune of 15,000 thalers when he left Leipzig. For their part the businessmen of Leipzig were not prepared to allow an outsider to tell them how to run a railway. Gustav Harkort and his associates were prepared to use List's talents to get the railway project started, but when that had been accomplished they had no regrets when he left Leipzig.

Although he was deeply involved in the work of the Leipzig–Dresden railway committee between 1834 and 1837, List never lost sight of his main objective, which was to promote the construction of a network of railways for the whole of Germany. He founded two journals, the *National–Magazin*[46] and the *Eisenbahnjournal*,[47] to propagate his views and he continued to write articles on railways for other reviews. His essays on the military aspects of railways which appeared in 1834–36 in the Darmstadt *Militärzeitung* were particularly significant.[48]

At the same time he was trying to secure concessions for lines in Prussia, Brunswick and Baden. In October 1833 he had sent a copy of his pamphlet on the proposed Leipzig–Dresden railway to K. G. von Maassen, the Prussian Minister of Finance, with a covering letter in which he advocated the building of railways from Berlin to Hamburg and from Magdeburg to Leipzig. Maassen asked Kühne (a senior Prussian official) for his views, and Kühne recommended that no action should be taken. Then in July 1834 List sent copies of the first three reports of the Leipzig railway committee to Freiherr von Rochow, the Prussian Minister of the Interior – again without success. In March 1835 he once more approached the Prussian authorities and submitted two reports on the advantages of lines running from Hamburg to Berlin, Magdeburg and Leipzig. He criticised a rival plan for the construction of a Hamburg–Berlin railway which had recently been submitted by a group of English entrepreneurs. On 26 April Christian von Rother replied that the Prussian government was not prepared to encourage railway building by guaranteeing the shares of joint stock railway companies.

On 14 May 1835 List believed his hour had struck. On that day shares in the Leipzig–Dresden railway company were offered to the public, and investors rushed to participate in the new venture. With characteristic impetuosity he left Leipzig for Berlin on the same evening, confident that the success of this flotation would lead the Prussian authorities to change their minds concerning his plans for the development of Berlin as a railway centre. He now expected that the king would give favourable consideration to his application for a railway concession.[49] But again List was doomed to disappointment. He was told that no concession could be granted to a single individual, and even when he gained the financial backing of a group of Berlin bankers his application was still turned down. The concession to build the Berlin–Magdeburg railway was granted to A. W. Francke, Burgomaster of Magdeburg, at the end of 1837, while no concession to build the Hamburg–Berlin railway was granted at the time.[50] The rejection of List's proposals was due to an adverse report which Christian von Rother had submitted to the king. Rother argued that the roads in Prussia were adequate to carry the existing traffic and that it was still open to question as to whether railways would pay their way.

Having failed in Prussia, List turned to the small state of Brunswick. Between June and August 1835 he was in correspondence with F. Vieweg, a publisher and bookseller, who had recently visited Leipzig to see what lessons could be learned from the scheme to link Leipzig and Dresden by rail. List hoped to secure a post in a future Brunswick railway administration. Although Vieweg was interested in List's plans for a 'Hanseatic-Hanoverian railway',[51] List was not offered any appointment in Brunswick.

Now Baden seemed to be his last hope. In 1833 L. Newhouse, an Englishman who had settled in Baden, had written a report urging the construction of a railway between Mannheim and Basel on the right bank of the Rhine, but his application for a concession to build the line had been rejected. In April 1835 List submitted a similar plan to the Baden parliament and he too applied for a concession. Neither Newhouse nor List was successful, and in 1838 it was decided to build a State railway at public expense. Baden was a small state and its government rejected the idea of leaving the construction of railways to private entrepreneurs lest foreign capitalists − such as the Rothschilds or the financiers of Basel − should secure an undue economic influence over the country. So the state raised the necessary capital itself and the Mannheim−Baden line was built as a nationalised railway.

With no railway concession in Prussia, Brunswick or Baden − and with no post in a railway adminstration − List gave up, for a time, his attempt to become a railway promoter or an official. He now devoted himself largely to journalism − contributing frequently to the Augsburg *Allgemeine Zeitung* − and endeavoured to influence governments and public opinion on railway policy through his writings. An article on transport which appeared in 1837 in the encyclopaedia edited by Rotteck and Welckler showed how thorough was his knowledge of the subject. List established for himself a considerable reputation not only as an authority on the planning and construction of railways but also as a man of vision who could see the future possibilities of the new form of transport.

List settled in Paris for the second time at the end of 1837 and remained there until the spring of 1840. In this period he pursued his studies in economics, which appeared in print in 1842 as *The National System of Political Economy*. But he had not lost his interest in railways. On his way to Paris he had seen King Leopold and he had attended the opening of the Malines−Louvain railway. He had had discussions on Belgium's railway policy with Jean-Baptiste Nothomb, the Minister of Public Works in Belgium, who had been responsible for constructing railways 330 km in length.[52]

In Paris List gained the confidence of Louis Philippe and Thiers, who accepted him as a recognised expert on railways.[53] In 1837 he submitted two memoranda to Louis Philippe in which he urged the construction of 'un système des chemins de fer en combinaison avec du papier monnaie et de banque dit joint stock banks'.[54] List also suggested that the postal service between the Continent and the United States could be greatly improved by establishing an agency in Strasbourg for the collection of letters and parcels. They could then be forwarded to Le Havre, where there was a monthly service of packet boats to New York.[55] When Thiers became Minister of Public Works in 1840 he offered List a government appointment but List declined the offer and shortly afterwards returned to Germany.

On returning to Germany in May 1840 he actively promoted the construction of railways in Thuringia. In a letter to Ernst I of Coburg–Gotha he claimed that he was well qualified to act as a railway consultant. He suggested that lines should be built through Thuringia from east to west and from north to south to link the railway networks of Prussia, Hanover, Saxony and Bavaria. He declared that, without these lines, the railway network of Germany – indeed, the railway network of the Continent – would be incomplete.

At this time two routes for a line running from west to east (Halle an der Saale to Cassel) were under discussion. The first would have followed the route of the old military and commercial highway running through Thuringia (Naumburg, Erfurt, Gotha and Eisenach), while the second was a more direct route through the Goldene Aue (Sangerhausen–Nordhausen). The Prussian government favoured the second route because it would be almost entirely in Prussian territory. But List strongly urged that the first route should be followed, since this was one which was 'as old as German culture itself'.[56]

List is entitled to some of the credit for bringing the three Thuringian states concerned[57] together to agree on a common railway policy. In April 1841 the Prussian government gave way and signed a convention with Hesse Cassel, Weimar and Coburg – Gotha which provided for the construction of a railway from Halle an der Saale to Cassel[58] that would run through Erfurt and Gotha. List hoped that his efforts would be recognised by some tangible reward but he received only £85 from the Thuringian states and an honorary doctorate from the University of Jena.

At the same time he was involved in another controversy concerning the route to be followed by a railway in central Germany. This was one which would provide a link between the railway systems of north and south Germany. One possible route ran through Saxony and the other through Thuringia. The government of Saxony was determined that the line should run through its territories from Hof (in Bavaria) to Plauen and Leipzig. But Prussia favoured a route through Thuringia along the valley of the river Saale to Halle, a route which would benefit Halle to the detriment of Leipzig.

Writing in the influential Augsburg *Allgemeine Zeitung*, List rejected both these proposals.[59] He had no love for Saxony in view of his treatment there in the past, and he poured scorn upon its government for selfishly threatening the efficiency of Germany's railway network in order to strengthen Leipzig's position as a centre of communications at Halle's expense. Nor did he favour the route proposed by Prussia. He suggested that the north–south Thuringian railway should follow the course of the river Werra. But this time no notice was taken of List's views, and in January 1841 Bavaria and Saxony agreed that the line should run through Saxony to Leipzig.[60]

List now devoted his energies to editing a journal (the *Zollvereinsblatt*), which he founded in 1843 to disseminate information concerning the progress of the German customs union. In an early number he declared that 'railways and Zollverein are siamese twins'.[61] The disappearance of many tariff barriers in Germany had stimulated trade between different parts of the country. Manufacturers and merchants had been able to take advantage of this situation only because railways were being built.

And List continued to take a lively interest in railway projects at home and abroad. In 1844 he was involved in a controversy between supporters of a line to run between Ludwigshafen, Worms and Mainz (on the left bank of the Rhine) and supporters of a line between Heidelberg, Darmstadt and Frankfurt am Main (on the right bank). In an article in the Augsburg *Allgemeine Zeitung* in September 1844 he demanded that the line from Ludwigshafen to Mainz should have priority.[62]

In 1843 and again in 1844 List had interviews with Metternich, who had once regarded him as a dangerous radical. They discussed plans for the expansion of the railway network of the Habsburg dominions. At the second interview Metternich asked List to send Kübeck, the President of The Royal Council (*Hofkammer*) a report on communications in Hungary. List did so early in 1845, but his report did not, as he had hoped, gain for him an official appointment in Austria.[63]

In the following year his mental powers declined. Robert Mohl, who met him in Munich in the spring of 1846, declared in his memoirs that List's nerves were shattered, that he suffered from a persecution mania, and that he was mentally unbalanced.[64] List died by his own hand at the end of November 1846. The extent of his influence at home and abroad at the time of his death may be judged by what Henri Richelot, a leading French economist, had written about him in 1845. 'There lives in Germany a man without public office, titles, or wealth, who has nevertheless become a veritable power in the land through his patriotism and his talents.'

In his day List had been a leading authority on railway planning. He had been directly concerned with the building of only two lines – the coal railway in Schuylkill County in Pennsylvania, and the line between Leipzig and Dresden. He never managed a railway company and he never became an official of a nationalised railway system. It was as a journalist and not as a railway promoter that he made his influence felt. His famous pamphlet on the Leipzig–Dresden railway and his articles on transport problems in various newspapers and periodicals gave his readers a better understanding of the importance of railways for the future. He saw a network of railways in Germany – indeed, a network of railways on the Continent – as a single transport system which would further the economic unification of Germany and stimulate the growth of modern industries throughout Europe. He was a visionary and a prophet whose dreams rarely came true in his lifetime but whose ideas influenced his countrymen long after his death.

Notes

1   See F. List, *Gesammelte Schriften* (ed. Ludwig Häusser, 3 vols, 1850: the first volume is a biography of List) and *Werke. Schriften, Reden, Briefe* (ed. Erwin von Beckenrath and others, 10 vols, 1927–35: cited as *Werke*); Hans von Schnurbein, *Friedrich List als Eisenbahnpolitiker* (1904); J. Westenberger, 'Friedrich Lists Wirken für ein deutsches Eisenbahnsystem', in *Archiv für Eisenbahnwesen*, 1920; Alfred van der Leyen, 'Friedrich List, ein Vorkämpfer des deutschen Eisenbahnwesens', in *Archiv für Eisenbahnwesen*, 1931, *Heft* 5; P. H. Bousquet, 'List et les chemins de fer', in *Revue d'histoire économique et sociale, Année* 21, 1933; P. Brock, 'Friedrich List und die deutsche Verkehrswirtschaft', in *Archiv für Eisenbahnwesen*, 1939; *Heft* 5; A. F. Napp-Zinn, *Friedrich List als Verkehrspolitiker* (1948); Elfriede Rehbein and Rudi Keth, 'Das Wirken Friedrich Lists für ein modernes Verkehrswesen in Deutschland', in *Wissenschaftliche Zeitschrift der Hochschule für Verkehrswesen 'Friedrich List'* (Dresden), 1961–62, pp. 307–32; P. Brock, 'Friedrich List und die deutsche Verkehrswirtschaft', in *Archiv für Eisenbahnwesen*, 1939, *Heft* V, pp. 1277–82.

2   Although the German railways were not unified in the nineteenth century, the need for close co-operation between railway administrations was recognised at an early date. The Association of Prussian Railway Administrations (ten railways) was set up in 1846. In the following year this organisation was expanded and became the Association of German Railway Administrations (forty railways). In 1848 an agreement on fares and freight charges was reached by the railways of north Germany. The railway associations included both private companies and nationalised railways.

3   Thus in the ten years after the opening of the first railway in Prussia – the Berlin–Potsdam line in October 1838 – 3,390 km of railways were built in that country.

4   On 10 April 1824 List wrote to his wife from Paris that he was leaving for London on the following day. He was in Paris again on 24 May 1824 (List archives 47, II, 57, and F. List, *Werke*, vol. VIII, pp. 287–9). A letter from Ernst Bolay (?) to List from Walker's Hotel, 9 May 1824, indicates that List was in London on that date (List archives, 41, I, 73). A letter from List to Johann Friedrich von Cotta, dated 16 May 1824, was written in London. List's statement in this letter that he had already been in London for four weeks was incorrect. And his statement, in a letter to the Duke of Coburg-Gotha dated 24 December 1840, that he had been in England in 1823 is also incorrect. Alfred van der Leyen was mistaken in supposing that List

was in England 'from the summer until the early autumn of 1824' (*Archiv für Eisenbahnwesen*, 1931, *Heft* 5).

5   John Bowring to F. List, 10 May 1824: photocopy in the List archives (Reutlingen), Fasc. 56/17; original in the Bavarian State Library in Munich.

6   List archives, Fasc. 24/13, and introduction to F. List, *Werke*, vol. III (Part 1), p. 5 (n. v). Fifteen years later in a letter to J. G. Cotta, 5 January 1839, List referred to this plan for the construction of a railway in Württemberg (*ibid.*, vol. III (Part 2), pp. 685–6).

7   Friedrich List's diary, 21 April 1825, in F. List, *Werke*, vol. II, p. 67.

8   For Friedrich List in the United States see Ludwig Häusser, *Friedrich Lists gesammelte Schriften*, vol. I (biography of F. List), chapter 4, pp. 138–90; W. F. Notz, 'Frederick List in America', in the *American Economic Review*, vol. XV, No. 2, June 1926, and 'Friedrich List in Amerika', in *Weltwirtschaftliches Archiv*, vol. XXI (2), 1925, and vol. XXII (1), 1925; Harry Hickel, 'Friedrich List, whom American history forgot', in the *Historical Bulletin* (No. 4, 1926) of the (Detroit) Concord Society; and R. W. Brown, *Friedrich List. The Father of German Railroads. His Residence in Dauphin and Schuylkill Counties, Pennsylvania* (address delivered before the Historical Society of Dauphin County, John Harris Mansion, Harrisburg, Pennsylvania, 18 September 1950).

9   F. List, *Mitteilungen aus Nordamerika* (1829): reprinted in F. List, *Werke*, vol. III (Part 1), p. 133.

10 The paper was popularly known as 'the Berks County Bible'.

11 For example, List bought coal-bearing land from Daniel Hotlz and Lewis Audienried in 1827 (List archives, 41, I, 100); from Audienried in 1828 (*ibid.*, 41, I, 129); and from B. R. Morgan and Isaac Hiester in 1829 (*ibid.*, 41, I, 132, and 41, I, 18). The contract between List and Morgan stated that a company would be established within three years to build a railway from the coal mines to the Schuylkill river. Morgan, then aged sixty-five, received an annuity of $2,000 for his land.

12 R. W. Brown, *Friedrich List. The Father of German Railroads* . . . (1950), p. 6.

13 In September 1828 List wrote that the proposal to build a canal had been abandoned in favour of a railway. See F. List, *Mitteilungen aus Nordamerika* (1829): letter to Joseph von Baader, 5 September 1828, in F. List, *Werke*, vol. III (Part 1), p. 109.

14 See List's expenses in the List archives, 41, II, 12.

15 Thomas Biddle had been described as 'a distant relative' of Nicholas Biddle, who was the president of the second Bank of the United States from 1823 to 1836: see T. P. Govan, *Nicholas Biddle* (University of Chicago Press, 1959, p. 196).

16 Ludwig Hausser, *op. cit.*, vol. I, p. 164.

17 H. Boetsch, *Einkommen und Vermögen von Friedrich List* (1936), pp. 66–9.

18 For the opening of the Tamaqua–Port Clinton coal railway see the *Berks County and Schuylkill Journal*, 3 December 1831, reprinted in F. List, *Werke*, vol. III (Part 2), pp. 686–7.

19 The locomotives *Comet* and *Catawissa* reached Philadelphia in the winter of 1833. Since the Schuylkill Canal was frozen, they were taken apart and conveyed to Tamaqua on carts drawn by oxen. They were the first locomotives in the United States to transport coal regularly. See W. W. Rhoads, 'When the railroad came to Reading' (Newcomen Society, American branch, New York, August 1948), and R. W. Brown, *Friedrich List. The Father of German Railroads* . . . (1950), p. 9.

20 E. von Beckenrath and Otto Stühler, introduction to F. List, *Werke*, vol. III
    (Part 1), p. 6. For the Tamaqua–Port Clinton railway (nucleus of the
    Philadelphia–Reading railway) see J. V. Hare, *A History of the
    Philadelphia and Reading Railroad* (1912). List described the line in the
    first footnote of his pamphlet *Über ein sächsisches Eisenbahnsystem* ...
    (Leipzig, 1833), reprinted in F. List, *Werke*, vol. III (part 1), pp. 155–95.
    See also F. List, *Mitteilungen aus Nordamerika* (1829) and *Nachtrag zum
    ersten Heft der Mitteilungen aus Nordamerika* (1829) (both edited by Ernst
    Weber and E. W. Arnoldi).

21 F. List, *Mitteilungen aus Nordamerika* (1828), No. 1, 1 September 1828, in
    F. List, *Werke*, vol. III (Part 1), p. 86.

22 F. List, in the Rotteck–Welcker *Staatslexikon*, vol. IV (1837), pp. 650–778
    and second edition (1846), pp. 228–87. For this encyclopaedia see H.
    Zehntner, 'Das Staatslexikon von Rotteck und Welcker', in *List-Studien*,
    Heft III, 1929. In 1831 List wrote that in Schuylkill County 'il y a jusqu'a
    six routes pour amener les produits des mines de charbon jusqu'an canal de
    Schuylkill' ('Idées sur les réformes économiques, commerciales et
    financières applicables à la France', in the *Revue Encylopédique*, March,
    April and November 1831, in F. List, *Werke*, vol. V, p. 88).

23 F. List to Ernst I of Coburg-Gotha, 24 December 1840, in F. List, *Werke*,
    vol. III (Part 1), p. 35.

24 In 1830 List deposited 1,070 shares with Thomas Biddle & Co. as security
    for a loan. The receipt is in the List archives (41, I, 60). In 1832 he
    deposited a futher 535 shares as security for another loan (41, I, 116).
    Early in September 1836 List wrote to Isaac Hiester, '. . . I want money and
    would thank you very much if you would dispose Mr Edward Biddle to
    make me a further loan of only 1,000 or 1,500 dollars on my coal interest
    . . .' (in F. List, *Werke*, vol. VIII, pp. 482–3).

25 Ludwig Häusser, *Friedrich Lists gesammelte Schriften*, vol. I (biography of
    List), p. 165.

26 Joseph von Baader, *Über die Verbindung der Donau mit dem Main und
    Rhein und die zweckmässigste Ausführung derselben* (Sulzbach, 1822).

27 Joseph von Baader, *Über die Vorzüge einer verbesserten Bauart von
    Eisenbahnen von den schiffbaren Kanälen mit besonderer Beziehung auf
    die vorgeschlagene Verbindung der Donau und des Rheins* (Munich, 1828).
    Baader had lived in England for eight years and had written a book on
    English machinery.

28 F. List, *Mitteilungen aus Nordamerika* (Hamburg, 1829) and *Nachtrag
    zum ersten Hefte der Mitteilungen aus Nordamerika* ... (Hamburg, 1829)
    in F. List, *Werke*, vol. III (Part 1), pp. 81–154. List's first letter to Joseph
    von Baader (27 April 1827) – and a note by Baader at the end of the letter
    – are printed in F. List, *Werke*, vol. III (Part 2), pp. 532–535. Weber and
    Arnoldi had been associated with List in running the Union of Merchants
    (Handels- und Gewerbsverein).

29 List referred to the Erie Canal as the New York Canal.

30 But in 1838 List wrote in favour of canals again. In the Rotteck–Welcker
    Staatslexikon he wrote enthusiastically about the construction of the
    Main–Danube canal, which had been begun in 1836, and advocated the
    linking of other German rivers by canals. See F. List, *Das deutsche
    National Transport-System* (1838), p. 34.

31 F. List, 'Idées sur les réformes économiques, commerciales et financières',
    in the *Revue Encyclopédique*, March, April and November 1831: reprinted
    in F. List, *Werke*, vol. V, pp. 59–79. A summary of List's articles appeared
    anonymously in German in the periodical *Ausland*, 16 and 17 April 1832,
    under the title 'Über ein allgemeines Eisenbahnsystem in Frankreich'. List

printed this article in a footnote to his pamphlet *Über ein sächsisches Eisenbahnsystem* (1833). See also F. List, *Werke*, vol. III (Part 2), pp. 564–73.

32 F. List, *Werke*, vol. V, p. 71.

33 L. Börne, *Gesammelte Schriften* (1862), vol. IX, p. 149 *ff*.

34 F. List, 'De la loi à faire sur l'expropriation', in the *Constitutionnel*, 4 and 21 November 1831: reprinted in F. List, *Werke*, vol. III (Part 2), pp. 555-63.

35 List's claim – in a letter to Ernst I of Saxe-Coburg-Gotha (24 December 1840) in F. List, *Werke*, vol. III (Part 1), p. 35 – that he had been largely responsible for the reform of the French law of expropriation in 1832 must be taken with a pinch of salt.

36 F. List to Ernst I of Saxe-Coburg-Gotha, 24 December 1840, in F. List, *Werke*, vol. III (Part 1), p. 35.

37 Friedrich Harkort, *Die Eisenbahn von Minden nach Köln*, 1833 (reprinted by the Harkortgesellschaft, 1961).

38 Ludolf Camphausen, (1) *Zur Eisenbahn von Köln nach Antwerpen* (*erste Eisenbahnschrift*, 1833); (2) *Zur Eisenbahn von Köln nach Antwerpen* (*zweite Eisenbahnschrift*, 1835); (3) *Versuchs eines Beitrages zur Eisenbahngesetzgebung* (*dritte Eisenbahnschrift*, 1838).

39 F. List to Ernst I of Saxe-Coburg-Gotha, 24 December 1840, in F. List, *Werke*, vol. III (Part 1), p. 35.

40 F. List, *Über ein sächsisches Eisenbahn-Systems* . . . (1933): reprinted in F. List, *Werke*, vol. III (Part 1), pp. 155–88. For List's activities in Leipzig in connection with the founding of the Leipzig–Dresden railway see Friedrich Schulze, *Friedrich List in Leipzig* (1927).

41 F. List, *Aufruf an unsere Mitbürger in Sachsen die Anlage einer Eisenbahn zwischen Dresden und Leipzig betreffend* (1834): reprinted in F. List, *Werke*, vol. III (Part 1), pp. 196–213.

42 F. Bülow, *Friedrich List* (1959), p. 48.

43 List was mistaken. Only seven reports were issued by the railway committee.

44 F. List to Ernst I of Saxe-Coburg-Gotha, 24 December 1840, in F. List, *Werke*, vol. III (Part 1), p. 35. List added with some satisfaction that Carl Tenner, one of his enemies in Leipzig, had 'gone bankrupt in so frightful and shameful a fashion that his good friends Messrs Carlowitz and von Winterheim had to send him to prison, where he is still serving his sentence' (*ibid*., p. 37). See also Friedrich Schulze, *Friedrich List in Leipzig* (1927).

45 The second section (Althen–Gerichshain) was opened on 12 November 1837.

46 The *National-Magazin* was a weekly. The first number appeared on 1 January 1834. It lasted for twelve months.

47 The *Eisenbahnjournal* was launched in 1835. Forty numbers appeared between 1835 and 1837. A ban on the journal in Austria in 1837 led to a drop in sales which proved fatal to its continued existence. In announcing the forthcoming issue of the first number List wrote, 'One of the main objects of this journal will be to prepare the way for a universal German railway system.'

48 F. List, 'Deutschlands Eisenbahnen in militärische Beziehung', in F. List, *Werke*, vol. III (Part 1), pp. 260–9. See also Georg Hoika, 'Lists Verkehrssystem unter militärische Gesichtspunkten', in *Wissen und Wehr*, vol. IX, 1938, pp. 402–13. Moltke was interested in List's views on the military aspect of railways. See *Essays, Speeches, and Memoirs of* . . . *Moltke* (New York, 1893), vol. I, pp. 225–63, vol. II, pp. 28–30.

49 List submitted two memoranda outlining his schemes: F. List, *Andeutung*

der Vorteile eines preussischen Eisenbahnsystems und insobesondere einer Eisenbahn zwischen Hamburg, Berlin, Magdeburg und Leipzig (1835) and *Über Eisenbahnen und das Interesse Hamburgs* (1835). See F. List, *Werke*, vol. III (Part 1), pp. 214–23 and 242–6.

50 When List's plan for a Berlin–Hamburg railway fell through, those who had supported the scheme put forward another project. This was for a line (127.5 km in length) from Berlin to Wittenberge on the river Elbe. Such a line could be regarded as the first section of a railway which could later be extended to Hamburg. A memorandum on this proposed railway was drawn up by G. F. Oppert (14 June 1836). But this plan too did not find favour with the Prussian government. It was not until July 1843 that the Berlin–Hamburg Railway Company was founded. In 1845 it secured concessions from the states through which the line would run. The line was opened on 15 December 1846.

51 F. List, 'Über die hanseatische-hannöversische Eisenbahn', 1835, in F. List, *Werke*, vol. III (Part 1), pp. 247–59.

52 For List's impressions of Belgium see F. List, 'Reiseberichte aus Belgien', in the Augsburg *Allgemeine Zeitung*, 4 September–11 October 1837: reprinted in F. List, *Werke*, vol. III (Part 1), pp. 270–89.

53 For List's views on French railway policy in 1839 see F. List, 'Die Eisenbahnen in Frankreich' in the Augsburg *Allgemeine Zeitung*, June 1839, pp. 1307 and 1314: reprinted in F. List, *Werke*, vol. III (Part 1), pp. 286–8.

54 F. List, 'Mémoire für Louis Philippe' (Leipzig, 12 June 1837), in F. List, *Werke*, vol. V, p. 97. The manuscript of List's second memorandum to Louis Philippe (November 1837) has not survived.

55 See 'Vorschlag Lists zu einer Privatpostverbindung zwischen Nordamerika und Europa' in F. List, *Werke*, vol. III (Part 2), pp. 908–9.

56 F. List, 'Die thüringische Eisenbahn', in the Gotha *Allgemeiner Anzeiger*, 19–28 June, and 'Die thüringische ostwestliche Zentralroute', in the Augsburg *Allgemeine Zeitung*, August 1840, pp. 1771 and 1778 (nom de plume Justus Möser, who was an eighteenth-century German historian); reprinted in F. List, *Werke*, vol. III (Part 1), pp. 294–305 and 312–20.

57 Coburg-Gotha, Weimar and Meiningen.

58 An extension of the line from Cassel to the Cologne–Minden railway was planned: see Hans Nordmann, 'Die ältere preussische Eisenbahn-geschichte', in *Abhandlungen der Deutschen Akademie der Wissenschaften zu Berlin* (Mathematisch-naturwissenschaftliche Klasse, *Jahrgang* 1948, No. 4, Akademie-Verlag, Berlin, 1950), p. 8.

59 F. List, 'Die thüringische nordsüdliche Zentralbahn' and 'Die bayerische-thüringische-Sächsische Frage noch einmal', 1840, in F. List, *Werke*, vol. III (Part 1), pp. 306-12 and pp. 320-30.

60 Hans-Friedrich Gisevus, *Zur Vorgeschichte des Preussisch-Sächsischen Eisenbahnkrieges* (1971), pp. 137–43. The line through Thuringia which List favoured, was not opened until 1882. See also Wilhelm Lins, *Die thüringischen Eisenbahnverhältnisse in ihrer geschichtliche Entwicklung* ... (1910), and Peter Beyer, 'Leipzig und der Plan einer Eisenbahnverbindung zwischen Sachsen und Bayern', in *Sächsische Heimatsblätter*, *Heft* II, 1965.

61 F. List, 'Das deutsche Eisenbahnsystem', in the *Zollvereinsblatt*, 6–7 November 1843.

62 See the correspondence between List and Dr Knyn (a member of the Mainz railway committee) in F. List, *Werke*, vol. III (Part 2), p. 1002 *ff.*

63 F. List, 'Über die Transport verbesserungen in Ungarn' (first report, 1
      January 1845; second report, 3 February 1845) in F. List, *Werke*, vol. III
      (Part 1), pp. 334–461, and F. List, 'Über die nationalökonomische Reform
      des Königreichs Ungarn', in F. List, *Werke*, vol. III (Part 1), pp. 462–527.
      See also G. Fittbogen, 'Friedrich List in Ungarn', in the *Ungarische
      Jahrbücher*, vol. 22, *Heft* 1–3.
64 Robert von Mohl, *Lebens-Erinnerungen, 1799–1875* (2 vols, 1902), vol. II.
      pp. 7–9.

Acknowledgements

The author wishes to thank the Leverhulme Trust and the Berlin Historical
Commission for the financial assistance which facilitated research in Berlin and
Reutlingen.

A Philadelphia textile merchant's trip to Europe on the eve of the Civil War

Robert Creighton, 1856–57

In writing the history of the British textile industry economic historians have tended to concentrate their attention on the supply of raw materials, changes in technological processes and the organisation of production in workshop and factory, to the neglect of the ways in which the goods so produced were disposed of both to the home consumer and in overseas markets. The literature on both aspects of textile consumption is therefore scanty. To cite a rare example, Brian Clapp has elucidated the world-wide merchanting activities of John Owens, Manchester merchant, between the 1820s and 1846. Owens, however, was not a specialised textile merchant but an exporter, as well as importer, of a wide range of manufactured goods and raw materials.[1] Two years later Dr Edwards, lamenting the fact that no attempt had been made 'to describe fully the marketing techniques used by those in the trade', went on to state:

Nor has an attempt been made to describe fully the marketing techniques used by those in the trade. The technological changes greatly increased the volume and variety of cottons. This threw a tremendous burden on those responsible for classifying, storing, and selling the various cotton goods. But very little is known about how those in the different markets responded to the challenge, and no one has said which were the most important centres. Did London call the tune, or was Manchester the more vigorous centre? How powerful were the dealers? How were goods sold overseas?[2]

This gap in our knowledge is particularly wide as regards the important export trade in textiles between Britain and the USA,[3] although Dr Buck's pioneer study of half a century ago still holds the field as a general account of how Anglo-American trade was carried on, mainly up to 1850, with particular reference to textiles, as recorded in official documents and printed sources.[4]

Fortunately the chance survival of a small letter-cum-memoranda book[5] which once belonged to Robert Creighton, wholesale textile merchant, of Philadelphia, covering the period from July 1856 to May 1857, throws the proverbial flood of light upon this trade, although his buying trip to Europe was clearly unusual, even accidental. Before considering the activities of Creighton, however, it is necessary to examine the way in which the export trade in British textiles was conducted. As late as 1869 it was estimated that 'at least sixty per cent of the textile fabrics and fancy goods imported into the United States were consignments from needy manufacturers or commercial speculators in Europe, and were destined to be sold, many of them, at auction'.[6] From about 1830 onwards, however, American importers themselves or their partners came over to Europe in increasing numbers 'to see the goods and make their purchases'.[7] Creighton's visit falls into this category, in spite of its accidental character, and the manner in which he financed the trip and his purchases bears out Dr Buck's view that the growth of the British banking and credit system after 1815 'much facilitated' the operations of American importers of British goods. William Brown, head of the Liverpool merchant banking house of Brown Shipley & Co. (of which Creighton was a customer) gave testimony before the Parliamentary Committee of 1847–48 on Commercial Distress as follows, indicating the method whereby British banking and commercial houses were financing these operations:

Mr A. in the United States goes to my brother, my partner in America, and states that he wants to import £1,000 or £2,000 value of goods. They look into the credit of the house, and if they are satisfied, a Credit is opened with us. The order goes to the manufacturing districts, to some individual who is authorized by us, when the goods are ready, to draw upon us for the Amount of this Credit.[8]

Robert Creighton (d. 1863) was of Presbyterian Ulster-Scottish stock, but by 1856 he was clearly an American by adoption, if not in law, with a flourishing textile merchanting business or 'store' (as he termed it in his will) at 10 South Front, Philadelphia. His private house, with its coloured cook, Mrs Davis, was at 1406 Spruce Street. The Philadelphia directories of 1858 and 1860 describe his firm as 'importers of dry goods'.[9] In his will dated 20 April 1863 he left reasonable annuities, fortunately in pounds sterling, to his brother William, of Newtownards, County Down, Northern Ireland, and to his sister, Mrs Mary Preston (formerly Blair) of Ballymena, County Antrim, Northern Ireland.[10] His buying trip to Europe, although exceptional in its circumstances, can hardly have been his first, but no positive evidence on this point has emerged. As from 1 June 1856 he had admitted as partners into the business his son, Hamilton Creighton, and a nephew, Hugh Creighton. The best available account of his motives for making the trip to Europe with his wife, Eliza, and their two daughters, Emily and Julia, is given in a letter he wrote from Belfast to James W. Murland of Castlewellan, a linen manufacturing and bleaching centre in County Down, twenty-five miles east-north-east of Newry:

... my being on this side at present was not contemplated by me until within a few days of my departure from Philadelphia. Mrs Creighton was somewhat depressed from having been bereaved of one son 21 years of age last winter and it has an effect on us all. I hoped by changing the scene a little that it would benefit us all and accordingly I embarked at New York for Havre with my wife and two daughters the latter end of July [1856].

Arrived at Paris, the Creightons installed themselves in the Hôtel du Louvre, 28 rue Notre Dame de Lorette, kept by a landlord or landlady who bore a name, Killaly, reminiscent of 'Ould Ireland',[11] and on 12 August Creighton drew 3,000 francs[12] from his Paris bankers, Greene & Co., on the strength of a letter of credit issued to him by Brown Shipley & Co., of Liverpool, almost certainly negotiated through their Philadelphia branch, Brown & Bowen,[13] which had a long-established connection with the linen import trade. When the Philadelphia firm of John A. Brown & Co., later Brown & Bowen, opened its doors in Philadelphia in 1818 a public announcement read:

John A. Brown & Co. take this opportunity of informing those who have been in the habit of purchasing linens imported by Alexander Brown & Sons of Baltimore, that the above firm is a branch of that concern and that both houses will import a constant supply of cheap linens.[14]

II

In August 1856 her parents settled Miss Julia Creighton in Paris at the 'Pensionnat Protestant' and school for young ladies kept by Mlles Nieman and Allemayer, 37 rue du Chemin de Versailles, quartier des Champs-Elysées; her board and tuition for 'the vacation of 2 months and 3 months school afterwards' came to 400 francs. Mr and Mrs Creighton and sister Emily then went on a long late summer tour to Martigny, (25 August), Lake Thun (28 August), Lucerne (1 September), Lake Hertenstein, Zug, Zurich (3 September) Romanshorn, Lake Constance, Schaffhausen, Basle, Kehl (opposite Strasbourg), Baden-Baden (10 September), Heidelberg, Frankfurt-am-Main, Hanau, and then down the Rhine (Mainz, Coblenz, Cologne (17 September)). By 29 September they were back in Paris after visiting Aachen, Brussels and Antwerp. It is not surprising that after this strenuous trip Mrs Creighton was suffering from an 'indisposition'.

Once back in Paris, business took over from tourism and visits to spas. Creighton wrote to Brown Shipley & Co. on 19 September acknowledging receipt of 'a circular letter of credit from Messrs

Heywood and Company of London dated 15th August to enable me to draw for what money I may require on the Continent, for my letters of credit on you for £1,500', and he was soon (6 October) in correspondence with A. & S. Henry, textile merchants, of 38 York Strand, off Portland Street, Manchester,[15] about a consignment of ginghams ordered by his Philadelphia house:

they write to me from Philadelphia to be very particular about keeping closely to the written instructions concerning the goods. I therefore request you to bear this in mind in the execution of the order, as the goods are intended to be sold to parties who are very particular; As I have not received any copy of the order from my House in Philadelphia I am at a loss to know the quantity of the ginghams that they have ordered, . . . it will be as well to send the smallest quantity that the order calls for . . .

He also received about this time a list of prices of cloths, with samples, from François Latard, of Verviers, in Belgium, but the Philadelphia firm does not appear to have traded in woollens and this approach does not appear to have resulted in an order.

Very soon the Northern Ireland linen connection appears in the correspondence. Early in October Creighton wrote to William Owens of Drogheda and R. & J. Workman of Belfast on the subject of brown drills.

We would like to have some of your [brown] drills to sell when the season comes and so as to keep your regular customers for them; perhaps therefore on this account you might be induced to send us a small consignment and we assure you that the best will be done with them in our power. [To W. Owens, 9 October 1856]

I received a letter recently from my House in Philadelphia stating that . . . you might possibly send us a small consignment of your 20 yd. pieces of soft drills. [To R. & J. Workman, 9 October 1856]

While making purchases for his store Creighton also tried to attract agency business from British firms exporting to North and South America. He wrote to Yates Brown & Howat,[16] cotton merchants, of Glasgow, on 23 October 1856:

I will thank you to inform me if there is a manufacturer of ginghams in Glasgow named John Baird. I am informed by my House that his Agent at Philadelphia died some time ago and that I might probably succeed in obtaining an Agency of his goods there.[17]

On 20 November he wrote to William Chaine & Sons, linen manufacturers, of Antrim, offering his services:

Being aware that you are extensive Manufacturers of Linen goods and having been informed that you ship a considerable quantity of goods to the U.S. and South America, I have taken the liberty of offering the services of my House at Philadelphia (Robert Creighton & Co.) for the transaction of any business of this nature, that you may be pleased to confide to it, should you not have any

Agent already at that place. Should you be pleased to make a consignment to them of such goods as you are in the habit of sending to New York or other parts of U.S., they will do the best in their power for your Interest in the sale of the goods, and you will be able to ascertain whether there would be any advantage or not in making further shipments of your goods. My House receives consignments of Linen goods from Jas. W. Murland, Esq., Castlewellan, Messrs John Patrick & Sons, Ballymena, and other parties in Ireland.

A month later he wrote to John Ferguson, linen merchant and manufacturer of Callender Street, Belfast: ' . . . My House at Philadelphia will be pleased to receive consignments of linen goods from you' (26 December 1856).

Agency work naturally brought problems differing from those connected with outright purchasing, e.g. the questions of ownership and insurance. For example, when Creighton became the agent for his friend John Patrick, it was necessary to get powers of attorney, to do a lot of letter writing and to make a journey to London, 'there being no American consul at Manchester'.[18]

When Creighton decided to leave Paris about 20 October Manchester, the textile capital of the world, became his British headquarters, with an address of convenience at Messrs A. & S. Henry, from whom his firm had recently (September) made extensive purchases of checks, jaconetts, chambrays and cambrics as well as ginghams:[19] 'Have everything you can shipped by *12 Nov*. *Packet*. *Fine goods* after that should come by steamer, but send nothing by transient vessels, as they save insurance rates considerably by Cope's line.'

Creighton also supervised from Manchester the execution of orders received by exporters direct from Philadelphia not only by other firms in Manchester but by other suppliers in Britain. For example, he wrote to Messrs Yates Brown and Howat, of Glasgow, on 23 October:

I have received letters from my House in Philadelphia in which they state that they have sent you a memorandum for sundry goods. I hope you will be able to execute all their memorandums sent you as they will expect the goods for their regular customers; in one of their letters they state that they hope you will send out a good supply of the old ones same as you sent to me last year at 6*d* per y[ar]d.

A good deal of work now began to fall on his Liverpool shippers, Messrs Langtry & Co.:

There are sundry goods to be sent down to you from this [place] to be shipped to my House in Philadelphia. I wish these goods to be shipped generally by the Packet Ship of the 12 Nov. from Liverpool to Philadelphia, a part to be shipped by the screw steamer *City of Washington* to sail on the 5 November from Liverpool to Philadelphia direct, but those to be shipped by the Screw Steamer as above, I will give you particular directions concerning, the greater part to be shipped by Sailing Packet of the 12 Nov.

I am thus particular because Maguire, Hyde & Co. inform me that they have
sent down a package of goods to you instructing you to ship it by the Ship
Hungarian. I do not wish any of my goods shipped by transient vessels . . .[20]

An interesting aspect of the correspondence is the entire absence of
reference to the US tariff rates on the goods imported, and indeed to the
whole tariff apparatus – with two minor exceptions, one being a
complaint that some goods ordered by Creighton had been shipped to
New York instead of to Philadelphia, which meant that he could be 'at
considerable expenses in having to employ a broker to enter the goods
and pass them through the Custom House in New York' prior to more
expense in transshipping them by rail to their final destination.[21] At this
period the American tariff was a comparatively low one, described by
Taussig as being characterised by 'moderated protection'.[22] By this time
American, and particularly New England, cotton manufacturing,
although well established and no longer an infant industry, was 'confined
mainly to the production of plain, cheap, staple cotton cloths, and was
not extended to the making of fine and "fancy" goods'.[23]

The rate of duty imposed by the tariff law of 1846 on 'manufactures
composed wholly of cotton' was a moderate 25 per cent *ad valorem*
(Schedule D), except for frame-knitted articles of cotton clothing, which
paid only 20 per cent *ad valorem* (Schedule E).[24] This may have led to
deliberate undervaluation on the invoices. There is, however, no direct
evidence of this in the correspondence, although it may explain in part
Creighton's insistence on purchases at rock-bottom prices, with
maximum discount and other allowances.[25] With regard to linens the
tariff of 1846 was even more favourable to the importer, for 'linens of all
kinds' and 'manufactures of flax not otherwise provided for' paid only 20
per cent *ad valorem*, so that the British competitive position was strong
indeed.[26] As late as 1890 'only the coarsest qualities' were being
manufactured in the USA, 'the finer being all obtained by importation',[27]
and in 1860 British linens imported into the USA amounted to £1.87
million by value.[28]

Now that Creighton was in Manchester an increasing amount of work
fell on Messrs Langtry & Co. and his Manchester suppliers. Particular
attention was to be given to packaging, labelling and dispatch by the fast
new screw steamers which within the space of twenty years had
transformed the North Atlantic trade. Instructions to John Siltzer of 9
Mount Street, off Peter Street, Manchester, one of the many firms of
German origin operating in the city during the nineteenth century, read
as follows:

Purchased from John Siltzer Manchester October 27th 1856. 2 cases each 84
Ends 14 yds each Black Tabby Velvets No. 2 quality 22 Inches Stretched at $9\frac{3}{8}d$
per yd. to be forwarded by 6th November to Liverpool to Langtry & Co. to be
shipped by the Packet Ship of the 12th Novr. from Liverpool to Philadelphia

direct making up with Boards, ticket, paper etc $4\frac{1}{2}d$ or $5d$ per end wrapped in thin Board in Ends of 14 yds.; put on a handsome ticket.

During late October and early November Creighton placed a spate of orders with such eminent Manchester cotton firms as Stavert Hunt Zigomala & Co., 40 Minshull Street, off Portland Street, and Thornton Huggins Ward & Co., Parker Street and Portland Street. Rylands & Sons, and Maguire & Hyde, American commission agents, of 29 Portland Street, both received very large orders for table cloths, probably of brown linen, although this is not absolutely clear. Rylands & Sons[29] were to supply 140 dozen table cloths[30] of sizes ranging from 47 in. by 56 in. (12s 6d per dozen) to 62 in. by 86 in. (25s 6d per dozen), while Maguire & Hyde were to furnish 150 dozen 'of the lower quality' (from 40 in. by 50 in. at 7s 8d per dozen to 62 in. by 86 in. at 19s $1\frac{1}{2}d$ per dozen), and 250 dozen of the best quality (from 40 in. by 50 in. at 8s 7d per dozen to 62 in. by 86 in. at 19s 8d per dozen). These were very low prices, even at wholesale rates. For the Maguire & Hyde order detailed instructions (29 October 1856) read:

A large handsome green ticket to be put on the outside piece of each Bundle and small tickets of the same color on every piece in the Bundle except the outside piece as before stated on which the large ticket is to be put: the sizes to be put on each ticket say 6/4, 7/4, 7/8, 8/4, 9/4, & 10/4, but the size in Inches only in the Invoice of the goods.[31] The goods to be *well* glazed and that side put out which will show the darkest shade of the Brown. The goods must be composed of a variety of patterns from the common pattern . . .

Reductions

Maguire Hyde & Co. will make a reduction of 1s. per doz. on the 20 doz. Table cloths 9/4 66 × 72 and which should have been 60 × 72 making them 16/– per doz in place of 17/3 and also a reduction on the Bloom Table Cloths of 2s per doz. 9/4 66 × 72 and which should have been 60 × 72 making them 19/6 per doz. in place of 21/6 per doz.

Evidence of strongly competitive conditions for freight on the Transatlantic route is revealed by Creighton's constant preoccupation with the subject, exemplified by a letter he wrote from Liverpool to Yates Brown & Co. of Glasgow on 4 November 1856 and one to James Smieton & Sons of Dundee on 24 November:

you had rather take care to have the goods Insured on this side (unless you have written to my House on the subject), as it is doubtful whether my policy would cover them in case of loss, it is also of importance that the goods should get early to market, and if any part remains to be shipped, it would perhaps be advisable to ship them by the Screw Steamers from this port to Philadelphia which depart every fortnight or by the steamer from Glasgow to New York; the freight by the Screw steamers from this port to Philadelphia has been reduced to 60/– per ton measurement.[32]

I could not get the Agent for the Screw steamers here to take my goods under 50/– and I have agreed with him at that rate for one year, this is to be for all goods on my own account; with regard to the goods that you may send to me on consignment they can either be shipped at 50*s*/– by the steamer or by sailing vessels as you may choose at whatever freight you may agree upon; you sometimes send goods to me on consignment, or leaving it optional with me to take them to my own account after having seen the goods, then you may either ship by screw or sailing vessel; if by the former at 50/– and if by the latter at whatever freight you may agree upon.

By 1 November Creighton had moved (c/o Messrs Langtry) to Liverpool, from which city he hurried up Thornton, Huggins & Co. and Stavert Hunt Zigomala & Co. in identical letters:

I will thank you to forward the goods that I purchased from you as early as possible, as it is of much importance that they should get to market early; send them to Messrs Langtry & Co. of Liverpool who will forward them to my House in Philadelphia – please to forward the Invoices of the goods by the Mail Steamer from Liverpool, addressed to Robert Creighton & Co. Philadelphia.[33]

From Liverpool he crossed over to Dublin shortly after 6 November 'to look after brown linen drills', and found some to his liking at Drogheda, Co. Louth, on 8 November buying both from William Owens of Laurence Street and from Richardson Flinn & Co., Linenhall Street. With the latter firm he arranged for a series of fortnightly shipments on a large scale.[34] The goods were of low quality and therefore 'entitled to be shipped at a low rate of freight'.[35] 11 November saw him installed in the Imperial Hotel, Belfast, after a visit to Newtownards (presumably staying with his brother William).[36] Clearly he felt at home in Northern Ireland, and it was from Belfast that he addressed the only letter in the collection which begins with a Christian name. It was to John Patrick of Ballymena, presumably a friend of his youth:

Dear John, I duly received your kind note of the 12th. and had the pleasure of an interview with your brother today. I am somewhat disappointed that you have not heard from my House in Philadelphia for some time, I hope you will hear from them soon. I suppose they were not selling Linen goods, but not withstanding they should have advised you. I am much obliged for your kind invitation but will have to forego it for the present, my stay here will only be for a few days. I left Mrs Creighton and my daughter at Liverpool where they will remain till my return there; it is possible they may have the pleasure of visiting Ireland some time next summer.[37]

After a very short stay ('a part of Monday' 19 November) in Glasgow Creighton arrived back in Liverpool on 20 November and opened up a correspondence with the rising Dundee merchant firm of James Smieton & Sons, with whom, to judge by the personal details in his letter, he was on very friendly terms:

I am offered by the Steam Boat Company here to take *all* my goods, both coarse and fine at 50/– per Ton provided I do not ship any goods by any other vessel than their Screw Steamers for Philadelphia which now sail regularly every fortnight for Philadelphia. I have [? some] idea of agreeing to this as I could perhaps get the Insurance effected lower. I therefore wish you on receipt of this to make this arrangement as your goods are so coarse and bulky and I would like to have your opinion on the subject as that would in some manner influence me and enable me to decide.[38]

After intense activity in Liverpool and Manchester seeing to the shipping of his orders by vessels leaving as late as 17 December the Creightons were back in the Hôtel du Louvre, Paris (via London), by 12 December. Robert was still occupied with shipping and financial business, but in addition was preparing for a winter trip to Italy. He wrote to Hamilton and Hugh Creighton in Philadelphia on 18 December acknowledging the receipt of the news that three bills of exchange amounting to £1,000 drawn on Brown Shipley & Co. of Liverpool were on their way to him:

I have written to them [R. Creighton & Sons, Philadelphia] that I would appropriate these Bills as follows: the £450 to Richardson, Flinn & Co. [Drogheda] and will draw on them for the amount of John Ferguson's Invoice. viz. £102–16–0. I will remit the Bill for £250 to Mr Owens and the Bill for £300 to Thornton, Huggins & Co., Manchester, requesting them to place it to the cr[edit] of Robert Creighton & Co., and that I will draw on their House in Belfast to pay whatever may be still due to Messrs Owens & Richardson, Flinn & Co. as soon as I ascertain what will be due these parties, so that you will have to remit to John Siltzer & Co., Stavert & Zigomala and the other parties from whom I have purchased goods.[39]

Shipping problems continued to plague him; he wrote to Thornton Huggins & Co. from Paris on 19 December:

I received a letter from Messrs. Langtry & Co. of Liverpool yesterday in which they do not mention your having forwarded any of my goods to go by the steamer of the 17th inst. for Philadelphia. I am a good deal disappointed at this, as the next Steamer of the Line does not go to Philadelphia but to New York. I feel quite vexed at the circumstance as the destination may cause us to miss a market for the goods. I am still in hope that they were sent by the steamer of the 17th.; please to say if you sent any by the steamer of the 3rd. inst. to Philadelphia; my address is to the care of Messrs. Greene & Co. Bankers, Paris; please to let me hear from you on receipt of this . . .[40]

At last the Italian trip began. After Christmas in Paris they left on 9 January 1857. On the 14th Creighton wrote to Hamilton from Marseilles, 'stating that we were going on that day by the steam boat *Ville de Marseilles* to Genoa'. By 21 January they were at La Spezzia and in Pisa three days later (Hotel Vittoria). From about 4 to 19 February they must have been sightseeing in Rome and were in Naples from 2 to 9 March. By 19 March they were back in Tuscany (Florence,

21st) and in Bologna by 26 March *en route* for Venice, where they had
arrived by 3 April. What is interesting is the chain of British banking
houses which existed to serve them in the days before specialised travel
agencies — Gibbs & Co. at Genoa, Magnay & Pakenham in Florence,
Pakenham & Hooker in Rome, W. J. Turner & Co. in Naples, and (less
obviously British) A. & C. Blumenthal at Venice. By Monday 13 April,
from Turin, Creighton wrote to Hugh Creighton:

stating that we would leave this [place] this evening to go over Mont Cenis and
that I would post this letter from Chambéry if we got there safe on Tuesday, that
we expected to arrive in Paris by the 17th April and that I would then see about
returning home either by Havre or Liverpool. Added a few lines from St Jean de
[Maurienne] stating that we had got over Mont Cenis after some difficulty.[41]

In the event Creighton booked a passage in Paris (23 April) to go from
Le Havre by the steamer *Arago* to New York on Tuesday 5 May, after
nearly a year's absence, in good time to experience the commercial crisis
of 1857.

He may have suffered losses in the crisis of 1857, and the outbreak of
the Civil War in 1861 would certainly not have made the conduct of
business less difficult for his firm. The disruption of raw cotton supplies
eventually had beneficial effects on the import trade in linens after the
disastrous year of 1861, when only just over $4 million worth of linens
were 'thrown on the market' through the port of New York as compared
with $11·2 million in 1859. However, during the last full calendar year of
Creighton's life, 1862, $8·2 million worth of imported linens were
released for domestic consumption by the New York custom house.[42]

Between 1857 and Creighton's death in 1863 we have little
information about his business or his family except what can be gleaned
from a reading of his will, which, naturally, is not an optimistic
document. Long and complicated, it shows him as a staunch, but not
bigoted, Presbyterian.[43] He left $5,000 in trust to his joint executors, Mrs
Creighton and his son Hamilton, to be devoted to religious societies,
among which were the two Boards of the Foreign and Domestic Missions
of the Old School Presbyterian Church, and other societies connected
with the Old and New School Presbyterians, the Episcopalians, the
Baptists and the Methodists. Out of the estate an annuity of $5,000 was
to be paid to his wife, and an annuity of $2,000 was settled on Emily,
who since the European tour had married Captain Joseph Bradish of the
British Indian Army. Robert expressed a wish that his wife, his second
daughter, Julia, and his two sons, Robert and Hamilton, should continue
living at 1406 Spruce Street. On the prospects of the firm of Robert
Creighton & Sons he was pessimistic. Should Hamilton wish to continue
the business he could have a loan of $20,000 out of the estate at 5 per
cent interest for the purpose, but, the will continues:

I do not recommend my son Hamilton to carry on business after my decease from my knowledge of its uncertainty, but I leave to himself to do what he chooses, at the time. I think twenty thousand dollars is too small a sum unless he does a small business, if he wishes to do a large business perhaps he could obtain some partner to put in forty thousand dollars such as has been spoken of between us and in case of such partnership I wish that he would give Robert my son a situation in the store at a very moderate salary.

Clearly Robert was not businesslike, but to guard against contingencies, e.g. Hamilton not going into business, both sons were to receive $750 a year.

There was a final warning: 'I beg of my son Hamilton not to form any partnership unless he is perfectly convinced of the [good] character of his partner and I would not recommend him to be concerned in any manufactory, nor to loan any money on factory buildings or machinery contained therein. Many commission merchants have become involved and finally got ruined by departing from this rule.'

Creighton had been worried in the closing months of his life by the depreciation of the American paper currency, which had fallen rapidly from $4.86 (par) to the £ in 1861 to over $8 to the £ early in 1863,[44] and it is noteworthy that his annuities to his brother and sister in Northern Ireland were expressed in British sterling in the will. These fears, with particular reference to legacies, are expressed in his will: '. . . on account of the domestic troubles in this country the exchange on England has risen to a most unprecedented rate, at one time being upwards of 70 per cent above par'.

The Philadelphia city directories for 1870, 1871 and 1872 provide the last glimpses of the business, which by then was trading in the names of James, Hugh and William Creighton, dry goods commission merchants (i.e. wholesale drapers), at 237 Chestnut Street, while Robert Creighton, Jr., still lived on at 1406 Spruce Street. The dynamism had clearly disappeared in 1863, and the firm is now forgotten in the 'City of brotherly love'.

Notes

1 B. W. Clapp, *John Owens, Manchester Merchant*, Manchester, 1965, *passim*.
2 M. M. Edwards, *The Growth of the British Cotton Trade, 1780–1815*, Manchester, 1967, p. 2.
3 Taking all exports into consideration, the USA was Britain's best customer throughout the boom years of the 1850s, taking £22·6 million of British exports out of a total of £115·8 million in 1856, and £20·1 million out of £122·1 million in 1857. (J. R. T. Hughes, *Fluctuations in Trade, Industry and Finance: a Study of British Economic Development, 1850–60*. Oxford, 1960, p. 40.)
4 N. S. Buck, *The Development of the Organisation of Anglo-American Trade, 1800–50*, New Haven, Conn., 1925. It is noteworthy that Dr Buck used only one set of manuscript business records, the Bostwick letter books

(pp. 176, 178), in the whole of this work. There are also useful studies by F. M. Jones, *Middlemen in the Domestic Trade of the United States, 1800–60*, Urbana, Ill., 1937 (*Illinois Studies in the Social Sciences*, vol. XXI, No. 3), reprinted New York, 1968, and E. J. Perkins, *Financing Anglo-American Trade: the House of Brown, 1800–80*, Cambridge, Mass., 1975.

5   The volume, a small notebook, 11·5 cm tall, 7·2 cm deep, and 1·1 cm thick, was item No. 845 in the April 1960 catalogue of David Low (Booksellers) Ltd, Emmington Chinnor, near Oxford, and is now in the possession of the author of this article, who wishes to thank Mr B. J. Avari, M.A., for making a transcription of the contents, and Professor Peter d'A. Jones of Illinois University (Chicago Circle) for great help in obtaining details of the Creighton family from various sources in Philadelphia.

6   Buck, *op. cit.*, pp. 151–2.

7   *Ibid.*, p. 153.

8   *Ibid.*, p. 155.

9   Information kindly supplied by the Historical Society of Pennsylvania. The store was possibly the large 'departmentized' Philadelphia dry goods store so graphically described in 1847 in *Hunt's Merchants' Magazine*, New York (F. M. Jones, *op. cit.*, pp. 49–50).

10 Mary was already to some extent dependent on him as early as 1856, for he instructed Hamilton Creighton shortly before 15 November 1856 'to send her the half-yearly money'.

11 Accommodation for the four at Hôtel du Louvre up to 13 August cost 221 francs.

12 According to the approximate rates of exchange obtaining at the time (£1 = 25 fr., 5 fr. = $1), this was the equivalent of 600 gold dollars or 120 gold sovereigns, worth about £2,400–£3,000 in modern paper money (July 1976).

13 A. Ellis, *Heir of Adventure: the story of Brown, Shipley & Co., Merchant Bankers, 1810–1960*, published privately, London, 1960, pp. 37–8, 42, 157. William A. Bowen, an American, who had for many years represented one of the American branches of the firm in Manchester, eventually became a partner in Brown Shipley & Co. from 1837 to 1859.

14 A. Ellis, *op. cit.*, p. 23. It is asserted by Ellis that A. Brown & Sons of Baltimore had at this time 'a virtual monopoly of the linen trade'.

15 For A. & S. Henry see anon. [James Burnley], *Fortunes made in Business*, vol. III, London, 1887, pp. 205–11, 'The Henrys of Manchester and Bradford' (reprinted from *London Society*, November 1880, pp. 446–52), and anon., *The Henry Group of Companies: A. & S. Henry & Co. Ltd*, n.d. (c. 1955), pp. 8–9. The firm had been founded in 1804–05 by an émigré Northern Ireland Scot settled in America, who sent his two nephews, Alexander Henry (d. 1862) and Samuel (d. 1840), to set up in business in Manchester.

16 This firm, specialising in muslins, of Newtownards, Co. Down, also had offices in Glasgow. (I. Slater, *Royal National Commercial Directories ... together with a ... Directory of Ireland, 1857*, pp. 47, 580.)

17 This may be linked with Creighton's letters to 'Mr [Jackson] Baird, care of Jas. W. Murland', Castlewellan, 13 and 15 November 1856, although Jackson Baird was already a supplier of cheap linens ('demis') to the Philadelphia house. They were selling rather slowly. Jas. W. Murland, one of the five sons of James Murland (d. 1850), was described in Slater as a barrister (p. 492). See also E. R. R. Green, 'James Murland and the linen industry', *Threshold*, autumn 1957, vol. I, No. 3, 6 pp. (unpaginated); and

E. R. R. Green, *The Industrial Archaeology of County Down*, HMSO, Belfast, 1963, pp. 32–3.

18   R. Creighton to Hugh Creighton, 25 November 1856, and to Hamilton Creighton, 2, 3, 4 December 1856.

19   Creighton to A. & S. Henry, 11, 15 October 1856. Mrs Creighton and Emily accompanied him to Manchester but did not cross to Ireland.

20   Creighton to Langtry & Co., Liverpool, 25 October 1856.

21   R. Creighton, Paris, 19 December 1856, to Messrs Langtry, Liverpool.

22   F. W. Taussig, *The Tariff History of the United States*, fifth edn, New York, 1910, pp. 114–15.

23   *Ibid.*, p. 142.

24   The text of the law of 1846, 'reducing the duty on imports', usually called the 'Walker tariff', is most easily found in US Congress, *Customs Tariff of 1846, with Senate debates thereon* ..., Washington, US Government Printing Office, 1911 (62nd Congress, first session, Senate document No. 71), pp. 264–72. See also Taussig, *op. cit.*, p. 114.

25   In connection with an order for 'high finished and handsomely ornamented' linens from John Ferguson, Belfast, 15 November 1856, Creighton wrote, '... the price to be 9d per year, which included all charges of boxes and ornament ... the discount, 2½%, to be taken off the invoice to be forwarded to Philadelphia.'

26   *Customs Tariff of 1846* (Schedule E), p. 269. Embroidered and tamboured linens, however, paid 30 per cent *ad valorem*, (Schedule C, p. 267), but presumably these were luxury items. The author is most grateful to Mr T. Kabdebo of the John Rylands University Library of Manchester and Mr E. N. MacConomy of the Library of Congress, Washington, D.C., for help in securing the exact text of the Walker tariff Act of 1846.

27   Taussig, *op. cit.*, p. 268.

28   A. J. Warden, *The Linen Trade, Ancient and Modern*, 1864, repr. 1967, p. 349.

29   For the history of this firm see D. A. Farnie, 'John Rylands of Manchester', *Bulletin of the John Rylands Library*, vol. 56, 1973–74, pp. 93–129. There is an amusing and very informative article (anonymous, but by James Lowe) in Charles Dickens's *Household Words*, vol. IX, No. 215, 6 May 1854, pp. 268–72, entitled 'A Manchester warehouse', which gives an excellent impression of the atmosphere and organisation of a great Manchester warehouse in the 1850s, such as those of A. & S. Henry & Co. and John Rylands & Sons, although the article itself describes 'Banneret & Co.', i.e. Henry Bannerman & Sons of 33 York Street (*The Century's Progress: Lancashire*, 1892, p. 102).

30   29 October 1856.

31   This was possibly to avoid complaints from literally minded retail purchasers in the USA who were too handy with their yardsticks or tape measures.

32   See also Creighton to Messrs Langtry, 11 November 1856, requesting that ' you will have an interview with the Agents of the Steamers to Philadelphia and endeavour to get them shipped at a reduction of freight; perhaps they would make an offer for all my goods both fine and coarse, as suggested before I left Liverpool at all events as I wish to get these goods to an early market, you will have to ship those you may receive at this time by the steamer from Liverpool to Philadelphia of the 19th inst. at the lowest rate of freight in your power. These goods will not bear a regular rate of freight and I hope the Agents will take this into consideration.'

33   3 November 1856.

34 Richardson Flinn & Co. were not always reliable, and their cloth had 'imperfections'. (Creighton to R.F., 28 November 1856.)

35 Creighton to Messrs Langtry & Co., 11 November 1856.

36 Creighton to J. W. Murland, Castlewellan, 11 November 1856.

37 Creighton to John Patrick, 14 November 1856.

38 James Smieton & Sons, of 55 Cowgate, Dundee, were linen and jute merchants. In 1857 they launched out to build the Panmure Works, a power loom factory for linen weaving at Carnoustie, about six miles from Dundee. (Warden, *The Linen Trade*, pp. 488–9, 716; information kindly supplied by the Chief Librarian, Dundee.)

39 Memo of 18 December 1856. On 26 December 1856 Creighton wrote from Paris to W. Owens 'with Brown & Bowen's draft [from Philadelphia] on Brown, Shipley & Co., Liverpool payable in London at 60 days' sight favor of Robert Creighton & Co. and accepted 15th inst. for £250.' From the mention of the use of inland bills of exchange in Anglo-American import–export trade (S. Nishimura, *The Decline of Inland Bills of Exchange in the London Money Market, 1855–1913*, Cambridge, 1971, pp. 34–5) it would seem that this procedure was unusual).

40 After his experience of the cheap British penny post Creighton was appalled at French postal tariff, which was 'calculated by weight and is very heavy' (R.C. to John Ferguson, Belfast, 19 December 1856). He advised correspondents to write on thin tissue paper! For similar complaints about French postal charges about this time see Thomas Jevons, Liverpool, to W. S. Jevons, 1 April 1855: 'In writing via Marseilles it is as well to write on thin paper as the French single postage only goes to $\frac{1}{4}$ oz while our English & Colonial single postage covers $\frac{1}{2}$ oz.' (R. D. Collison Black, ed., *Papers and Correspondence of William Stanley Jevons*, vol. II, London, 1973, pp. 132–3.)

41 Neither in the account of the Continental tour in 1856 nor in the one made in 1857 is there a single mention of the railway.

42 See table in Warden, *op. cit.*, p. 350. After 1861 the consumption of linens by the confederate states was to some extent supplied via the West Indian islands.

43 Registers Office, City and County of Philadelphia. Will dated 20 April 1863, proved 26 June 1863. I am indebted to Professor P. d'A. Jones for securing me a copy of this document.

44 I. Unger, *The Greenback Era: a Social and Political History of American Finance, 1865–79*, Princeton, 1964, p. 15. At its lowest point in 1864 the rate was fourteen paper dollars to the British gold sovereign.

Appendix Specimen orders by Creighton

(*a*)   October 23rd. 1856 [ordered] from Maguire Hyde & Co. [Manchester]
... 1 case rolled Jaconetts
[?is] 40 yds each to sell at 6$\frac{3}{4}$ cost about 2$\frac{1}{4}$[*d*]
or 7/6 per piece
of 40 yds.

(*b*)   Order to Maguire Hyde & Co. Manchester 23rd October 1856
20 pieces 5/4 check Muslins A23 to be A10 at 3/10$\frac{1}{2}$

40	„	*do*	*do*	No. 25 to be A12 at 4/4$\frac{1}{2}$
25	„	*do*	*do*	No. 26 „ „ 14 „ 4/7$\frac{1}{2}$
20	„	*do*	*do*	No. 27 „ „ 16 „ 5/–
20	„	*do*	*do*	No. 28 „ „ 18 „ 5/3
20	„	*do*	*do*	No. 29 „ „ 20 „ 6/–
20	„	*do*	*do*	No. 30 „ „ 22 „ 6/9
13	„	*do*	*do*	No. 31 „ „ 24 „ 7/9

12 „   *do*   *do*   No. 32 „ „   26 „ 8/9
10 „   *do*   *do*   No. 33 „ „   28 „ 9/9

200 „ to be put up with yellow papers under first fold to be Numbered A10–28 as stated, and a small ticket put in each piece besides the Ornamental ticket, marked as follows:–
"Manufactured for Dunham & Kearfitt, Baltimore" to be shipped by 12 Novr. packet, and goods to [be] in Liverpool 6 Nov^r.

(*c*)   Purchased from Thornton, Huggins & Co. Manchester, Oct. 30th. 1856.
1 case Brilliantes as follows:–

No.

A64 – 10 pieces   3515, 3520, 3522, 3516, 3524 at $3\frac{1}{8}^d$
              2   2   2   2   2

70 – 10   „   3527   3528   3530   3533   3536 „ $3\frac{5}{8}^d$
              2   2   2   2   2

8 – 10   „   3537   3529   3527   3529   3531 „ $3\frac{3}{4}^d$
              2   2   2   2   2

78 – 10   „   3541   3544   3548   3542   3545 „ $4\frac{1}{2}^d$
              2   2   2   2   2

59 – 10   „   3552   3554   3556   3562   3540 „ $4\frac{7}{8}^d$
              2   2   2   2   2

79 – 5   „   3562   3563   3565   3566   3567 „ $5\frac{3}{8}^d$
              1   1   1   1   1

62 – 5   „   3577   3592   3591   3595   3598 „ 7^d
              1   1   1   1   1

to be cut into ends of about 28 yd. each say the above pieces of about 50 yds. to be cut in two to be put up in Book fold same as Victoria Lawns with 2 Ribbands on each piece, handsome ticket, to be forwarded to Langtrys & Co. Liverpool; Say 1 case 120 pieces 25 yds each to be shipped if possible by 12 Nov. Packet or 19 Screw steamer high finish 5 pieces.

(*d*)   Order from Robert Creighton & Co. of Philadelphia to Messrs. Richardson, Flinn & Co., Drogheda, Nov. 8th. 1856.
1 case 30 pieces each, each piece about 48 yards, Brown Linen drills
       at - $5\frac{1}{4}^d$
   3 cases more of the same
     in 2 weeks
2 cases 30 pieces each *do. do.* at $5\frac{1}{2}^d$
   2 cases more of the same
     in 2 weeks
1 case 30 pieces each *do do*   at 5/^{d}
1 –   30 pieces *do do*   at 6^d
   2 cases more of the same
     in 2 weeks.
all the above to be the same as the samples given to me
Let the invoice be made out as stated say 1 case 1400
                    1 „ 1400
                    1 „ 1400
                        ———
                        4200
                        $113\frac{1}{2}$
                        ———
                  $4086\frac{1}{2}$ at $5\frac{1}{4}$ [*d*]

[Allowance] 2/37%

&c and discount deducted 2½%. Ship by first class steamer from Drogheda to Liverpool at as low a rate of freight as possible, addressed to Langtrys & Co. Liverpool who will have my instructions respecting the shipping of the goods. Send the first goods off by the steamer by Wednesday to Liverpool at the latest, the remainder in the course of 2 weeks afterwards. Send an Invoice of the goods by the Mail Steamer from Liverpool to the U.S. addressed to Robert Creighton & Co. Philadelphia and a duplicate Invoice addressed to Robert Creighton care of Langtrys & Co. Liverpool.

(e)   Paris 26th Dec. 1856.

Mr. John Ferguson.,
   [Belfast]   Dear Sir,
   I am in receipt of your favor of the 23rd. and note the contents; my House at Philadelphia will be pleased to receive consignments of Linen goods from you and perhaps you could send out denim pieces 4/4 at from 9d. to 11d. which might answer to fill up our assortment, as we receive but few goods as low as 9d; some at 8½d might likewise suit. It is the custom of my House at Philadelphia to remit something on Account on the arrival of the goods at Philadelphia. If you mean to get such advance I do not see how they could hold over your goods at your limits for an indefinite time, but if you did not require an advance on them, they would abide by your instructions on your writing to them fully to that effect; at all events they will obtain the best prices for the goods that the market will afford; if you wait till the goods are sold and sales rendered you; they will make a trial with a small parcel of your goods and then you will be better able to form an opinion, what they can do for you.
                              I remain

The Manchester Ship Canal
1894–1913

During the four years 1880–83 twenty-five maritime canals were projected under the influence of the delusively high dividends which were paid by the Suez Canal Company in order to win support for the associated venture of the Panama Canal Company. One of those schemes was intended to transform the centre of England's main export industry into a second Liverpool. The idea of a Manchester Ship Canal matured under the influence of friction between two world markets, generated by the increasing divorce of Liverpool from Lancashire as it passed under the influence of the New York cotton market, and exacerbated by the cotton corners of 1879 and 1881. The ambitious plan for such a waterway stemmed from a growing aversion in Manchester to carriers as middlemen, deemed comparable almost to landlords in their parasitism, and from a determination to reduce the cost of carriage to industry, to avoid the payment of dock and town dues at 'the Liverpool toll bar' and to by-pass the three Liverpool–Manchester railways as well as the port itself. The projectors assumed that the cost of transport was as important to the cotton industry as to the heavy industries, and aspired to place that staple trade within carting distance of the outside world, to transfer the raw cotton market to Manchester and to link Lancashire directly to its markets in Asia by a waterway dug to the same depth as the Suez Canal and designed to take the largest vessels then afloat. In that venture they lacked the support of the elite of a city which had given its name to a school of sober, practical and realistic thought. They were bitterly opposed by all the corporate interests they threatened to subvert, i.e. the railway companies, the shipping lines, the merchants, the port and the corporation of Liverpool and all the Manchester mercantile interests inseparably allied to Liverpool. Their hopes were drastically modified even before the cutting of the first sod. The estimated reduction in the cost of carriage of cotton was revised from 80 per cent in 1882 to 67 per cent in 1883 and then to 50 per cent in 1886, after precautionary rate reductions had been made in 1883 and 1885. Estimates of the potential dividend were reduced from the 10 per cent of 1882 and the 18 per cent of 1885 to 5 per cent in 1887. The intense opposition frustrated three successive attempts, in 1885, 1886 and 1887, to raise the necessary capital of £9 million. Daniel Adamson (1818–90) resigned as chairman in favour of Lord Egerton after the rejection of his idea that capital should be raised locally and especially from small investors. J. C. Lee (1832–95), the chairman of Tootal's, became the financial saviour of the enterprise by enlisting the aid of London capital. In July 1887 Baring's and Rothschild's took up £4 million in perpetual preference shares to supplement the £3,312,000 subscribed in the Manchester district and to permit the Manchester Ship Canal Company to be floated.

The Canal Company exhausted its capital of £8 million within four years in completing half the work of construction. In order to avoid bankruptcy it appealed for financial aid to Manchester corporation, which on 4 February 1891 established a special Ship Canal Committee destined to remain in existence until 1910.[1] On the recommendation of that committee the corporation decided on 9 March, amidst general astonishment, to lend the company the necessary £3 million at $4\frac{1}{2}$ per cent and thus brought to its aid a corporation which could borrow at 3 per cent and was prepared to pledge its credit upon an heroic scale in order to preserve the prestige of the city. Manchester deliberately excluded other local authorities, and Salford in particular, from participation in that loan and declined even to consider the conversion of the company into a public trust representative of the district served by the canal. In return for the loan the corporation appointed on 5 August five directors, who comprised one-third of the fifteen-member board of the company. A new financial crisis was precipitated when the company twice raised its estimate of the sum necessary for completion, on 1 September 1891 and on 1 June 1892. As an emergency measure an executive committee was appointed on 11 December 1891, with four corporation directors and three Ship Canal 'ordinary directors' under Alderman Sir John Harwood (1832-1906) as chairman, and vested with plenary powers to carry out all works, so effectively excluding both Egerton and Lee from the administration of the company. Harwood's report of 27 July 1892 sharply condemned the past administration of the company and inspired the Ship Canal Committee to resolve on 14 October, without any discussion with the company, that the corporation should have an absolute majority upon the board of directors and upon its various spending sub-committees in return for an additional £1·5 million. In fulfilment of that resolution the committee decided on 13 March 1893 that the board should comprise twenty-one directors, including eleven corporation directors. On 7 June the corporation duly appointed its eleven directors and nominated Harwood as deputy chairman of the company. On 12 June it secured majorities upon five of the six sub-committees of the board, leaving only the traffic and rates committee with a majority of shareholders' directors. The Ship Canal Shareholders' Association established in 1892[2] could not prevent the appointment of a majority of corporation directors but successfully opposed a proposal made in 1894 for their direct election by the ratepayers.

Such a bold extension of the sphere of civic enterprise made within the cradle of individualism alarmed Herbert Spencer, who rebuked Manchester for exceeding the function of a municipal government established primarily for the local maintenance of order. The loan of £4·5 million to the company increased the municipal debt steeply by 67 per cent[3] and raised the municipal rates by 26 per cent between 1892 and 1895. The company secured the necessary capital and completed the canal, whose construction required seven years rather than the four originally anticipated and cost £15·25 million instead of the estimated £9 million. For that achievement it paid a high price in the loss of its independence, in its effective transformation into a diarchy and in its assumption of a heavy burden of fixed-interest payments. Harwood carried the enterprise to a successful completion and then before resigning launched a new attack upon the administration of the company in his report to the corporation on 6 June 1894. That report evoked Lord Rothschild's letter of 12 June insisting in the interests of the preference shareholders that a full-time manager should be appointed at an annual salary of £3,000 for the new canal. On 20 July Lord Egerton resigned as chairman[4] and was succeeded by John Kenworthy Bythell (1840–1916), who became 'the second founder of the Manchester Ship Canal'[5] and developed the company's operations on the basis of harmonious co-operation between corporation directors and shareholders' directors. The successful completion of the great cut represented a joint triumph for private initiative and for civic vision. Manchester corporation did not indeed secure the fulfilment of all its aims and had to accept minority representation upon the Mersey & Irwell Joint Committee, created in 1891, and upon the Port Sanitary Authority, created in 1896. The constitution of the Port of Manchester with effect from 1 January 1894 nevertheless entailed a large westward expansion of Mancunian influence and a corresponding withdrawal of the limits of the Port of Liverpool to some eleven miles beyond Warrington. The new port was not taken under municipal administration but was entrusted to the management of the company and, as a profit-oriented undertaking, became unique amongst the major ports of England. The Canal Company became the lord of a gigantic fief and operated as port and harbour authority, canal proprietor, pilotage authority, tug company, dredging agency, dock company, employer of dock labour, warehousing, forwarding and shipping agent, railway company, landlord and banker. As a distinct triumph for civic patriotism the Ship Canal aroused the envy of other towns such as Bristol, Birmingham and Sheffield.[6] In Lancashire Preston was stimulated by the example of Manchester to improve from 1883 the navigation of the Ribble and to open in 1892 the Albert Edward Dock. The capital of the weaving district, Blackburn, was urged in vain to build its own ship canal in order to shake off 'the grip of the Mancunian octopus' and so to become in some degree a combined Liverpool and Manchester instead of 'a struggling town, with one branch only of a great trade, and the most elementary department of that branch'.[7] In the spinning district the projectors of a Chadderton–Royton–Castleton canal in 1894 hoped to reduce the high transport costs of Oldham and Rochdale but failed to secure support for such a venture. The fortunes of the Manchester Ship Canal did not encourage the promoters of similar schemes. The most determined opponents of the new waterway remained the railways and the ship owners, upon whom the Canal Company became dependent for the success of its venture.

The railways controlling the great highway of commerce between Manchester and Liverpool were very powerful enterprises, enjoying the lowest costs and the highest rates in the kingdom. They became more than ever the prisoners and defenders of their own capital, after they became subject to the statutory control of rates in 1888–94 and to rising costs from 1896. They had bought up the canals to eliminate their competition and could not permit the Ship Canal to breach their semi-monopolistic position by undermining their control of the route from Liverpool or by encouraging the inland extension of coastal shipping. Thus they firmly opposed all attempts to integrate the new port into the transport network of the country. They survived attempts to weaken their monopoly by the projectors of a Lancashire Derbyshire & East Coast Railway in 1891, intended to create a 130-mile east–west link between Warrington and the North Sea, and of a Manchester Newcastle and Glasgow Grand Trunk Railway in 1892 and 1897. They neglected to complete their rail connections with the new docks for the opening day. Only the Cheshire Lines Committee had established on 1 October 1891 a connection from the south-west at Cornbrook, near the new Pomona Dock in Manchester. The two main railway companies, the London & North Western and the Lancashire & Yorkshire, proved slow to follow that example. They even asked the Canal Company to permit all rail traffic to be carted until all the railways were connected with the docks. The Cheshire Lines Committee first accepted traffic for Lancashire & Yorkshire stations, then yielded after less than a month to pressure from the other railways and declined all such traffic, being persuaded to relent only by a formal application to the Railway Commissioners.[8] The LNWR completed its link line from Eccles to the north-west to Mode

Wheel and Weaste on 4 November 1895, so giving the canal direct access to the whole of the LNWR system. The Lancashire & Yorkshire Railway proved the most determined opponent of the canal, and became the last of the three companies to undertake, from 26 September 1895, the construction of a branch line to the docks, although it was the great cotton railway and the sole potential link to the main docks in Salford. Such connections were less important than the rates levied on traffic carried by rail from the new docks.

For six long years until 1898 the railways delayed the fixing of reasonable through rates and quoted prohibitive rates to traders. The Canal Company had begun negotiations with the railways two years before the opening of the waterway, and its manager held five meetings in fourteen months with the railway managers, to no avail.[9] Manchester was thus denied the same mileage rates in relation to its new geographical position as competing ports, so that the canal was restricted merely to the service of the city and of places within carting distance. The railways exploited their control of carting services in order to embarrass the company. For thirty months from 5 December 1893 they claimed the right to cart all traffic to or from the docks and charged for that service a special carting rate thrice the normal. After the lines to the docks were completed the railways rerouted goods via their stations and then charged extra for cartage from the station to the docks. The policy of procrastination pursued by the railways compelled the company to devise its own through rates under the Euston agreement of 8 June 1894,[10] which had settled the rates for general traffic and class rates. The railway companies, however, still held under consideration the exceptional rates, which were based upon the class rates, were granted at ports for articles such as grain, timber and cotton carried in great bulk and weight, and were applicable to most of the canal's traffic. Nor would they agree that the Canal Company was a railway company in respect of its dock railways for the purpose of interchanging traffic, fixing rates and sharing terminal charges. In their memorandum of 28 June 1894 the railway companies declined to be parties to any such through rates issued by the Canal Company and declared such rates inclusive of Ship Canal toll and handling charges as well as the railway rate to be illegal. They developed their competition vigorously from November 1894 and charged from 1 December unacceptable rates for general traffic to towns within carting distance of Manchester as distinct from towns beyond that radius. They conceded beneficial through rates to all railway ports, to the disadvantage of Manchester. They granted through rates from Hamburg and Rotterdam via the ports of the east coast to towns in the West Riding very near to Manchester and denied the Ship Canal similar through rates until 1898–99, so effectively restricting to a minimum the hinterland of the new port.[11] The unexpected failure of the canal to acquire the staple trades in raw cotton and piece goods originating within carting distance of the docks made it wholly dependent upon the railways for its hinterland. The continued delay by the railways in the establishment of reasonable rates prevented liners from securing full cargoes at Manchester, disheartened steamship owners, reduced the tonnage carried to a small amount and made Manchester merely a local port instead of the great centre of distribution envisaged by the projectors of the canal. [12]

The railways compelled the company to follow their example in granting traffic credit accounts and to become a virtual banker through the extension of overdrafts to its clients. [13] They also granted traders extra facilities as well as lower rates in order to preserve their custom, including increased facilities, accommodation without extra charge and preferential traders' tickets. Their competition with the canal restricted the development of the export of coal and piece goods, the expansion of the import trade in iron ore, raw wool, raw cotton, dyewoods, frozen meat and beet sugar and the growth of direct trade with Ireland, which would have adversely affected the railway ports. The railway companies were so powerful that the company could not afford even to contemplate the possibility of a rate war and was forced to refuse business rather than provoke the railways to retaliatory rate cutting. [14] The refusal of the railways, especially the Midland Railway, to reduce their rates for the benefit of the company inspired Bythell's public denunciation of the railway companies on 26 February 1896 as 'one of the most serious hindrances' to the development of the trade of the port of Manchester. [15] A meeting in London on 26 March 1896 with the railway companies failed to avert a resort to litigation. On 2 June 1896 the Canal Company applied to the Railway Commissioners for the grant of through rates on grain and timber to Birmingham from the Midland Railway and secured a verdict in its favour, so persuading the railways to remove the boycott on carting and to undertake the construction of large goods yards in Manchester. A second appeal to the Railway Commissioners for the grant of the vital exceptional rates from the Midland Railway was heard on 4, 5, 6 and 8 February 1897 and made possible a final settlement on 15 July, when the railways finally agreed to recognise the Canal Company as a railway company and to make the rates agreed upon retrospective to June 1894. [16] During the next seven months about 18,000 rates to 1,114 stations were fixed, and virtually all rates had been agreed upon by August 1899. The completion by the Lancashire & Yorkshire Railway of its costly tunnel line from Windsor Bridge to Salford Docks on 28 March 1898 enabled the company to project the construction of its ninth and greatest dock, separated by a marshalling yard from dock No. 8, and to secure its construction by the Manchester Dock & Warehouse Extension Company Ltd, which was registered in 1902 and renamed in 1968 the Bridgewater Investment Trust Ltd. The Lancashire & Yorkshire Railway not only stimulated the export trade in coal from the coal depot opened in 1902 but became also the main vehicle for the carriage of imports from the great railway goods depot built up at the docks. Thus the railways finally conceded the right of the canal to exist and to handle upon agreed terms a limited amount of traffic.

Ship owners proved most reluctant to use an inland route which, as a locked cul-de-sac rather than a sea-level isthmian highway, militated against the speed and dispatch essential to the successful operation of a maritime steamship line. As lords of the ocean highways they regarded the new waterway simply as a barge canal, had no wish to assimilate their vessels to mere coasting steamers and could not subject them to the ordeal and indignity of inland navigation along a polluted ditch, especially when the prospect of high freights was absent. They could secure the same freight at the Mersey ports without attempting a thirty-five-mile inland navigation at a maximum speed of six knots, around a sharp curve at Runcorn, through five sets of locks, past five swing bridges and beneath five high-level rail bridges, whose height allowed masts a clearance of only 75 ft. The absence of terminal facilities lengthened the time of turn-round of vessels, and the shortage of return freight reduced the income from such ventures. The canal lacked the depth of 26 ft necessary for India and China ships drawing 24 ft and was restricted on its opening to vessels with a draught of less than $21\frac{1}{2}$ ft. On 9 January 1894 the board of directors ordered its engineers to dredge the waterway to a minimum depth of 23 ft and then to 26 ft, depths which required respectively three months and seven months to attain.[17] Shipowners were daunted by the limited depth and informed the company that they had no steamers small enough to make use of the canal. They were also deterred by the lack of passing stations, the absence of compulsory pilotage, the unlimited liability attaching until 1897 to a voyage along the confined waters of the canal and the high rates accordingly exacted by marine insurers. In self-protection they succeeded, against the uncomprehending opposition of the company, in assimilating for purposes of insurance a voyage up the canal to one on the high seas.[18]

The Canal Company did all it could to attract traffic. It made Manchester a free port as regards ships, charging no canal toll, no dues on ships and no quay rent until 1901, supplying free towage for large vessels and providing cheap dock labour and warehousing. It could not, however, offer remunerative freights in order to attract and retain the regular custom of established lines of steamships. Ship owners were concerned primarily to protect their sole source of income, could never accept 'the General Philosophic Manchester Principle that all freight is robbery'[19] and remained opposed to any innovation which might depress freights. By strengthening their conference organisation they therefore reduced uneconomic competition within their ranks. By extending their use of the deferred rebate, especially from 1895, they capitalised upon the

intense competition amongst shippers and ensured their unwavering
loyalty. The discreet use of the rebate bound the merchants of
Manchester to the shipowners as effectively as publicans of tied houses
were linked to their brewers. Thus shipowners extended their pecuniary
power over shippers and effectively deprived them of any incentive to use
the new route. Their conferences discouraged the use of the canal in
various ways. They dissuaded shippers from inducing steamship owners
to come for cargo to Manchester and prevented merchants from using
lines sailing from Manchester. They warned shippers against favouring
Manchester steamers lest they should suffer for it in connection with their
other shipments.[20] They cut rates sharply but temporarily when outside
vessels came up to Manchester. They even threatened to poach upon the
home preserves of such lines and so drove them away. They also
discouraged foreign steamers from loading in Manchester. They
prevented member lines from succumbing to the blandishments of the
Canal Company, from coming for cargo to the new port and from
departing from established pooling arrangements. When they permitted
conference liners to load in Manchester they imposed strict conditions
and compelled them to charge the same freight as if they were sailing
from Liverpool. They even asked for a higher rate on freight from
Manchester than on the same cargo from Liverpool, so that only the
Bombay conference carried goods at the same rate from Manchester and
Birkenhead. They also prevented conference steamers using Manchester
from loading any other cargo than piece goods or from accepting more
than a small quantity of piece goods in proportion to their carrying
capacity, so reducing the revenue of the Canal Company, which was
derived solely from cargo and not from ships. They effectively restricted
major freight reductions to the coasting trade, wherein outward rates
from Manchester were reduced to Glasgow by 25 per cent and to
London by 35 per cent at the expense of the railways rather than of
themselves.

Such conferences controlled the export trade and retarded the growth
of exports from, in comparison with imports to, Manchester. They
debarred the canal from participation in the export trade to Asia save for
Bombay and the Persian Gulf and especially from that to Calcutta,
China, Australia, New Zealand, South Africa and South America. They
prevented the diversion of Eastern shipments of machinery from
Liverpool and Birkenhead except for those consigned to Bombay and
Shanghai. They competed out of commercial existence the experimental
Manchester lines established to Turkey, the Persian Gulf, China,
Australia, West Africa, the river Plate and the USA. By their control of
the export trade they also repressed indirectly the development of many
valuable import trades. Thus they excluded from the canal a wide range
of trades in imported produce, such as dairy produce from Denmark,
wheat from the Black Sea for two and a half years, wheat from India,

wool from Australia, cattle, meat and grain from the Argentine, nitrate
from Chile and cattle and general produce from North America. They
delayed the inauguration of a direct line to Australia until 1904,
restricted the Houlder Line thereafter to outward sailings from
Manchester and so ensured that its frozen meat was carried to Liverpool,
although cold storage buildings had been completed at Mode Wheel in
1898 by the Colonial Consignment and Distributing Company Ltd. They
could not, however, influence imports directly or to the same degree as
exports, because foreign shippers had such large amounts to send that
they could practically charter their own vessels and because importers of
produce were fewer in number than exporters and dealt with larger
quantities. Nor did the Canal Company find conferences as much a
threat as did merchants in the Cape trade. Thus it declined in 1897 to
join the South African Mercantile Association of London in demanding a
select committee to investigate the influence of shipping rings upon
British trade. [21] It also refused to give evidence in 1907 before the Royal
Commission on Shipping Rings, thereby hoping to conciliate the shipping
interest and especially Liverpool.

The Ship Canal was no mere waterway but a symbolic declaration of
economic independence by Manchester and an instrument of commercial
revolution designed to undermine the whole complex of interests vested in
a major axis of transport. As such it represented the greatest challenge
ever made to the established interests and the corporate pride of the
mercantile community of Liverpool. That port was wholly dependent
upon its function as a non-industrial entrepôt between the outer world
and its manufacturing hinterland. Its mercantile elite had initiated every
improvement in transport facilities extending that hinterland, especially
along the Mersey and Irwell, and had insensibly acquired a proprietary
attitude towards 'their' river. Inevitably the construction of the Ship
Canal created deep and abiding hostility between the two world markets
of Lancashire, deprived Manchester of any co-operation from Liverpool
in the development of its traffic and ensured that Liverpool concentrated
its energies upon denying it any oceanic commerce. The implacable
opposition of Liverpool therefore compelled Manchester to turn for aid in
the development of its shipping services to the ports of the north-east
coast, the pioneers of economical shipping and shipbuilding. From that
region was enlisted the enterprise of George Renwick of Newcastle in the
establishment of the dry docks of the Ship Canal,[22] of James Knott of
Newcastle in the development of the Prince Line's service to Egypt, and
of William C. F. Bacon (1855–1931)[23] and Christopher Furness
(1852–1912) of West Hartlepool in the development of trade with
Montreal. From Sunderland emanated the proposal for a Manchester,
Newcastle and Glasgow Railway intended to strengthen the Irwell–Tyne
axis. [24]

In any contest for oceanic trade between the two cities Liverpool

enjoyed very great advantages. As a major port with a large and
expanding fleet in local ownership it could offer fixed and regular sailings,
with fast and frequent passages. It was not merely the home of great
shipping lines but also the seat of the conference organisation pioneered
from 1868 and extended from 1895 under the influence of the dynamic
genius of Alfred Jones. Its shipowners had made substantial investments
in the railway companies serving their port and could thus quote the
through rates denied to Manchester. They had powerful allies in the canal
companies which extended the influence of Liverpool into the Midlands
along the Ellesmere and Chester canals and the Weaver Navigation.
They were determined to preserve their hard-won hinterland, to deny the
new artery of commerce any ocean shipping and to reduce it to the level
of a mere barge canal, subservient to their own world harbour. They
enjoyed the support of all the highly developed mercantile and financial
facilities of such a port, its large importing firms, its well established
produce markets, its extensive warehousing facilities, its great banks
adapted to the needs of the shipping trade and, above all, those close
links with the hinterland that enabled Liverpool to supply outward cargo
in coal to tramps and even to ship Lancashire goods by vessels which
had left Manchester forty-eight hours earlier.

The foreign trade of Liverpool was undoubtedly affected by the
competition of Manchester but had in fact reached a peak value in 1889,
five years before the opening of the canal. Its re-exports did not surpass
their level of 1889 until 1897, its exports sank in value below its imports
from 1891 and did not surpass the level of 1890 until 1904, while its
imports had declined from their peak proportion of 1875 and did not
exceed their level of 1891 until 1900. The receipts of the Mersey Docks
and Harbour Board did not surpass their level of 1892 until 1899,
declining between 1892 and 1897 at an average annual rate of 0·93 per
cent. From 1894 the volume of tonnage paying harbour rates only at
Liverpool and therefore using the canal inevitably expanded much faster
than the volume of tonnage paying full tonnage rates at Liverpool. The traffic
of the canal expanded its share of the tonnage entering the Mersey
continuously until 1901 but supplied only 15·9 per cent thereof in
1894–98 and 20·3 per cent in 1899–1913.

Liverpool had undertaken the competitive improvement of its port
facilities as soon as the construction of the canal began. The Mersey
Docks & Harbour Board was transformed into a veritable hive of
activity and enterprise: it began to increase the depth of its docks from
1886, to dredge away the Mersey bar from 1890, to undertake the
radical reconstruction of its northern docks and to construct the new
Canada Docks with a depth of $27\frac{1}{2}$ ft from 1891. The building of bigger
cargo steamers, especially by the White Star Line, effectively
demonstrated the difference between a deep-water port and a great inland
ditch, although it led to the transfer of that shipping line in 1907 to the

true deep-water port of Southampton. The Ship Canal never fulfilled its intended function of taking the largest steamers afloat: the average size of ocean steamships entering Manchester was only one-quarter that of steamers using the Suez Canal in 1894 and only one-third thereof in 1913. The speedier turn-round of vessels further enhanced the competitive advantages of Liverpool. That port intensified its opposition after the inauguration of the new waterway, as Alexandria had increased its hostility to Port Said after the opening of the Suez Canal. It appointed the first general manager of its docks in 1894 and extended its investment thereafter in lairages and in grain silos. Its close contacts with London ensured the wide diffusion of bitterly hostile reviews of the canal's progress[25] but failed in 1894 to bring the canal under the jurisdiction of the Railway Commissioners and the Act of 1888 so as to compel a reduction in its minimum toll and impair its competitive capacity. Liverpool did not reform the structure of its dock dues, but reduced their rate upon commodities imported to Manchester. It sought to inhibit any development at its expense of lighter traffic from Manchester in overseas produce and successfully imposed town dues upon Hungarian flour barged from Manchester to Liverpool importers.[26] It sought to preserve its own entrepot trade by reconsidering the idea of a 'lurry railway' for the transportation by rail of loaded lorries in competition with the canal[27] and even by boldly offering to buy the Bridgewater Canal from the Canal Company.[28] The Manchester & Liverpool Transport Company Ltd was registered on 12 April 1898 to develop the transhipment trade by barge between Liverpool and Manchester under an agreement of 19 October 1897 with the Canal Company.[29] That enterprise represented an imaginative effort by Liverpool interests to preserve the position of their port at the expense of the railways and disturbed the shareholders of the Canal Company as an apparent reversal of policy and change of front by their directors. The venture had great difficulty in raising the necessary capital and failed to halt the decline in barge traffic using the canal from its peak tonnage of 1898.

The trade of Liverpool was first affected in its exports rather than in its imports or in its re-exports. Its imports surpassed their value of 1893 in 1896 but its exports did not exceed their level of 1893 until 1900. Its exports declined in value between 1893 and 1898 by 10·4 per cent, or by 2·08 per cent per annum, and its share of the total exports of the country sank from 38·3 per cent to 32 per cent. That decline in the value of its exports was due not to the decline in prices but to the growth of direct shipments from Manchester. The decline in Liverpool's share of total imports from 24 per cent in 1893 to 23·5 per cent in 1898 amounted to only one-seventh of the decline in its share of total exports. The long-term decline in its share of exports from the peak of 41·2 per cent in 1889 to 32·4 per cent in 1913 reflected the comparative stagnation in textile shipments and was caused as much by the competition of other ports as by that of Manchester. The tonnage of shipping clearing Liverpool had been permanently exceeded since 1884 by that clearing London. Liverpool and Manchester were thus competing for a smaller share of the country's exports than the ports of the Mersey had enjoyed before the construction of the canal. As exports declined in their relative importance imports increased therein, so that Liverpool and Manchester increased their joint share of total imports from 23·98 per cent in 1894 to 27·4 per cent in 1913.

Table 7.1.   Trade of the ports of Manchester and Liverpool, 1894–1913

| | Value of the trade of Manchester | | | Proportion of trade of UK of Manchester and Liverpool | | | | | | Proportion of NRT paying harbour rates only at Liverpool |
| | | | | Imports | | Domestic exports | | Re-exports | | |
Year	Imports	Domestic exports	Re-exports	M	L	M	L	M	L	
1889–93 average					25·6		39·5		20·1	
1894	2,790,129	4,019,344	109,205	0·7	23·3	1·9	36·2	0·2	18·1	11·8
1895	4,220,792	8,836,999	165,935	1·0	22·9	3·9	34·6	0·3	20·9	15·9
1896	7,732,416	8,338,447	280,982	1·8	23·4	3·5	34·1	0·5	20·4	16·2
1897	8,311,878	7,408,430	267,102	1·8	22·6	3·2	32·9	0·5	22·5	17·3
1898	9,163,977	7,933,542	283,985	2·0	23·6	3·4	32·1	0·5	21·8	18·1
1899	10,714,369	8,609,516	324,067	2·2	22·7	3·3	30·7	0·5	24·7	18·7
1900	16,159,954	7,416,873	407,394	3·1	23·8	2·5	30·0	0·7	23·9	19·1
1901	14,901,401	7,929,148	330,970	2·9	25·2	2·8	32·2	0·5	23·2	18·0
1902	17,620,772	8,001,563	308,873	3·3	24·1	2·8	32·2	0·5	26·8	17·3
1903	20,279,255	8,856,100	440,965	3·8	23·8	3·1	32·9	0·7	27·2	18·6
1904	21,468,225	10,869,790	1,054,196	3·9	25·0	3·6	35·6	1·5	25·4	20·1
1905	23,290,796	11,956,514	1,653,348	4·1	24·7	3·6	35·7	2·1	26·5	19·8
1906	26,536,274	12,920,812	1,366,196	4·4	24·1	3·4	34·5	1·6	24·4	21·0
1907	30,402,229	15,754,398	1,072,229	4·7	24·8	3·7	33·6	1·2	25·0	21·1
1908	25,647,640	14,498,684	257,439	4·3	23·7	3·8	32·4	0·3	24·9	21·8
1909	28,943,444	14,315,329	249,296	4·6	23·8	3·8	33·2	0·3	26·4	21·9
1910	29,944,905	17,277,429	211,872	4·4	25·1	4·0	32·8	0·2	28·3	22·5
1911	32,502,954	21,375,265	265,254	4·8	23·5	4·7	32·9	0·3	26·5	22·7
1912	35,111,128	21,182,625	424,216	4·7	24·1	4·4	33·6	0·4	27·2	21·2
1913	35,290,606	20,630,339	378,107	4·6	22·8	4·0	32·4	0·3	23·0	21·2
1894–8 average				1·46	23·17	3·18	33·96	0·40	20·74	15·86
1894–1913 average				3·35	23·85	3·46	33·22	0·64	24·35	19·2

Source. Annual Statements of the Trade of the UK, 1894–1913.

Liverpool retained all its great produce markets and the vast bulk of its trades, including the import of raw cotton and the even more valuable export of piece goods. It sacrificed very little commerce to Manchester, and acquired new trades in the import of rubber and rice. The mere increment in the value of its imports between 1894 and 1913 amounted to almost treble the total imports of Manchester in 1913, while the

increment in the value of its exports was more than four times the value
of Manchester's exports in 1913. From 1902 the value of its exports
expanded faster than that of its imports: from 1906 the combined value
of its domestic exports and re-exports gave the port a sustained export
surplus for the first time since 1890. Above all, it developed in the re-
export trade the one branch of commerce which Manchester as an inland
port was least adapted to handle. Thus Liverpool increased its share of
the country's re-exports from 1899, raising it from 21·8 per cent in 1898
to 27·2 per cent in 1912 and even raising that share above its share of
total imports from 1899 until 1913. The borough expanded its population
in 1891–1901 faster than Manchester, as it had in 1801–71 and was to
do again in 1911–31. In the Edwardian era it enjoyed a great building
boom and made its university, through the establishment of schools of
tropical medicine in 1899 and of civic design in 1909, into 'the most vital
and progressive university of Great Britain, in the last half-generation'.[30]
The port remained until 1922 a larger exporter than London and became
thereafter a major beneficiary of the development of road transport and a
great industrial centre in inevitable response to Manchester's determined
bid to become a port.

   The failure of the Ship Canal speedily to attract the expected trade
made the foundation of a Manchester shipping line essential to ensure its
development and to avoid a fatal dependence upon roving tramps or the
liners of other ports. The necessity of 'the control of steamers by the
Company' had been recognised by Bythell from 1896,[31] especially after
the failure of Furness in 1895 to purchase the Beaver Line and the
defection of the lines sailing from Manchester to West Africa and China.
Two schemes were mooted in 1896 for a Manchester steamship
company, backed respectively by £1 million and by £600,000,[32] but
neither could secure the support of enough capital. Then Furness and
Alexander Henderson agreed to run a line of steamships to Canada in
summer and to North America in winter.[33] The direct trade of
Manchester with America had thitherto been carried on by Lamport &
Holt of Liverpool, who had established a service to Brazil in March
1894. That firm brought their vessels back from Brazil via New York on
a triangular route but, in deference to their fellow ship owners, they
refused to carry general cargo or quoted prohibitive rates for it. Their
steamers were not fast enough to secure the best class of provisions nor
large enough to carry cattle, and brought in very little toll to the Canal
Company because of the cost of the special tugs they needed.[34] The cattle
trade was the key to the development of the American trade, because
freights for general cargo from America to England ruled so low in the
most competitive market in the shipping world. In turn the American
trade was regarded as the key to the development of Mediterranean
trade, since a supply of American apples was essential to the successful
operation of the new Manchester fruit market and thus to the large-scale

import of oranges from the Mediterranean.[35] The cattle trade could not, however, develop before the necessary lairages were available. The delay of over two years in their completion was caused by difficulties in drainage and was then followed, after their opening on 26 August 1896, by a delay of eight months before the first cattle steamer arrived from New York on 26 April 1897.[36] The Canal Company was thus compelled by the opposition of the Liverpool importers to take the initiative in negotiations in Ottawa, London and Manchester for the establishment of a Manchester steamship line to America[37] and may well have benefited therein by the contemporary revival of imperial sentiment.

Manchester Liners Ltd was registered on 3 May 1898 but was faced by the same problem of the lack of capital as the Canal Company: it could raise only £350,000 of its nominal capital of £1 million, had to accept half of that in 5 per cent preference shares and then had to issue debentures in 1899. It could not secure a quotation on the stock exchange until 1915, since it had not raised the necessary half of its capital, even after a supplementary issue in 1902. It remained virtually a fief of Furness, who subscribed 35·8 per cent of the total capital, including 57 per cent of the ordinary shares, while Manchester supplied with difficulty £200,000, or 57 per cent thereof. The new company was granted by the government of Canada a subsidy of £8,000 per annum for three years in return for a fortnightly service to Montreal in summer and to St John, N.B., and Halifax, N.S., in winter, which was intended to develop the potential of the Manchester area as a centre of consumption of Canadian produce. It was also granted by the Canal Company free towage and exemption from ships' dues.[38] Seven new vessels designed to the dimensions of the canal and built in yards on the north-east coast were delivered only between December 1897 and February 1900. For the first year the line received only half the promised subsidy, because in the absence of a full complement of steamers its service had not been fully maintained, and it experienced 'exceptional difficulty' in collecting even that half.[39]

The establishment of Manchester Liners dismayed Liverpool as much as had the inauguration of the Ship Canal. The safe arrival of the *Manchester City* on 16 January 1899 proved that the canal could be used by a large steamer with a tonnage of 8,500, a length of 461 ft and a draught of 25 ft. Under the able management of R. B. Stoker (1859–1919) the line extended the import of American produce, the largest import trade of England and Liverpool, and the consumption thereof in the country's largest single centre of consumption. It developed the import of provisions and stimulated the formation of a wholesale provision trade association in Manchester to free the city from commercial dependence upon Liverpool. It extended its services successively to New Orleans during the cotton season from 1899,[46] to Philadelphia from 1901 with a subsidy from the Philadelphia & Reading

Railroad and in co-operation with the Leyland Shipping Company[41] and to Quebec from 1902 in association with the Great Northern Railway Company of Quebec, established in 1900. The new line proved much more successful in the carriage of imports than of exports and did not prevent the Lancashire cotton industry from losing the Canadian market to its competitors in the USA. It extended the import of the staples of grain, timber, wood pulp and cotton to Manchester and brought in 90 per cent of the cattle imported. The foreign cattle trade imported 23,307 head per annum on average between 1900 and 1910, and reached a peak in 1905 before the setback caused by the publication of Upton Sinclair's *The Jungle* in 1906. During its first decade the line handled almost one-tenth of the canal's traffic. Its service was less influential in reinvigorating the trade in green fruit than the inauguration by Elders & Fyffes of the import of bananas from Jamaica in 1902. It did not succeed in making Manchester a centre either of ship owning or of shipbuilding, in giving the new port a position in the world of shipping commensurate with the magnitude of its waterway and docks or in earning the desired dividends for the Canal Company. Nevertheless it paid an average annual dividend of 6 per cent for its first four years from 1899 to 1903, then paid no dividend from 1904 until 1912 during the prolonged depression in the freight market which succeeded the boom of the Boer war. The line linked free-trade Manchester to protectionist Canada and retained its Canadian subsidy until 1917 but considered it 'absolutely inadequate' in relation to the 'poor results' of its service.[42] It therefore began a service to the river Plate in 1904 in association with the Central Northern Railway of Argentina, so expanding far beyond its initial service to the St Lawrence. The new service was maintained for only four years against the fierce opposition of the River Plate conference and the lack of support from Manchester shippers before it was discontinued from 1 January 1908. In this connection the company had begun to employ firemen from West Africa who took up residence in Moss Side, the home of the Manchester Moors, and so endowed the city with the nucleus of a coloured community. The abandonment of the Plate venture enabled the line to double the frequency of its Montreal service from fortnightly to weekly and so to fulfil its original intention. From the year 1912–13 it resumed the payment of dividends, which soared during the Great War to heights not to be reattained until 1974. In R. B. Stoker it furnished the Manchester Chamber of Commerce in 1916 with its first protectionist president of the twentieth century.[43] Although it remained a small steamship company it brought into association with the port of Manchester Furness Withy & Co. Ltd, which was ultimately to absorb within its group the Prince Line, the Houlder Line and the Manchester Dry Docks Company Ltd.

The traffic of the canal increased much more slowly than had been anticipated by its supporters or feared by its opponents. It did not reach

Table 7.2.   Traffic of the Manchester Ship Canal, 1894–1913

			Proportion of imports		Proportion of			Gross receipts of the Canal Co. (£)
Year	Tonnage of exports	Tonnage of imports	Vol.	Value	Coast wise shipping	Runcorn ship- ping	Barge tonnage	
1894	299,407	386,751	56·4	40·3	63·5	76·3	25·9	97,901
1895	494,862	592,581	54·5	31·9	46·1	49·2	20·0	137,474
1896	565,100	944,558	62·6	47·3	39·0	39·1	17·3	182,330
1897	616,842	1,053,637	62·0	52·0	38·4	35·9	17·7	204,664
1898	995,880	1,222,125	55·1	52·7	43·9	31·3	14·6	236,225
1899	993,751	1,435,417	59·1	54·5	39·9	23·0	12·6	264,775
1900	1,106,464	1,678,379	60·3	67·4	36·0	21·3	9·0	290,830
1901	1,012,836	1,671,997	62·3	64·3	37·5	19·8	8·8	309,517
1902	1,161,597	1,975,751	63·0	68·0	35·7	20·5	8·2	358,491
1903	1,385,700	2,168,936	61·0	68·6	32·4	18·2	7·6	397,026
1904	1,438,463	2,179,541	60·2	64·3	31·2	19·7	7·7	418,043
1905	1,748,238	2,244,872	56·2	63·1	31·2	19·1	6·1	449,436
1906	1,951,326	2,489,915	56·1	65·0	30·8	17·3	5·5	498,837
1907	2,354,659	2,573,125	52·2	64·4	33·8	16·1	5·4	535,585
1908	1,820,747	2,497,218	57·8	63·5	30·8	18·7	5·8	506,975
1909	1,810,312	2,480,453	57·8	66·5	37·3	12·7	6·0	534,059
1910	1,990,444	2,627,626	56·9	63·1	39·2	12·9	6·5	555,735
1911	2,032,415	2,862,255	58·5	60·0	38·1	13·0	6·2	580,841
1912	2,025,445	2,996,246	59·7	61·9	37·1	8·7	6·0	605,179
1913	2,254,968	3,202,250	58·7	62·7	37·7	8·5	5·6	654,937
1894–8 average			58·1	44·8	43·6	46·4	19·1	
1894–1913 average			58·5	59·1	37·3	24·1	10·1	

Source. Manchester Ship Canal Company, Statements of Account, 1894–1914; Annual Statements of Navigation and Shipping, 1894–1913.

the volume of 3 million tons forecast in 1885 for the first year of operation until its seventh year in 1900: nor did it reach the level of 4·4 million tons forecast for the second year of operation until its thirteenth year in 1906. The revenues of the Canal Company expanded even more slowly than the traffic of the canal, and did not reach the amount of £800,000 forecast in 1885 for the second year of operation until 1916, nor the amount of £1·5 million forecast for its seventh year until 1926. Traffic did not reach the volume of 9,650,000 tons forecast for the seventh year of operation until 1950. The company was so disappointed that it published no returns of traffiic for the first six months[44] and sought to attract custom by appointing traffic canvassers and by reducing tolls to established lines.[45] Traffic expanded continuously in volume until 1901, as did revenue until 1908. In 1897, however, the value of the total trade carried along the canal suffered its first recession, and the rate of growth of both traffic and revenue was sharply reduced. In response the company limited its monthly traffic returns simply to revenue receipts, on the pattern of railway companies,[46] and sought to raise funds by the appointment in 1896 of an advertising agent, by the issue of mortgage debentures from 1896, by the sale of chief rents from 1897, by the large-scale mortgage of its surplus lands from 1898 and by the sale in 1900 of the Duke's Dock in Liverpool.

The traffic of the canal was composed of barges, coasting vessels and ocean-going ships. Barges supplies 26 per cent of the tonnage of the waterway during its first year, 19 per cent during its first quinquennium 1894–98, and 10 per cent during its first twenty years, but were largely confined to the estuary section and proved relatively unremunerative. The coasting trade benefited by a 20 per cent reduction in toll from 1 July 1894 and during 1894 supplied 50·8 per cent of the tonnage entering Manchester and 81 per cent of that entering Runcorn. Its contribution to the shipping tonnage of the canal remained substantial, declining only from 43·6 per cent in 1894–98 to 35·2 per cent in 1899–1913. Its rate of expansion between 1894 and 1913 was, however, only half that of the ocean shipping using the canal. Runcorn remained the main destination of coasting vessels, which carried china clay from Cornwall for onward transmission via the Bridgewater Canal to Preston Brook and thence via the Trent and Mersey Canal to the Staffordshire potteries. Its traffic furnished 76 per cent of the canal's tonnage during 1894 but suffered increasing competition from the Weaver Navigation after the reorganisation of its Trust in 1895. Runcorn's traffic reached its peak tonnage in 1908, and its contribution to the canal's tonnage declined from 39 per cent in 1895–98 to 16·6 per cent in 1899–1913.

The Canal Company had neither the statutory powers nor the capital to attract trade to the new port of Manchester. It could not afford to compete for traffic with the railways on the Liverpool–Manchester route lest it should precipitate a rate-cutting war which it could not win, reduce tolls to an unremunerative level, sacrifice revenue essential for the expansion of its services and find it impossible ever again to raise tolls. Above all, it remained wholly dependent upon those same railways for the effective expansion of the hinterland of the port of Manchester. Thus it determined to avoid any such suicidal policy of establishing cheap carriage between Manchester and Liverpool upon the Ship Canal[47] and firmly maintained that its essential function was to facilitate the bringing of goods direct to Manchester without breaking bulk at Liverpool. It rejected all general appeals to charge lower rates as a means of attracting traffic.[48] The failure of the canal to reduce costs explains in part the lack of support from Manchester merchants. Those traders were exporters rather than importers, and included a substantial foreign contingent with a strictly pecuniary motivation. They lacked in general the corporate sense and the civic pride of the mercantile elite of Liverpool. They also had close business links with the railway companies as well as with Liverpool. They bore with patience the constant rebukes of Bythell for

their 'lethargy and lukewarmness' and for their incorrigible desire to
cheapen their carriage costs without changing their trading routines. The
limitations upon the company's freedom to reduce transport costs have,
however, been concealed by constant reliance upon the rhetoric of cost
reduction as the canal's reason for existence, by the traditional
association of water transport with low costs of carriage and by the
apologias of quasi-official spokesmen for the enterprise., The canal had in
fact accomplished its essential function of reducing rates between 1883
and 1894 and could not afford thereafter to do so. Thus it did not
produce results comparable to the achievement of the Anti-Corn Law
League and could not moderate the general rise in prices which began in
1896. The new waterway nevertheless remained a potential route for
commerce, a bridle upon both railway rates and shipping freights and a
guarantee against any return to the monopolistic position of 1872–82.

Manchester did not attract foreign or ocean shipping as did seaboard
ports and even had difficulty in retaining the loyalty of Mancheser
Liners. It failed to acquire a diversified export trade and so forced
departing vessels to load with ballast when the desired outward cargoes
were lacking. It neither attracted high-class freight nor acquired any
staple import trade other than those in lamp oil and bananas. The import
trade in bananas was retained for only nine years, from 1902 until 1911,
before it was captured by Garston. The import trade in oil began to tilt
the whole balance of Canal traffic westward from Salford to Stanlow.
Manchester failed to acquire as extensive a hinterland as that of
Liverpool. It supplied imported fruit, oil, and iron ore to the West Riding,
and timber, grain, fruit, oil and iron ore to the Midlands, which perhaps
benefited more than Lancashire by the increase in the competition for its
commerce between the four great estuaries of the kingdom. It never
became, or even seemed to be about to become, 'a second Liverpool'.[49] In
the total value of its trade the port of Manchester rose in status from the
sixteenth port of the realm in 1894 to the fourth in 1906. During the
twenty years from 1894 to 1913 it imported, however, only 3·35 per cent
of the total value of the imports of the UK, or one-seventh of the share of
Liverpool, exported only 3·46 per cent of the total value of British
exports, or one-tenth of the share of Liverpool, and handled only 0·64 per
cent of the value of British re-exports, or one thirty-eighth of the share of
Liverpool.

What may seem to require explanation is not the comparative failure
of the Ship Canal but the unquenchable vitality of the myth of its success.
In part the explanation may lie in an uncritical reliance upon a limited
range of committed sources and especially upon the work of Fletcher,
McConechy and Leech.[50] In part it may derive from the exaggeration of
the role of Manchester and of the cotton industry in the life of the nation
characteristic of the pre-war era and from the interpretation of the
Mancunian renaissance of the 1890s as a presumptive response to the

stimulus afforded by the opening of the canal. In part it may originate from a studied neglect of the bases of the commercial empire of Liverpool, from the use of a simple rank order of ports to inflate the importance of Manchester and from the difficulty in estimating even approximately either the economic or the social savings effected by the enterprise. The influence of technological monomania has tended to concentrate upon the heroic period of construction rather than upon that of operation and to equate the economic benefits of the enterprise with the magnitude of the engineering involved in the creation far inland of a man-made port. The hypnotic attraction of the means of transport and communication for many historians may have encouraged an implicit inflation of the actual economic achievement of the canal. The role of transport and communications has undoubtedly been of key importance in the history of a region with a frontier society, a relatively immobile population, an export-oriented industry and a peripheral cultural life. The successive improvement of the Mersey–Irwell axis by means of river navigation, road, canal and railway may have encouraged the automatic assumption that the Ship Canal was at least as effective a means of transport as the Bridgewater Canal or as the Liverpool–Manchester railway. For Manchester in particular the development of communications supplied essential compensation for the disadvantages of its geographical location and became the key to its historical development and to the evolution of its world outlook, so establishing the dominant tradition of thought within which the Ship Canal tended to be subsumed. The construction by private and civic enterprise of a non-strategic canal in independence of the State embodied a timely reaffirmation of the pacifist and voluntarist tradition of the Manchester school during the imperial renaissance of the 1890s. The upsurge of navalist sentiment during that decade manifested itself in Manchester in the distinctively humanitarian institution of Lifeboat Saturday, devised in 1891 by the textile magnate C. W. Macara. The tacit assumption of the commercial success of the canal may thus have been simply a ritualised gesture of faith in the values of the Manchester school and in the relevance of the philosophy of free trade.

The Manchester Ship Canal was an expensive luxury for an island power and for a region with a highly articulated structure of transport and communication. It was undoubtedly a high-cost canal and had required an investment in its construction of £430,000 per mile, in sharp contrast to the £4,000 per mile of the inland canals of England, to the £43,600 per mile of the railways of Britain, to the £185,000 per mile of the Suez Canal and to the £160,000 per mile of the Panama Canal. Manchester was saddled from 1894 with all the expenses of a first-class and old-established port but was restricted to the trade of a new and undeveloped one. The revenues of the Canal Company were limited in direct proportion to the traffic of the canal. They accrued mainly from tolls levied upon cargo, since ships paid no tax before 1901 and passenger traffic declined sharply after the first few months of operation, so that the Ship Canal Passenger Steamer Company Ltd, established in 1893, was forced to wind up its operations in October 1895. Even the revenues of the Bridgewater Canal declined, as traffic was diverted from 1895 to the Ship Canal, and sank by 28·6 per cent from an annual average of £61,636 in 1887–93 to one of £43,982 in 1894–98. Those receipts nevertheless supplied 25·6 per cent of total revenues in 1894–98 and were maintained at a high level by the continued carriage of coal and by the service performed from 1898 of linking the docks to the new factories in Trafford Park. Gross revenue proved more resilient than either shipping or cargo tonnage and suffered only one annual decline, in 1908, during the first twenty years of operation.

The ordinary shareholders in the Canal Company were nevertheless denied any material return for twenty-five years after they had sacrificed in the financial crisis of 1891 the right to receive interest during construction. The incapacity of the company to pay dividends on its ordinary shares was caused by the slow development of traffic, by the prior claims of the three-quarters of its capital supplied by preference shares and debentures and by Bythell's ascetic commitment to the development of port facilities out of income. The debenture interest was not even equalled by the gross income of the company until 1902 and was not paid in full out of revenue until 1907. The corporation continued to extend generous financial aid and permitted the company to fall into arrears on the interest due upon its debentures. An Act of 1904 accomplished a financial reconstitution of the diarchy: it cancelled £854,492, or 47 per cent, of the company's arrears of interest, funded the remaining £951,498 in the form of $3\frac{1}{2}$ per cent non-cumulative preference shares and authorised the corporation to accept such shares in satisfaction of all past and future arrears of interest. It also linked the fortunes of city and company together by making the original £5 million of debentures perpetual and reduced the interest due thereon by 29 per cent from $4\frac{1}{2}$ per cent to $3\frac{1}{5}$ per cent, or from £225,000 to £160,000. The corporation was thus enabled to end the levy of its Ship Canal rate and to ease the burden imposed on the ratepayers by 'Lancashire's white elephant'.[51] Ordinary dividends were the last to appear, and remained low in amount. They did not materialise until the Great War disrupted the established patterns of shipping and raised the revenues of the company by 52·5 per cent between 1914 and 1918. Not until Bythell had been unseated from the board did the ordinary shareholders receive a first dividend, for the year 1915, while Trafford Park Estates had begun the regular payment of such dividends from 1909 and Manchester Liners from 1912. The potential dividend of the Ship Canal had been estimated in the sober climate of 1885 at 5 per cent, which was not in fact reached until 1923–27 and not again thereafter until 1956. Over the sixty years from 1915 to 1974 the Canal Company paid to its ordinary shareholders an average annual dividend of only 4·5 per cent, while Trafford Park Estates paid one of 9·9 per cent and Manchester Liners one of 12·8 per cent. The social savings effected by the canal cannot, however, be measured by the dividends paid by the Canal Company, since its true returns were non-financial.

The trade of the waterway comprised mainly exports and imports, since re-exports enjoyed only a brief boom in 1904–07 under the stimulus of the new Australian connection and were limited to raw cotton and wool. Exports did not develop on the same pattern or to the same extent as imports. They were surpassed by imports in volume from 1894 and in value from 1897, so that Manchester acquired a permanent import surplus. Until 1899 exports expanded more rapidly in volume but more slowly in value than imports. They did not experience a gradual increase in value so much as a sharp increase therein during 1895 with the advent of piece-goods exports. Then they suffered a recession in 1896–97 and remained relatively stagnant after the 1898 boom in coal exports until 1902. The value attained by exports in 1895 was surpassed only in 1903, and their share of the total exports of the UK attained in 1895 was exceeded only in 1910. In 1899 they experienced their first recession in volume, while imports did not suffer such a recession until 1901. From 1899 exports expanded in volume more slowly than imports and so departed from the national trend of exports expanding faster than imports. The unit value of exports also sank below that of imports from 1900, so that the port of Manchester thereafter exported goods worth even less per ton than those it imported, and acquired a structure of trade resembling that of a colonial port. Unlike imports, its exports expanded faster in volume than in value as shipments of coal increased.

Manchester remained the market for England's chief export industry, but its shippers were firmly linked by mutual interest to the port of Liverpool and were even freed by the railways from dependence upon their nearest port by the grant of differential rates upon goods routed via London, Southampton or Hull. Thus the Ship Canal failed to tap the staple industries of the region and in particular the cotton industry, which was indeed becoming progressively less important in its contribution to the export trade. The direct exports of Manchester remained more limited in volume and range than its imports, being dominated by coal. They comprised much smaller parcels than the imports and were more liable to suffer from cyclical depression. They declined in volume below the level of the preceding year in five years out of the twenty between 1894 and 1913, while imports suffered such a recession only thrice. They declined in value below the level of the previous year in seven years during those two decades, while imports underwent such a recession only twice, in 1901 and 1908. The tonnage of exports reached in 1907 a pre-war peak which was not surpassed until 1949. The growth in traffic was thus

dominated by imports. After 1895 and 1898 the canal never experienced
an export-led boom, and the company was denied the revenues accruing
in toll from high-rated exports.

Coal exports languished for the first nine months of the canal's
existence, although an export station had been created at great expense at
Partington, within eight miles of the Lancashire coalfield. Only when
through rates were settled by the railway companies, first by the
Manchester Sheffield & Lincolnshire Railway in September 1894 and
then by the Midland Railway in November 1894, did the trade begin to
develop. The coalfields of south Yorkshire profited from the creation of a
shipping port thirty miles nearer than any other and became a main
contributor to the mineral traffic of the canal. During 1895 coal exports
increased by only 41 per cent, to the disappointment of the Canal
Company, because the Bridgewater Canal carried in 1894 four times as
much coal as the Ship Canal. The trade suffered keen competition from
Garston, with which Lancashire collieries had developed close links.
Lancashire coal had thitherto been consumed mainly within the shire and
was comparatively unknown in outside markets, so that it would not sell
for bunkering purposes and had to be passed off as 'Cardiff steam coal'
by tramps calling at Cardiff after loading in Manchester. The increased
export of coal depended upon the development of a larger import trade
carried in tramps requiring coal as a return cargo. During 1898 exports
increased under the influence of the strike in South Wales by 260,000
tons, or by 93·6 per cent, supplying 73·5 per cent of the increase in
export tonnage during the year: during 1907 they increased by 379,000
tons, or 35 per cent, as shipments of Yorkshire coal were captured from
the traffic-blocked eastern ports, and supplied 94 per cent of the
increment in export tonnage during the year, boosting export tonnage to
the highest level reached during the first fifty-five years of the canal's
history. In 1907 coal production in Lancashire and Cheshire reached its
all-time peak tonnage, and coal exports via the canal also reached their
all-time peak six years before the pre-war national peak of 1913,
although they supplied only 2·3 per cent of the total volume of British
coal exports. Coal exports had expanded faster than exports in general
since 1894 and had supplied 65·5 per cent of the total increment in export
tonnage betwen 1894 and 1907: in 1908 they declined sharply by 46 per
cent and thereafter remained relatively stable until 1914. From 1903 until
1914 they supplied more than half the total tonnage of exports. Their
value was so low that from 1900 the average unit value of exports sank
below that of imports. Coal paid less toll than any other commodity save
salt and earned the company revenue from a small toll levied upon a
large aggregate volume.

Salt provided another bulk export but was shipped in increasing
amounts only from 1899, although it had ben one of the first
commodities carried on the canal from the Weaver Navigation, with the

establishment of Saltport in 1892. Shipments along the Weaver had, however, suffered a sharp decline from their peak volume of 1881, and were carried to Liverpool by the barges of the Salt Union established in 1888, being delivered there at an inclusive price. Salt exports developed via the Ship Canal only after the Salt Union agreed in November 1895 to deliver salt f.o.b. ship at Manchester at the same price as at Liverpool. They expanded from 1896 and rose from the fourth largest export in 1895–98 to the third after coal and textiles in 1899. They increased faster than any other export and grew at an average annual rate of 51 per cent between 1895 and 1913, while shipments along the Weaver declined during the same period by almost 1 per cent per annum. Manchester rose in status from the eighth largest exporter of salt in 1895 to that of the third in 1896, and first surpassed Middlesbrough in the exceptional year of 1913, to rank second to Liverpool. Salt was not a very remunerative commodity, yielding only half the toll on coal, but proved a very useful cargo, enabling steamers to leave fully laden instead of partly laden and also supplying a ballast cargo.

In the export of cotton manufactures Manchester succeeded in capturing much more of the trade in yarn than of that in piece goods and in reducing the freight on yarn much more than that on piece goods, sharply cutting that on yarn shipped to the Continent by 38·5 per cent. In 1894 Manchester surpassed Hull in its volume of yarn exports and ranked second therein to Liverpool, handling 17 per cent of the total quantity exported from Britain and almost half the quantity exported from Liverpool. The trade had, however, been in slow decline since 1885 and lay largely outside the control of Liverpool, unlike the trade in piece goods. The export of cotton textiles was a much more valuable trade than that in yarn, being large, regular and increasing in volume, but was largely monopolised by the conference lines of Liverpool and Glasgow. Manchester could enter that trade only by attracting non-conference vessels or by persuading the conference lines to send vessels up the canal. Shipments of piece goods by the new route during 1894 were so restricted that they were discreetly recorded by the company under the uninformative heading of 'general cargo'. They developed only during 1895, when Manchester surpassed London, Southampton and Glasgow and rose in status from the fifth to the second port for the export of piece goods. The first attempt to link Manchester directly to its largest single overseas market was made in February 1894 when D. & C. MacIver tried to establish a Manchester and Liverpool Steamship Company to operate a line to Karachi and Bombay but failed for lack of capital. A second attempt made by Furness and some London ship owners in November 1894 proved more successful. The formation of the Manchester Bombay & General Navigation Company Ltd compelled the shipping lines of Liverpool and Glasgow for the first time to take the canal seriously.[52] The new line sought to abrogate the monopoly of the

Bombay piece-goods trade held by the four powerful members of the
Bombay conference, the Clan, City, Anchor and Hall lines. Bythell, a
former merchant of Bombay, secured the support of the Bombay Native
Merchants' Piece Goods Association, which had procured within a year
of its foundation in 1882 a reduction in net freight by 36·5 per cent and
which determined in October 1894 to play off Manchester against
Liverpool in order to obtain a new reduction. The Bombay conference,
however, bought off its potential competitor in return for a reputed
£11,000 and recouped itself by a reduction in the through rate by 10 per
cent rather than by the expected 20 per cent, agreeing also on 29
December 1894 to send three steamers a month to load in Manchester.[53]
Thus the new Manchester and Bombay company under Captain W. C.
Bacon was diverted from April 1895 from the Indian to the Canadian
trade.

Three of the four conference lines duly sent their vessels up to
Manchester between January and April 1895, but the Hall Line did so
only in October and only after strong representations from the Canal
Company. Those vessels carried mainly piece goods to Calcutta, Karachi
and Bombay, and created an export trade, swelled from July 1895 by the
direct shipment of piece goods to the Persian Gulf, first by the Bucknall
Line and then by Strick & Co. Manchester's exports expanded during the
exceptional year of 1895 more than its imports in volume and much
more in value. The company's hopes of developing the complementary
import of tea from India were reinforced by experimental shipments but
remained unfulfilled by the development of any regular trade therein. The
competition of London as the chief market for Oriental produce and as
the main destination for homeward-bound steamers from the East proved
far more effective than that of Liverpool in excluding the new port from
the import trade in the produce of Asia. Manchester could not hope to
succeed in entering the valuable tea trade in competition with London
where Liverpool had failed. The Canal Company had, however, missed
in 1894 an exceptional year in the export of cotton manufactures, as in
the import of raw cotton. Exports of piece goods to Bombay, which had
risen in volume by 30 per cent during 1894, declined in 1895 by 36 per
cent, and the conference became increasingly reluctant to send the
stipulated three steamers a month up to Manchester,[54] especially as the
export of piece goods from Liverpool declined in the same proportion as
they increased from Manchester. The restraining influence of the
Bombay importers nevertheless ensured that Manchester retained its new
direct trade to Bombay.

The successful entry into the Bombay trade encouraged efforts to
secure for the new port a share in the shipment of piece goods to China.
The China conference had emerged victorious from the *Mogul* case in
1891 as a more formidable oligopoly than ever under the leadership of
the Ocean Steam Ship Company: it declined to lower its rates but

capitulated to a request from the China shippers in Manchester, made on 20 November 1894, in order to avoid any recourse to non-conference lines and thereby any threat to established freight rates. The first Holt vessel loaded in Manchester rather than in Birkenhead in January 1895, and was followed in March by a large new steamer of the China Mutual Line, established in 1882. These vessels proved that the canal was perfectly navigable by steamers over 350 ft in length and could safely be used by vessels up to 410 ft in length, so refuting the misleading assertions of Liverpool shipowners. The China conference lines reduced freights by 16 per cent from May 1895, but their steamers would not carry a full load of piece goods from Manchester, ostensibly for fear of provoking retaliation by the shipping lines of London.[55] The growing use of the canal by Bombay and China steamers deprived the bye-carriers on the Bridgewater Canal of the bale and case goods traffic, sending them out of business and so reducing the revenue of that undertaking.[56] The China lines reduced their Manchester service in December 1895 to a single sailing as exports to China declined,[57] discontinued the service in mid-1896 and raised freights to their former level from November 1896. Manchester's share of the total volume of exports of piece goods from Britain declined from 12 per cent in 1895 to 9·6 per cent in 1898, or to one-sixth of the 60 per cent thereof expected in 1885. Thus the new port did not share in the fast-expanding trade with the Far East and paid a large quasi-rent or surtax in freights to Singapore, China and Japan. The China conference was publicly reproved before the British Association by a Manchester engineer[58] but retained the support of most of the China shippers of Manchester and especially of those with agencies of steamship lines at Eastern ports. It continued to carry American cotton goods at lower freights than English calico, and ended that discriminatory practice only in June 1902, when net freights to China were halved. Manchester remained excluded from the export of piece goods to Bengal, Burma, the Straits, the Dutch East Indies and the Cape, and was much less successful in capturing the export of cotton manufactures than in encroaching upon the import of raw cotton. Its shipments of textiles enjoyed the lowest coefficient of expansion of any of the major exports along the canal and expanded at one-sixth of the rate of export tonnage in general and at one-twelfth of the rate of the imports of raw cotton. Manchester's exports thereof between 1894 and 1913 were less than half the expected quantity and represented only 6·8 per cent of the total volume of exports of British cotton manufactures but supplied 13 per cent of the total volume of exports via the canal. Those exports developed in harmony with the national trend and reached their peak in 1913, when cotton manufactures supplied 24·1 per cent of the value of British exports, 41·6 per cent of the value of Liverpool's exports and 63·5 per cent of the value of Manchester's exports.

The export of machinery, like that of piece goods, was virtually a new trade inaugurated in 1895. It began in October 1894, when Brooks & Doxey, the textile engineers, of Gorton, chartered a vessel to load a full cargo of machinery and to sail direct to China, at little over half the conference rate. The successful departure of the *Rosary* in December 1894 compelled the China conference to halve its rates for machinery in order to prevent other ships coming to Manchester, and inspired efforts to secure Indian shipments of machinery for Manchester. The trade developed to a limited extent to Bombay and Shanghai and helped to equip the foreign competitors of Lancashire. Exports rose in 1898 to a level surpassed only in 1905 and reached a new peak in 1907–08, surpassed only in 1927. These shipments developed under the influence of the four engineers, S. R. Platt, C. J. Galloway, W. H. Bailey and W. J. Crossley, who served as directors of the Canal Company. They were, however, restricted by the established practice of machine makers in quoting the same price f.o.b. at all ports, so giving a buyer the choice of any port of shipment but depriving him of any advantage in shipping via Manchester. During the initial phase of expansion machinery exports increased in importance from fifth among Manchester's exports in 1896 to fourth in 1897 and, stimulated by Platt's offer of a rebate to shippers of machinery from Manchester, even temporarily displaced salt from its position in third place in 1898. They remained much more important for their value than for their volume, supplying in 1913 3·2 per cent of the tonnage of exports but 9·6 per cent of their value.

Imports were slow to develop, because of the initial lack of warehouses and of such specialised facilities as grain silos, cattle lairages, oil tanks and cold storage works, which were essential to attract their particular trades. The Canal Company lacked the dock land, the capital and perhaps even the spirit of enterprise necessary to provide such facilities. 'We had no idea that we should have to do almost everything for everybody in order to obtain traffic.'[59] Bythell proved at first reluctant to sink valuable capital in warehouses and preferred first open-air storage and then transit sheds to storage sheds proper. Under his guidance the company relied upon both the corporation and private enterprise to provide the necessary investment and hoped thereby to secure the establishment of facilities for both storage and processing. The corporation responded magnificently to the needs of the company, and constructed such essential ancillary establishments as a fruit sale room in 1894, a cold-air store in 1895, cattle lairages in 1896 and oil storage tanks in 1897. Salford corporation failed to follow the example set by Manchester, and left a void filled by private agency. The Manchester Ship Canal Warehousing Company Ltd (1895–1949) established multi-storeyed warehouses from 1896 and leased them to the Canal Company.

Imports experienced a distinct boom from 1898 after the completion of the port's basic terminal facilities, the inauguration of the Lancashire & Yorkshire rail link and the establishment of Manchester Liners. Under such encouragement imports rose to form 61·6 per cent of the volume of the canal's trade and 67 per cent of its value in 1900–03. They increased in value even faster than in volume, expanding between 1894 and 1913 at almost thrice the rate of exports. Manchester became more important as a port of import than as one of export, and ranked by 1903 as the fourth importing port but as the eighth exporting port of the realm. The import trade proved of great benefit, directly and indirectly, to the working classes and to their representative organisation, the CWS. The increase in imports extended employment rather than destroyed it, supplying foodstuffs as well as raw materials and creating a boom in employment in road and rail transport within Lancashire. The associated development of Manchester's function as a distributive centre was facilitated by the organisation of produce exchanges and trade associations and was actively encouraged by the CWS and by the local banks.[60] That trend reinforced the commercial position of the city within the north-west at the expense of Liverpool and Preston, the older capitals of Lancashire: it compensated Cottonpolis for the relative decline of its home trade in textiles and of its trade in domestic grain, fostering in their stead the development of the city as a regional metropolis.

During the first twenty years of the canal's operation imports supplied 58 per cent of traffic tonnage and 59 per cent of the value of its trade. A small group of commodities, timber, wood pulp, paper-making materials, grain, cotton, oil and iron ore furnished 56·4 per cent of the total volume of imports. Timber became, as had been expected, a most important element in traffic and represented the ideal cargo for the canal, being heavy and bulky in proportion to its value, requiring no elaborate wharfside installations for its storage and paying a good toll to the company. It supplied the largest volume of imports of any commodity from the opening of the canal, exceeded the imports of general cargo during 1896 and maintained its premier position until 1910, supplying material for the building industry of east Lancashire and for the manufacture of the packing cases used in the shipment of textiles. These imports came first from the Baltic and then from America, especially Canada, after the establishment of regular lines from the American ports and the completion of the lairages in 1896. They were brought first by sailing vessel to Runcorn and by lighter to Manchester and then, especially from 1897, by steamer direct to Manchester, so increasing the revenues of the company. The trade was essentially seasonal and supplied the bulk of cargo on the canal in summer, when traffic reached the peak level of its activity. It was encouraged by the company's grant of free wharfage until 1 April 1895, and brought Manchester into competition with Hull as well as with Liverpool. As a timber port Manchester rose from the position of the seventh largest importer in 1898 to that of the fourth in 1907, but its imports were dominated by the cheaper woods, while Liverpool experienced no difficulty in retaining the trade in the finer and more valuable varieties.[61] The trade had established itself on such a firm basis during the first summer of the canal's existence that it expanded thereafter more slowly than any other major import. Together with wood pulp and paper-making materials, timber supplied 29 per cent of the tonnage of imports during the canal's first five years and 24·7 per cent thereof during its first twenty years of operation. The timber trade was liable to fluctuate more than the grain trade, and was mainly responsible for the slight recession in imports in 1901, but provided a solid foundation for Manchester's Canadian connection.

Imports of grain proved slow to develop before 1896 because of the absence of storage space, the failure of successive attempts to form companies for the construction of grain silos and the lack of support from Manchester merchants as well as from Liverpool merchants and millers. The new port had no grain merchants accustomed to buy full cargoes of grain abroad and to distribute them to millers. Its small buyers, whether merchants or millers, proved reluctant either to buy full cargoes or to combine in order to import cargoes jointly. Grain imports were thus restricted during 1894 to oats from the Baltic and during 1895 to maize feed grains for horses and cattle while Liverpool retained the much more valuable import trade in food grains for human consumption. The arrival of the first cargo of Hungarian flour from Fiume in February 1895 marked a first encroachment on the monopoly of the Liverpool millers. In April 1895 corn merchants and millers agreed to arrange for direct imports to Manchester from the Argentine and the USA. The arrival by sailing vessel of the first cargo of wheat from California in May 1895, discharged at Runcorn and barged up to Manchester, encouraged the Mersey Docks & Harbour Board to decide on 13 June to lower its charges on wheat by 25 per cent, so as to force the Canal Company to make further concessions. During 1896 grain imports were developed by Liverpool grain merchants and were carried as ballast in cotton ships during the cotton season. They doubled in volume and assumed the third place amongst imports after timber and wood pulp, so creating an acute blockage at the docks because of the lack of storage space and of rail connections.

The Manchester Ship Canal Warehousing Company filled the gap left by the defection of Salford corporation and agreed on 28 July 1897 to erect an elevator on Trafford Wharf with a capacity of 43,000 tons, or the equivalent of half the imports of 1896. An immense ten-storeyed structure was built at a total cost of £89,000 on the American pattern and according to the plans of John S. Metcalf, of Chicago, 'the cleverest elevator engineer in America'.[62] The building of the largest elevator in Europe took twice as long to complete as had been estimated, because its foundations had to be sunk much deeper than had been expected. It was first used on 4 July 1898 and immediately began to return in rent to its proprietors $4\frac{3}{4}$ per cent on its cost and to benefit the local milling trade.

During 1898 grain imports rose in volume by 50·7 per cent to exceed 10 per cent of the total tonnage of imports, to take second place to timber and to increase the liner traffic of the canal, since freight by chartered steamers generally remained too dear. In response to the competition of Manchester, Liverpool built its own new silo granaries, quoted cheaper freights for grain from New York than were available to any other British port and so remained the premier port for imports of grain until 1921, maintaining its extensive milling industry in full employment. The volume of grain imports to Manchester surpassed those of timber in 1910 and retained their primacy in tonnage until 1934. They expanded much more rapidly than those of flour but furnished in 1894–1913 only 3·4 per cent of the total volume of imports of grain into the country and only 5·5 per cent thereof in 1913, so that the first elevator did not require a companion until 1915.

Imports of raw cotton were more valuable than those of grain and had been expected to provide a major contribution to traffic, since Manchester had 80 per cent of the spindles of the cotton industry within a radius of twelve miles and thus lay within carting distance of the consumers of the bulk of the cotton imported. The first direct import of cotton from Galveston to Manchester on 15 January 1894 posed no threat to Liverpool's monopoly of the cotton market, although the through rates on cotton from the Manchester docks were one-third less than those via Liverpool. The estimated proportion of cotton imports expected by the canal had, however, been revised downwards in 1891 from 74 per cent to 44 per cent. The estimated saving on such direct imports was revised downwards in 1894 from the £500,000 estimated in 1885 to £150,000, or 30 per cent of the cost via Liverpool instead of the anticipated 50 per cent: such a saving to employers was still equivalent to a 5 per cent reduction in wages.[63] Manchester, however, had no cotton importers, no market for cotton, and especially no futures market, and no warehouses for its storage. Liverpool enjoyed all the advantages of an old-established world market, reinforced by the reforms of 1883. The shipowners and shippers of New Orleans and Galveston were closely linked to the city by ties of mutual interest and were strongly prejudiced against the new route, preferring to ship in bulk and at Liverpool rates and demanding higher freights on small consignments for Manchester. The cotton importers of Liverpool feared a boycott of their stocks by the buying brokers if they shipped any cotton to Manchester for sale. The efforts of the Canal Company to persuade the reinvigorated Liverpool Cotton Association to permit the storage of cotton in Manchester and to make the two cities into one market[64] were doomed to failure. The close links between the spinning firms of Lancashire and the brokers of Liverpool could not be easily broken, being based upon old-established connections, family ties, the extension of credit and the investment of capital during the 1880s in limited liability spinning companies. Spinners

were reluctant to by-pass Liverpool and to buy direct in the USA. Their
weekly visit to Liverpool was sanctioned by a tradition of over fifty
years, and remained of great economic value to small spinners because of
the wide range of choice available in the world's largest market for cotton: it
was also an enjoyable social occasion, especially when combined with a
weekend excursion to the Isle of Man. Their dependence upon Liverpool
was reinforced by the long decline in cotton prices, which amounted to
43 per cent between 1890 and 1895 and encouraged spinners to reduce
their stocks, to avoid making large purchases, to buy only when they
needed raw material and thus to increase their reliance upon the
Liverpool market and its warehousing facilities. Thus the lucrative cotton
trade was not transferred to the canal, and the Canal Company was
denied the large revenue anticipated by the original promoters of the
enterprise.

The new port opened at the tail end of the cotton season of 1893–94
and thus could not begin to divert the main crop from its traditional
market. The Spinners' Federation delayed for six months until the
opening of the next season before asking the Liverpool Cotton
Association to include Manchester on equal terms in the scope of its
operations. The refusal of the Association to recognise the new port on
24 September 1894 was indeed followed by the retaliatory establishment
of 6 November of a Manchester Cotton Association as a rival to the
Liverpool organisation. The new association was, however, joined by
firms owning only 33 per cent of the industry's spindles and remained
hampered by the absence of support for the establishment of a spot
market in Manchester, by the lack of capital, by the slow subscription of
its shares and by the absence of any local importing company and
shipping company to buttress its operations. The creation of two
duplicate markets forty miles apart for the same commodity was as vast
and uneconomical a task as the construction of the canal itself or the
creation of two separate shipping fleets. The large crop of 10 million
bales in 1894–95 offered the prospect of a golden harvest which was
reaped by Liverpool rather than by its rival. In both 1894 and 1895 the
Bridgewater Canal carried much more cotton from Liverpool to
Manchester than the Ship Canal.

The announcement by the Canal Company of a discount of 10 per
cent upon all cotton landed at Manchester during the 1895–96 season[65]
evoked a prompt response from Liverpool. Its shipping lines informed
spinners that whatever the cost via Manchester they would lay down
cotton at the mills at the same price. The Mersey Docks & Harbour
Board reduced the dock dues on cotton by 42 per cent in 1895 and
1896,[66] and the railways reduced the rate on cotton carried to
Manchester by 10 per cent, so making direct import even less economic
than before. Then a great advance in the price of cotton, by 45 per cent
between February and September 1895 in anticipation of a small crop,

discouraged spinners from importing at dearer prices than they could buy in Liverpool and encouraged them rather to buy on the spot in Liverpool.[67] The short crop also caused an almost unprecedented collapse in the American freight market and reduced exports to Liverpool by some 37 per cent during 1895, forcing Bythell to conclude that a Manchester shipping company was essential to secure the cotton trade.[68] Egyptian cotton had, however, been successfully imported from Alexandria by the Prince Line since 1894 against the determined opposition of the Moss Line of Liverpool and accounted for the whole of the increment in cotton imports to Manchester during 1895, when imports via the canal almost doubled in bulk and supplied the new port with what remained for almost sixty years until 1952 its most valuable single import. From 1896–97 the Canal Company abandoned its reliance upon American charterers, chartered steamers at its own risk from the cotton ports of the USA and succeeded in developing the imports of American cotton, which first surpassed those of Egyptian cotton during 1896. Manchester had been the fourth cotton port in 1894 but rose to be the third in 1895, surpassing London in the volume of its imports, and became the second in 1896, when it surpassed Hull. Cotton became the fourth largest import of Manchester in 1896 and the third after timber and grain in 1898. The volume of direct imports increased in harmony with the general flow of cotton imports to the UK and reached an all-time peak in 1912, when cotton supplied 7·7 per cent of the volume of imports to Manchester but 43·4 per cent of their value. Manchester developed a small re-export trade from 1904 but could never rival Liverpool, whose standards remained the basis of all European transactions in cotton until 1923. During the twenty years 1894–1913 the canal handled 15·18 per cent of the total volume of cotton imports into England – only one-third of the anticipated volume. Its share of Egyptian cotton, imported for the medium–fine trade of Bolton, increased from one-third of total consumption in 1897 to one-half in 1900 and remained much higher than its share of American cotton imports, enhancing the local interest in the maintenance of the occupation of Egypt and in the reclamation of the Sudan for the cause of 'commerce and civilisation'.

Oil became the sixth largest import of the canal from 1898. The oil trade was relatively new but had been pursued by the company without avail for almost three years: it was conducted on a very small scale and confined to the case trade until the establishment of oil tanks. The first attempt in 1895 to establish a local oil storage company failed for lack of capital, and both Russian and American oil companies declined at first to erect their own tanks and to use Manchester as a centre for distribution.[69] The contract concluded by the Standard Oil Company in August 1895 with Lamport & Holt to ship 12,000 tons in twelve months at three-weekly intervals placed the trade upon a firm footing. The arrival in October 1895 of the first shipment of oil in barrels direct from New York

for the Anglo-American Oil Company, the English subsidiary of
Standard Oil,[20] encouraged small independent firms to conclude on 4
September 1896 and 21 May 1897 the first agreements for the
construction of oil tanks, of which four were completed by August 1898.
The real expansion of the trade began with the admission to the canal of
oil tankers under regulations approved by the board of directors on 16
July 1897,[71] restricting them for reasons of safety to the section below
the Mode Wheel locks. The corporation of Manchester brought up the
first tanker in July 1897 to the oil gas depot at Mode Wheel, where it had
erected its own tanks. The first oil tanker from Batum arrived in
September 1897, so opening up another source of supply. The new trade
expanded rapidly: the volume of cask oil imported was exceeded in 1897
by the volume imported in tankers and continued to expand, though at a
slower rate than that of bulk oil. Between 1895 and 1913 imports of oil
expanded faster than any other major import, rising seven times as fast
as imports in general and ten times as fast as the imports of timber and
wood pulp. In the import of petroleum Manchester rose from the position
of the seventh port of the realm in 1896 to that of fifth in 1897, third in
1898 and second after London in 1899, when the volume of its imports
of lamp oil first surpassed those of Liverpool – which, however, was not
exceeded in the value of its petroleum imports until 1907 and preserved
unchallenged its vast import trade in palm oil from West Africa. By 1906
imports were running at double the storage capacity available and the
canal had acquired a firm hold on a trade which was as remunerative as
that in timber. From 1911 oil ranked next to cotton as the second most
valuable import via the canal. From 1934 it displaced grain as the source
of the largest tonnage of imports. The real development of the oil trade
took place at the western end of the waterway, where the first oil dock
was built at Stanlow in 1916–22 and the five-mile Eastham–Stanlow
section was deepened in 1927 below the depth of the remaining thirty
miles of the canal. Not until 1952 did oil imports surpass in value those
of raw cotton and so assume primacy in the import trade.

The construction of the canal altered the pattern of land use in the
flood plain of the Mersey and Irwell. It drained much moss land and
reduced the severity of the floods to which Salford, Flixton and
Warrington had thitherto been liable. It also raised the potential value of
agricultural land alongside the waterway by making it available for
industrial use and enhanced the Canal Company's expectations of
revenue from what was less a canal than an elongated harbour or dock
thirty-five miles in length. New units of local government were created
between Eccles and Runcorn, and future-oriented town planners
envisaged the emergence of a 'city region' or urban province of
'Lancaston' extending from the Mersey to the Pennines and comparable
to Greater London.[72] Manchester and Liverpool nevertheless remained
separated by the extensive moss land east of Warrington and by the

broad belt of loamy soil to the west. The growth of industrial sites and
the development of flanking wharves along the deep-water frontage of the
canal proved slow before the petro-chemical boom of the 1950s. Such a
pace of development was not necessarily unfortunate, since the canal was
to repel middle-class residents from its banks and was to serve as a
vehicle of social segregation as the canalside towns from Ellesmere Port
to Irlam became purely working-class communities. At Irlam the CWS
established a soap works in 1894 but increased its output markedly only
from 1907 and did not begin to manufacture margarine until 1917. Near
by the Partington Steel and Iron Company, a subsidiary of Pearson &
Knowles of Warrington, opened a new works in 1914 close to a
convenient supply of coal and ore. Warrington was by-passed by the
canal, as it had been by the Bridgewater Canal, and became more
isolated than ever. Its corporation waged a perpetual feud with the Canal
Company but failed to secure the facilities deemed essential to the
prosperity of its commercial community, especially a dock. Its
population nevertheless increased between 1891 and 1901 by 16·3 per
cent, or twice as fast as that of Manchester. The chemical industry of the
lower Mersey for long made no contribution to the traffic of the canal:
chemical exports did not develop upon any scale until 1903, nor chemical
imports until 1913. Saltport failed to fulfil the expectations of its founders
and developed neither as a timber port nor as a salt port. Ellesmere Port
declined in population between 1891 and 1901, like Widnes and Irlam, as
it lost the navvies engaged in the construction of the canal. It nevertheless
acquired a new function in addition to its role as a canal port and began
gradually to develop its manufacturing capacity, especially in the iron
and steel industry established in 1884, so prospering at the expense of
Eastham.

The main development of industry took place at the eastern end of the
canal, where the influence of the old Catholic family of the de Traffords
was undermined. Trafford Park was transformed into a virtual island,
bounded by the Bridgewater Canal to the south and by the wide bend of
the Ship Canal to the north. The disposition of that estate remained a
matter of debate for three and a half years from 1 February 1893, when
Manchester corporation established a special committee to consider its
acquisition. The 1,200 acres had acquired a high potential value because
of the proximity of the canal but could provide an ideal public park for a
swelling population in dire need of recreational space. If the park were
not so preserved it would be rapidly built upon and dedicated to
manufacturing pursuits. Thus it would pollute the purest atmosphere in
the district with the 'incense of industry' and, from its strategic position
to windward, would deepen the 'devil's darkness' beclouding Manchester.
In the final decision upon its fate the pecuniary calculus triumphed over
social considerations. The corporation was heavily committed in other
directions and was not prepared to pay more than £260,000, so deciding

on 3 October 1894 against the purchase. The park would undoubtedly
have been an invaluable asset to either the Canal Company or the
railway companies but was sold for £360,000 to the company promoter
E. T. Hooley, who floated Trafford Park Estates Ltd on 17 August 1896
and resold it the park for £650,000 in 'one of the biggest and the most
profitable deals I ever did'.[73] The new company recruited as its general
manager Marshall Stevens (1852–1936), who had been the manager of
the Canal Company since 1885 and who became, with Bythell and
Stoker, one of the co-founders of the prosperity of the port of
Manchester. Stevens determined to develop the area as an industrial
estate and especially as a site for new firms and new factories without
any of the financial and family ties to Liverpool importers, brokers and
exporters of the older industrialists. Thus Trafford Park, like Manchester
Liners, was intended to provide the canal with the traffic denied to it by
established interests and was not developed as a site for a racecourse, a
villa estate or 'a Greater Hyde Park for Greater Manchester'.[74] It became
the first industrial estate in Europe, but was not dedicated wholly to
manufacturing pursuits, since it included a model housing estate laid out
by Trafford Park Dwellings Ltd. Stevens survived the bankruptcy of
Hooley in 1898 and reached agreement with the Canal Company on 28
October 1898 for the construction of a railway connection to the docks
and for the levy of a very low rate of sixpence per ton, which extended
the advantage of a dockside site throughout the whole park and remained
unchanged until 1950.[75] For the provision of essential services to this
extensive fief of the industrial age he encouraged the establishment of a
number of associated companies, including the Trafford Brick Company
Ltd (1897–1900), the Grain Elevator Estate Ltd (1899), Trafford Park
Dwellings Ltd (1899), Trafford Power & Light Supply Ltd (1899–1920)
and the West Manchester Light Railways Company (1899–1904), which
became in 1905 the Trafford Park Railway Company.

The park developed so slowly that Trafford Park Estates spent more
than it earned from 1898 until 1906 and resorted to financial speculation,
purchasing the Manchester Racecourse in 1899 in anticipation of the
Canal Company, which required the land for the construction of its large
new dock. The park did not become a centre of the cycle and rubber
trade, as intended by Hooley, nor of the patent fuel industry, as intended
by Stevens and the Manchester Patent Fuel Works Ltd (1897–1909).
Nor did it attract the flour milling industry before 1903. It rather became
the home of heavy industry and especially of electrical engineering. Its
development inaugurated a shift of the industrial centre of gravity from
the north-east to the rural south-west of the city and ushered in a new
industrial era in the history of Manchester in succession to the
commercial era of 1820–1900. Indirectly it helped to reduce the
importance of the cotton trade in the industrial life of Cottonopolis, since
no cotton mills, no cotton spinner and no cotton manufacturers were

attracted to 'Traffordville'.[76] American influence in Manchester was
notably extended through the establishment of British affiliates of
American concerns, the building of large factories by large firms, the
introduction of American techniques of building, manufacture and
industrial training, the adoption of a grid pattern for roads and the import
of the American custom of numbering avenues. The British
Westinghouse Electric Company was established in 1899 and built at
high speed a huge machine shop, modelled on American lines and
equipped with gigantic machine tools at a total cost of £1·7 million. The
firm employed American foremen, retrained English engineers at
Pittsburgh and became the largest employer in the park but suffered from
a high turnover of labour, from the failure of British railways to adopt
electrification on the American pattern and from the absence of any
extensive demand for electric motors in the textile industry. As a financial
venture it proved disastrous and paid no dividend to its ordinary
shareholders until 1919, after its reorganisation as Metropolitan-Vickers
Electrical Company. In contrast Trafford Park Estates paid a first
dividend on its ordinary shares for the year 1909 and passed increasingly
into the ownership of Rothschild's.

The eastern terminal of the canal lay largely outside the limits of
Manchester, because Salford controlled the north bank of the Irwell and
had declined in 1889 to amalgamate with its neighbour. The new county
borough of Salford became the site of the main terminal docks, with
twice the length of quay of Pomona Docks and with the only suitable
docks for ocean-going vessels, and would have been even more important
if the projected Ordsall docks had been constructed. The corporation of
Salford had, however, turned hostile to the great enterprise as it became
Mancunianised, and its finance committee had even resolved on 31 May
1889 to secure a refund of its contribution to the initial legal expenses.
Salford was undoubtedly concerned at its lack of control over a major
new influence upon the livelihood of its citizens, and was offended by its
calculated exclusion from the loans extended to the company in 1891 and
1893 and by the consequent denial of any representation upon the board
of directors. It became alarmed by the threatened impounding of the
polluted waters of the Irwell by the locks at Mode Wheel and by the
consequent danger to the health of its inhabitants. It also feared
competition with its cattle market from the Foreign Animals Wharf at
Mode Wheel sanctioned in 1893 by the Board of Agriculture, which
rejected Salford's scheme for such a wharf on its side of the canal at
Weaste. The borough nevertheless became the main recipient of the rates
paid by the company and increased them substantially in 1895, 1896 and
1901, so increasing its ratable value faster than Manchester during the
1890s. On two occasions the company sought financial aid from Salford.
In 1896 Salford decided to erect a large grain silo at a cost of £120,000[77]
but encountered much opposition from the Labour Party and abandoned

the scheme in May 1897. In 1899 Salford was asked by the company to
extend a ten-year interest-free loan of £250,000 for the construction of
transit sheds in its docks but declined, accusing the company of having in
the past favoured Manchester at its expense. The division of function
between the two cities gave Salford the docks, the dock population and
their low-rated housing but denied it the high-rated industrial estate of
Trafford Park. The town acquired a new focus for its road system and
became more than ever a through route as traffic to and from the docks
increased the congestion in its streets. The rapid building-up of south-east
Salford from Ordsall to Weaste took place during the two decades after
the beginning of the construction of the canal. In the salient between
Pomona and Salford docks Ordsall Hall, restored in 1896–97, became
closely encircled by working-class housing as no other country house in
the realm was. The district acquired the stigmata of a proletarian ghetto,
despite its inclusion of a public park and a square of model three-
storeyed artisans' dwellings laid out under an Act of 1900. The large-
scale immigration of Irish as dock workers supplied the social hierarchy
of the whole quarter south of the Liverpool–Manchester railway with a
new lower stratum, strengthened the old Catholic tradition of the city and
helped to secure the return of Salford's first Catholic MP in Hilaire Belloc
(1906–10).

The unloading of cargo generated employment in a labour-intensive
industry which remained under the complete control of the Canal
Company as it was in no other port. The company wished to keep its
labour costs to the minimum in order to attract and retain traffic so that
it might offer ship owners a substantial rebate on labour charges and so
avoid making any irreversible concession regarding tolls or wharfage
rates. Its labour charges were under constant pressure from the
Manchester Steamship Lines Association, founded in 1894.[78] The
dockers were recruited from the ranks of ex-navvies released from work
on the canal, from skilled stevedores drawn from Glasgow, Barrow and
Liverpool and from local labourers, who asserted their right to
preferential employment over 'foreigners' within ten days of the opening
ceremony.[79] The company declined to accept such a demand and decided
to engage labour in future outside rather than inside the docks, to end
public access thereto by the erection of hoardings and barriers, and to
recruit its own police force. In February 1894 it successfully introduced
payment by piece work in an occupation previously accustomed to
payment by time rates.[80] The formation in 1895 of a local branch of the
Liverpool society of the National Union of Dock Labourers began the
slow process of the unionisation of unskilled labour in Salford. The union
profited by the solidarity of an isolated single-class community,
reinforced by a large Irish contingent, and unionised 300–400 of the 800
dockers by the time of the first strike (27 May–24 June 1895).[81] It failed
nevertheless to secure recognition by the company or the restriction of

employment to union members only. The company imported labourers from outside and declined an offer of arbitration made by the Manchester Joint Board of Conciliation. It agreed to the discreet wearing of the union badge and to the entry of union officials to the docks but declined a bold request made on 12 August 1895 by the Manchester and Salford Trades and Labour Council for direct representation upon its board by two directors.[82] It continued to recruit non-union labour, enlisted the aid of the National Free Labour Union established in 1893[83] and benefited from the intense competition for employment at the docks. The Salford dockers never became as militant as those of Liverpool, because their employment opportunities were more limited, and they secured the full recognition of their union only after the two-week strike of 1911.[84]

Under the influence of the Ship Canal Manchester experienced in the 1890s a distinct revival of economic activity and a building boom, which paved the way for the marked growth of population in the 1900s. A large inland town could not, however, be transformed into a maritime community simply by the construction of a canal and the legal constitution of a 'port of Manchester'. The city added to its economy a new and highly specialised sector, whose activities tended to be segregated from the daily life of the majority of its inhabitants. The population remained essentially insular in their way of life and in their world outlook. The influence of Mancunian liberalism was, however, weakened by the relative decline of the cotton industry and by the growth of the local influence of London. That transformation was accelerated by the professionalisation of education, the diffusion of the higher journalism, the development of the cult of history and the agitation for social reform. As the cotton industry ceased to expand Manchester extended its influence increasingly within Lancashire rather than within the wider world. It became one of the great 'tentacular cities' of the modern age not only through its commercial and financial functions but also through its distributive trades, its new electric tramways, its control and sale of water from Thirlmere and its expanding educational institutions. The city became more than ever the centre of a network of communications as well as of transport, and extended its distributive function from the sphere of commerce to that of culture, high and low. The successive establishment of the Royal Northern College of Music in 1893, of the Whitworth Park Art Gallery in 1896 and of the John Rylands Library in 1899, and the expansion of the Hallé Orchestra under the Wagnerian Richter (1897–1911) made the city in the eyes of Lancashire a Mecca of culture such as it had never been before. The extension of Mancunian influence served to sap the cultural vitality of many cotton towns. The new journalists of the *Manchester Guardian*, through their self-conscious cultivation of 'style', imported the superficies of the deferential aristocratic culture of southern England into a region proud of the blunt directness of its speech. The spread of a new historical consciousness began to erode the anti-historical essence of Manchesterdom and was reflected not only in the inauguration from 1893–94 of the teaching of economic and industrial history within the university and in the reorganisation from 1895 of the school of history by the Tory Tout but also in the formal celebration in 1896 of the jubilee of the repeal of the corn laws and in 1897 of the centenary of the Manchester Chamber of Commerce.

Social reformers helped to erode the traditional values of the community and to reorient its loyalties from liberalism to collectivism, from individualism to municipal socialism and from economic to non-economic aspirations. They found an expanding audience for their secular gospel of the healthy life within the City Beautiful and preached a crusade against the slum as both an environmental and a eugenic menace. Their rhetoric was imbued by an insidious hostility to modern industry, by a quasi-religious reverence for the arts and crafts and by a quest for a renewed sense of brotherhood with Nature in harmony with the agrarianism of the 1890s.[85] The surrender to a land company for industrial development of one of the city's very few parks diffused a widespread sense of shock and generated an intense debate over the impolicy of such a transaction, which was condemned as tantamount to 'municipal suicide'.[86] The reluctant sacrifice of Trafford Park to Mammon inspired first the corporation's decision in 1896 to secure the rebuilding of the Infirmary in the suburbs and the creation of gardens upon its site in Piccadilly and then the purchase in 1903 of the extensive Heaton Park. The reawakening of social conscience and of an interest in the condition-of-Manchester question also inspired the establishment in 1895 of the University Settlement in Ancoats, the refoundation in 1898 of Ordsall Hall as a kind of university settlement and the publication in 1904 of the first housing survey of the city.[87] The activity of such social reformers served only, in combination with the aesthetic movement of the 1890s, to enhance the traditional repellent image of Manchester, which still appeared to be 'the ugliest place on the earth', expressing 'only the worst qualities of our race' and dimly resembling a grimy, water-girt 'Venice in Hell'.[88]

Notes

1 Manchester Corporation, *Proceedings of Special Committees*, vol. 2 (1890–93), 27–8, 3 February 1891.
2 *Manchester Guardian*, 16 December 1891, 5 vii–viii; 13 February 1892, 9 iv–vi.
3 J. R. Galloway, 'The Municipalities of Manchester and Hamburg', *Transactions of the Manchester Statistical Society*, 8 December 1897, 61.
4 Manchester Ship Canal Company, *Board of Directors, Minutes* (hereafter cited as 'B.O.D.'), 115, 159, 20 July 1894.
8 *Manchester Guardian*, 19 August 1916, 6 i–ii, 9 i.

6   S. Lloyd, *England Needs Inland Steam Navigation* (London, Pickering, 1885, 89 pp.), 63. Id., *A National Canal between the Four Rivers a National Necessity* (London, Hogg, 1888, 64 pp.). *Manchester Guardian*, 20 March 1895, 8 vi, 'A Yorkshire Ship Canal'.

7   *The Bee. The Magazine of the Blackburn Technical School*, March 1891, 26–7, 'The Blackburn Ship Canal. An argument in three chapters'.

8   Manchester Ship Canal Company, *Traffic and Rates Committees, Minutes* (hereafter cited as 'T.R.C.'), 55, 1 February 1894; 65, 9 February 1894.

9   On 5 December 1893, 24 May and 8 June 1894, 11 January and 7 February 1895.

10 T.R.C., vol. 3, 253–4, 14 June 1894; vol. 4, 3–4, 21 June 1894; 16–24, 5 July 1894.

11 B.O.D., 10, 25 August 1896.

12 *Ibid.*, 88–97, 8 June 1894, J. K. Bythell's report of 30 May.

13 T.R.C., 14–15, 12 January 1894. B.O.D., 180, 19 October 1894.

14 B.O.D., 176, 19 October 1894.

15 Manchester Ship Canal Company, *Report of the Directors*, 26 February 1896, 4–9; 25 August 1896, 7–10.

16 B.O.D., 289, 16 July 1897.

17 T.R.C., vol. 3, 152, 5 April 1894; 244, 7 June 1894; vol. 4, 54, 2 August 1894.

18 B.O.D., 54–6, 31 January 1896; 105–7, 19 June 1896; 167–8, 4 December 1896.

19 F. E. Hyde, *Shipping Enterprise and Management, 1830–1939. Harrison's of Liverpool* (Liverpool University Press, 1967), 80, quoting T. & J. Harrison to Hoare Miller & Co., 7 February 1896.

20 B.O.D., 95, 8 June 1894.

21 *Ibid.*, 315, 8 October 1897.

22 The Manchester Ship Canal Pontoons and Dry Docks Company Ltd was established in 1891 and opened two docks in 1894 but paid no dividend to its ordinary shareholders until 1897, vainly seeking financial relief from the Ship Canal Company, and became the Manchester Dry Docks Company Ltd from 1906.

23 *Manchester Guardian*, 13 January 1931, 6 iii–v. Bacon became a director of the Canal Company in 1902 and the successor of J. K. Bythell as its chairman from 1916 to 1931.

24 *Manchester Guardian*, 11 October 1892, 8 ii.

25 *The Times*, 30 November 1894, 6 iii–iv, 9 v–vi; 9 January 1895, 4 iv–vi.

26 B.O.D., 198, 29 January 1897; 328–9, 16 November 1897; 409, July 1898.

27 *Manchester Guardian*, 23 October 1896, 7 vii.

28 B.O.D., 190, 15 January 1897.

29 *Ibid.*, 268–9, 18 June 1897; 321, 22 October 1897; 375, 11 March 1898; 419–20, 29 July 1898.

30 P. Geddes, *Cities in Evolution* (London, Williams, 1915), 275, 297.

31 B.O.D., 107, 19 June 1896.

32 *Ibid.*, 93, 8 May 1896.

33 *Ibid.*, 218, 26 February 1897.

34 T.R.C., 58, 2 August 1894. B.O.D., 300, 5 April 1895; 465, 22 November 1895.

35 B.O.D., 436, 25 October 1895.

36 *Manchester Guardian*, 27 April 1897, 9 vii.

37 B.O.D., 218, 26 February 1897; 262–3, 4 June; 315, 8 October; 332, 19 November; 338, 3 December; 342, 17 December; 359, 11 February 1898; 369–70, 25 February; 393, 6 May 1898. T. M. Young, *Manchester and the*

Atlantic Traffic (Manchester, Sherratt, 1902), reprinting seven articles from the *Manchester Guardian*, 24 July–20 August 1902.

38 B.O.D., 413–14, 15 July 1898.
39 Manchester Liners Ltd, *Minute Book* [of the Board of Directors], vol. I, 81, 7 October 1899; 115, 11 August 1900.
40 *Ibid.*, 77, 9 August 1899.
41 *Ibid.*, 110, 14 July 1900; 127, 17 November 1900.
42 *Ibid.*, 224, 25 April 1903; 242, 30 October 1903; vol. II, 196, 11 October 1917.
43 *Manchester Guardian*, 4 September 1919, 12 vi.
44 B.O.D., 48, 30 March 1894. T.R.C., 59, 2 August 1894.
45 T.R.C., vol. 3, 258–9, 14 June 1894; vol. 4, 56–7, 2 August 1894.
46 B.O.D., 181–2, 22 December 1896; 204, 12 February 1897.
47 Manchester Ship Canal Company, *Report of the Directors*, 24 August 1897, 16.
48 *The Manchester Ship Canal, and How to Make it Pay a Dividend. The 'Robert Jones' Scheme* (Manchester, Sherratt, 1902, 24 pp.).
49 B.O.D., 97, 8 June 1894, J. K. Bythell.
50 A. W. Fletcher, 'The economic results of the Ship Canal on Manchester and the surrounding district', *Transactions of the Manchester Statistical Society*, 10 February 1897, 83–108; July 1899, 155–69. J. S. McConechy, 'The economic value of the Ship Canal to Manchester and district', *ibid.*, 13 November 1912, 2–126, with fifty-four tables and eighteen charts. B. T. Leech, *History of the Manchester Ship Canal from its Inception to its Completion, with Personal Reminiscences* (Manchester, Sherratt, 1907, two vols.), which was savagely reviewed in a first leader, probably written by an infuriated C. P. Scott, in the *Manchester Guardian*, 7 September 1907, 8 i–iii, and was excoriated for its 'disorder, diffuseness, repetition and triviality' and for 'its literary defects, which are defects of design, selection of material, and construction, as well as of expression'.
51 *Manchester City News*, 13 July 1896, 4 vi, 'Manchester's advance'.
52 B.O.D., 178, 19 October 1894; 195, 16 November; 210, 7 December 1894.
53 T.R.C., 65–7, 4 January 1895. B.O.D., 233–6, 18 January 1895.
54 B.O.D., 12, 20 December 1895; 41, 17 January 1896.
55 F. E. Hyde and J. R. Harris, *Blue Funnel. A History of Alfred Holt and Company of Liverpool* (Liverpool University Press, 1956), 107–9.
56 B.O.D., 439, 25 October 1895.
57 *Ibid.*, 41, 17 January 1896.
58 J. R. Galloway, 'Shipping rings and the Manchester cotton trade', *Journal of the Manchester Geographical Society*, July 1898, 241–63.
59 Manchester Ship Canal Company, *Report of the Directors*, 16 February 1899, 6, J. K. Bythell.
60 *Manchester Guardian*, 5 February 1902, 10 ii–iii, 'Manchester banks and the Ship Canal. The financing of imports'.
61 J. M'Farlane, 'The port of Manchester: the influence of a great canal', *Geographical Journal*, November 1908, 496–503.
62 B.O.D., 245–6, 3 June 1897; 259–61, 4 June; 276–81, 2 July; 346–7, 31 December 1897. *The Engineer*, 7 October 1898, 354–6, 'American elevator on the Manchester Ship Canal'.
63 *Textile Manufacturer*, August 1890, 395; July 1894, 290; November 1894, 461, 472.
64 T.R.C., 136–7, 29 March 1894.
65 *Ibid.*, 85, 2 June 1895. B.O.D., 350, 21 June 1895.
66 *Textile Manufacturer*, September 1896, 321.
67 B.O.D., 414, 27 September 1895; 433–5, 25 October 1895.

68 *Ibid.*, 7, 20 December 1895.

69 *Ibid.*, 332, 24 May 1895; 350, 21 June 1895.

70 *Ibid.*, 412, 27 September 1895; 432, 25 October 1895.

71 *Ibid.*, 288–9, 16 July 1897.

72 P. Geddes, *Cities in Evolution* (1915), 31–2.

73 E. T. Hooley, *Hooley's Confessions* (London, Simpkin, 1925), 26–31.

74 *Manchester City News*, 8 April 1893, 4 v; 27 June 1896, 6 i–ii.

75 B.O.D., 274, 2 July 1897; 296, 13 August 1897; 455, 4 November 1898.

76 J. Dummelow, *1899–1949* (Manchester, Metropolitan-Vickers Electrical Co. Ltd, 1949), p. 7.

77 *B.O.D.*, 148, 23 October 1896; 173–4, 10 December 1896; 205–6, 12 February 1897.

78 Manchester Steamship Lines Association, *Minutes*, 16 February 1894–29 September 1897.

79 T.R.C., 7, 12 January 1894. *Manchester Guardian*, 16 January 1894, 5 viii, 'Manchester Ship Canal. Serious disturbance at Salford docks'.

80 T.R.C., 106, 1 March 1894.

81 B.O.D., 329, 24 May 1895; 343–6, 21 June 1895. *Manchester Guardian*, 13 June 1895, 8 iv–v; 15 June 1895, 8 vii–viii.

82 B.O.D., 389, 16 August 1895.

83 *Ibid.*, 431, 8 September 1898.

84 *Manchester Guardian*, 29 June 1911, 9 ii–iii; 10 July, 6 iii, 7 i–iii; 11 July, 5 iii, 8 ii.

85 C. Rowley, *Fifty Years of Work Without Wages (Laborare est Orare)* (London, Hodder, 1912), 47.

86 H. Philips, 'Open spaces for recreation in Manchester', *Transactions of the Manchester Statistical Society*, 9 December 1896, 60. A. W. Fletcher, 'On municipal trading in Manchester', *ibid.*, 20 March 1901, 105.

87 T. R. Marr, *Housing Conditions in Manchester and Salford. A Report Prepared for the Citizens' Association for the Improvement of the Unwholesome Dwellings and Surroundings of the People* (Manchester, Sherratt, 1904, 114 pp.).

88 George Moore, *Evelyn Innes* (London, Unwin, 1898), 122, Sir Owen Asher. T. C. Horsfall, 'The government of Manchester', *Transactions of the Manchester Statistical Society*, 13 November 1895, 6–7. Id., *An Ideal for Life in Manchester Realisable if —* (Manchester, Cornish, 1900), 8. *Manchester Guardian*, 24 October 1892, 8 v, William Morris, 'Town and country'. C. E. Montague, *A Hind Let Loose* (London, Methuen, 1910), 3.

The development of a tariff reform policy during Joseph Chamberlain's first campaign
May 1903–February 1904

Few dates of the Edwardian era are better remembered than 15 May 1903. On that day, in a speech at Birmingham, Joseph Chamberlain launched a campaign to widen the commodity base of Britain's import duties, partly for protection for its own sake and partly as a necessary prerequisite for granting preferential treatment to the colonies. Though there is no realistic way of quantifying the importance of any motivating factor in a decision to embark upon a programme of this kind, there can be no doubt that both political and economic motives weighed heavily in Chamberlain's mind, and since he saw his policy as the means of obtaining both his economic and his political objectives it matters little which of those objectives he regarded as paramount.[1] But, though the 'ends' of the policy might be both political and economic, the 'means' were not. As the campaign developed, the policy had to be formulated in more detail than had emerged from the Birmingham speech, and had to possess *economic* validity, since without this they would possess no political credibility. Where did the specific measures, the economic tools to bring about the tariff reformers' desires, come from? The many autobiographies, even Chamberlain's collected papers, give us little idea. Indeed, in Amery's *Life of Joseph Chamberlain*, the most detailed political biography of the period, the economic measures at the heart of the campaign emerge quite late, almost as a bolt from heaven, at Glasgow in October.[2]

It is the intention of this essay to argue that the detailed measures – and they really were not very detailed, nor were they considered so by the tariff reformers – emerged from the public debate that immediately surfaced in the wake of the Birmingham speech, and which dominated the columns of the press in the ensuing months. There is perhaps insufficent evidence to regard them as having *originated* in the debate, though it seems that way at times. But at least they were conditioned and moulded by the course of the debate into the form which they possessed by February 1904.

In the public controversy a conflict between policy objectives and policy measures, between 'ends' and 'means', was evident. Chamberlain hoped to win acceptance of his policy in terms of objectives, since these were the less controversial. His opponents would not – indeed, could not – let him; they sought constantly to illuminate the weaknesses contained in the specific measures which, they asserted, he would have to advocate. In the debate over measures Chamberlain was less convincing, and had to advocate a new methodology. The most significant event establishing a terminal date for the first campaign was not so much, as is commonly supposed, Chamberlain's departure on a Continental holiday after a particularly gruelling series of major speeches but the establishment of a new organisation, the Tariff Commission. Partly intended as a propagandist body, partly as an investigating committee of more noble purpose, the task of the commission was to bring new methodologies to bear in the formulation of policy, to enable the discussion to break out of a closed loop of controversy which revolved around imponderables. The commission's scientific task was to find answers; its propagandist task was to be *seen* to be finding answers.

I

In terms of its content the Birmingham speech did not formulate new proposals and policies. Chamberlain was content to start off his movement by appealing that the time had come to review thoroughly Britain's commercial arrangements and the place of the colonies in them.[3] Indeed, in a *literal* sense he did not so much advocate imperial preference as urge that people should *discuss* the issue in what later became known as the 'great inquiry'.[4] In this, people took him up immediately. Whatever backstage manoeuvring was going on, the immediate effect on the public was their bombardment by an unprecedented volume of tariff reform and free trade material. Speech-making was a primary weapon here – in the series of great speeches of summer 1903 the fiscal debate seldom took second place to the 1902 Education Act, and any such reversal of priorities was usually practised by second- rather than first-rank political figures. But it should be remembered that the biggest meetings reached directly only some 5,000 or 7,000 people, and much of this was preaching to the converted. The only contact of most people with the debate was through the press. Here not only were major speeches reported verbatim but there were also widespread reporting of minor speeches, even on a very local level, endless columns of editorial comment, and thousands of letters. And in a controversy with so many participants, dealing with economic issues and their political implications,

political issues and their economic implications, it was inevitable that
there was much confusion and uncertainty.

Chamberlain's aim as expressed in the Birmingham speech was
imperial unity in the face of a changing world order and the rise of new
economic super-powers. But he knew that such unity could be promoted
by means only of reciprocal preferences, since other methods (closer co-
operation in imperial defence, and the proposal of the 1890s for a 'Council
of Empire') had already been vetoed by the self-governing colonies at the
previous two colonial conferences.[5] Very quickly the free-traders began
to formulate possible schemes from the implications of Chamberlain's
generalised statements. Asquith was one of the first to suggest that the
plan involved taxation not only of imported food but also of imported
raw materials.[6] Furthermore, since only 20 per cent of Britain's food
imports and only 33 per cent of her raw-material imports came from the
colonies, British costs of production would be bound to rise even if
colonial products were allowed in free. A few days later Dilke hammered
this lesson home in the Commons' debate on fiscal policy, in the process
adding semi-manufactures to the list.[7]

Chamberlain was reluctant to concede on this issue. In the Commons
debate he again stressed that imperial preference was raised only as an
issue for discussion. He merely:

... called attention ... to the opportunity existing at the present time ... of
making preferential arrangements in the nature of a reciprocity treaty with our
colonies ... [and] to the fact that under our existing system we are helpless ... to
bring any influence to bear on foreign countries if they attack our colonies or if
they attack us in any manner which ... would seriously endanger our
industries.[8]

Though seeking to perpetuate his idea of the reality of any discussion,
Chamberlain did on this occasion admit that any step towards imperial
unity via preference had little room for manouevre. In the carefully hedged
climax of the Commons debate he remarked, 'Therefore we come to this:
if you are going to give a preference to the colonies – I do not say that
you are – you must put a tax on food.'[9]

Chamberlain had invited discussion: now he had admitted the
necessity, under his scheme, of taxing food. But further than this he had
said little, in spite of the *Times's* prediction that in the Commons debate
he would have a chance to develop his ideas 'with greater fullness and
precision'.[10] His critics, that newspaper announced, had misrepresented
him and made wild inferences about his intentions, to the extent that 'he
has been credited with the visionary idea of forcing some cast-iron
scheme of preferential tariffs upon all our colonies at once ... he has been
charged with plotting universal aggression upon the commercial world'.[11]
Chamberlain's statements in the Commons debate seemed to confirm
such remarks about misrepresentation. Indeed, in the first exchange he

had replied to Dilke's assertion that his plan was to tax food and raw materials with the words 'I must ask the right hon. gentleman not to quote me as committed to this, that, or any other proposition.'[12] But his subsequent remarks surely left the *Times* disappointed: after the Commons debate his plan still possessed neither 'fullness' nor 'precision'.

Chamberlain's reluctance to indulge in detail has been applauded by his official biographer, who sums up the situation thus: 'The Opposition had called for a detailed statement of the new policy. They hoped to hear a set of proposals which could be subjected to every kind of criticism. Chamberlain had no intention of falling into the trap.'[13] Indeed, the reluctance was understandable, and there was perhaps little else that Chamberlain, a self-confessed novice in economics, could do. But any hopes of the success of silence on this aspect were unreal. The campaign could not for long be conducted on the basis of extreme generalities. And the opposition were not likely to impose upon themselves the restrictions on the debate over details hoped for by Chamberlain.

By August Chamberlain had still gone no further than to admit the necessity of taxing food. In a published letter to Griffith–Boscawen, a tariff reform MP, he put on record that he thought taxation of raw materials would be unnecessary.[14] Free-traders, however, capitalised on the Asquith–Dilke argument that, in such a case, the scheme would rest on too narrow a base. The *Standard* published the views of John Charlton, a member of the Canadian House of Commons of thirty-one years' standing, who maintained that a preference on wheat alone would benefit directly only the north-west provinces of Canada. Ontario in particular would gain little. Charlton felt that 'it would be as well for British politicians to understand that preference confined to one or two articles would not be likely to command a favourable response in Canada'.[15] To be fair to Chamberlain, from 28 May onwards he had by implication not confined his remarks to wheat alone, but nevertheless free-traders were delighted when Charlton elaborated a desirable list from the Canadian point of view – all grainstuffs, flour, butter, cheese, meats, other farm produce, and *timber*, one of the industrial raw materials that Chamberlain had declined to include in his scheme.

At Cinderford in October Asquith pretended to take Chamberlain's reluctance to mention raw materials as an indication that he intended to exclude such commodities from taxation. Asquith wondered how the Canadian lumber exporter, already in bitter rivalry with Norway in the British market, would react to the news that he was to be denied the preference granted to his compatriot wheat farmer. Perhaps more dangerously, he pointed out that such a Canadian situation would have an Empire-wide parallel. South African food exports were negligible: the colony's principal export to Britain was raw wool, the raw material of one of our great industries.[16] In fact Asquith was not the pioneer of this argument. The *Free Trader* had anticipated his speech, illuminating the inconvenient fact that after raw wool (exports to Britain in 1902 of £3·15 million) Cape Colony's only exports of any consequence to Britain were skins (£484,000), copper (£339,000) and hides (£83,000).[17] The lesson was simple: either raw materials would have to be taxed or the result would be a scheme with huge inequalities of treatment both between colonies and within colonies.

Without waiting for the tariff reformers to concede that taxation of raw materials would be necessary, the free-traders proceeded to show that most products were in some circumstances raw materials. Though they surprisingly made relatively little play of agricultural products in this part of the debate, numerous propagandists made the general point. But the *Free Trader* took the laurels for pedantry when it printed excerpts from two papers, one by free-trader Harold Cox and the other by protectionist Ernest E. Williams, in parallel columns as if in shocked surprise that the two camps could ever agree about anything. It hoped that Chamberlain would enlighten the country 'as to why he does not intend to tax raw materials, and . . . why his reasons do not apply with equal cogency to manufactured materials'.[18]

Let us, for a moment, consider manufactured goods in general. There can be little doubt that Chamberlain, because of his endeavours at the Colonial Office, because of the capture of his imagination by the 'illimitable veldt'[19] during his trip to South Africa, had a sincere autonomous interest in the success of a colonial policy and was not merely using the Briton's sentiment for Empire as a vehicle for industrial protection. If this is so, it does raise the question as to whether Chamberlain, in his policy, would have therefore accepted a 'second best' solution, that of preference to the colonies but with no duties on manufactured goods, if it had been forced upon him. In this respect it is well to remember that the train of events was pulling manufactures more into the centre of the controversy, whether they were dispensable to Chamberlain or not. Bernard Semmel is correct in saying that the first six months of Chamberlain's proposals were 'exclusively imperial in scope'[20] if by that he means that Chamberlain's second public speech on the issue took place six months after his first. But this neglects what had been going on in the public debate. There, duties on manufactures had made an oblique entry, not only through the development of a protectionist policy but also through revenue considerations. And whatever the *intentions* of the tariff reformers, free-trade criticism played no small part in conditioning the role of duties on manufactures in the evolution of the tariff reform programme.

Many free-traders seemed determined to ignore the fact that Chamberlain did not intend to exclude agricultural products other than wheat from his plan, in order to show that it could not succeed. Sir William Harcourt, after a homily on the dangers of over-reliance on imperial wheat supplies, informed Chamberlain in the press that any scheme to finance old-age pensions would require duties on manufactured goods as well as on wheat.[21] In fact Chamberlain had already widened the alternative possibilities in his programme, a step which in the long run was to result in the dropping of pensions from the scheme. At the Constitutional Club on 26 June he had mentioned the possibility of a series of compensatory reductions on existing food duties, and stated that working men would have a choice – they could opt either for such compensations or for longer-term social benefits:

That is a matter which will come later. When we have the money then will be the time to say what we shall do with it: and if the working classes refuse to take my advice ... if they prefer the immediate advantage ... if, for instance, they are called to pay 3*d* a week additional on the cost of their bread, they may be fully, entirely relieved by a reduction of a similar amount in the cost of their tea, their sugar, or even of their tobacco. In this case, what is taken out of one pocket could be put back into the other.[22]

Almost immediately certain tariff reformers proceeded to neglect Chamberlain's advice too. It is not impossible that they were prompted by a Chamberlain anxious to formulate a policy that would avoid the political stumbling block of an increase in working-class living costs, but, whether or not they were secretly guided from above, their actions ironically gave free-traders more ammunition rather than less, this time on the other front of manufactured goods. The *Daily Telegraph* and 'A Revenue Official' in the *Times* attempted to review the whole scheme to show how bread and meat could be taxed without affecting the budget of the working man.[23] The two schemes were quite similar, though using slightly different figures, and we can therefore concentrate on the one which excited most comment. 'A Revenue Official' found that a 5 per cent tax on imports of foreign foodstuffs would yield to the Exchequer £7·5 million. But, as free-traders were quick to point out, the cost to the consumer would be more than this, since the price of home-grown produce and colonial imports would also rise. The *Free-Trader*, using a different estimate that a 5 per cent duty would yield some £5·8 million in revenue, assumed that the real cost to the consumer would be as high as £14–15 million. This meant that to keep the family food budget unchanged the existing food taxes (some £13·6 million in 1902) would have to be taken off in their entirety, and a residual amount (£0·4 million–£1·4 million) would have to be taken off the tobacco duty.[24] Whether 'A Revenue Official' agreed that a tax which yielded only £7·5 million (or £5·8 million) to the Exchequer would actually cost the consumer as much as £14 million–15 million he did not say, but he certainly did advocate the removal of the whole of the existing £13·6 million revenue duties on food imports.

As noticed by free-traders, the implication of the scheme thus far was to leave an Exchequer shortfall of between £6·1 million (£13·6 million minus £7·5 million) under 'A Revenue Official's' conditions and £8·7 million (£14·5 million minus £5·8 million) under those deemed likely by his opponents. 'A Revenue Official' proposed to raise the necessary revenue by a 7 per cent *ad valorem* duty on imports of foreign manufactures, this rate producing a slightly larger amount than that necessary to cover the shortfall.[25] 'Already, therefore,' remarked the *Free Trader*, proud of its Machiavellian skill in exposing the ungodly, 'the controversy gravitates towards the central point of the Protectionist ideal.'[26]

Such rather precipitant schemes brought with them other, related difficulties. 'A Revenue Official' was taken to task in the *Times* for failing to mention that, of the £37·8 million of Britain's food imports already subject to revenue duties, about 30 per cent were from the Empire, thus rendering an equitable system of preference between colonies more difficult.[27] It was further pointed out that nearly half the existing duties were yielded from sugar, a tax that had been imposed under emergency conditions in the Boer war and which many regarded the Unionist government as pledged to repeal. Other critics related this back to the question of manufactures, whilst yet others wondered whether even taxation upon manufactures was enough to recover the revenue lost to the Exchequer in view of the fact that, if 'crudely manufactured raw materials' and 'domestic appliances and personal necessaries' were excluded, duties under this heading would rest upon only 15 per cent of Britain's total imports.[28] The implication was that either duties on manufactures would have to be very high or else taxation would have to spill over into raw materials and semi-manufactures.

Had the plan been just to tax corn and meat, leaving revenue duties untouched, the Exchequer would have gained. Not perhaps by the £7·5 million suggested by 'A Revenue Official' (the tariff reformers almost always assumed that sources of supply would shift from foreign to colonial countries, but that they would continue to collect duty on the food that no longer came from the foreign countries!) but by some positive amount.[29] But since, in order to stifle political hostility to an increase in the cost of food, Chamberlain felt the need, as early as June, to offer a choice between pensions and 'compensatory' reductions, he was indeed committing himself either to leaving the Exchequer short (and thus, given the unlikelihood of any reduction in government expenditure, having to increase internal taxation) or to duties on manufactured goods.

Nevertheless, in spite of one or two loose statements, the tariff reform leaders and most of their supporters were by no means as forthcoming on the possibility of taxing manufactured goods, at least on the sustained basis necessary to satisfy the revenue considerations, as the free-traders would have had the public believe. Though Chamberlain's remarks from Birmingham onwards advocated a policy of 'retaliation' and the re-establishment of Britain's ability to negotiate, he was never specific.

Phrases like 'not being bound by any purely technical definition of Free Trade', 'power of negotiation', and words like 'freedom', all used in the Birmingham speech, hardly had the power, the solid reality or the permanence of the forbidden word 'protection'. Furthermore the *least* euphemistic passage from that speech ('... if necessary, retaliation, whenever our own interests or our relations between our Colonies and ourselves are threatened by other people') had direct reference to the imperial situation through Germany's proposed reprisals against Canada following the unilateral preference granted by the Dominion to Britain in 1897. All this could be interpreted as periodic, *ad hoc* countervailing power rather than sustained protection. Chamberlain had not *quite* burned his bridges. But, by the same token, he had left the question of government revenue very much in the air.

In June C. A. Vince, Secretary of the (Birmingham) Imperial Tariff Committee and probably in as good a position as any to know in advance what really lay behind Chamberlain's statements, interpreted the policy as an essentially moderate one of eliminating unfair conditions of competition. In particular the granting of bounties, 'direct or indirect', would be discouraged by the imposition of a duty corresponding to that bounty.[30] Vince forecast in the *Times*:

Mr. Chamberlain would adhere in every case to Cobden's principle of free interchange at the natural price. According to this, *if he did put on a duty* it would not necessarily give a claim to any other manufacturer. If Mr. Chamberlain found that the Germans earned their success legitimately, he would leave the home manufacturers to find out how they did it and to beat the Germans with their own weapons.[31]

The use of the phrase 'if he did put on a duty' in Vince's letter highlights the refusal of the Chamberlainites to recast their general policy in terms of any concrete structure. Where the tariff reformers had come closest to presenting specific proposals, these proposals had not received the endorsement of Chamberlain himself. The free-trade press was not at a loss to suggest a reason for his silence in the face of the criticism of schemes put forward by his supporters but apparently without his authority:

While committing himself as little as possible he [Chamberlain] allows his lieutenants to put forward scheme after scheme and argument after argument, so that he may see which will take with the public, and hastily drop, all without prejudice to himself, those which obviously will not do ... [This] will enable him to start his campaign in October with a tolerably clear idea of the line of least resistance on which he has to move. For example, he has already learnt that the promise of Old Age Pensions will fall on incredulous ears, and that the nation will not stand any proposal admittedly increasing the cost of food.[32]

If the precise structure of Chamberlain's policy was the subject of heated debate, so too were its likely effects. We must bear in mind that, since the effects were discussed in the absence of any definitive statement of policy, this was inevitably to heighten the prevailing confusion even more.

A fundamental element of the controversy, of course, was the effect on prices of a duty on wheat. At the extremes of opinion certain opposition speakers, such as Harcourt, argued from the beginning that the price would be raised by the complete amount of the duty,[33] whilst some tariff reformers even argued that the price would fall.[34] The press debate was as unconvincing as the views of important public figures. Two correspondents in the *Times* conducted an absurd debate over the supposed effect of the French duties on the price of bread in Paris. The periodical *Free Trader* saw fit to intervene in this debate to correct the arithmetical errors, but the only thing it succeeded in proving conclusively was that its expert statistical staff thought that there were 2 kg in 1 lb, not 2 lb in 1 kg.[35]

It is generally recognised that the difference of opinion among academic economists over tariff reform reflected the division within the emergent profession between marginalists and historical economists.[36] In the public debate no such niceties of methodology were involved. Free-traders frequently resorted to supposed historical proofs of the effects of a duty. At its crudest this approach is illustrated by a Gloucester correspondent who ascribed the dismal position of the labourer before 1846 to the evils of protection. When Chamberlain responded that the two situations afforded no parallel the West Countryman had sufficient guile to recall a speech of Chamberlain's in 1885 in which he had talked of the labourer's 'hopeless' position under a 'prohibitive protective duty'.[37] Another free-trader discovered the 246-year run of wheat prices in volume 29 of the *Encyclopaedia Britannica* to be nothing less than a Book of Revelations.[38] Elderly men enjoyed a brief period of popularity in being allowed to reminisce upon the terrible conditions of life under the corn laws.[39] Examples of such simplistic approaches were to be found in great numbers. On a more serious level 'Diplomaticus', in the *Westminster Gazette*, was one of several who made a detailed historical analysis of colonial preference before 1846, comparing the world and British market prices of sugar and timber and ascribing solely to the timber preference the short-lived supremacy of the US shipbuilder before the Civil War.[40] Even when dealing with more recent events the free-traders showed a strong affinity for the historical method. The editor of the *Corn Trade Year Book* sent to the *Times* information for the years 1890–97 to show that the French price of wheat, in that period, had always been greater than the English by more than the amount of the French duty. The *Free Trader* took these 'conclusive figures from France' to prove that any corn tax would increase prices by more than the amount of the tax itself.[41]

Such over-simple analyses, in which the tariff was accredited with monocausal importance in the determination of price differences, are completely unsatisfactory in hindsight. And Chamberlain too sought frequently to stress that other factors had to be taken into account, not least to explain his retreat from his free trade position of the early 1880s.[42] But not all tariff reformers were able to sense the illegitimacy of the method, all the more since many of them were using similar arguments themselves. Indeed, to many tariff reformers historical method was taken as a central method of investigation.

Furthermore the tariff reformers' case was weakened by a duality of objectives. Chamberlain's Birmingham speech had virtually coincided with Chaplin's deputation to Balfour protesting at the removal of the corn registration duty, and it was hard for many to see why agriculturalists should agitate so strongly for the retention of a measure which they maintained would not increase the price of corn.[43] The Hon. Thomas Brassey, in his well publicised change of allegiance to the Conservative Party, expressed the view that tariff reform would tend to arrest the decline in the agricultural population, thus inferring that he expected the profitability of British farming to increase under a duty.[44] But another wing of tariff reform ideology maintained the reverse. Both Sir Vincent Caillard and Sir Gilbert Parker argued that the supply of corn from the colonies would be so increased under a preferential scheme that in a few years the price in the home market would fall.[45] The free-trade press made the most of these conflicting approaches.[46] This apparent inconsistency had its parallel in another sphere too. Whilst many tariff reformers took the line that the price of bread would not rise, others argued with Arnold-Forster that a small increase in the cost of living would not be too high a price to pay for closer relations within the Empire.[47] Usually such speakers denied that there was any certainty of a price increase, but in admitting the possibility they contributed to the confusion, a confusion that was only increased when the financial orthodoxist Robert Giffen, in arguing that this might well be a situation where political conditions were more important than economic ones, remarked in a weighty letter to the *Times* that 'something we may not quite approve may become expedient'.[48]

In such a situation the public looked eagerly to the expert for judgement. But as Professor Coats has pointed out, so too did Balfour, himself relatively well versed in economic matters, and the advice he received from the Treasury on the effects of a duty on the price of corn was diametrically opposed to that from three Board of Trade officials.[49] The academic community was also divided, and some economists, like Marshall, were reluctant to enter the debate. The famous 'manifesto' of the 'fourteen professors'[50] did not prove an outstanding success in settling the debate:

3. The injury which the British consumer would receive from an import tax on wheat might be slightly reduced in the possible, but under existing

circumstances very improbable, event of a small proportion of the burden being thrown permanently on the foreign producer.

4. To the statement that a tax on food will raise the price of food it is not a valid reply that this result may possibly, in fact, not follow. When we say that an import duty raises price we mean, of course, unless it is overborne by other causes operating at the same time in the other direction. Or, in other words, we mean that in consequence of the import duty the price is generally higher by the amount of the duty than it would have been if other things had remained the same.[51]

This was hardly the clear and simple answer the public was hoping for. In hindsight, too, it seems a particularly deficient statement. The expectation that it would be improbable that the price of wheat would rise by any amount less than the duty was a relatively brutal simplification of the theory of the time, and the objectivity of the assertion was doubtful. In addition the postulate of a *ceteris paribus* situation was not very helpful in assessing the probable effects of a policy which would, if the tariff reformers' most sanguine expectations were realised, produce radical and dynamic changes in the production possibility curves of Empire wheat growers.[52] In the *Times* A. C. Pigou later avoided these pitfalls, but in order to show that a probable increase in price of slightly less than four-fifths of the amount of the duty could be expected he had to confront his public with terms like 'the elasticities of production in taxed and untaxed sources respectively', and to hope that his readers would follow his reasoning that:

... to justify [the] ... assertion that the 'major part' of the tax will be borne by the consumer [*sic*], it is necessary to assume that the elasticity in the United Kingdom and the Colonies together is not merely equal to, but is nearly six times as great as, the elasticity in foreign countries — an assumption which it is impossible to defend.[53]

II

Finally, on 6 October, at Glasgow, Chamberlain gave details of his policy. In brief, the tax on corn was 'not to exceed 2s a quarter', whilst maize was to be exempted because it was a food of the poor and a raw material for pig farmers. A 'corresponding tax' was to be put on flour. A 'small tax of about 5 per cent on foreign meat and diary produce' was suggested, though bacon was to be excluded again because of its importance in the budgets of the poor. There would be a preference on colonial wines and perhaps colonial fruits. And, in compensation, a remission of 'three-fourths of the duty on tea and half of the whole duty on sugar, with a corresponding reduction on cocoa and coffee'.[54] Using Board of Trade figures of household budgets, Chamberlain estimated the maximum effect of this proposal to be 4d a week to the labourer, 5d a week to the artisan, the extra expenditure being totally remitted by the compensating reductions.

But the maximum effect was unlikely. Chamberlain had presented his figures on the assumption that prices would rise the full amount of the duty. But he did not believe that this would in fact be the result:

I have gone to one of the highest official experts whom the Government consult ... and in his opinion the incidence of a tax depends on the proportion between the free production and the taxed production ... if, for instance, the foreigner supplies, as he does in the case of meat, two-ninths of the consumption, the consumer only pays two-ninths of the tax. If he supplies, as he does in the case of corn, something like three-fourths of the consumption, then the consumer pays three-fourths of the tax ... This is a theory, like any other ... but I believe it to be accurate.[55]

Thus, argued Chamberlain, if the price of bread or other taxed articles rose by less than the amount of the duty, the consumer would gain, since goods relieved from revenue duty would fall by the total amount of the duty remitted, since there was no home production of such goods.

As we have seen in earlier free-trade criticism, any such scheme would have resulted in a loss to the Exchequer. Chamberlain's remission of revenue duties was less sweeping than were forecasts of his policy, but he still calculated a shortfall of some £2·8 million per annum. To make this good, and to more than make it good, he proposed an average duty of 10 per cent on manufactured goods, 'varying according to the amount of labour in these goods', and yielding an estimated £9 million–15 million per annum.[56]

Chamberlain's scheme had apparently now emerged. But if anyone had expected what Chamberlainites had insisted were misconceptions surrounding the policy to disappear, they were disappointed. Though Glasgow was the most detailed formulation to date, it differed little in outline from the various forecasts that had been circulating weeks beforehand. In this sense, therefore, the free-trade criticisms of all the projected schemes from 15 May onwards still had relevance.

Nevertheless the revelations at Glasgow do show some development in the policy. Chamberlain's admission that the price of wheat could well rise by 75 per cent of the amount of the duty – an estimate well in advance of, and little different from, Pigou's estimate of rather under 80 per cent – perhaps indicates that he no longer regarded this issue as critical to the campaign. Suspect as was the theory of Chamberlain's 'official expert'[57] about the effects of food taxes upon prices, perhaps he felt that the inclusion of 'compensatory duties' in the plan was hitting home.

Perhaps it was to avoid Chamberlain's adroit handling of food taxes that free-traders thereafter changed their emphasis somewhat towards taxation of manufactured goods. Or perhaps it was that, now defined in a little more detail, and endorsed by Chamberlain, the scheme's provisions with regard to manufactures were more susceptible to criticism. The close follow-up of the speech at Glasgow by those at Newcastle and Tynemouth later in October provided ample material for discussion of this issue. It was, of course, noted by the opposition that in hoping to raise £9 million–15 million on manufactures Chamberlain was working on Board of Trade estimates of manufactured imports, which included semi-manufactures. Indeed, this was by Chamberlain's own admission; in the Glasgow speech he said just that.[58] Asquith pointed out that the proposal to reduce imported manufactures, and increase imports of raw materials to make exports with, suffered from the old problem of the definition of a raw material. At Paisley he cited Sir Robert Giffen's definition that raw materials were anything that entered the country to be worked on by British labour and British capital.[59] Here, of course, was a fundamental difference of approach – Chamberlain regarded semi-manufactures as manufactures, whilst the free-traders regarded them as raw materials, and they were not to tolerate Chamberlain's concession that they should be subjected to a lower rate of duty. Besides, this meant that the rate on wholly manufactured goods would have to be higher than 10 per cent. Following the free-trade maxim that 'one manufacture is but the raw material of another',[60] Hicks Beach forecast dire consequences of a possible 20 per cent duty on agricultural machinery upon the sorely depressed agricultural sector.[61]

These objections to the plan were reinforced with four further considerations. Firstly, Asquith and Giffen attacked what Asquith regarded as the tariff reformers' tendency to 'panic' over the increase in imports of manufactures.[62] Giffen, whilst admitting the great difficulties in using government statistics that were often poorly tabulated and loosely defined, thought that in his speech at Glasgow Chamberlain's use of table 1 of the 'Fiscal Blue Book'[63] was misleading and subject to about 70 per cent error, since that table included semi-manufactures and manufactures together in one total.[64] Secondly, though Asquith discounted dumping as being of no long-term importance,[65] it was realised that to stop it according to Chamberlain's wishes would require duties far higher than a maximum of, say, 20 per cent. In this sense it was perhaps unfortunate for the tariff reform cause that Ashley's book *The Tariff Problem* was published so near in time to the Glasgow speech.[66] For in that volume, commonly regarded as one of the finest statements of the tariff reform case, Ashley expressed the opinion that duties of 50–75 per cent might well be necessary to prevent a determined campaign of dumping.[67] Thirdly, it was noted – and this not only in relation to manufactured goods – that, once protection was established, its level had a tendency to rise. At Cinderford Asquith used a phrase popular with Goschen when he said, 'Protection is an inclined plane. Once you put your foot on it there is no logical halting place until you get to the bottom.'[68] And fourthly, it did not go unnoticed that Chamberlain, in asserting that his 10 per cent tariff would raise some £9 million–15 million, was assuming that there would be no reduction in the volume of manufactured goods imported. The tariff reformers were caught both ways: either a reduction of import volumes would narrow even more, the base on which to place duties, or else the maintenance of import volumes would cast doubt upon the promise, carried for week after week by the *Daily Express* on its front page, that 'Tariff Reform Means Work for All'.[69] (It must be said that it is possible that Chamberlain had in mind a situation where imports of semi-manufactures would rise, in spite of a duty, owing to the *differential* duty between semi-manufactures and wholly manufactured goods. But there is no real evidence for this, and such a view would not have been very compatible with his nationalistic sympathies towards British industry when it is considered that a large proportion of those imports of semi-manufactures were iron and steel products.)

The free-traders also criticised Chamberlain's statement, in justification of duties on manufactures as a bargaining weapon, that British exports had been stagnant for the previous thirty years. Giffen's argument, that the export figures should be presented after deducting the value of imported raw materials, seems to have been a refinement neglected by free-trade spokesmen.[70] Rosebery and Asquith were both more in tune with the popular debate when they criticised Chamberlain for comparing 1902 with the abnormal year of 1872,[71] though Chamberlain took pains to point out, at Newcastle on 20 October, that this criticism was oversimplified.[72] But tariff reformers affected bemusement at being pilloried for using what, after all, were the official returns, and they could take comfort from Giffen's warning that for many purposes these were exceedingly difficult to use.[73] And Asquith and barcourt both made mistakes similar to Chamberlain's in the technique of historical comparison, Asquith glibly changing the years under discussion from 1872–1902 to 1877–1902, and Harcourt deciding that 1892–1902 was quite sufficient.[74]

Though free-traders did not, as far as an admittedly and inevitably incomplete survey of the debate has revealed, criticise Chamberlain's assertion that exports were stagnant on the grounds that exports valued at current prices would tend to conceal increases in real volumes, at least until 1896, they did criticise the tariff reformers' tendency to omit coal from the figures, perhaps highlighting a difference between the nationalist and the cosmopolitan outlook on the economic situation. And they did introduce, to a greater extent after Glasgow than before, the vexed question of invisible exports, which the *Morning Post* rather unconstructively dismissed as a 'kind of providence for the rescue of distressed Free Traders'.[75] And the matter of paying for imports with the dividends on overseas capital was, as a particular aspect of this, spotlighting a basic difference in philosophy to confuse the public. 'We

should be glad' (again the *Morning Post*), 'if Mr. ASQUITH would go
carefully into the question of foreign investments, and explain in detail
the advantage of the transference of British manufacturing enterprise to
foreign countries.'[76] But it is doubtful whether many of the public could
have followed Felix Schuster, in a widely reported paper before the
Institute of Bankers in December, when he pointed to the inherent
tendency to exaggerate the visible import surplus through the valuation
of exports as f.o.b. and of imports as c.i.f., and to the fact that an 'undue'
import surplus could not exist because of the strength of the exchanges
and the stability of interest rates.[77] Hidden in his analysis, however, was
the assumption that Britain was not 'living on her capital', an assumption
which was, of course, substantiated some years later,[78] but with which
many tariff reformers would not have agreed at the time.

    This is not to say that food taxes were forgotten. If Chamberlain's
'compensation' argument had some plausibility, what better way to
undermine it than to argue that the duties required on wheat and meat
would be so much larger than the tariff reformers anticipated that a
reduction of existing revenue duties could not possibly compensate for
them? Thus Dilke argued that a preference, to achieve the imperial
objective, would have to be much larger than the proposed 2s per
quarter.[79] Hicks-Beach tried to damage the neatness of Chamberlain's
model by arguing that even though it might work in theory the price
reductions would not filter down to the consumer because 'middlemen
are extremely astute individuals'.[80] But he did admit that his experience
as the architect of the corn registration duty had led him to believe that
part of the tax was paid by 'the great railway companies in the United
States, who lowered their rates to a certain extent in order to relieve the
flour producers in the Western States of America in order to place them
on an equality with the home producer here'.[81]

    Thus the Glasgow speech, whilst an important stage in the progress of
the campaign, had not produced any decisive victories for the tariff
reformers in their great mission of educating the country. It did not clear
up the unanswered questions that preceded it, and it provoked new
criticisms to be answered. Many, especially those who adhered to some
variant of 'National Efficiency', thought with Chamberlain that the main
cause of the uncertainty and obscurity that clouded each successive
contribution was the party element. Pleas for objective, non-partisan
discussion had been heard right from the beginning of the campaign.
Chamberlain had asked for such a discussion at Birmingham.[82] After this
it took only two weeks for Vincent Caillard to write in exasperation to
the *Times* that 'one might as well discuss Euclid on party lines as this'.[83]
In June Walter Long, then president of the Local Government Board,
announced that the partisan way in which Chamberlain's proposals were
being discussed was an indictment of the party system.[84] And still, in
December, Chamberlain, in a published exchange of correspondence,

clung to his view that the fiscal question was one of 'National and Imperial interest, which ought not to be discussed as a matter of party politics'. [85]

Partly, of course, it was a propagandist stratagem that prompted some to raise the cry that the tariff should be taken out of politics – after all, the tariff reformers could only stand to gain in the unlikely event of this being achieved. Certainly it is true that the majority of those advocating this course were tariff reformers. But there *were* others who took a similar view. At Burnley, Rosebery had forecast that tariff reform would cut 'diagonally' across partly lines, [86] though he was subsequently to discover that, in the case of his own Liberal imperialists, this diagonalism was to be manifest in the defection of a small but significant minority to the Conservative camp. [87] The effort to remove the binding and blinkering party element was, however, in part the reflection of a sincere belief that the intricacies of the problem could be unravelled, that solutions and answers could be found, by objective enquiry along 'scientific' lines. Thus it was that subsequent opponents of tariff reform – Devonshire, looking for a ray of light in his perplexity, Rosebery for a way of deciding his divided loyalties – had endorsed such attempts.

But Balfour's 'inquiry by the Cabinet for the Cabinet', [88] which resulted in the publication of the famous Board of Trade 'Fiscal Blue Book', [89] satisfied no one, and was commonly regarded as merely a collection of statistics with no attempt to draw conclusions. [90] And nor would the appointment of a Royal Commission have been the answer. If the commission had been shunned by free-traders it would have been criticised as having a protectionist bias. If it had been constituted according to party strength in the House of Commons it would have produced at least two alternative reports, each convincing no one who was not already convinced. There can be little doubt that Balfour, in resisting pressure from the press and advice from the king downward, correctly divined the likely course of events should a Royal Commission have been appointed:

I have always had grave doubts about the value of a Commission to examine what I may call 'fundamentals' ... when the inquiry is finished, it probably produces a series of widely divergent Reports upon all the really important issues. The Labour Commission, for example, dealt with, on the whole, far simpler problems ... what degree of agreement has followed from its protracted labours? [91]

III

Here, therefore, was a debate about a policy whose precise measures were still unclear, even after the Glasgow speech. It was a debate in which the effects of those measures would, quite naturally, depend on the measures themselves. And the effects even of given, assumed measures were not known, or were at least hotly disputed. It was a debate that raised fundamental questions about the use of statistics in proving causation: more than this, it raised serious doubts about the reliability of even the best British statistics extant. It was a debate which, however reluctant were the politicians to enter into the realities of a complex international economy, was pushing the public comprehension into areas well beyond all normally accepted limits. It was a debate which was apparently not amenable to examination by those traditionally regarded as expert in economic enquiry: the civil service was divided, the academic economists were not only divided, albeit unequally, but in many cases unwilling to participate, and the idea of a Royal Commission was passed over because of its probable inability to reach any firm and unanimous conclusions.

Furthermore, in the sense that by October–November 1903 neither side was obviously winning in the war of propaganda, things were going rather worse for the tariff reformers than appeared on the surface. In spite of a great volume of propaganda material organised and distributed by the Tariff Reform League and the Imperial Tariff Committee there were already indications that the free-traders' belief in overwhelming working-class support was to be vindicated. Harmsworth's opinion poll of 2,000 people in August showed a great mass of hostility towards Chamberlain's scheme.[92] By late November similar indications were coming from organised labour. The writing on the wall was discounted by Chamberlainites, who preferred to use the recent works of Sidney and Beatrice Webb to argue that the TUC and its parliamentary committee did not represent the views of the rank and file.[93] It is doubtful whether they convinced even themselves. But, more than this, the tariff reformers were fighting against ideas and beliefs, reasoning and prejudice, established and entrenched for over half a century.

Fundamentally, what the tariff reformers had failed to do was to propose a policy that was unequivocally superior to the existing policy: not only that, but one which could be *seen* to be unequivocally superior by an audience that was rapidly losing its grip as the debate became more complex. In hindsight we might consider it absurd that they should have expected to be able to do so. Nevertheless this is precisely what they *did* expect to be able to do. Moreover the tariff reformers thought it axiomatic that such a policy existed. But to develop this policy a radical new approach was necessary; a continuation of the controversy along existing lines would eventually result in a stalemate which, combined with the inertia of the voting masses, would lead to defeat at the polls. It was as much with hope as with conviction that the *Morning Post* anticipated Chamberlain's forthcoming speech at Leeds with the words 'We do not agree with the critics on either side who say that as far as the general aspects of the controversy are concerned there is nothing more to be said.'[94]

The new thrust came in combining the need for a 'scientific', impartial enquiry with the belief that 'business principles' and the hard-headed pragmatism of the businessman could succeed where politicians and economists had failed. On 11 November the Tariff Reform League had issued a statement that they had received enquiries from all over the country asking how Chamberlain's proposals would affect particular trades and industries. Sutherland and Chamberlain[95] had replied that the duties put forward in the Glasgow speech:

... must not be treated as anything but tentative. It is an essential part of his [Chamberlain's] policy that whenever the principles he advocates are accepted the details should be submitted to a committee, which will take evidence and will carefully consider the conditions of each trade, only fixing a tariff after having heard all that was to be said.[96]

To the tariff reformer Chamberlain's Glasgow programme had been received as less than conclusive only because it had not been worked out in sufficient detail; because it had been presented in a way suitable for delivery from a platform rather than rigorously formulated in terms of a 'scientific' tariff. (This is not to say that he did not regard the Glasgow proposals as infinitely more 'scientific' than anything the free-traders had yet had to say on the issue.[97]) The time had now come to move in the direction of a specific formulation through which everyone could see the bearing of the new proposals upon his own particular circumstances. In the speech at Leeds on 16 December Chamberlain announced his new departure:

Let us make a tariff, let us make a scientific tariff ... Let us make a tariff, if that be possible – and I think it is – which shall not add by one farthing to the burden of any taxpayer, but which by the transference of taxation from one shoulder to another ... may not only produce the same amount of revenue which will always be necessary for our home expenditure, but may incidentally do something to develop and extend our trade ... It is true we are told we cannot make a scientific tariff. We cannot distinguish between the raw material and manufactures, that we cannot be fair all round, that if ... we prevent the dumping of iron below cost, we shall ruin the tinplate trade, that if we stop the excessive importation of cheap foreign labour we shall ruin the boot and shoe trade, that if we stop the excessive importation of foreign yarn there will be an end of the clothing industry ...
Why should we suppose that our scientific economists, that our manufacturers cannot do what every other country had been able to do without finding their way into exaggerated difficulties? Now we are going to try to do it ... We are going to form, nay, have gone a long way in the direction of forming, a Commission, not a political Commission, but a non-political Commission of experts ... to consider the conditions of our trade and the remedies which are to be found for it.[98]

As the speech unwound, the public learned for the first time that the new commission would consist of 'leading representatives' of all the principal industries of the UK and of representatives of India, the Crown colonies and the Dominions, and that it would:

... invite before it witnesses from every trade, and it will endeavour, after hearing all that can be said, not merely in regard to the special interests of any particular trade, but also in regard to the interests of all the other trades which may be in any sense related to it – it is going to frame a model tariff.[99]

Throughout the campaign the tariff reform press had ridiculed the body of orthodox economists, portraying them as 'musty theorists', 'evangelists of a fossilised doctrine', and so on.[100] Thus when, soon after the Leeds speech, it was announced that the secretary of the new commission was to be from the ranks of what tariff reformers commonly called the 'modern' or 'younger'[101] school of political economy there was perhaps little cause for surprise. Professor W. A. S. Hewins had been Director of the London School of Economics since its foundation in 1895, and had for some time been an active supporter of the imperial cause, though he had felt it expedient not to come to the forefront of the controversy. His largest contribution to the propaganda war up to December 1903 had been a series of sixteen articles in the *Times* under the pseudonym 'An Economist'.[102] Now he was out in the open he was frequently applauded in the tariff reform press as an economist who had 'always tried to base the study of economics on a study of industry and commerce' and had been in 'close contact with business all his life'.[103] At the same time, he had close relations with certain German scholars, particularly von Halle of Berlin, and had published several articles in German academic journals, including Schmoller's *Jahrbuch*.[104] He was thus very much influenced by the close relationship between industry and the State in Germany, and was aware of the close intercourse and elaborate discussion of detail between businessman and bureaucrat which went into the formulation of a tariff. Here, therefore, was an ideal link between the business approach to complex problems and the technical expertise required to draw up a scientific tariff.

In the weeks following the Leeds speech the Chamberlainite newspapers sought constantly to emphasise the virtue of direct action at a practical level. The *Sheffield Daily Telegraph* expressed contempt at the new outburst of cries that Chamberlain's announcement had provoked from free-traders about the increased urgency of appointing a Royal Commission: '... that is not Mr Chamberlain's way. He has no intention of having the great subject 'hung up' indefinitely. The question demands attention, and that without delay.'[105] Another tariff reform leader announced that:

Throughout the enquiry ... one sole object will be kept steadily before its [the Commission's] members. This is not to multiply difficulties and stifle action with academic objections, but to arrange a practicable scheme which can be carried into effect with the least possible delay.[106]

In this way the tariff reformers sought to stress that direct and immediate action was far divorced from the unhelpful, equivocating realm of theory. What they perhaps were really doing was hoping that progress would be achieved by removing controversy. The distaste for the theoretician in the public mind could be played upon by emphasising the 'representative' quality, the common sense and the stature of the business members of the commission.

Thus the early organisation of the commission was carried on in what was apparently a wilful disregard of free-trade hostility. Every few days tariff reform newspapers proudly carried the press release of the latest industrialists who had consented to serve, until by the middle of January 1904 the commission was announced to be complete. This eulogising of the businessmen who had agreed to serve was brought to a peak by Chamberlain himself when, at the opening meeting of the commission, he described them as:

'... these fifty-eight gentlemen, princes of commerce, who have grown grey and bald in the trade fight for success, have ever their feelings under perfect control, and allow only the doorway to reason to remain open'.[107]

Though tariff reformers were trying to stand all of from objections in order to try to push their movement ahead, free-traders had, of course, not failed to provide those objections. Condemnation of the commission was developing along two lines, which were not entirely compatible. The first, and rather more simple, criticism was of its composition. The fifty-eight members were represented as 'a ring of vested interests ... of managing directors who have hundreds of thousands of pounds to gain by the imposition of a skilful tariff'.[108] To this the tariff reformers answered that to whom should the task of formulating a tariff be given but to the most prominent industrialists in the land? These men were well known in all the countries of the commercial globe. Their political affiliations were not taken into account when the choice was made, only their ability to represent authoritatively the trade or industry concerned.[109] A related free-trade criticism was that the commission was not representative of the whole sphere of British economic activity. It became almost a hobby to find gaps in the list – in the House of Commons it was asked 'Why it was that not a single banker of repute sat on the Tariff Commission?' and Lloyd George asked why no workingmen were represented.[110] At Halifax Winston Churchill pointed to the absence of the cotton trade, the professions and the free-traders.[111]

But criticism along these lines ran the danger of establishing the principle that if the commission was composed in a representative way, one which met such objections, then perhaps the whole exercise would be legitimatised. The second line of criticism was more fundamental. The opposition press was quick to deny that the commission was in any way an answer to the agitation of previous months for a Royal Commission.

The *Echo* noted that 'it is certainly not an impartial inquiry. The question to be put before it is not whether Protection should be adopted or not, but how can the Protective Tariff be best framed in the interests of those who are advocating it'.[112] The *Standard* reminded its readers of its long-standing support for an impartial enquiry, but by this it had not meant 'an "ex parte" inquiry by a tribunal starting with preconceived opinions, and pledged, beforehand, to a particular conclusion'.[113]

But of course the tariff reformers agreed that the intention of the commission was to draft a tariff. That was what it had been set up to do. As for the idea of its having preconceived ideas, the only one held was that *some kind* of modification of policy was required, and as far as that was concerned tariff reformers usually assumed that everyone in the country felt this.[114] It was the task of the commission to find out *what* kind. As the *Morning Post* put it, much of the free-trade criticism was irrelevant:

The Tariff Commission will do what must have been done either by Mr. CHAMBERLAIN individually or by the industrial and commercial classes on their own initiative, for obviously the details of a tariff must be worked out before, not after, the country expresses its final judgement.[115]

IV

What had happened here was a complete rift between the two sides, not about the substance of the controversy itself but about the way in which the controversy should continue. As the next two months went by, as details emerged in the press about the commission's increasing activity in collecting information and examining witnesses from the first industry to come under its scrutiny, iron and steel, the free-traders watched the proceedings with incredulity.

In March 1904 there was a short exchange of letters in the *Times* between Hewins and L. T. Hobhouse, in which Hewins sought to prove that the methods of the commission rested on a more scientific basis than did those of the Free Trade Union.[116] This led to an exchange of letters between Hewins and Herbert Gladstone, which illustrates perhaps better than anything else the irreconcilable gulf over method which now lay between tariff reformers and free-traders.

Gladstone took the Leeds speech as evidence that Chamberlain now considered his case proved, and that the next step was to set up a commission to work out a tariff. If this was the case Chamberlain's scheme must have been proved, to the satisfaction of the tariff reformers, by the propaganda that preceded the Leeds speech, and thus the methods of the tariff reformers were to be condemned on the same criterion – that of lack of a scientific method – as that on which Hewins had condemned the methods of the Free Trade Union. If this was not the case, and the Tariff Commission was reopening what Gladstone termed the 'main issue', that of free trade versus protection, then, argued Gladstone, its composition militated against its ability to conduct an unbiased examination of the relative merits of each.[117]

But Hewins's reply was to show that, in public at least, he did not consider Chamberlain's policy proved. Nor was the commission to discuss the relative merits of free trade and protection. He argued that his opponents were inclined to make dogmatic statements as to the effects of any proposal for a tariff without justifying them. Such criticism assumed that the free-traders had already constructed a tariff and found out that it would not work. If this was so, bantered Hewins, the nation should be told the results. It should be allowed to see whether this hypothetical free-traders' tariff had been drawn up in the most beneficial way – for instance, what goods were to be put on the free list, how the free-traders had decided between the merits of specific and *ad valorem* duties, and whether they had reached their conclusions after proper consultation with manufacturers.[118]

It is here that the tariff reform approach becomes understandable. Free-traders were attacking a policy that had still not been fully worked out in detail. Of course, to the free-trade mind this was of no account, since free trade, even the most 'one-sided' free trade, was inevitably superior in a welfare sense to any form of protection that could possibly have been devised. But to the tariff reformer, or to anyone occupying a mid-way position, anyone who did not accept the superiority of free trade as an axiomatic truth, the free-trade case did indeed seem to be assuming a certain protective policy against which to measure the superior benefits of free trade. As Hewins remarked:

Mr Chamberlain has described a practical situation, with regard to which it is desirable to take action. The figures on which that description is based have not, so far as I know, been disputed ... If we are to deal with the situation described by Mr Chamberlain, you will, I feel sure, agree that we must have a policy. It is open to the free-traders to sketch an economic and commercial policy, which will deal with actual problems, alternative to that suggested by Mr Chamberlain. But they have not done so ...[119]

Of course, Chamberlain's figures *had* been disputed. Hewins was accepting Chamberlain's assumption that something was wrong with British industry. His answer, therefore, would not have carried any conviction with a free-trader who thought the economic situation was healthy. (Indeed, at this point, Hewins appears not to have been regarding free trade as a policy at all). But in defence of Hewins it should be remembered that by no means all free-traders held the view that Britain's economic condition was so sound that no action would be required in the foreseeable future. Free-traders may have accused Chamberlain of gross exaggeration, but even Asquith had been prepared to admit that the situation was not perfect. As early as May he had counselled, 'Until some better substitute [for free trade, than Chamberlain's policy] could be discovered, let us stick to our well-tried policy of free markets and an open door.'[120] There were many people who were not complacent, and not all of them were tariff reformers – most common among the others were supporters of one or another of the various forms of 'National Efficiency', advocating here the remedy of improving technical education along Charlottenburg lines, advocating there the remedy of improving the consular service. To them, perhaps, Hewins's reasoning was understandable. Certainly it was at them, at the middle ground, that it was directed. The Tariff Commission was to examine how the industrial situation could best be remedied by means of a tariff: it was up to others to suggest alternative remedies to compare that tariff with.

The tariff reformers had conceded little to their opponents. One of their number admitted publicly that the appeal was to emotion rather than to reason.[121] This is too strong – it underestimates the case for tariff reform. But what the propaganda campaign had done was to leave a demanding legacy for the Tariff Commission. Chamberlain's proposals had been cast as utopian. He had refused to admit that any sector would not have its condition improved through his policy (though it is true that he seldom mentioned the financial sector in his campaign). Today we would consider as accepted the idea that protection may – indeed, usually will – raise the community welfare function overall. But, in effect, Chamberlain had promised that everyone within that community would be benefited. He had not been able to show how it was to be done. But, by definition, it *could* be done. That was the function, that was the *meaning*, of a 'scientific tariff'.

The principal model on which the 'scientific tariff' was to be built was that of Germany. Just why the German tariff was regarded as 'scientific' is not, in hindsight, particularly clear. Though tariff reformers were not very specific during the first campaign, they appear to have had in mind fairly superficial administrative and structural features – the grading of duties according to labour content, the choice between *ad valorem* and specific duties, the granting of drawbacks on exports. What they failed to consider was the importance of economic pressure groups in determining even Germany's 'scientific' tariff, in spite of the fact that they sometimes castigated the 'log rolling' tactics endemic to the formulation of the US tariff as a prime example of bad practice.

Precisely how the Tariff Commission was to accomplish its task Hewins left unsaid. Though the much-talked-about 'scientific' tariff had not yet been rigorously defined, its objectives were clear. It had to devise a system of agricultural preference which, when combined with compensating reductions in British taxation, would not increase the cost of food. It had to grade the spectrum of duties on raw materials through semi-manufactured goods to finished manufactures so that the consequential changes in production levels at home would have little effect on the prices of industrial products, or would at least increase wages to compensate for that. It had to increase employment. And if it did increase employment and wages, it had to avoid damaging the export trade. It had to harmonise the interests of industry and agriculture. It had to do all this and still produce a scheme containing preferential terms acceptable to every single colony, no matter what its economic base. The project had to be carried out under the methodology of the day, without the sophisticated calculating equipment and statistical techniques of later generations. But this was the sublimely optimistic objective that the tariff commissioners had in mind as they embarked upon their eighteen years of labour. [122] If we think Chamberlain asked too much of them it is only fair to remember that they undertook the task willingly.

Notes

1   It is recounted by a biographer of Bonar Law that the deciding factor in Chamberlain's decision was the imperial rather than the protectionist issue, which he 'should have left ... to younger men'. But this helps little in an assessment of the importance of economic and political factors in the desire for Empire consolidation. See Chamberlain's remarks, quoted in H. A. Taylor, *The Strange Case of Andrew Bonar Law* (London, n.d. but *c.* 1929), p. 78.

2   J. Amery, *The Life of Joseph Chamberlain*, (vols 5 and 6): *Joseph Chamberlain and the Tariff Reform Campaign* (London, 1969), chapters 100–10.

3   Chamberlain, at Birmingham, 15 May 1903; reprinted in *Times*, 16 May 1903, p. 8.

4   This phrase had sufficient currency at the time to be chosen as the title of Hilaire Belloc's satirical pamphlet *The Great Inquiry* (London, 1903).

5   The conferences of 1897 and 1902. For a good short summary see S. H. Zebel, 'Joseph Chamberlain and the genesis of tariff reform', *Journal of British Studies*, VII (1967), pp. 138–41.

6   Asquith, at Doncaster, 21 May 1903; reprinted in *Times*, 22 May 1903, p. 5.

7   *Parliamentary Debates*, 4th ser., CXXIII, 28 May 1903, cols. 143, 144, 147.

8   *Ibid.*, cols. 178, 179.

9   *Ibid.*, col. 185.

10   *Times* (editorial), 28 May 1903, p. 7.

11   *Ibid.*

12   *Parliamentary Debates*, 4th ser., CXXIII, 28 May 1903, col. 143.

13   J. Amery, *op. cit.*, vol. 5, p. 232.

14   Chamberlain to Arthur Griffith-Boscawen, 15 August 1903; published in *Standard*, 18 August 1903, p. 3.

15   John Charlton, quoted in *Standard*, 17 August 1903, p. 3.

16   Asquith, at Cinderford, 8 October 1903; reprinted in T. L. Gilmour (ed.), *All Sides of the Fiscal Controversy* (London, 1903), p. 70.

17   *Free Trader*, 28 August 1903, p. 34.

18   *Ibid.*, p. 37.

19   Chamberlain, at Birmingham, 15 May 1903; *loc. cit.*

20   B. Semmel, *Imperialism and Social Reform* (London, 1960), p. 93.

21 *Free Trader*, 31 July 1903, p. 4.
22 Chamberlain, at the Constitutional Club, 26 June 1903; *Free Trader*, 4 September 1903, p. 45.
23 *Daily Telegraph, Imperial Reciprocity. A Study of Fiscal Policy*, (London, n.d. but 1903), pp. 76–83; 'A Revenue Official' to ed., *Times*, 28 July 1903, p. 6.
24 'The proposed gamble in food', *Free Trader*, 7 August 1903, pp. 10–11.
25 'A Revenue Official' to ed., *Times*, 28 July 1903, p. 6.
26 'The proposed gamble in food', *Free Trader*, 7 August 1903, pp. 10–11.
27 'Questioner' to ed., *Times*, 7 August 1903, p. 5.
28 *Free Trader*, 7 August 1903, p. 11.
29 The yield from a duty on corn and meat would also have depended on the extent of any preference granted to colonial produce. This was to remain an unspecified, indeed largely unmentioned, feature of the tariff reform proposals throughout the campaign.
30 The principal example used by Vince was German machinery exports. Countervailing duties on direct bounties were quite widely accepted in principle: indeed, at that precise time the question of the sugar duties was being discussed by Parliament. But Vince must have realised that 'indirect' bounties was a term which could have been used to cover any financial assistance given by the German government to exporters or transport concerns in the form of subsidies, exemptions from taxation or tax remissions. Indeed, taken to its logical conclusion, the term could even have embraced Germany's superior educational facilities. In view of the positive role of the State in pre-1914 German economic development such a policy, taken literally, could have given the implementers of a tariff *carte blanche* with regard to provisions against Germany. See C. A. Vince to ed., *Times*, 10 June 1903, p. 12.
31 *Ibid.* (my emphasis). Vince's letter had been sent to the *Times* only after consultation with Chamberlain's private secretary. Furthermore it is worthy of note that when, later in the year, Vince published his book *Mr Chamberlain's Proposals. What they Mean and What we shall Gain by Them* (London, 1903), the volume's authority was increased by the inclusion of a preface by Chamberlain himself.
32 *Free Trader*, 7 August 1903, p. 11.
33 Sir William Harcourt, 'Mr Chamberlain's proposals', *Free Trader*, 31 July 1903, p. 4. See also *Free Trader*, 7 August 1903, p. 9.
34 Sir Gilbert Parker to ed., *Times*, 6 August 1903, p. 9.
35 A. Branscombe Wood to ed., *Times*, 28 July 1903, p. 6; R. Gamman to ed., *Times*, 4 August 1903, p. 2; *Free Trader*, 7 August 1903, p. 16.
36 A. W. Coats, 'Political economy and the tariff reform campaign of 1903', *Journal of Law and Economics*, XI (1968), p. 224.
37 *Free Trader*, 4 September 1903, p. 45.
38 'M.B.' to ed., *Times*, 4 June 1903, p. 9.
39 See, for example, G. Chambers to ed., *Free Trader*, 21 August 1903, p. 29.
40 Cited in *Free Trader*, 21 August 1903, p. 28.
41 George J. S. Broomhall to ed., *Times*, 29 August 1903, p. 5; *Free Trader*, 4 September 1903, p. 42.
42 *Free Trader*, 4 September 1903, p. 45.
43 *Times*, 16 May 1903, p. 9. See also editorial, p. 11, where the *Times*, whilst asserting its opinion that the reinstitution of the corn registration duty would not increase the price of corn, admitted that 'possibly what was done a year ago by SIR MICHAEL HICKS BEACH suggested to

the agricultural classes that they had a chance of obtaining protection, in the future, though not in the present . . .'.

44 Hon. T. A. Brassey to the chairman of the Conservative and Unionist Association of the Rye division of Sussex; *Times*, 7 August 1903, p. 6.

45 Sir Gilbert Parker to ed., *Times*, 6 August 1903, p. 9; Sir V. H. P. Caillard, *Imperial Fiscal Reform* (London, 1903). Caillard's book was based on three articles which had appeared earlier in the *National Review*.

46 Referring to Brassey and Parker, the *Free Trader* felt that 'the task of reconciling these two Dromios of Protection is frankly beyond our power'; 14 August 1903, p. 17.

47 Arnold Forster, at Belfast, 18 August 1903; reported in *Free Trader*, 28 August 1903, p. 40.

48 Sir Robert Giffen to ed., *Times*, 28 May 1903, p. 5.

49 A. W. Coats, *loc. cit.*, pp. 191–3.

50 'Tariff Reformer' [L. S. Amery] to ed., *Times*, 18 August 1903.

51 C. F. Bastable, A. L. Bowley, E. Cannan, L. Courtney, F. Y. Edgeworth, E. C. K. Gonner, A. Marshall, J. S. Nicholson, L. R. Phelps, A. Pigou, C. P. Sanger, W. R. Scott, W. Smart and Armitage Smith to ed., *Times*, 15 August 1903, p. 4.

52 It is true that elsewhere in the 'manifesto' the possibility of increasing imperial supplies was doubted, but not denied. See *ibid.*, para. 6.

53 A. Pigou to ed., *Times*, 3 December 1903, p. 5, quoted in A. W. Coats, *loc. cit.*, p. 216 n.

54 Chamberlain, at Glasgow, 6 October 1903; reprinted in J. M. Robertson, *The Collapse of 'Tariff Reform'. Mr Chamberlain's Case Exposed* (London, 1911), pp. 52, 54.

55 *Ibid.*, p. 58.

56 *Ibid.*, pp. 61–2.

57 *Ibid.*, p. 57.

58 *Ibid.*, p. 62.

59 Asquith, at Paisley, 31 October 1903; in *Morning Post*, 2 November 1903, p. 4.

60 L.G.C.M. [L. G. Chiozza-Money], 'Preferential tariffs and British trade, II, The fear of imports – materials, raw and other', *Free Trader*, 7 August 1903, p. 15.

61 Hicks Beach, at Manchester, 5 November 1903; in *Morning Post*, 6 November 1903, p. 7.

62 Asquith, at Paisley, 31 October 1903; *loc. cit.*

63 *British and Foreign Trade and Industry. Memoranda, Statistical Tables, and Charts Prepared in the Board of Trade, with Reference to Various Matters Bearing on British and Foreign Trade and Industrial Conditions*, Cd. 1761 (1903) (hereafter cited as *British and Foreign Trade and Industry . . .*), p. 5, table 1.

64 Giffen to ed., *Times*, 24 October 1903, p. 12; Chamberlain to ed., *Times*, 27 October 1903, p. 9; Giffen to ed., *Times*, 29 October 1903, p. 6. See also Chamberlain to Giffen, 24 October 1903, and Giffen to Chamberlain, 26 October 1903, in J. Amery, *op. cit.*, vol. 6, pp. 479–80.

65 Asquith, at Paisley, 31 October 1903; *loc. cit.*

66 W. J. Ashley, *The Tariff Problem* (London, 1903).

67 *Ibid.*, p. 133.

68 Asquith, at Cinderford, 8 October 1903; *loc. cit.* See also Goschen, at Passmore Edwards Settlement, Tavistock Place, London, 16 October 1903; in *Times*, 17 October 1903, p. 8.

69 B. Semmel, *op. cit.*, p. 112.

70 Giffen to ed., *Times*, 29 October 1903, p. 6. Giffen had made this point as

long before as 1877. See *Essays in Finance*, 1st Ser. (London, 1877), p. 145.

71   Rosebery, at Sheffield, 13 October 1903; reprinted in T. L. Gilmour (ed.), *op. cit.*, p. 110. Asquith, at Cinderford, 8 October 1903, *loc. cit.*

72   Chamberlain, at Newcastle, 20 October 1903; reprinted in *Times*, 21 October 1903, p. 10.

73   Giffen to ed., *Times*, 29 October 1903, p. 6.

74   *Morning Post* (editorial), 2 November 1903, pp. 5–6. Austen Chamberlain, at Aberdeen, 3 November 1903; in *Morning Post*, 4 November 1903, p. 4.

75   *Morning Post* (editorial), 2 November 1903, pp. 5–6.

76   *Ibid.*

77   See, for example, 'Bankers and the fiscal question', *Morning Post*, 17 December 1903, p. 4.

78   See G. Paish, 'Great Britain's capital investments in other lands', *Journal of the Royal Statistical Society*, LXXII (1909), pp. 465–80, and discussion, pp. 481–95.

79   Dilke, at Normanton, 2 (?) November 1903; in *Morning Post*, 3 November 1903, p. 3.

80   Hicks Beach, at Manchester, 5 November 1903; in *Morning Post*, 6 November 1903, p. 7.

81   *Ibid.*

82   Chamberlain, at Birmingham, 15 May 1903; *loc. cit.*

83   Sir Vincent Caillard to ed., *Times*, 28 May 1903, p. 5.

84   Walter Long, in Lincolnshire, 3 June 1903; in *Times*, 4 June 1903, p. 4.

85   Chamberlain to Sir W. Treloar (of the City of London corporation), 4 December 1903; in *Morning Post*, 11 December 1903, p. 6.

86   Rosebery at Burnley, 19 May 1903; in *Times*, 20 May 1903, p. 12.

87   Including the Duke of Sutherland, Sir Charles Tennant (Asquith's father-in-law) and Thomas Brassey. See H. C. G. Matthew, *The Liberal Imperialists* (London, 1973), p. 101.

88   A. W. Coats, *loc. cit.*, p. 200.

89   *British and Foreign Trade and Industry . . ., op. cit.*

90   See the remarks of Devonshire and Edwin Cannan in A. W. Coats. *loc. cit.*, p. 206 n.

91   Balfour, quoted in A. W. Coats, *loc. cit.*, p. 204.

92   'Our walking inquirers', *Daily Mail*, 29 August 1903, p. 4. See also A. Gollin, *Balfour's Burden* (London, 1965), pp. 87–8.

93   S. and B. Webb, *Industrial Democracy* (1st edn, London, 1897), especially vol. I, chapters 1 and 2; a new one-volume edition had been published in 1902. In this connection see *Morning Post*, 11 November 1903, p. 5; 12 November 1903, p. 5; 23 November 1903, p. 6; 25 November 1903, p. 3; 28 November 1903, p. 4; 30 November 1903, p. 4.

94   *Morning Post* (editorial), 14 December 1903, p. 6.

95   President and vice-president of the League respectively.

96   *Morning Post*, 11 November 1903, p. 5.

97   See, for instance, the *Morning Post* editorial on Morley's speech at Nottingham on 3 November 1903; *Morning Post*, 4 November 1903, p. 4.

98   Chamberlain, at Leeds, 16 December 1903; reprinted in *Sheffield Daily Telegraph*, 17 December 1903, pp. 7–8.

99   *Ibid.*

100 A. W. Coats, *loc. cit.*, p. 210.

101 *Ibid.*, p. 211.

102 All the articles bore the same title, 'The fiscal policy of the Empire', and appeared in the *Times* at uneven intervals between 15 June and 19 September 1903.
103 *Morning Post* (editorial), 18 December 1903, p. 4.
104 Including one prophetic article on Britain's future trade policy, 'Der Imperialismus und seine voraussichtliche Wirkung auf die Handelspolitik des Vereinigten Königreichs', *Schriften des Vereins für Socialpolitik*, XCI, 1900.
105 *Sheffield Daily Telegraph* (editorial), 18 December 1903, p. 6.
106 *Morning Post* (editorial), 18 December 1903, p. 4.
107 Chamberlain at the first meeting of the Tariff Commission, 15 January 1904; reprinted in *Sheffield Daily Telegraph*, 16 January 1904, p. 9.
108 'A committee of directors', *Echo* (editorial), 18 December 1903, unpaginated but p. 2.
109 See, for example, *Morning Post* (editorial), 16 January 1904, p. 6.
110 *Parliamentary Debates*, 4th ser., CXXIX, 9 February 1904, col. 822; 10 February 1904, col. 954.
111 Churchill, at Halifax, 20 December 1903; in *Sheffield Daily Telegraph*, 21 December 1903, p. 9.
112 'A committee of directors', *Echo* (editorial), 18 December 1903, unpaginated but p. 2.
113 *Standard* (editorial), 17 December 1903, p. 6.
114 Chamberlain at the first meeting of the Tariff Commission; *loc. cit.*
115 *Morning Post* (editorial), 23 December 1903, p. 4.
116 L. T. Hobhouse to ed., *Times*, 14 March 1904, p. 6; W. A. S. Hewins to ed., *Times*, 15 March 1904, p. 8; Hobhouse to ed., *Times*, 16 March 1904, p. 2.
117 H. J. Gladstone to Hewins, three letters, 18 March 1904, 15 and 19 April 1904; reprinted in *Times*, 20 April 1904, p. 4.
118 Hewins to Gladstone, two letters, 30 March 1904 and 15 April 1904; reprinted in *Times*, 20 April 1904, p. 4.
119 Hewins to Gladstone, 30 March 1904; *loc. cit.*
120 Asquith, at Doncaster, 21 May 1903; *loc. cit.*
121 Weymss Reid, in *Nineteenth Century*, cited in A. W. Coats, *loc. cit.*, p. 199 n.
122 The commission was finally disbanded in 1921.

Control of the liquor trade in Great Britain
1914–21

Though the regulation of the sale of intoxicating liquor is older than Parliament itself, the form of control established during the first world war was very much more extensive and more stringent than anything that had existed hitherto. It involved not only extensive regulation of the trade and the consumers but it also included the penetration of the State into the ownership of licensed premises. The legacy of the latter remained in evidence until very recently when the remaining State houses were put up for sale.

On the whole the institution of wartime control was not motivated by the most obvious forces: that is, the need to conserve food supplies,[1] the prospect of high brewery profits or pressure from the temperance reformers. In fact the primary reason was to reduce the danger of the forces and munitions workers soaking themselves in alcoholic drink and thereby lessening the efficiency of the war machine. This is evident from the first steps taken to control the trade. The first regulation relating to liquor (12 August 1914) under the Defence of the Realm Act (DORA) stated that 'the competent naval and military authority may by order require all premises licensed for the sale of intoxicating liquor within or in the neighbourhood of any defended harbour to be closed except during such hours as may be specified in the order'. Further important regulations relating to the armed forces were subsequently promulgated, and by the end of August the first steps to control the civilian trade were introduced. The Intoxicating Liquor (Temporary Restriction) Act gave licensing Justices wide powers over the sale and hours of opening in areas where it was thought to be necessary.[2] Initially, however, primary emphasis was given to regulating the supply of liquor to the armed forces, and the need for controlling drink consumption throughout the country was never seriously considered much before 1915, and even then only because voluntary action had been tried and found wanting.

After the army the next area calling for immediate attention was around the munition centres. High wages and the influx of migrant workers had served to push up the rate of drunkenness in these areas; one of the worst places was Carlisle, where, it was alleged, 'almost every alley was littered with prostrate drunken men'.[3] The gravity of the situation was expressed by Lloyd George in February 1915 in a speech at Bangor. 'Drink is doing us more damage than all the German submarines put together . . . We have got great powers to deal with drink and we are going to use them.'[4] His solution to the problem was for the State to buy out the drink trade, but this plan failed to receive a warm reception in the Cabinet.[5] Instead a compromise solution was adopted which involved extensive regulation of the trade and a limited degree of State ownership. Under the Defence of the Realm Amendment Act of May 1915 the government was given powers, in areas to be defined by order in council, to sell, supply or control liquor, take over any premises, either temporarily or permanently, or establish its own refreshment rooms. These activities were to be exercised through a newly created Central Control Board which had very wide powers of control.[6] In fact the Board could do almost anything, from closing or acquiring premises and regulating the conditions of sale to the prohibition of treating and the establishment of refreshment rooms.[7]

Initially attention was directed at controlling the consumption of drink in those areas deemed essential to the war effort, that is, the ports and the munition centres. But the Board used its direct powers sparingly and only in three or four key areas did it actually acquire existing premises. These were in Enfield Lock, near London, Gretna and the Carlisle area on the west Scottish border, and Invergordon and Cromarty on the north-east coast of Scotland. All were taken over in 1916 at the instigation of the Ministry of Munitions or the Admiralty. These districts were all considered to be of vital necessity to the successful prosecution of the war, and the implementation of direct control was seen as the best way of reducing insobriety rather than as a first step towards a policy of wholesale State purchase of the liquor trade.[8] The Board's policy was to reduce drunkenness not merely by limiting the amount of drink but also by providing food with any liquor consumed, improving the condition of public houses, prohibiting the advertising of liquor and introducing disinterested management.

Outside these special areas the rest of the population steadily came within the Board's directions regulating the sale of alcoholic beverages. During 1915 about half the population of Great Britain had been covered by the Board's orders, while by the end of 1917 its sphere of control had been extended to some 38 million people out of a total population of 41 million.[9] At the same time measures were taken to restrict output, and dilute its quality, reduce the hours of sale and increase taxation. For example, the Output of Beer (Restriction) Act of 1916 limited beer production to 26 million standard barrels for the year to March 1917, that is, ten million less than the output in 1914. Subsequent cuts in production reduced output to little more than 10 million barrels for a time in 1917. At the same time restrictions on strength were implemented. An order of July 1917 stipulated that one half the quantity of beer brewed in Britain was to be at a gravity not exceeding 1,036 degrees, while in 1918 the War Cabinet decided that all beer brewed should be of a specific gravity of not more than 1,030 degrees.[10] There were also numerous other orders restricting the conditions of sale of liquor, while during the course of the war the opening hours of licensed premises was reduced drastically, from around sixteen to nineteen to no more than five hours per day. In addition, the enormous rise in the duty on beer and spirits had a considerable effect on the amount of beer and spirits consumed. In the autumn of 1914 the duty on a standard barrel of beer was increased from 7s 9d to 23s and by 1920 it had reached 100s. During the same period the duty on spirits per proof gallon rose from 14s 9d to 72s 6d. These changes in duty were not fully reflected in retail prices, since the latter were controlled from 1917 onwards. Even so, retail prices probably more than trebled during the course of the war; the price of a glass of spirits, for example, rose from 4d to 1s 2d.[11]

There can be little doubt that wartime control produced a very much more sober nation. The total number of convictions for drunkenness in England and Wales fell from 135,811 to 29,075 between 1915 and 1918, after which they rose again.[12] But the shift towards increasing sobriety was not solely due to wartime restrictions. Since the 1880s the position had been improving, and the rate per 10,000 of persons found guilty of drunkenness fell sharply between 1905 and 1916, from 59 to 25·27, with a further dramatic drop to 8·88 in 1918.[13] Several factors were responsible for this trend. The Royal Commission on Licensing of the 1890s listed the work of the temperance reformers, the spread of education and the recent intensive development of the 'passion for games and athletics'. This last activity, it was stated, served as a powerful rival to 'boozing', which was at one time almost the only excitement open to working men.[14] In the early twentieth century counter-attractions such as the cinema, radio, allotments and improved travel facilities brought about less drunkenness, coupled with the fact that by that time drunkenness had gone 'out of fashion'.[15]

The Board's success in the direct control districts was not specially greater than elsewhere. In the principal area, Carlisle, drunkenness was reduced considerably after 1916 but other places recorded a greater proportionate fall. Thus, for example, the number of convictions in Bootle fell from 495 to eighty-two between 1914 and 1918, against a decline of 275 to eighty in Carlisle. Admittedly there was a very much sharper drop between 1916 and 1918 in Carlisle, but this was largely accounted for by the dramatic boost to convictions in 1916 as a result of a large influx into the area of workers with a high propensity to consume liquor. In any case more than fifty county boroughs out of a total of eighty-four had a lower conviction rate than Carlisle for each of the years between 1916 and 1924, while the record for insobriety among women was especially poor in Carlisle. By 1929 convictions for drunkenness in England and Wales had fallen to 27·5 per cent of the 1913 level and in Carlisle to 22·8 per cent.[16] In other words, State control did not produce all the benefits expected, and the claim that the sharp drop in convictions in Carlisle from the very high levels reached in 1915–16 was due to the introduction of disinterested management is not valid.[17] The improvement began before direct control became effective and it synchronised with the exodus of the migrant workers who had been largely responsible for pushing up the rate of convictions.

If anything, therefore, restrictions on hours of sale and the quantity of beer brewed were more effective in reducing insobriety than a nation-wide policy of State ownership and control of the trade. This is hardly surprising when one examines the figures for output and consumption. Between 1915 and 1918 beer production feel from 33·1 million standard barrels to 13·8 million, and spirits distilled declined from 50·1 million to 37·1 million gallons over the same period. Consumption per head of beer fell from 25 to 10 gallons and of spirits from 0·74 to 0·31.[18] Despite the restrictions on production and consumption, brewery profits rose sharply, from £10·0 million in 1913–14 to £24·4 million in 1917–18 and to £32·4 million in 1919–20.[19] The number of licensed premises continued to decline, but at no faster rate than before the war, despite the Central Control Board's almost unlimited powers of suppression.

The success of the wartime control of the liquor trade, as regards both sobriety and the saving of valuable food resources, is hardly in question. The more interesting issue is what was to happen after the war. Should all restrictions be abolished, the Board wound up and the trade thereby revert to the system of local control as practised before the war? Or should some attempt be made to retain control in the national interest, and if so what form should it take? In actual fact most of the wartime restrictions on output, gravity and hours of sale were lifted in the immediate post-war years, the Board was eventually abolished and only a few legacies of the wartime experience remained. But not before there had been considerable debate about the whole issue, a debate which centred around the existence of the Control Board and the question whether the State should penetrate further into the liquor business. Nationalisation was a very live issue during the latter half of the war and immediately thereafter, and at one time it seemed possible that the liquor traffic, along with the railways, coal mines and one or two other things, would be acquired by the State. The fact that the trade eventually remained in private hands was due not so much to any ideological

aversion on the part of the government to a policy of State purchase but
to the fact that there were so many varied and conflicting interests
involved that eventually the best solution appeared to be to leave well
alone.

Though wartime control of the liquor trade was regarded as a
temporary expedient it was almost inevitable that more permanent
regulation should be considered in the light of wartime experience.[20] Few
people were, of course, opposed to a course of action which involved a
larger measure of control than had existed before the war, but the
controversial issue was whether the state should be directly involved in
the business of liquor.

The question of State purchase certainly cropped up frequently during
the course of the war, and for a time it gained considerable backing.
Several committees reported on the matter in this period. The first of
these, an advisory committee under Lord Samuel, was given the specific
task of examining the financial implications of State purchase in the event
of such a policy being adopted. Since the report was signed before the
Central Control Board was established it could not be taken as referring
to proposals for a permanent policy in the light of practical experience.
Briefly, the committee concluded that such a policy would be financially
feasible, the cost of transfer being estimated at some £250 million.[21]

At the time no specific action was taken on this matter, largely because
the Cabinet did not share Lloyd George's enthusiasm for State purchase.
But during the latter half of the war the prospects become considerably
brighter. Early in 1917 a Home Office committee had reported in favour
of State purchase, and subsequently the Prime Minister was presented
with a plan for the complete control of the trade during war time with a
view to probable State purchase after the war.[22] That the matter was
under very serious consideration at this time is indicated by the fact that
in June a series of three committees (one each for England and Wales,
Scotland and Ireland) were set up 'to inquire and report on the terms
upon which these interests should be acquired and the financial
arrangements which should be made for the period of control', the
assumption being that wartime control would inevitably involve purchase
of the brewery trade after the war.[23] The main recommendations applied
to the whole country, and the Scottish and Irish committees dealt with
the differences in law, custom and trade organisation compared with
England and Wales.[24]

Since most retail outlets were 'tied' to the brewers, the committee
recommended that both the manufacture and the supply of alcoholic
liquor should be acquired by the State, together with most off-licence
premises. The sale of intoxicants in hotels, restaurants, railway
refreshment rooms and in clubs would be excluded and the State would
not acquire wholesale businesses in wines and foreign spirits. The cost of
acquiring the main interests, that is, the brewers, free houses, on-licence

holders and retail off-licences but excluding distillers and rectifiers, was put at £350 million, and at well over £400 million if Scotland was included. The terms of purchase were to be based on pre-war values, the average annual profits of the four years 1910–13 being taken as the basis of valuation for brewery undertakings, while in other cases the purchase price was to be fixed by a tribunal in default of agreement. The purchase price was to be paid in government stock, and a purchasing body or tribunal would be established to carry out the acquisition.

Meanwhile the Central Control Board had been exerting pressure in the same direction. At the end of 1916 the Board had submitted a memorandum to the government which favoured a policy of State purchase.[25] Doubtless it based its advice on the favourable reports isued in 1915 and 1916, to the effect that its work had been nothing short of a great success.[26] 'State control,' it noted, 'has come to be regarded with more and more favour as being the policy which offers the most rapidly effective and best permanent solution of the problem.'[27] The Board had considered the possibility of assuming control of the drink traffic for the period of the war only, or as a preliminary to purchase at some later date, but it was satisfied that on both financial and administrative grounds a policy of purchase outright was by far the most desirable course to adopt in the particular circumstances of the liquor trade. In its third report the Board was able to state emphatically that by extinguishing private interests in the sale of liquor and establishing a strict system of control and inspection of public houses it had been possible to reduce excessive drinking to a very marked degree, and to ensure that restrictions such as those imposed by the Board's orders were effective to an extent impossible under conditions of private management.[28] Clearly the Board was under no illusions as to the benefits of direct control.[29]

The Board had some cause for self-satisfaction with the results achieved in the direct control areas, though undoubtedly it exaggerated them and not all could be attributed simply to the imposition of State management. Certainly it had done some very good work in the way of improving the conditions under which alcohol was sold. Its policy was fewer and better houses, the provision of food and non-intoxicants, a general improvement in the conditions under which the whole trade was carried on, and the elimination of private interests in the sale of intoxicants.[30] A few examples will serve to illustrate this point. In the Enfield Lock area the Greyhound and Royal Small Arms taverns had been reconstructed and as a result some thousands of workers were provided with rest, recreation and refreshment in hygienic and pleasant surroundings in premises in which formerly less than a quarter of the number could find sitting or standing space, being herded together in small rooms, staircases and corridors. Upwards of 250,000 meals had been provided at these two taverns since the completion of the schemes of renovation.[31] A similar policy had been followed at Gretna; a number of taverns were improved and provision was made for the sale of food, with teas served at some country inns. Longtown provides a typical example. This was a small town near the Gretna munition factory which had seven licensed premises when the Board began operations. Four of these were subsequently closed down and a fifth, the Globe, was entirely reconstructed to comprise a large beer hall with kitchen, dining, billiard and reading rooms. An off-sales shop also formed part of the scheme. The Graham Arms Hotel, in 1916 nothing more than a squalid drinking house, was transformed into a first-class country hotel which was chiefly frequented by fishermen and motorists. The bars were abolished and a new smoking room was opened. In Carlisle itself eight food taverns were established from which hot meals were dispensed, a total of 570,000 being served in the year ending 31 March 1920.[32] These taverns also sold food for consumption off the premises, and hot pies and soup were served to many workers, who benefited from a good meal rather than cold intoxicants, especially in winter. Rationalisation also brought considerable economies. By 1920 Carlisle had only one brewery instead of four, while bottling was carried on in only one establishment as against twelve prior to the Board's inception. It was estimated that up to £40,000 was saved on the wholesale and retail side.[33] With the institution of salaried managers an effective check was kept on credit, treating, profit and the 'long pull' practice of giving generous measure to attract custom, all of which were common when the trade was in private hands. As a result the Board managed to make a reasonable return on capital employed.

The general manager for the Carlisle area was in no doubt that the experiment had been a success. It showed that the transfer from private to public ownership could be carried through without undue friction and without loss to the national exchequer.[34] Moreover he questioned the wisdom of handing the trade back to private enterprise, since it would not be welcomed by the inhabitants. 'What appears to be incontrovertible is that any proposal to hand back the licensed trade to private interests would be received with dismay by the great majority of the inhabitants.'[35] Support for the Board's work was not lacking. The chief constable for Carlisle welcomed it on the grounds that it kept the amount of drunkenness down, while trade unionists and Labour Party members were very satisfied with what they saw in Carlisle. A meeting of organised labour in the area passed a unanimous resolution in November 1919 in favour of the extension of public ownership to the whole country.[36]

Though the government never formally adopted a policy of nationalisation it seems very certain that for a time the possibility of extending the 'Carlisle experiment' was under serious consideration by the Cabinet. Lloyd George, Winston Churchill and other members of the government were known to favour a policy of further acquisition.[37]

Indeed, in its report for 1918 the War Cabinet paid tribute to the activities of the Central Control Board in such a manner as to imply that nationalisation might well form part of the government's post-war legislative programme. 'The continued progress of the Board's work has proved that in the areas concerned, strict control of the liquor traffic and financial success are not irreconcilable under the conditions of State ownership with a development of enlightened and constructive policy.'[38] Furthermore the King's Speech in February 1920 indicated that legislation would be forthcoming, and while no specific mention was made about State purchase there was nothing to suggest that such a policy had been ruled out of court. 'Experience during the war showed clearly the injurious effects upon national efficiency of the excessive consumption of strong drink and the amelioration both in health and efficiency which followed appropriate measures of regulation and control. A Bill will accordingly be presented to you providing for the development of a suitable system for the peace-time regulation of the sale and supply of alcoholic liquor.' The King's Speech of 1921 also promised legislation dealing with the sale of alcoholic liquor in the light of experience gained during the war.

Yet it was not until the summer of 1921 that legislation dealing with the matter was presented, and then it became clear that no further acquisitions would be made by the State. It was a fairly weak compromise which merely transferred the properties of the Board to the Home Office and placed certain limitations on conditions of sale. The fact that it took so long to produce the legislation would seem to indicate that the government was still contemplating the possibility of a more radical measure. The question is, why did the government back down at the eleventh hour from nationalising the drink trade?

The more obvious reasons for rejecting nationalisation as a solution may first be considered briefly. It is probable that by 1920 the government was rapidly losing any appetite it may have once had for revolutionary policies. State purchase of the coal mines had been rejected as early as August 1919 and the railways were relieved of the same threat soon afterwards. In any case it would have been difficult to force such a radical measure through Parliament at the time, though no doubt the purely ideological opposition to putting the drink trade under State control was less strong than in the case of the coal mines or the railways. More important, the financial cost of acquisition had escalated as a result of rapid inflation. By 1920 Snowden reckoned it would cost £1,000 million to implement, that is, far more than double the estimate made during the latter half of the war.[39] Such a high price was hardly likely to appeal to the government, which by then was busily trying to cut down national expenditure.

But in the case of the liquor trade the cross-currents of informed and political opinion were probably crucial to the outcome. There were so

many differing shades of opinion on what should be done that
nationalisation never received substantial backing from one particular
quarter for any length of time.[40] Most parties were agreed that something
should be done to regulate the trade in the light of wartime experience,
but there agreement ended. Even within any one particular movement
unanimity of opinion was sometimes difficult to reach. The Labour
Party, for instance, never threw its wholehearted support behind the
nationalisation cause. Initially the Labour Party did favour State
purchase, but it is doubtful whether it was ever very enthusiastic about
the idea. More likely its support was a convenient expendient in an
attempt to manoeuvre the government, which had been toying with the
question anyway, into taking a radical step at the 'shallow end' so that
the party could then press forward its claim for the nationalisation of
other industries. However, once the government had rejected
nationalisation of the mines the way was clear for the Labour Party to
modify its programme with respect to the drink trade. State purchase was
watered down to local option largely through the influence of Snowden,
who had started out as a supporter of nationalisation but who, for
various reasons — one being that he did not wish to annoy the
prohibitionists — had changed his views.[41] Thus at the Labour Party
conference in June 1920 a policy of State purchase was rejected:
1,352,000 votes for, and 1,672,000 against. Total prohibition was also
turned down overwhelmingly, but a local option resolution was carried
by 2,003,000 votes to 623,000.[42] But the Labour movement as a whole
was far from united on this issue. Early in 1920 the annual conference of
the Independent Labour Party at Glasgow carried motions in favour of
nationalisation of the drink trade and municipalisation of the retail trade
as well as one on prohibition. The Trades Union Congress also passed a
resolution in favour of public ownership, but the Scottish TUC rejected
nationalisation in favour of prohibition.[43]

Once the support of the Labour Party had dissolved there seemed little
point in the government pressing on alone with a policy which was bound
to create considerable controversy within the coalition government. Had
the Labour Party and Lloyd George waged a more concerted campaign
on this front there is a good chance that a nationalisation measure would
have been presented to Parliament. It is true, of course, that a number of
prominent government members were favourably inclined towards State
ownership or at least some form of State control over the brewery trade,
but any such action along these lines would undoubtedly have produced
considerable opposition within the government. Since the latter half of the
nineteenth century the brewing industry had been closely identified with
the Conservatives and the temperance movement with the Liberals.[44]
Neither could therefore afford to give much support to a policy of
nationalisation. Though parliamentary representation of the brewery
interests was less conspicuous than formerly, the trade still had twenty-

eight spokesmen in the House of Commons,[45] most of whom were totally opposed to State purchase or any real form of control, but they were disinclined to favour a return to pre-war conditions for fear of giving the temperance reformers an even greater weapon to wield in their campaign for prohibition.[46] The natural inclination of most Conservatives was, of course, against State control, though their most influential spokesman, Bonar Law, was a teetotaller and appeared indifferent on the matter. Since State purchase would not have satisfied the temperance interests,[47] the most that could be hoped for from the Liberals was some support for a policy of local option, towards which at least half the Liberals were known to have leanings.[48] Asquith himself had, only a few days after the armistice, made known his opposition to nationalisation.[49]

Whether the Prime Minister was ever really committed to a policy of nationalisation is difficult to determine, since Lloyd George was not noted for consistency in either his statements or views. There is no doubt that he had no ideological bias against State control and there seems no reason to believe that he would not have been prepared to take drastic steps had the conditions been right. It is true that in April 1915, when asking the House of Commons to give the Central Control Board unlimited powers, he did acknowledge that these were for the period of the war only: 'We do not want to raise any issue beyond that'. And by June 1919 it seemed very likely that the issue would go no further, since Bonar Law announced to the House that the government intended to terminate the existence of the Board and replace it by a Minister responsible to Parliament.[50] The absence of enabling legislation to follow this statement was later explained by the fact that the government was still considering how best to reap the benefits of wartime experience.[51] In fact the government had already given the matter a great deal of consideration and it is more than likely that the delay was caused by the fact that Lloyd George had not given up the idea of introducing a more radical alternative. In March 1920 he made a statement which, though not official, gave reason to believe that he not yet abandoned the notion of State purchase. Addressing a meeting of Liberal MPs at Westminster Hall on 18 March he was asked whether he was still in favour of the disestablishment of the drink traffic by putting it in the hands of disinterested management, 'a matter very dear to the heart of Liberals'. Lloyd George replied that it was the first time he was aware that the Liberals felt this way and ended by saying that 'it would be very welcome to me if it were so and I shall wait until I hear officially what the view is.' What is more significant is that earlier in his speech he had expressed regret that the opportunity to nationalise the trade had been missed during the war. 'I believe that in 1915, when I first proposed it, you could have purchased [the liquor traffic] at a price which subsequent events have shown would have produced an enormous revenue to the State and which the Carlisle experiment proved would have improved the sobriety

of the areas in which it would have worked.'[52] Yet by October 1920
Lloyd George had abandoned all thoughts of public ownership, believing
by then that nationalisation would lead to the evils evident in other
countries, namely personal, class and local sectional favours.[53]

Once Lloyd George had given up the cause the issue of nationalising
the drink trade was more or less dead. There are several possible reasons
why the Prime Minister changed his mind on the matter. The cost of
acquisition would have been prohibitive by 1920 and it certainly would
not have gone down well with the coalition government, which was bent
on reducing public expenditure. The lack of a strong body of support,
especially from the Labour and Liberal parties, and the divided and
sectional interests involved on this matter, were hardly likely to inspire
Lloyd George to plough a lone furrow. Moreover to bring the liquor
trade under the tutelage of the State was more likely to exacerbate
political controversy over the drink question than reduce it. As *The Times*
noted in 1919, 'The greatest objection to nationalisation ... is that it
would make the liquor question an incomparably more acute political
issue than it is already, because the advocates of prohibition and other
nostrums would only have to capture the Government to secure their
object.'[54] A Prime Minister bent on holding together a crumbling
coalition, which had not been particularly successful with its post-war
reconstruction policies,[55] would scracely wish to raise the political
temperature by a policy which was likely to feature prominently at the
next election.

A final factor, no doubt, was the absence of any firm popular
support in the country at large for State control. During the war the
public had acquiesced in the Board's restrictions as a necessary evil but
they became increasingly irksome in peacetime and their continued
existence led to the feeling that the best solution was to get rid of the
Board itself.[56] During 1919 and 1920 the Board came under increasing
fire from various quarters; a meeting of 2,000 people at Bradford in April
1919 demanded its abolition and attributed labour unrest in the area to
the fact that the Board's actions had not taken account of local
sentiment.[57] In December 1920 it was reported that transport workers at
the breweries were contemplating strike action in protest against its
continued existence.[58] There were also signs that the people in the
Carlisle area were becoming dissatisfied with the Board's management,
while the chairman of Tottenham magistrates even thought that the
Liquor Control Board was running England into revolution.[59]

The trade, of course, exploited popular sentiment. The implication that
full State control or even the continued presence of the Liquor Board
might lead to some form of prohibition or restriction on drinking habits
was used to counter the propaganda of the prohibitionists. Effective use
of placards was made by display in wineshops, clubs and bars. One of
these, for example, referred to America, where people had laughed at the

thought of the country going 'dry', but prohibition came and their glass of wine had gone. 'Your glass of wine will go too, if you do not defend it. Help yourself. The citizen, not the trade, can win this fight.'[60] The brewers were anxious to get rid of the Control Board and many of the wartime restrictions, though they had no wish to return to pre-war conditions – at least, not the long opening hours![61]

Inevitably, therefore, the solution adopted was a typically British compromise. As *The Times* foreshadowed in 1918, 'One of the best results of liquor control during the war is that it has pointed a middle way between the extremists on either side.'[62] On 12 May 1921 Lloyd George announced the government's decision to abolish the Central Control Board and transfer its properties to the Home Office.[63] Subsequently a round-table conference of seventeen MPs, under the chairmanship of Sir Gordon Hewart (Attorney General), was convened 'to consider with reference to the law of licensing how best to adapt in time of peace the experience obtained during the period of war'.[64] The proceedings were kept very secret, and the conference never issued a report except one for official circulation. Pending the outcome the Liquor Board was requested to suspend further relaxation of wartime restrictions, though many of the most important ones had already been removed. By the end of June it had finished its deliberations, having reached agreement as to the lines on which a non-contentious licensing Bill could be framed with the prospect of reaching the statute book that session. Recommendations as to hours of opening, licensing arrangements and the properties of the Board were embodied in the licensing Bill introduced on 19 July. The Bill was given a second reading on 22 July and it became law, without drastic amendment, a month later (17 August 1921).

Part I of the Licensing Act of 1921 outlined the conditions of sale. These were more rigorous than those which had applied before the war. Hours of opening, for example, were reduced by about half. For all licensed premises the hours of sale were fixed at eight (11 a.m. to 10 p.m., with a break of two hours at noon),[65] though in the Metropolis one hour extra was allowed (until 11 p.m.). For any district outside London the licensing Justices could vary the hours slightly if they felt that conditions warranted any alteration. Sunday opening hours were left as amended by the Board in 1920, that is, not more than five, and closing at 10 p.m.[66] Provision was also made for the extension of hours in the evening on certain premises, including clubs in which meals were served, provided specific application was made by the licence-holder. Conditions as to the sale and distribution of alcoholic liquor were made more stringent than before the war, since some of the wartime restrictions were retained. No one could sell (that is, a trader) liquor from a van, cart or vehicle without prior order. Other clauses restricted the granting of credit – everything bought had to be paid for – and prohibited the 'long pull' and house canvassing for orders. But restrictions on the supply of drink to residents on licensed premises and on the ordering of liquor for delivery were abolished.

The second part of the Act dealt with the Central Control Board and its properties. The Board was wound up and the four State management districts – Carlisle, Enfield Lock, Cromarty Firth and Gretna – were taken over by the Secretaries of State for England and Scotland. They could dispose of the properties or administer them until Parliament determined what might be done with them, but no new premises could be acquired except in the Carlisle area. In fact the Enfield Lock premises were sold in 1923, but most of the remaining properties continued to be managed by the State until quite recently.[67]

Thus a subject which had excited such a great deal of controversy during the war and early afterwards finally ended on a calm and virtually uncontentious note. As *The Times* noted, the strength and acceptability of the new legislation lay in the fact that it was a partial return to pre-war and a compromise at that.[68] Possibly too most people were heartily tired of the liquor dispute by 1921.

Not a great deal really remained from the wartime experience. The licensing Justices regained most of their former powers, though conditions relating to the supply and sale of alcohol were made more stringent than formerly, most notably the sharp reduction in the length of time each day during which liquor could be sold. The nationalisation of the trade, which looked a distinct possibility at one stage, failed to materialise, largely because of the fragmented and half-hearted support for such a policy and the conflicting opinions as to how the drink question should be dealt with. Hence a compromise solution was inevitable and the State simply ended up with the management districts which the Central Control Board had taken over during the war.

However, though the legacies of wartime control were fairly limited the experience did have one beneficial effect in that it helped to produce a much more sober nation. The consumption of liquor rose again after the restrictions were relaxed but it never attained anywhere near its pre-war level. During the early 1920s consumption per head of spirits was nearly 50 per cent down on the immediate pre-war years, while beer consumption was also appreciably lower (16·6 gallons per head in 1924, as against nearly 27 just before the war).[69] Convictions for drunkenness reached a low point of under nine per 10,000 persons in 1918 and then rose steadily to a peak of over twenty-one in 1924, after which they declined steadily. By the early 1930s the rate was less than one fifth that of the immediate pre-war years.[70] Of course, as mentioned earlier, not all of this improvement can be attributed to the wartime crisis, since there had been a steady downward trend in drinking since the last quarter of the nineteenth century. But there is little doubt that the wartime check to imbibing produced a beneficial response in peacetime.

Notes

1 60–70 per cent of the barley used in brewing could be made into flour suitable for bread making. T. N. Carver, *Government Control of the Liquor Business in Great Britain and the United States* (1919), p. 26; *Report of the Food (War) Committee*, Cd. 8421 (1917), p. 31.
2 H. Carter, *The Control of the Drink Trade* (1918), p. 30.
3 J. Rowntree and A. Sherwell, *State Purchase of the Liquor Trade* (1919), p. 30.
4 *War Memoirs of David Lloyd George* (1934), vol. 1, p. 194.
5 *Ibid.*, pp. 196–200.
6 For details regarding the establishment of the Board see Carver, *op. cit.*, pp. 69–75.
7 *Second Report of the Central Control Board*, Cd. 8243 (1916), pp. 7–8.
8 Though the question of State purchase of the trade was by no means a dead issue, as we shall see presently.
9 A. Shadwell, *Drink in 1914–22. A Lesson in Control* (1923), p. 36.
10 *Brewers' Almanack*, 1925, p. 82.
11 Carver, *op. cit.*, pp. 105–6; Shadwell, *op. cit.*, pp. 86–7.
12 *Licensing Statistics*, Cmd. 2496 (1925) p. vii.
13 G. B. Wilson, *Alcohol and the Nation* (1940), p. 432.
14 *Final Report of the Royal Commission on Licensing of 1896*, Cd. 9379 (1899), p. 2.
15 F. W. Hirst, *Consequences of the War to Great Britain* (1934), pp. 64–7; *Final Report of the Royal Commission on Licensing, 1929–31*, Cmd. 3988 (1932), p. 9.
16 Wilson Stuart, *Drink Nationalisation in England and its Results – the Carlisle Experiment* (1927), pp. 37–8; G. E. G. Catlin, *Liquor Control* (1931), p. 183.
17 On the basis of the Carlisle experiment Miss B. Picton-Turberville advocated State purchase as the best policy. See *Fortnightly Review*, 108 (1920), pp. 340–2.
18 *Brewers' Almanack*, 1925, pp. 85, 112, 117.
19 Wilson, *op. cit.*, p. 89; *The Economist*, 4 September 1920, pp. 356–7. Brewery profits had, however, been depressed before the war.
20 The general feeling that profit should be derived from the wartime control experience was not confined to the liquor trade. The railways provide a good example in this respect.
21 *Report of the Advisory Committee on the Proposal for the State Purchase of the Licensed Liquor Trade*, Cd. 8283 (1916). A separate report on Scotland was issued, dealing mainly with the differences in licensing laws between England and Scotland. For the *Scottish Report* see Cd. 8319 (1916).
22 *The Economist*, 20 January 1917, p. 82, and 10 November 1917, p. 763.
23 See Paper on the *Appointment of Committees to consider the Financial Aspect of Control and Purchase of the Liquor Trade by the State*, Cd. 8619 (1917).
24 *Reports of the English, Scottish and Irish Committees on the State Purchase and Control of the Liquor Trade*, Cd. 9042 (1918).
25 *Memorandum submitted to the Government by the Central Control Board (Liquor Traffic)*, Cd. 8613 (1917).
26 *Reports of the Central Control Board*, Cd. 8117 (1915), Cd. 8243 (1916).
27 Cd. 8613 (1917).
28 *Third Report of the Central Control Board*, Cd. 8558 (1917), p. 16.

29　Curiously enough, the exact position of the head of the Board, Lord D'Abernon, is somewhat unclear. He certainly did not want to see a return to pre-war conditions of sale, but it is very unlikely that he favoured a policy of nationalisation, or the continued existence of the Board in peacetime. He realised that it was not so much the policy of direct control which had reduced drunkenness but the restrictions imposed on output, hours of sale, etc. See *Alliance News*, May 1919, pp. 33–4, and *The Times*, 28 August 1919.

30　*General Manager's Report to the Central Control Board for the Year ending 31 December 1920 – Carlisle and District Control Area*, Cmd. 1252 (1921), p. 4.

31　*Fourth Report of the Central Control Board*, Cd. 9055 (1918), p. 14.

32　Cmd. 1252 (1921), p. 6.

33　*Ibid.*, p. 7.

34　*General Manager's Report to the Central Control Board for the Year ending 31 December 1918*, Cmd. 137 (1919), p. 20.

35　*General Manager's Report to the Central Control Board for the Year ending 31 December 1919*, Cmd. 666 (1920), p. 20.

36　A. Greenwood, *Public Ownership of the Liquor Trade* (1920), pp. 173–88. *The Times*, 14 November 1919.

37　*Brewers' Almanack*, 1920, p. 86.

38　*War Cabinet Report for 1918*, Cmd. 325 (1919), p. 294.

39　*The Times*, 26 June 1920.

40　Except from ardent socialists such as Sir Leo Chiozza Money.

41　Snowden was also unhappy with the wartime experiment in State control, partly because of the high profits made by the Central Control Board. Before the war he had supported State ownership only as a step to local veto or prohibition on the basis of a popular vote. *The Times*, 26 June 1920 and *Alliance News*, July 1920, p. 100.

42　*Alliance News*, July 1920, p. 100. During the previous year J. H. Thomas had been campaigning vigorously in favour of public ownership. *The Times*, 14 November 1919; *Brewers' Almanack*, 1920, p. 86.

43　*The Times*, 7 April 1920; Greenwood, *op. cit.*, p. 29.

44　R. C. K. Ensor, *England 1870–1914* (1936), pp. 70–2; P. Mathias, 'The brewing industry, temperance and politics', *Historical Journal*, 1 (1958).

45　*Brewers' Almanack*, 1920, p. 50.

46　The temperance movement was greatly strengthened by the fact that America went 'dry' in 1919–20.

47　They were particularly grieved at the much higher consumption of beer per head than of milk. *Alliance News*, April 1919, p. 25, October 1919, p. 79, January 1920, p. 27.

48　*Alliance News*, October 1919, pp. 77–85.

49　*Brewers' Almanack*, 1920, p. 86.

50　*H. C. Deb*, 2 July 1919, vol. 117, cols. 958–60.

51　*H. C. Deb*, 24 February 1920, vol. 125, cols. 1609, 1642–7.

52　*The Times*, 19 March 1920; *Alliance News*, April 1920, p. 55 – though in his *War Memoirs*, vol. 1, pp. 197–8, Lloyd George later stated that he deemed State purchase to be inexpedient in 1915 as yet.

53　*Brewers' Almanack*, 1921, p. 59.

54　*The Times*, 18 November 1919.

55　On this matter see P. Abrams, 'The failure of social reform, 1918–20', *Past and Present*, 24 (April 1963); P. K. Cline, 'Reopening the case of the Lloyd George coalition and the post-war economic transition, 1918–19', *Journal of British Studies*, 10 (1970); P. B. Johnson, *Land Fit for Heroes. Planning for Reconstruction, 1916–19* (1969).

56   *H. C. Deb.*, 18 May 1920, vol. 129, col. 1213.
57   *Brewers' Almanack*, 1920, p. 55.
58   *H. C. Deb.*, 9 December 1920, vol. 135, col. 2438.
59   *Brewers' Almanack*, 1920, p. 55.
60   *The Times*, 24 May 1920.
61   *The Times*, 1 July, 16 November, 3 December 1920. *Brewers' Almanack*,
     1920, p. 89. Though one brewer, W. Waters Butler, chairman of Mitchell's
     & Butler's, must go on record for expressing the belief that State purchase
     offered the best solution to the problem. See *The Statist*, 16 August 1919,
     pp. 323–5.
62   *The Times*, 4 December 1918.
63   *H. C. Deb.*, 12 May 1921, vol. 141, col. 2118.
64   *H. C. Deb.*, 14 June 1921, vol. 143, col. 241.
65   That is, the time range within which the eight hours could be operated.
66   Monmouth was added to Wales for Sunday closing.
67   The act also abolished any remaining wartime restrictions on the output
     and supply, etc, of alcoholic liquor.
68   *The Times*, 23 July 1921.
69   *Brewers' Almanack*, 1925, p. 117.
70   See G. B. Wilson, *op. cit.*, p. 432.

Clydeside revisited

A reconsideration of the Clyde shipbuilding industry 1919–38

If there is one product apart from whisky which epitomises the Scottish economy in the popular consciousness it is ships, and just as Lancashire is associated with cotton, South Wales with coal and Devon with dairy products, the geographical area in Britain most immediately connected with shipbuilding and marine engineering is almost certainly Clydeside. The Clyde-built ship and the Glasgow marine engineer are two of the standard clichés of British maritime fiction.

Like the Lancashire cotton industry and the South Wales coal mines, the Clydeside shipbuilding industry lives on, but in much reduced circumstances. In the years immediately before the first world war, however, the Clyde was the foremost shipbuilding and marine engineering centre not only of the United Kingdom but of the entire world. In the last full year of peace, 1913, the shipyards strung out along both sides of the Clyde and its estuary, with two principal concentrations around Glasgow and Greenock, accounted for more than 35 per cent of the total gross tonnage of merchant shipping launched in the United Kingdom: this represented over 20 per cent of the world's merchant shipping output at that time. In addition British warships totalling some 66,000 displacement tons – nearly 35 per cent of the total tonnage added to the Royal Navy in 1913 – were launched from Clyde shipyards.[1] But in 1913 the Clyde was at the zenith of its career as a shipbuilding centre: after that date things were never to be quite the same again. During the first world war itself, it is true, activity in the shipyards and marine engineering shops of Clydeside considerably exceeded the level of 1913 under the stimulus imparted by the emergency conditions of wartime.[2] But once the war was over the Clyde – like other British shipbuilding centres – entered into what even the most optimistic commentator would be obliged to characterise as a twenty-year period of depression. The naval construction programme initiated in wartime was virtually completed in 1919, and in no year of the period 1920–38 did the warship tonnage launched on the Clyde exceed two-thirds of the 1913 level: indeed, in some years not a single warship went down the ways from a Clydeside yard. Merchant ship construction fared less badly, but even so only in 1920 during the entire inter-war period did the gross tonnage of merchant ships launched on the Clyde come anywhere near the 1913 figure. The rest of the time the annual tonnage launched never exceeded 85 per cent of the 1913 figure, and in nine out of the twenty inter-war years it was less than 50 per cent of that figure.

It is not difficult to build up a fairly detailed and comprehensive picture of the rise of the Clyde as a shipbuilding and marine engineering centre before 1914, though it is fair to say that the definitive history even of that phase has yet to be written. But the troubled waters of the Clyde in the inter-war period are far from being as well charted by economic historians, though the chart is by no means completely blank. This essay attempts, not to complete the picture (far less to present any definitive view), but simply to fill it in a little more by supplementing and to a certain extent revising existing studies.[3]

I

The years between the two world wars were difficult for shipbuilders everywhere. Not only did the Clyde shipyards find it impossible to surpass the level of tonnage launched in 1913 but so, for most of the time, did shipbuilders elsewhere. Shipbuilding output in the rest of the United Kingdom, apart from the Clyde, never regained the 1913 level throughout the period 1919–38. In the rest of the world, outside the UK, the tonnage of merchant shipping launched in 1913 was exceeded only occasionally, in the period 1919–22, in 1930 and in 1937 and 1938.[4]

The economic circumstances affecting shipbuilding in general during the inter-war period are too well known to require detailed recitation here: a bare outline will suffice.[5] The fact was that throughout the inter-war period there was a surplus of merchant shipping in the world. The volume of world trade tended, on the whole, to stagnate throughout the period, with occasional dramatic slumps. In the very best years, which were few, it never rose above the 1913 level by a margin of more than 20 per cent. The world merchant fleet of the inter-war period, on the other hand, was substantially larger than the pre-war fleet. By 1929 the gross tonnage of merchant shipping in service in the world was 38 per cent greater than in 1914; in 1937 it was still, in spite of a significant decline in the slump years between 1929 and 1933, about 35 per cent greater than in 1914. But mere tonnage figures do not tell the whole story: technical improvements had considerably increased the efficiency of shipping between 1914 and 1937, and the carrying capacity of the world merchant fleet over the period had in fact grown by some 50 per cent. The great bulk of the increase in merchant shipping tonnage had been brought into being in the early years of the period, between 1917 and 1922, so that right from the start there was more shipping space available than was required in the conditions of world trade that persisted between 1920, when the post-war reconstruction boom collapsed, and 1939, the greatest proportion of it being tramp (i.e. general cargo) tonnage. In these conditions shipbuilders found it difficult to obtain orders even to replace old ships which were being scrapped. Nor could they expect to find any compensation for the depressed state of demand for merchant ships in the form of naval orders. Wartime construction had left the naval powers with larger fleets than they could conceivably need in peacetime (which most naval authorities, before 1931 at any rate, considered would be the normal state of international relations in the foreseeable future), and this surplus of warships, together with the effects of the Washington treaty and other naval armament limitation agreements, meant that naval construction in the '20s and early '30s was at a low ebb virtually everywhere.

British shipbuilders experienced the depressive effects on their industry of the economic conditions of the inter-war period perhaps in a more severe form than most others. Their best customers, not surprisingly, had always been British ship owners, who had represented nearly 80 per cent of their pre-war market. But British ship owners in the years between the wars were in an increasingly insecure position, and their propensity to order new ships suffered accordingly. For a start, Britain's import and export trades – the carriage of which had always been the principal business of British ship owners – were markedly less buoyant than world trade in general. And whereas foreign governments took steps to protect their domestic shipping industries by such means as outright subsidies, low-interest building loans and regulations restricting at least part of their countries' overseas trade to their own ships, the British government was very behindhand in making any special provision for the merchant marine that sailed under its flag. Britain's relatively unprotected merchant marine found it increasingly difficult to compete with foreign ships for such cargoes as were available, and not only was the proportion of world trade carried in British ships lower in the inter-war period than it had been before 1914 but the proportion of Britain's own trade carried in British ships was also substantially lower. As a result of all this the British merchant fleet, upon which British shipbuilders depended for most of their work, expanded less rapidly than the merchant fleet of the world as a whole between 1914 and 1929 (by $4\frac{1}{2}$ per cent as against 38 per cent) and contracted more sharply between 1929 and 1937 (by $13\frac{1}{2}$ per cent as against $2\frac{1}{2}$ per cent).[6]

The stagnation and decline of the domestic market served by British shipbuilders between 1919 and 1938 was compounded by the decline of their foreign markets. Merchant tonnage built on foreign account had amounted to over 22 per cent of the total merchant tonnage launched in Britain between 1909 and 1913; but only 15 per cent of the total merchant tonnage launched in Britain in the period 1920–38 was built in response to foreign orders. Foreign governments rarely, indeed, directly subsidised their domestic shipbuilders, but the measures they took to protect their shipping interests generally had the not unintended effect of strengthening the hands of their shipbuilders as well. So effectively did some governments act in this respect that British shipbuilders occasionally found that their own best customers, British ship owners, were deserting their traditional allegiance to British yards and placing orders abroad. The number of cases was not particularly large,[7] but such episodes as the order for five ships placed with a German yard in 1925 by the Furness Withy line had a moral effect far beyond the significance of the number and size of the orders concerned.

With their traditional market severely depressed, and facing considerably increased competition for both foreign and domestic orders, the British shipbuilders' share of world output would almost inevitably have declined during the inter-war period in any case. This tendency towards decline was, however, aggravated by certain adverse factors within the industry itself. Basic raw material costs, for instance, were often higher in Britain than in competing countries.[8] Nor can there be much doubt that foreign shipyards were in many respects more progressive technologically than their British counterparts – for example, in the substitution of welding for riveting, which speeded up the process of constructing hulls and their upper works and reduced their production cost.[9] On both the demand and supply sides, therefore, the tide was running against British shipbuilders between the wars. Britain remained the world's leading shipbuilding country between 1918 and 1939,[10] but her lead was being steadily reduced and the qualitative basis of her pre-1914 position was fast being undercut as the development of shipbuilding and marine engineering technology progressed more rapidly abroad than it did in Britain.

Within the United Kingdom the Clyde maintained its pre-war position as the most important shipbuilding centre between the wars. Indeed, as table 10.1 indicates, not only did Clydeside hold its own against the rest of the country as far as its share of total UK merchant shipping output was concerned, it actually improved somewhat upon its pre-war position, with the consequence that the region's share of world output fell less far below its pre-war level than did the rest of the country's. This improvement in the Clyde's position within the structure of the United Kingdom's shipbuilding industry as a whole is the basic phenomenon which this essay seeks to explain. It will also explore the question whether the Clyde could have done even better in the inter-war period, or (to put it another way) whether there were any easily defined or readily corrected

Table 10.1   Proportions of aggregate merchant tonnage launched (gross tons)

Years	Clyde % total		Rest of UK % world
	UK	World	
1909–13	33·00	20·10	39·05
1919–23	33·04	10·61	21·50
1924–28	39·45	20·74	31·83
1929–33	33·99	15·27	29·65
1934–38	37·93	14·13	23·12

Source. *Lloyd's Register of Shipping. Annual Summaries of Merchant Ships launched in the World.*

deficiencies within the shipbuilding and marine engineering industries of Clydeside which can be considered – without exercising the wisdom of hindsight to an undue extent – to have hampered their competitiveness or efficiency.

In seeking to explain the relative buoyancy of Clyde shipbuilding as against the rest of the United Kingdom during the years between the wars Mr Buxton evidently considered that two circumstances operated particularly in the Clyde's favour. First, and in his view foremost, was the emphasis placed by Clyde shipbuilders on the production of passenger liners and the smaller passenger cargo liners, for which demand after 1918 was generally more favourable than the demand for general cargo or tramp shipping. Britain's liner fleet had suffered greater wartime losses in proportion to its size than her tramp fleet; the liner trades were less depressed during the inter-war period than the tramp trade (which suffered most severely from the decline of British coal exports after the first world war); and liners were subject to a higher rate of obsolescence than tramps, so replacement demand for the former tended to be substantially more elastic. Secondly, and conferring a more marginal advantage on the Clyde in Mr Buxton's view, there was the fact that the Clyde took a lead over other British shipbuilding centres in the development and application of the diesel engine as a propulsion unit for ships.[11]

While not, in essence, disagreeing with Mr Buxton's suggestions, one wonders whether they do not represent a degree of oversimplification of the Clyde's position and whether, in any case, they tell the whole story. He appears to be suggesting that during the inter-war period the market for new ships moved in a direction less unfavourable to the traditional specialisation of Clyde shipbuilders than to those of other important shipbuilding centres in the United Kingdom, most notably perhaps those of the north-east of England. But to maintain as he did that the Clyde specialised in liner, and to a lesser extent warship, construction is to oversimplify matters to the point of distortion. It is true that specialists in liner and warship construction existed on the Clyde, and that among them were to be found some of the largest and most important firms on the river, such as Scott at Greenock, John Brown, Stephen, Fairfield and Barclay & Curle in and around Glasgow and Denny at Dumbarton. But in fact specialisation over a much wider spectrum of products was exhibited by the shipyards of Clydeside. Yarrow and Beardmore were primarily warship specialists; the yards around Paisley and Renfrew concentrated on the construction of dredgers and harbour service vessels such as tugs, hopper barges and pilot boats; there were coastal cargo ship specialists at Paisley and Old Kilpatrick, tanker specialists in Glasgow and, in what was probably numerically the largest group on the river, yards which specialised in the construction of general cargo ships of the tramp variety and cargo liners (which did not usually differ very substantially from tramps in size, design or construction). It was this last group that had formed the backbone of the pre-war Clyde shipbuilding industry. 'As a rule,' a *Glasgow Herald* editorial remarked in 1921, 'tramps predominated in the production of pre-war years, and the largest tonnages were usually to the credit of firms who specialised in such vessels.'[12] The most consistently successful Clyde shipbuilding firm in the inter-war years was not a 'liner and warship' specialist such as John Brown or Fairfield but Lithgow of Port Glasgow,[13] a 'tramp and cargo liner' firm whose subsidiaries – Wm. Hamilton & Co. and Robert Duncan & Co., both also of Port Glasgow and both sharing Lithgow's specialisation – also produced a substantial proportion of the Clyde's total output between the wars.

Mr Buxton is rightly inclined not to attach too much significance to the Clyde's lead in the field of diesel propulsion. One wonders, in fact, whether any significance need be attached to it, for not a single original contribution of any importance appears to have been made by Clydeside engineers in the field of marine diesel technology, in spite of the self-congratulatory air of contemporary comment on the subject such as is to be found, for example, in the columns of the *Glasgow Herald Annual Trade Review* in the early '20s.[14] One would look in vain for a Clydeside marine engineering firm producing diesels of its own design: in fact the only British marine engineering firm of any significance so employed appears to have been Doxford at Sunderland. Contemporary technical publications clearly reveal that Clyde-built motor ships in the inter-war years were overwhelmingly equipped with engines of Continental design, built under licence by Clyde engineers – the most common varieties being the Swiss Sulzer and Burmeister & Wain engines of Danish origin. The Glasgow firm of North British Diesels, which apparently played an important part in pioneering marine diesel engine construction on Clydeside in the early '20s, started life as a wholly-owned subsidiary of Burmeister & Wain of Copenhagen.[15]

Shipbuilders were in any case not entirely free agents in the choice of power plant for the ships they built. During the '20s and '30s shipbuilding firms might occasionally undertake the construction of vessels on a speculative basis, in which case they would have a free hand in their design, construction and equipment; but by and large the shipyard worked on the basis of commissions received from ship owners, who, since they were presumably better acquainted than the builder with the actual conditions under which their ships were required to operate, retained final control over a vessel's specification.[16] By no means all ship owners were convinced of the superiority of diesels over more traditional prime movers in relation to their own particular requirements. Thus, for example, the Harrison line of Liverpool remained unimpressed by both diesels and oil-fired steam engines (whether turbine or reciprocating) and continued to place their faith in coal-fired triple-expansion reciprocating steam engines for their ships right up to the outbreak of the second world war. In their estimation this old-fashioned form of propulsion suited their specific pattern of trade best, and since the Harrison line was one of the most successful British shipping lines during the inter-war period it would have been a brave shipbuilder indeed who said their decision was wrong.[17] In any event, the fact that the Clyde led the United Kingdom shipbuilding industry in the construction of motor ships was arguably due less to those who built the ships than to those who ordered them. As far as liners (both cargo and passenger) and warships were concerned, the nature of the individual product seems to have been substantially determined by the buyers (who maintained their own staffs of naval architects, marine engineers, etc) rather than by the builders, who worked under the close supervision of their customers' technical experts.

III

If the buoyancy of Clyde shipbuilding relative to the rest of the United Kingdom in the period 1918–39 is not to be satisfactorily explained by the river's specialised production and technical progressiveness, then wherein did the Clyde's advantage lie? It is well nigh impossible to answer this question with any certainty, but it does seem possible to suggest, in a decently tentative fashion, a number of possibilities hitherto largely unconsidered by serious students of economic history. While some of these potentially useful lines of enquiry are of a kind which would be recognised by most economic historians as professionally respectable, since they involve the consideration of suitably impersonal economic forces and might even be susceptible to quantitative analysis, the others carry the risk of accusations that one has succumbed to the romance of ships and the sea instead of submitting to the proper rigours of an academic discipline. The latter, unfortunately, somehow seem to be the more attractive and interesting, and could conceivably be the more reliable in explaining why the Clyde's record in the inter-war years was more fortunate than that of the rest of the UK.

To take the more respectable category first, one wonders whether the Clyde might have enjoyed a very narrow, but in the circumstances of the inter-war period nevertheless significant, cost advantage over its competitors in other shipbuilding centres in the United Kingdom by reason of the high degree of concentration in the west central part of Scotland of the coal, iron and steel, shipbuilding, marine and ancillary engineering and other industries relevant to the construction of ships. Shipbuilding is above all an assembly industry in which a very large number of components bought in from specialist manufacturers is fitted together to assume the form of a ship. These components – plates, frames, angles, prime movers of whatever type, metal castings, forgings and fabrications, insulating materials, valves, pumps, condensers, evaporators, auxiliary engines, cargo-handling equipment, navigational instruments and many other items – could readily be obtained for the most part within a twenty-mile radius or so from Glasgow itself, from suppliers who were in some cases the market leaders in the United Kingdom in their particular trades.[18] There is insufficient evidence available relating to the economics of fitting out a ship, but it is not inconceivable that better access to the whole range of materials and components for ship construction might have given the Clyde a slight advantage in the prime cost of construction over, say, Merseyside, Barrow, Belfast and other centres whose shipbuilders often relied upon the same sources (in their cases more distant, and therefore involving higher transport charges) for some at least of the parts they required. Even a very narrow cost advantage over other centres accruing to the Clyde from the very close proximity of major suppliers of shipbuilding components could have been of considerable commercial significance at a time when, as a contemporary remarked, 'initial costs weigh heavily with ship owners: with British ship owners, it would seem, even more than with foreign owners'.[19]

It also seems possible that Clyde shipbuilders enjoyed a certain margin of advantage over other British shipbuilders because they were somewhat more progressive technically, in a general way rather than in any specific aspect of their craft. Mr Robertson's study of technical education in the British shipbuilding and marine engineering industries *before* 1914 seems to indicate that, while Britain lagged a considerable way behind America and some European countries in this respect, the Clyde was the most advanced of the British centres.[20] It seems probable that the Clyde's lead in this field was not entirely dissipated before 1939, even though there is not much evidence of any marked broad-front advance in the related technologies of ship design and construction on the Clyde during the inter-war period. Even if the technical education of entrants into the shipbuilding industry in the period improved significantly (and there are few obvious signs that it did), the senior management and production workers in the yards in the '20s and '30s would be likely to be men who had been brought up in the pre-war tradition, when, as Mr Robertson has observed, 'formal technical training had been disdained by the men and their employers alike'.[21] But yet again, in the commercial conditions prevailing in the inter-war period, the retention of even a fairly marginal advantage in technique by the Clyde could have assumed a significance of some magnitude when it came to competing for orders against other UK shipbuilding centres.

IV

Anyone perusing the contemporary technical journals such as *The Shipbuilder and Marine Engineer*, newspaper commercial supplements or the published histories of shipping and shipbuilding companies in the inter-war period might perhaps be forgiven for speculating about the utility of an analysis of the history of shipbuilding during that unsettled era which is based entirely upon impersonal economic factors such as cost advantages, market structures or technological innovation. For the shipbuilding and shipping industries in the period both exhibit certain common characteristics which are not readily susceptible to that particular kind of approach; it may leave unexplained a residuum as significant in influencing the pattern of the industries' development as any analysis derived from more purely economic considerations. One such non-economic characteristic is tradition, which was important to ship owners and shipbuilders alike, and which appears to have exercised a not insubstantial role in determining the placing of shipbuilding orders. Another is what might loosely be described as the personal touch, deriving from the powerful spirit of individualism that permeated British shipping and shipbuilding circles.

In both the shipping and shipbuilding industries of the '20s and '30s the overriding characteristic of organisation – in spite of the existence of some quite large public companies with their attendant bureaucracies in both sectors – was individualism. The great majority of concerns appear to have been of the comparatively small 'family firm' variety, human in scale, in which powerful individual personalities could exercise a decisive influence. On the shipping side, for example, there were what might be described as the civilian Sea Lords, Kylsant, Inverclyde, Inchcape and Maclay, together with numerous baronets and plain esquires. On the shipbuilding side one finds similar figures, the Stephen brothers, Lord Pirrie of Harland & Wolff, Sir James Lithgow. Both sides exhibit a sense of close community at both the business and the social levels, and the communities were far from being mutually exclusive. When it came to the placement of an order for a new ship, personal contacts – sometimes of a most casual kind – could be decisive. Thus, for example, the construction of the three largest British liners for the North Atlantic route before 1914, the White Star Line's *Olympic* and her ill-fated sisters

Titanic and *Britannic*, was initiated as a result of a meeting over dinner in Belgravia between Lord Pirrie of Harland & Wolff and J. Bruce Ismay, son of Lord Ismay, the founder of the White Star Line.[22] More directly relevant, perhaps, to this study is the case of the 6,000 ton cruise liner *Nerissa*, completed in a record seven months after her keel was laid in November 1925 at William Hamilton's yard in Port Glasgow. Hamilton's was a Lithgow subsidiary, and the £164,000 order came to the yard as a consequence of a chance encounter in London between Sir James Lithgow and Sir Frederick Bowring of Liverpool's Red Cross Line.[23] Some Clyde shipbuilders, Lithgow among them, valued these personal contacts so highly that they were very resistant to suggestions that the salvation of their industry in the depresed conditions of the inter-war period lay in amalgamation, merger and the rationalisation of capacity.[24] When some form of rationalisation seemed unavoidable it was accepted only with the greatest reluctance even by Lithgow, who has ironically gone down in history as the arch-rationaliser who murdered Jarrow in the process. Characteristically, the chosen instrument for rationalisation – National Shipbuilders' Security Ltd, with Lithgow himself as chairman – allowed the individualism of the shipbuilders quite a full rein. 'The scheme,' it has been remarked, 'was not an amalgamation of shipbuilding interests. Nor was it a merger. There was no compulsion on any firm either to join or to sell. It was a purely voluntary co-operative effort to improve matters for the industry as a whole.'[25] Given the spirit of individualism which pervaded both shipping and shipbuilding, the importance shipbuilders attached to personal contacts with ship owners and the evidence (admittedly slim) that such personal contacts – even at a social level – did influence ship owners' decisions to order from particular yards, one may ask whether it was in this area that the Clyde's advantage over other shipbuiding centres lay. Did Clyde shipbuilders simply have more and better personal contacts with ship owners than builders in other areas, and did this determine that they therefore obtained a larger share of the reduced number of orders which were being placed in a time of decided difficulty for shipowners? It does not seem inconceivable that they might have done, given the Clyde's position as the country's principal shipbuilding centre.

This possibility is reinforced by the apparent existence in shipping circles of what, in modern marketing terms, might be described as a strong tendency towards 'brand loyalty' in the choice of builders of new ships. It is noticeable, for instance, that the White Star Line tended to have its new passenger liners built by Harland & Wolff at Belfast, whereas Cunard tended to go to John Brown at Clydebank. The Canadian Pacific Railway's shipping branch divided its favours between John Brown and Fairfield, and the latter firm also counted the Bibby Line among the regular patrons of its Govan shipyard. The P. & O. and British India lines, with their subsidiaries, were regular customers of

Alexander Stephen's Linthouse yard, as were the Glasgow-based shipping firm of Maclay & McIntyre and the Union Steam Ship Company of New Zealand. Glasgow was itself a major centre of the British shipping industry, and Glasgow ship owners would not unnaturally tend to favour local builders, but the Clydeside shipbuilders' contacts evidently extended well beyond their immediate locality, and some of their best customers were based in areas which were themselves shipbuilding centres of some note, like Merseyside.[26] The key to the apparent continuity of relationships between particular shipping companies and particular shipbuilders was probably partly to be found in the personal contacts that some shipbuilders valued so highly: it is human nature to do business with somebody whom one knows well and trusts, and such considerations can transcend questions of rational economic advantage. Partly also it lay in tradition: some ship owners had always done business with a specific shipyard and would continue to do so out of a combination of sentiment, inertia and satisfaction with the arrangement. Is it possible that the Clyde's ability to improve its position in the inter-war period at the expense of other centres resulted from the fact that its shipyards were fortunate enough to number among their regular clients a higher proportion of those shipping companies which were sufficiently successful financially in the trying circumstances of the times to be able to place orders for new ships?[27]

Finally, one may ask, could the traditions of Clydeside itself have been a factor in the expansion of the region's share of the United Kingdom's total output of merchant shipping? If the term 'Clyde-built' still stood in the inter-war period for the highest standards of quality and durability in ship design and construction and in marine engineering (in the UK, at any rate), then it is quite conceivable that those fortunate ship owners who were in a position to order ships would prefer to place their orders – other things, such as prime cost, delivery date and so on being equal – with builders in what was still widely considered, with or without real justification, as the place where the best ships were built. And the Clyde's reputation could not have been wholly undeserved: many of its firms were indeed the leading specialists in the United Kingdom in the production of certain specific types of ship.

The shipbuilding industry of Clydeside was obviously not completely insulated against the operation of purely economic, impersonal forces such as the state of world seaborne trade, measurable changes in the pattern of demand for new merchant ships, and so on. But the industry's development in the inter-war period was equally clearly not so adversely affected as the rest of the United Kingdom's shipbuilding industry in general. That economic circumstances in the '20s and '30s were less unfavourable to the Clyde than to the rest of the UK, as Mr Buxton has suggested, is not to be entirely gainsaid, but non-economic factors such as advantageous personal contacts, tradition and reputation may well have played their part too in protecting the Clyde to a certain extent against the full rigours of the economic elements. It is not possible to be certain of this, nor to define the extent of the protection thus obtained, and perhaps it will never be possible. But, while certainty is lacking, one may at least take the view that it would not be impossible for such non-economic factors to have exercised an influence perhaps as decisive as that which was brought to bear on Clyde shipbuilding by the more specifically economic forces.

V

The Clyde's position as the leading shipbuilding centre of the United Kingdom, and for that matter of the world, before 1914 may well have been, as Professor Campbell has suggested,[28] the result of the area's pre-eminence in the late nineteenth century in the field of marine engineering. On to this there came to be grafted a willingness to innovate in techniques of hull construction and other aspects of the actual building of ships. Even before 1914, however, there appeared to be signs that the initiative in innovation in both shipbuilding and marine engineering was passing from the Clyde.[29] And during the first world war itself a tendency (by no means confined to the Clyde) actually to resist the application of technical innovation in shipbuilding manifested itself. When the standardisation of ship design, prefabrication and other methods of simplifying and speeding up merchant ship construction were advocated as means of rapidly replacing merchant shipping losses sustained in the face of the German submarine campaign, most shipbuilders wanted nothing whatever to do with such new-fangled notions, which 'did not appeal to shipbuilders with pride in their craft, and they were relieved when the Armistice removed that threat'.[30] It was left to the Americans to demonstrate the advantages of the new techniques, which were the basis of the enormous expansion of US merchant shipping output of 1917–21. For a time the Clyde was worried by what was evidently considered a serious threat from America,[31] but when the American shipbuilding bubble burst at the end of the post-war reconstruction boom the relief of Clydeside was probably mingled with a strengthened attachment to technological tradition. Nothing justifies the rejection of change better than the discomfiture of those who have accepted it.

In matters of technology Clyde shipbuilders and marine engineers were probably in most respects at least as good as any in the kingdom in the inter-war period. The main British centre of marine diesel development was in the north-east of England, as has already been noted, and the Burntisland Company's yard on the east coast of Scotland was probably the most progressive in Britain in construction techniques,[32] but with these exceptions there is no reason to assume that the Clyde lagged behind other British centres in technological terms. It may even, as suggested above, have retained a slight general technological lead. In no area of technology, at any rate, was the Clyde shipbuilding industry completely static.[33] Equally clearly, however, it was by no means as advanced as its Continental competitors, for example in the case of substituting welding for riveting. Another aspect of shipbuilding in which, during the inter-war period, Continental countries established a clear lead over the Clyde and the rest of the United Kingdom was hull-design. This is perhaps best exemplified in the case of the large Transatlantic liners put into service between the wars. *Queen Mary*'s hull was not, as has been suggested, simply a larger version of the earlier *Aquitania*'s, but it was not as radically different from *Aquitania*'s as the hulls of the German liners *Bremen* and *Europa* and the French *Normandie*. These three ships, all launched in the inter-war period before *Queen Mary* herself and all (like the Cunarder) the highest expression of the shipbuilder's craft in their respective countries, were better designed, more efficient and in all respects more modern in the configuration of their hulls than their British rival. *Normandie*, slightly larger than *Queen Mary*, required 40,000 fewer horse-power from her engines to more or less match the Cunarder's cruising speed.[34] Even if hull design on the Clyde had matched or surpassed that in France or Germany, however, it may be doubted whether any significant change in the placement of shipbuilding orders would have resulted: the Compagnie Générale Transatlantique would have been no more disposed to order their *Normandie* from John Brown's yard than Cunard were to order their *Queens* from Penhoët or Hamburg. Tradition and sentiment, to say nothing of government policy, would not have permitted it.[35]

VI

It is convenient, and arguably necessary, to deal with naval shipbuilding on the Clyde during the period under discussion separately from merchant shipbuilding. For one thing, although Clydeside managed to maintain and even improve upon its pre-war share of British merchant shipping output, the same was not true of the river's record as far as naval construction was concerned, as table 10.2 demonstrates. Admiralty orders for new warships were fulfilled from two sources, which might be described as the competitive and non-competitive sectors of the shipbuilding industry.[36] The royal dockyards comprised the non-competitive sector, being under complete and direct Admiralty control: traditionally, before about 1850, they had enjoyed a virtual monopoly of warship construction for the Royal Navy. A variety of pressures developing after 1850, however, had obliged the Admiralty to make more use of private shipyards for the construction of warships, and on the eve of the first world war warships built under contract to the Admiralty by

Table 10.2. Proportion of tonnage launched on the Clyde for Royal Navy service (displacement tons)

Years	Clyde % of all RN construction	Clyde % of RN tonnage launched from private shipyards
1898–1908	25·61	–
1913	34·46	59·80
1918	41·17	41·41
1919–23	35·60	38·71
1924–28	30·05	40·72
1929–33	9·96	19·74
1934–38	36·08	42·84
1919–38	31·27	39·23

Source. L. Jones, *Shipbuilding in Britain, mainly between the Wars*, 125 (table XXXIII). The more significant figures in this table are those in the second column

private shipbuilders constituted the bulk of the naval tonnage launched in Britain; and of the private shipbuilders employed by the Admiralty, Clydeside shipyards – contributing nearly 60 per cent of the contract-built tonnage launched for Royal Navy use in 1913 – were by far the most important. What appears to have happened is that, during the 1914–18 war, naval capacity in shipbuilding centres other than the Clyde underwent the most rapid expansion, and the need to maintain as much as possible of that capacity in being during the inter-war period resulted in a shift in the focus of the Admiralty's contract building activities which was unfavourable to the Clyde. In any case, Admiralty work was concentrated as far as possible during the '20s and '30s in the royal dockyards, as the naval authorities understandably desired to ensure the maximum possible use and continuity of work for the establishments under its own direct control. Only the need to maintain established contacts with private shipbuilders, the need to maintain a reserve of efficient private capacity for naval construction and the fact that the size of ship capable of being handled by the royal dockyards appears to have been limited to a maximum of about 20,000 displacement tons kept a highly erratic flow of orders moving towards the private naval shipbuilders between 1920 and about 1934. For several years during that period Clyde yards on the Admiralty's list secured no naval orders at all; in others the naval tonnage launched amounted to the few hundred tons represented by a single river gunboat for service in China or a single Fleet destroyer. Only once between 1920 and 1935 did the Clyde launch more than 50 per cent of its 1913 naval tonnage figure: this was in 1925, when warships totalling 35,000 tons went down the ways. Under the impetus of the rearmament programme initiated by Baldwin's National

Government naval construction picked up considerably, but even so the Clyde never came near to approaching, between 1935 and 1938, the figure for naval tonnage launched into the river in 1913. And although in every year from 1935 to 1938 the Clyde improved upon its 1913 performance in terms of its proportion of total naval output from British shipyards of all types, it never approached its 1913 position as producer of some 60 per cent of the contract-built tonnage launched for the navy.

As far as naval construction in the inter-war period was concerned, the Clyde yards could do little to improve the state of affairs they experienced. In the case of British naval orders they were entirely in the hands of the Admiralty, which exercised absolute rule and was not readily susceptible to any pressure from private shipbuilding interests. Foreign orders could be sought, and were indeed obtained, but the days of the great international naval race – when European, South American and Oriental countries of even the most modest maritime pretensions indulged in the bulk buying of British naval hardware – were over, and what before 1914 had been a stream of potential foreign customers was reduced to a trickle.

It can, perhaps, be argued that Admiralty shipbuilding policy ought to have been different. There was some scope, even under the provisions of the international agreements on the limitations of naval forces in operation during the period, for a more ambitious programme of new naval construction than was actually followed. But economic and political conditions in Britain before 1936 constituted a serious practical barrier to this. On the outbreak of war in 1939, however (or at least very soon afterwards), some serious deficiencies in Britain's naval armaments were revealed. There were not enough Fleet destroyers, anti-submarine escort vessels or up-to-date aircraft carriers at the Royal Navy's disposal in 1939–40 for the war it was called upon to fight.[7] In addition, Britain's oil supplies were threatened by a serious shortage of tanker tonnage.[8] One way or another these deficiencies were dealt with, but at a considerable cost in cash and above all in blood during the massacre of inadequately escorted convoys which occurred between 1940 and 1943. Had the Admiralty been less under the domination of the battleship school and more aware of the lessons of the previous war (particularly as regards anti-submarine warfare and convoy protection) during the years between the two conflagrations the naval construction programme might have started earlier, proceeded on a larger scale and followed a pattern more closely conforming to Britain's strategic needs. In addition, the ineffectual scrap-and-build policy towards tramp shipping implemented by the government in the '30s should perhaps have been dropped in favour of a policy designed to encourage tanker construction by British owners. These alternative policies – none of them unrealistic in terms of the information that was available to the Admiralty and the government at the time – would have served the country's needs better than the policies actually implemented. They might also, incidentally, have served the interests of the Clyde in its role as a leading centre of warship and tanker construction.[9]

VII

Much work remains to be done on the economic history of shipbuilding and marine engineering on the Clyde and elsewhere. There is a wealth of published contemporary source material covering the twentieth century at least, in the technical and commercial press, in the reports of official enquiries, and so on, and it is rather surprising that Scottish economic historians especially have not in the past devoted more attention to industries which were of such crucial importance to the national economy of their country in the hundred years before 1950. There are signs, however, of a growing interest in the subject in Scotland, which has been assisted, ironically, by the decline of Scottish shipbuilding since about 1960. The records of many old and famous firms – among them John Brown, Denny, Stephen, Barclay-Curle and Fairfield – are becoming available for study as a result of the disappearance by merger or liquidation of the firms themselves. These valuable source materials are indeed beginning to be utilised by historians. It is to be hoped that the fruits of their efforts will not be too long in ripening, and that relatively unambitious studies such as the present one may be of some modest assistance to them by at least suggesting some questions worthy of their attention. In particular it may be worth hoping that new, detailed studies based closely on the business records of shipbuilding firms may enable more light to be cast upon the relationships between shipbuilders and their customers and component suppliers, since it seems possible that in this wider sphere – rather than within the shipbuilding industry itself, narrowly defined – the explanation of the record of the shipbuilding industry in the inter-war years and at other times may be found.

Notes

1 Unless otherwise stated, all figures relating to merchant shipping are in gross tons and are drawn from *Lloyd's Register of Shipping. Annual Summaries of Merchant Ships launched in the World*. Annual displacement tonnage of warships launched for the Admiralty are to be found in L. Jones, *Shipbuilding in Britain mainly between the Wars* (1957), table XXXIII, 125

2 See W. R. Scott and J. Cunnison, *The Industries of the Clyde Valley during the War* (1924), 74 f.

3 Few existing studies of either phase relate to Clydeside specifically. In practice, however, studies of *Scottish* shipbuilding are inevitably heavily biased towards the Clyde, which accounted for roughly 90 per cent of all Scottish shipbuilding output in 1870–1939. The same bias, though obviously not to the same extent, is present in studies of UK shipbuilding, of which the Clyde in the same period was the leading centre of production

Table 10.3. The performance of Clyde shipbuilding in the inter-war period

Year	Merchant shipping launched on Clyde (gross tons)	Clyde % total UK merchant output	Motor ships % Clyde merchant output	Tankers launched on Clyde (gross tons, ships over 1,000 g.t. only)	Clyde % total UK tanker output	Warships launched on Clyde (RN only, displacement tons)	Clyde % total UK warship output
1919	525,747	32·5	n.a.	n.a.	—	99,997	41·3
1920	680,466	33·4	n.a.	n.a.	—	429	1·6
1921	505,189	32·9	11·4	n.a.	—	nil	—
1922	392,068	38·0	14·7	n.a.	—	nil	—
1923	172,931	26·8	19·1	n.a.	—	nil	—
1924	532,072	37·0	20·5	7,898	12·2	nil	—
1925	506,717	46·7	27·5	46,450	34·5	35,000	50·0
1926	267,645	41·8	18·8	33,740	33·7	11,225	20·9
1927	423,723	34·6	31·5	76,825	25·1	1,054	5·0
1928	571,948	39·5	33·4	103,644	34·5	21,540	28·0
1929	532,379	35·0	39·7	49,117	28·1	6,860	17·0
1930	508,392	34·4	42·6	132,713	24·1	2,660	10·3
1931	148,392	29·5	43·5	72,125	29·8	nil	—
1932	52,196	33·1	0·6	6,427	100·0	2,750	7·2
1933	48,760	36·6	17·4	nil	—	875	8·2
1934	237,631	51·7	34·8	8,807	12·8	25,635	30·2
1935	160,600	32·2	28·2	52,610	100·0	8,895	38·0
1936	282,182	33·0	50·7	60,019	40·3	31,080	35·9
1937	335,897	36·5	51·4	96,816	67·0	42,970	39·3
1938	412,422	40·0	44·6	60,145	26·0	31,409	37·6

Source. Lloyd's Register of Shipping. Annual Summaries of Merchant Ships Launched in the World (1919–38); L. Jones, Shipbuilding in Britain, 103, 125; Shipbuilders and Repairers' National Association for Clyde tanker tonnages, 1930–38.

and, very largely, of technology. On the development of Clyde shipbuilding and marine engineering before 1914 the following works are particularly useful: W. S. Cormack, 'An economic history of shipbuilding and marine engineering' (unpublished Ph.D thesis, University of Glasgow, 1930); S. Pollard, 'The economic history of British shipbuilding, 1870–1914' (unpublished Ph.D thesis, University of London, 1950), on which the same author based articles in *Economic History Review*, 2nd ser., V (1952), and *Journal of Economic History*, XVII (1957); R. H. Campbell, *Scotland since 1707. The Rise of an Industrial Society* (1965), 225–31, provides a good summary of developments before 1914, but his treatment of the inter-war period (256–61) is rather superficial and disappointing; P. L. Robertson, 'Shipping and shipbuilding: the case of William Denny and Brothers', *Business History*, XVI (1974), 36–47, and 'Technical education in the British shipbuilding and marine engineering industries, 1863–1914', *Econ. H. R.*, 2nd ser., XXVII (1974), 222–35. On the inter-war period Jones, *op. cit.*, contains much useful detailed information about developments on the Clyde, but the scope of his analysis is much wider; Cormack's unpublished thesis, in so far as it relates to the inter-war period, must be regarded as a contemporary source rather than as a mature historical study, as indeed must the Board of Trade, *Industrial Survey of the South West of Scotland* (1932), 34–40; N. K. Buxton, 'The Scottish shipbuilding industry between the wars: a comparative study', *Business History*, X (1968), 101–20, is the best recent study relating largely to Clydeside, but is still some way from being the definitive study to which the author evidently aspired.

4   These generalisations, of course, conceal variations (often considerable) in the performances of individual shipbuilding districts within the UK and of individual countries elsewhere in the world. In Japan and Spain, for example, merchant tonnage launched each year more often than not exceeded the pre-war level by a considerable margin: the same was true of Norway, Denmark, Sweden and Italy. In Germany, France, Belgium and the United States, on the other hand, the pre-war level was rarely exceeded. Mr Buxton (*op. cit.*, 104–7) notes that the performance of the east coast of Scotland's shipyard was generally better than that of the Clyde industry, and on one occasion at least (in 1937) the tonnage launched in the north-east of England (Tyne, Tees and Wear districts) exceeded the figure for the two Clyde districts (Glasgow and Greenock).

5   See especially Jones, *op. cit.*, 27–60; also Buxton, *op. cit.*, 101–4, for fuller surveys. I have found no reason to differ from their views.

6   British Association (Economic Science and Statistics Section), *Britain in Recovery* (1938), 352.

7   326 ships totalling 737,680 gross tons were built in foreign countries for British owners between 1920 and 1938 (Jones, *op. cit.*, table 23, 87). This represented the equivalent roughly of half the total output of British shipyards in a single good year during the period, such as 1929. The trouble, of course, was that good years were rare between the wars, and even they were not particularly good by pre-war standards.

8   Steel plates, for example, were substantially more expensive in Britain than in Germany, France and Belgium throughout most of the period 1921–38: see D. L. Burn, *The Economic History of Steel Making, 1867–1939* (1940), 427, 454.

9   Jones, *op. cit.*, 84–5.

10   In the years 1918–21 the USA was, in fact, the world leader in terms of tonnage launched but this was a purely temporary phenomenon stemming from the first world war.

11 Buxton, *op. cit.*, 110–13. On the effects of the declining coal export trade on
tramp shipping see Jones, *op. cit.*, 50–1. In 1918 Lord Inverclyde had
advocated a policy of concentration on liner production rather than tramp
construction for just the reasons suggested above: *Glasgow Herald Annual
Trade Review*, 28 December 1918.

12 *Glasgow Herald Annual Trade Review*, 30 December 1921.

13 In the decade 1929–38, for instance, Lithgow headed the annual Clyde
'league table' of tonnage launched no fewer than five times: see the January
issues of *The Shipbuilding and Marine Engineer*, 1930–39.

14 See, for example, *Glasgow Herald Annual Trade Review*, 30 December
1921, in which it was remarked that '. . . in this new movement in the world
of shipbuilding and shipping the part played by the Clyde is the foremost',
and in which James Richardson of Beardmore, the Dalmuir shipbuilders,
submitted that 'It is a matter of sincere congratulation . . . that in this – the
latest development of marine propulsion – we are taking such a prominent
and promising position, and of all the shipbuilding and marine engineering
centres of the world . . . the Clyde is pre-eminently first'.

15 See yet again *Glasgow Herald Annual Trade Review*, 30 December 1921;
also Cormack, *op. cit.*, 386.

16 At the annual general meeting of the P. & O. line in 1929 the Earl of
Inchcape (chairman) described a new liner as reflecting 'the greatest credit
on our Naval Architect, our Superintending Engineer, our Nautical
Advisers, our Superintending Pursers *and* [his italics] the Builders, Messrs
Alexander Stephen & Sons.' (J. L. Carvel, *Stephen of Linthouse,
1750–1950* (1950), 123.) The builders did manage in the case of this ship –
Viceroy of India (19,648 tons gross) – to persuade the owners to fit turbo-
electric power plant instead of the geared turbines originally specified, but
Stephen's next three ships for the P. & O. line (*Corfu* and *Carthage* in 1931
and *Canton* in 1938) reverted to geared turbines. The order in which Lord
Inchcape assigned the credit for *Viceroy of India* is interesting.

17 F. E. Hyde, *Shipping Enterprise and Management, 1830–1939. Harrisons
of Liverpool* (1967), 149–55. Harrison's were far from being hidebound
traditionalists. They had tried other methods of propulsion but, having
monitored the performances of their ships very carefully, came to the
conclusion that oil firing, geared turbines and other such innovations were,
in the particular context of their operations, less economic than coal-fired
triple-expansion engines, which were, however, latterly fitted with the new
Bauer-Wach exhaust turbine. Harrison's record of profitability during the
inter-war period was substantially better than that of the larger and more
technically progressive Blue Funnel Line (Alfred Holt & Co.), also of
Liverpool.

18 It is difficult to cite hard, detailed evidence in support of this suggestion.
Advertising matter in technical publications such as *The Shipbuilder,
Shipbuilding and Shipping Record*, the annual *Shipping World Year Book
and Port Director* and *Jane's Fighting Ships* conveys an impression that it
is probably valid enough, and it would certainly be logical for the leading
centre of the world's shipbuilding country to have developed around it a
greater concentration of suppliers of all the materials and components
necessary for ship construction than other centres. Some such suppliers –
for instance, G. & J. Weir & Co. and James Howden & Co., both Glasgow
fims – undoubtedly led the country, and even the world, in their fields.

19 Cormack, *op. cit.*, 320.

20 P. L. Robertson, 'Technical education', *Ec. H. R.* (1974).

21 *Ibid.*, 235.

22 J. Maxtone-Graham, *The North Atlantic Run* (1972), 47. The fate of

Titanic is well known. *Olympic* survived at least two serious collisions, only to be scrapped in the mid-'30s. *Britannic* never saw service as a liner; completed as a hospital ship in 1915, she was mined and sunk in the Mediterranean the following year.

23 J. M. Reid, *James Lithgow. Master of Work* (1964), 107–8.

24 See, for example, the reaction of Sir Alexander Kennedy of Fairfield in 1928 to such a suggestion (emanating from a director of Beardmore, whose Dalmuir yard was in difficulty): in Sir Alexander's view the personal element in contacts between builders and their customers was of crucial importance. The exchange was reported in *The Shipbuilder*, January 1929, 93.

25 On Lithgow's attitude to rationalisation see especially Reid, *op. cit.*, 129–30. The description of National Shipbuilders' Security Ltd is from Carvel, *op. cit.*, 125.

26 Alfred Holt & Co. (the Blue Funnel Line) and T. & J. Harrison, both of Liverpool, were regular customers of the Scott and Lithgow shipyards respectively in the '20s and '30s. The connection between the Liverpool-based Bibby Line and Fairfield's Govan shipyard has also been noted.

27 It has been noted that shipbuilding firms frequently held shares in shipping companies, and *vice versa*, and such financial links undoubtedly did influence the placement of shipbuilding orders. No clear correlation between the size of shareholding and the scale of ordering seems to exist, however. Before 1914 the best customer of William Denny's Dumbarton shipyard was the British India line, in which Denny's holding was a minimal £250. Such links could, indeed, be disadvantageous, as in the case of Alexander Stephen & Sons, in which a controlling interest was held after 1918 by the Inchcape family of the P. & O. line: other lines were reluctant to order from a builder controlled by one of their rivals, while the Inchcapes were unwilling to appear to be exerting influence within the P. & O. line for orders to be placed with a shipbuilder their family controlled. See P. L. Robertson, 'Shipping and shipbuilding', *Business History*, XVI (1974), especially 43 n. 1 and 47. For a more general analysis of financial links between shipping lines and Scottish shipbuilders see Cormack, *op. cit.*, 383–7.

28 R. H. Campbell, *op. cit.*, 225–31.

29 Clyde shipbuilders may have been among the first in the world to build ships powered by steam turbines and diesels, but these prime movers – unlike the earlier compound and triple-expansion reciprocating steam engines – owed little in their conception and design to Clydeside engineers. The reaction turbine was the brainchild of Charles Parsons of Tyneside, the impulse turbine of an American named Curtiss, though some of the credit for applying reduction gearing to marine turbines may belong to Professor Biles of Glasgow University. The diesel, or course, was of German origin, and Continental engineers – in Germany, Holland, Scandinavia and Switzerland – were the technological leaders in its adaptation to marine use. So in marine engineering between 1890 and 1914 the technological pendulum seems clearly to have been swinging away from the Clyde.

30 Carvel, *op. cit.*, 113; see also Reid, *op. cit.*, 67–70.

31 In the *Glasgow Herald Annual Trade Review*, 28 December 1918.

32 The Burntisland Company's founder, Sir Amos Ayre, was a Tynesider whose approach to technical problems was evidently more scientific and systematic than that of more traditional shipbuilders like Lithgow. He was also rather more receptive to new ideas such as standardisation than his fellows. Lithgow's biographer remarked of Burntisland that 'Its methods

were strikingly progressive. Even in the years of slump, the business grew.'
(Reid, *op. cit.*, 193–4.) See also Buxton, *op. cit.*, 107.

33   An impression of technological stasis might be generated by, for example,
Maxtone-Graham's comparison between the Cunarders *Queen Mary*
(launched by John Brown in 1934) and *Aquitania* (launched from the same
yard in 1912): *Queen Mary* he characterised as 'a larger and bulkier
Aquitania ... reminiscent of any number of Clyde-built hulls. Her sole
distinction was size.' (Maxtone-Graham, *op. cit.*, 289.) This assessment is
less than fair to the builders: a superficial and admittedly inexpert
comparison of the hull lines of the two ships does not confirm it.

34   Maxtone-Graham, *op. cit.*, 289. One still modern feature of the three
Continental ships which *Queen Mary* lacked was the bulbous line of the
bow below the waterline. In fairness to John Brown & Co., it should
perhaps be said that it is extremely doubtful whether there was anything to
be learned by them from *Normandie*'s builders (Penhoët, St Nazaire) as
regards shipyard technique, however advanced the French may have been
in matters of scientific hull design.

35   Though the CGT numbered several Clyde-built ships among the smaller
and more prosaic units of its fleet between 1920 and 1939. See Marthe
Barbance, *Histoire de la C.G.T.* (Paris, 1955), appendix.

36   One recognises the limitations of such a description, however. The royal
dockyards could not afford to be too uncompetitive, or the Admiralty – to
obtain value for its large but still limited budget – would probably have
been obliged to make more use of private shipbuilding resources. On the
other hand, access to Admiralty orders was far from being subject to
entirely free competition among private yards: contracts were awarded by
the Admiralty only to those private shipyards on a very restricted approved
list, which included in 1913 Scott of Greenock, John Brown at Clydebank,
Fairfield at Govan, Beardmore at Dalmuir, Yarrow of Scotstoun and
Denny of Dumbarton from among the Clyde shipyards.

37   See A. J. Marder, *From the Dardanelles to Oran. Studies of the Royal
Navy in War and Peace, 1915–40* (1974), especially chapter II ('The
influence of history on sea power: the Royal Navy and the lessons of
1914–18').

38   The tanker shortage is explored by the official historian of wartime oil
supply, D. J. Payton-Smith, *Oil. A Study of Wartime Policy and
Administration* (1971), pp. 54–61, 72, 104–5.

39   Naval policy between the wars, and particularly in the 1930s, was largely
terra incognita until the publication of S. W. Roskill's *Naval Policy between
the Wars, vol. I, 1919–29* (1967), *vol. II, 1930–9* (1976), and Marder, *op.
cit.*, Armies are traditionally always ready to fight the last war rather than
the next, but it is arguable that in anti-submarine and convoy protection
equipment the preparedness of the Royal Navy in 1939–40 was not even as
advanced as that. The low priority accorded to Coastal Command by the
Air Staff did not help matters.

Exports and the Scottish economy in the depression of the 1930s

In 1934 the greater part of the industrial area of the Scottish Lowlands was designated a 'Special Area' and deemed to require extraordinary measures to restore its economic life. The low level of employment which culminated in this step was a result of the contraction of a few important industries upon which the Scottish economy was heavily concentrated. Unemployment ran at a very much higher rate in lowland Scotland than the average for the whole of Great Britain. In 1933 an average of 26·1 per cent of insured workers in Scotland were unemployed, compared with 19·1 per cent in the whole of Great Britain.[1]

It has been commonly assumed that this state of affairs arose from Scottish industry's high degree of dependence on the export market: this rendered the Scottish economy particularly vulnerable to the vicious forms of economic warfare practised in the inter-war period. 'Scotland's basic industries,' reported the Scottish Economic Committee in 1939, 'under normal conditions, depend mainly on the export trade.'[2] Referring to the Scottish shipbuilding areas, the same source expressed the view that 'the future depends much more on the state of international commerce'. 'It is fair to say,' it went on, 'that before the War Scotland compared very favourably with England in industrial activity and equipment ... In order to reach this position, Scottish industrialists had perforce concentrated primarily on developing their export markets, a process which was carried through in Scotland to a greater extent proportionately than in England.'[3] Similarly, the Scottish industrialist Sir Steven (later Lord) Bilsland was reported in 1936 as saying that 'when one considers the effect of the depression on Scotland in comparison with England, two factors affecting employment must be borne in mind – that Scotland, proportionately, had formerly the larger export trade, and made a greater contribution to emigration.'[4]

As an explanation of the particular severity of the depression in Scotland this would appear to be very reasonable. The basic heavy industries – coal, steel, engineering and shipbuilding – formed the core of the structure of industry in the lowland belt, and it was with these industries very much in mind that the generalisations quoted in the preceding paragraph were commonly formulated. This essay aims to investigate the accuracy of this analysis both as a broad generalisation and in relation to the individual principal industries. It is not assumed, of course, that a possible failure of export markets was the *sole* explanation of the severity of the depression in Scotland. Other possible explanations – a too heavy concentration on the production of capital rather than consumer goods, the exhaustion of local raw material resources, a decline of local entrepreneurial drive, or a drying up of the flow of investment capital – call similarly for investigation. But because the 'export bias' explanation was probably the most favoured one at the time of the depression itself this essay will focus its attention upon it.

The exact assessment of the role of exports in the Scottish economy of the inter-war period, however, presents formidable, if not insoluble, problems. There are not today, and have never been at any time previously in the nineteenth or twentieth centuries, any official statistics of Scotland's imports or exports. Since the Union of 1707 the Scottish economy has been entirely integrated into the larger entity of the United Kingdom, and although certain Scottish Customs series of statistics were separately prepared in the second half of the eighteenth century, exports emanating from Scotland have ever since been grouped together with those from England and Wales (and, for much of the time, from Ireland as well).

Since 1854, however, the Board of Trade has published an annual series of statistics relating to the trade of individual ports.[5] Until 1895 only a selected group of principal ports was covered by this series, but from 1896 details of the trade of every port were published. In addition to the total value of the import and export trade of every port, these tables also list the quantities and values of the principal commodities in the trade of each port. There are no indications of the directions of the trade: this information is available only for the United Kingdom as a whole. This source permits the calculation of the total value and quantities of the overseas trade of Scottish ports. This, of course, is a very different figure from that of Scottish overseas trade. An unknown, but certainly significant, proportion of Scotland's overseas trade passes through ports in other parts of the United Kingdom, the goods leaving Scotland by road, rail and coastal shipping.[6] Though trade associations and chambers of commerce have produced statistics in respect of a small number of individual industries, there is absolutely no means of assessing the volume of 'Scottish' imports and exports passing through non-Scottish United Kingdom ports.

In these circumstances the analysis of Scottish overseas trade may seem a hopeless task. But this would be taking an unnecessarily gloomy view of the situation. The *Annual Statements* contain a wealth of information which it would be foolish to dismiss, while for commodities the whole United Kingdom output of which was produced in Scotland, such as Scotch whisky or jute, it is possible to take account of the quantities passing through non-Scottish ports. Similarly, the bulky nature of other commodities — grain, timber, iron ore, unrefined sugar, crude petroleum among the imports, and coal and ships among the exports — makes it reasonably certain that the whole 'Scottish' trade passed through Scottish ports. It is with these possibilities and limitations in mind that the following analysis has been undertaken. On account of the incompleteness of the data, much of the analysis must inevitably be tentative and inadequate.

As a first step in the analysis of the behaviour of Scottish overseas trade in the depression of the 1930s a volume index of exports through Scottish ports has been calculated. This can then be compared with the similar index available for the trade of the United Kingdom as a whole[7] to indicate any significant differences in the Scottish experience. The preparation of a separate Scottish volume index was judged to be desirable on account of the differences in commodity composition of the Scottish and United Kingdom trades, and the variability of these differences over time. For this index thirty-two commodities have been selected, representing a proportion of the trade which is never less than 66 per cent and is mostly a much higher percentage. The resulting weighted price index permits the construction of a table in which the volume of exports is calculated from the total values of the trade of all Scottish ports on the basis of the 'prices' ruling in each year. The average of the prices ruling in the period 1925–29 has been selected as the base, since this period seemed to offer the most stable base from which to examine the developments of the following decade. There are, of course, no series of export *prices*, and it is customary for this purpose to substitute 'average values' derived by dividing the quantities of goods traded into their total value as shown in the *Annual Statements*, and the index was weighted annually according to the share of the value of each commodity in the total value of exports.

Before turning with the aid of the statistics and index just described to an examination of the dynamics of the export trends in the 1930s let us first examine the reality of the 'export bias' generalisation in relation to the period immediately preceding the depression. Though, in looking back from the 1930s, many commentators may have had in mind some ideal period before 1914, the short-run position in the 1930s can effectively be compared only with the immediately preceding period. It is, of course, true that, to the extent that the depression of the early 1930s was as much the outcome of secular developments as it was of cyclical trends, explanations of the situation in the 1930s must also be sought in the developments of several decades before the 1930s; but to investigate the secular as well as the cyclical elements in the Scottish industrial situation of the 1930s would involve a study well in excess of the bounds of a short essay. Thus, though reference must necessarily be made from time to time to longer-run trends, in this essay developments in the 1930s will be related for the most part to the situation in the pre-depression quinquennium 1925–29.

In this quinquennium exports from Scottish ports amounted to 16·3 per cent of the estimated national income of Scotland, compared with 18·2 per cent for the United Kingdom.[8] There are certain disparities between the data that produce these percentages, the most important of which is undoubtedly the fact, already discussed, that the figures of exports through Scottish ports are obviously less, and may be substantially less, than the figures for domestic exports with which they are being compared in the United Kingdom percentage. Given, also, that there was certainly some difference between Scotland and the United Kingdom as a whole in the proportion of gross national product contributed by mining and manufactures,[9] it would clearly be unwise to assume that global figures of this kind either confirm or deny generalisations about the greater reliance of the Scottish economy upon exports than the English or Welsh economies.

When one turns to individual industries, moreover, the picture becomes more complex. As we noticed earlier, the 'export bias' generalisation was commonly offered in a context linking it with the heavy industries of the central belt. Yet, on the whole, it is less true of these industries than it is of others. In the relatively normal quinquennium 1925–29 only 20 per cent of the Scottish coal output was exported and 19 per cent of new ships,[10] neither of these being trades in which there were likely to be significant 'leaks' of Scottish trade through English ports. It is virtually impossible, on account of the diverse nature of the products, to make any valid estimate from trade and production figures as far as the iron and steel industry is concerned but there was little in the history of this industry in Scotland in the inter-war years to suggest that it was likely to be a very successful competitor overseas: it was also, of course, closely linked with the local shipbuilding and engineering industries. Many of the remaining industries that contributed significantly to Scotland's exports in this period, however, come much closer to fitting the 'export bias' category. Though there are not, and cannot be, from the heterogeneous nature of the class, any relevant figures for the whole class of machinery exports, it was claimed, for example, that between 80 and 90 per cent of sewing machines from the huge Singer works at Clydebank was exported in the late 1920s.[11] Thirty-five per cent of the whisky produced was exported in the quinquennium 1925–29. The textile industries were generally heavily committed to the export market: the jute industry exported 46·3 per cent of its output in 1924 and 47·0 per cent in 1928.[12] The woollen industry, it was claimed, exported as much as 80 per cent of its output before 1914, and still, in the 1930s 'as high as 60 per cent and no lower than 50 per cent';[13] as late as 1938 it was possible for one observer to claim that the Scottish woollen industry was 'largely dependent on its export trade'.[14] The cotton sewing thread industry, concentrated in Paisley, relied heavily on the export market: 81 per cent of its output was exported in 1919.[15] It would, of course, be as easy to produce a similar series of high export figures of single industries in England and Wales: the manufacture of cotton piece goods is an obvious example. By themselves, therefore, these figures tell us very little.

Among the principal export commodities there was, therefore, a very wide range in the scale of the relative importance of the export market to the industry concerned. For some industries the export trade was of overwhelming importance; for others the home market predominated heavily. How important were these different categories in the export trade as a whole? The industries in which exports played a relatively minor role (probably no more than 20 per cent of total output) in the quinquennium 1925–29 – coal, ships, iron and steel – accounted for just under one-third of total exports through Scottish ports – 32·1 per cent; whisky accounted for 11·8 per cent, and machinery, impossible to place exactly on the scale, for 15·6 per cent. The textiles, mostly with a very high proportion of their output exported, accounted together for 22·4 per cent.

The simple generalisation that attributed the misfortunes of the Scottish economy in the 1920s to its heavy dependence on exports turns out, therefore, on closer examination to mislead through over-simplification. It is clearly least true in respect of the heavy industries with which it was most commonly associated in the 1930s, and most true in relation to the textile industries.

Let us turn now to examine the impact of the depression itself on the dynamics of the export trade during the 1930s. Fig. 11.1 shows the volume index for the exports of Scottish ports described above, set beside the London and Cambridge Economic Service's index for the United Kingdom.

There is a discrepancy in the base periods between the two sets of figures, but this does not materially affect a comparison of trends. Two important characteristics of the export trade of Scottish ports emerge clearly. First, this trade began to decline sooner, and continued to decline for a longer period, than that of the United Kingdom; and, second, the extent of the decline was greater in the case of Scottish ports than of United Kingdom ports. Since recovery in the Scottish case was little greater than in the United Kingdom as a whole, it is clear that exports

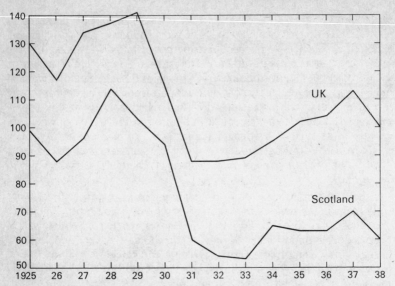

Fig. 11.1 Export volumes, Scottish ports and United Kingdom, 1925–39. (Scotland, 1925–29 = 100; United Kingdom, 1938 = 100.) For sources see pp. 192–3.

from Scottish ports were relatively less successful than United Kingdom exports generally in recovering the ground lost in the downswing.

It is not to be expected that the export trade of each industry would necessarily reflect these general trends closely. Exports during the 1930s of the principal commodities, except textiles, are shown in fig. 11.2. Owing to the diverse nature of the textile group these exports have been set out separately in fig. 11.3. The figures plotted are those of indices (based, as before, on 1925–29) of *quantities* exported. The volume curve at the foot of each figure for purposes of comparison is the same as that shown in fig. 11.1. In general, the turning points conform with those of the total volume curve, which is, of course, a weighted average of all the commodities in the index. The extent of the fluctuations of individual commodity exports, on the other hand, shows some important variations. Very broadly, three types of experience may be noted: first, industries whose exports were not too seriously affected by the depression of the early 1930s and were maintained at a fairly steady level throughout the period; second, those whose exports fell off more seriously during the depression but recovered reasonably well in the late '30s; and, third, those whose exports declined severely and remained at the new low level throughout the remainder of the decade. In the first category were coal, cotton sewing thread and cordage; in the second, machinery, whisky, ships, and jute manufactures; and in the third, iron and steel

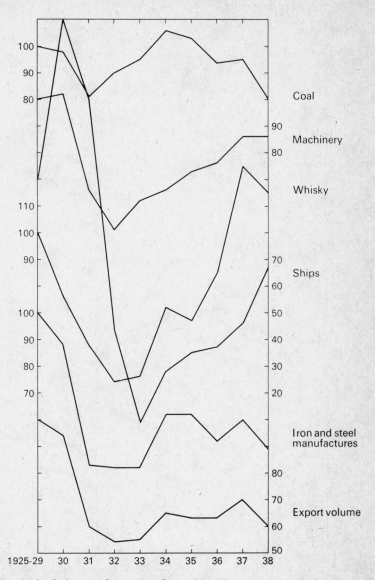

Fig. 11.2 Indexes of exports from Scottish ports, principal non-textile commodities, 1925–29, 1930–38. (1925–29 = 100.) Source: Annual Statements of the Trade of the United Kingdom.

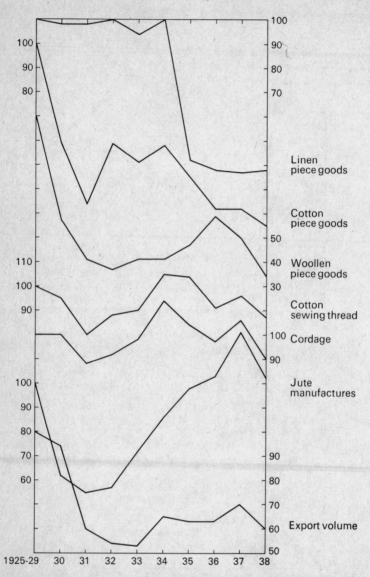

Fig. 11.3 Indexes of exports from Scottish ports, principal textile commodities, 1925–29, 1930–38. (1925–29 = 100.) Source: Annual Statements of the Trade of the United Kingdom. Note that in the case of jute manufactures the figures are of total exports from the UK.

manufactures, linen, cotton and woollen piece goods. In the pre-depression base period (1925–29) the first group accounted for 14·6 per cent of total exports, the second 38·4 per cent, and the third 30·0 per cent. By the peak of the general recovery in 1937 the first group had advanced its share to 16·6 per cent of total exports from Scottish ports, the second to 39·5 per cent, while the third had fallen away to 16·7 per cent.

In view of the high unemployment in the Scottish coalfields the comparative stability of coal exports may at first seem surprising. The Scottish coal export trade, however, had already taken its most serious knocks in the immediate post-1918 period. In the last pre-war quinquennium (1909–13) exports from Scottish ports averaged just over 10 million tons annually. Apart from the exceptional year 1923, this level was never remotely reached again. And for this particular commodity the base period 1925–29 unfortunately introduces an important distortion: the coal strike of 1926 resulted, *inter alia*, in unusually low exports in that year, thus reducing the base-period average and leading to an understatement of the decline to the nadir of 1931.

It remains the fact, nevertheless, that in comparison with the later 1920s the performance of Scottish coal exports in the 1930s was not as bad as might have been expected. Scotland, however, was fortunately served by the terms of the trade agreements with the Scandinavian countries of 1933 and 1934. The development of the Polish export trade in the 1920s through the port of Gdynia, aided, first, by highly subsidised rail freights, and, second, by the marketing opportunity afforded by the British coal strike of 1926, had severely cut into the valuable British export trade in coal to the Scandinavian countries, much of which, in the pre-1914 period, had fallen to the Scottish coalfields exporting through Scottish east coast ports. The British coal delegation to Scandinavia of 1930 had drawn attention to the near monopoly position of the British coal trade in Scandinavian markets in 1913 – about 93 per cent in the case of Denmark, over 95 per cent in Sweden and nearly 98 per cent in Norway. By 1929, however, the British share of these markets had fallen to 54 per cent, 47 per cent and 62 per cent respectively, nearly all the loss being accounted for by Polish competition.[16] By the 1933 and 1934 agreements, however, Denmark agreed to take 80 per cent of all her imports of coal from Britain, Sweden 45 per cent and Norway 70 per cent. While these proportions did not necessarily represent any very great advance on the position at the time of the agreements, they at least protected British exporters against further losses. That this fillip to the coal export trade of the east coast ports was of real importance is shown by the figures for the exports of coal from Scottish east coast ports: these averaged 3·7 million tons annually in the years 1930–32 before the agreements, and 4·3 million tons in the years 1934–36. The coal–cattle pact with the Irish Free State in 1934 was credited with a comparable, if lesser, effect on the Scottish west coast ports.[17] Similarly, Scottish coal exporters were less adversely affected than were the English and Welsh exporters by French import restrictions, by the economic sanctions on Italy, and by the Spanish Civil War.[18] Offsetting these advantages, however, there was a widespread feeling in the later '30s that Part I of the Coal Mines Act of 1930 was detrimental to the interests of the Scottish coal export trade. Economic recovery, and particularly rearmament, was driving up home demand, and increases in home quotas were made only at the expense of the export trade, and were beginning to lead to delays in delivery, and even, astonishing as it may seem for the 1930s, to the refusal of export orders. In 1935 Denmark had to be relieved of its obligation to take up its quota of British coal and allowed to buy coal elsewhere.[19] It was possibly the concentration on the home market that lay behind the slight decline in exports of coal in the second half of the decade.

Cotton sewing thread, also in the first category of exports that were relatively slightly affected by the depression, and an important Scottish specialisation within the broader framework of the textile industry as a whole, was not enumerated separately in the trade returns for the individual ports until 1925. Thereafter, however, its exports through Scottish ports showed a degree of steadiness quite untypical of the period. There was a 20 per cent decline to 1931, but the level of the late '20s was recovered by 1934 and subsequently broadly maintained. Cotton sewing thread, however, is a commodity whose value is high in proportion to its bulk, and it is distinctly possible that a significant proportion of the trade in Scottish-produced thread passed through English ports. Though the share passing through Scottish ports may not have fluctuated sharply in the short run, nevertheless it would clearly be unwise to assume too much from these figures alone.

The exports in the second category — those that made a good recovery from the depths of the early '30s — all shared a high volatility. Machinery exports halved between 1930 and 1932, but climbed steadily back thereafter to something approaching their pre-depression level by the later 1930s. Whisky exports behaved similarly, though the fall to 1932 was even greater and the subsequent recovery more vigorous. Exports of manufactured jute are perhaps the most surprising member of this group. By 1936 the trade had recovered its pre-slump level; but that year was still accounted a bad one in Dundee. Jute exports in the late '20s, although the best since the early years of the century, showed an appreciable decline from the peak period at the end of the nineteenth century. The quantity of jute piece goods exported in 1925–29 was only 87 per cent of that of 1896–1900. In fact the complaints in the jute industry in 1936 concerning the poorness of trade were in no way exceptional; they recurred throughout the 1930s with monotonous regularity. The depression of the 1930s in the Dundee jute industry served merely to stress the fact that trends in the world jute industry had been unfavourable to Dundee for many years. The trouble lay not so much in the difficulty of maintaining a steady level of output as in maintaining the trade at a reasonably profitable level. The rate of decline of the industry may be said to have been retarded by the willingness of the Dundee manufacturers to accept trade at little or no profit over a surprisingly long period rather than see the trade disappear entirely.

Production and export in the industry are difficult to estimate over long periods, owing to the varied nature of the output and to changes in the units used in official returns. Perhaps the best guide to the level of activity in the industry is the consumption of raw jute (total United Kingdom retained imports). In the base period 1925–29 these had averaged 186,000 tons per year. In the quinquennium 1934–38 164,000 tons were imported yearly, but in 1910–14 the average level had been 203,000 tons; further back still, in 1896–1900, the figure was 217,000 tons. This suggestion of secular decline in the industry is confirmed by the employment figures: the 43,000 employed in 1890 had fallen to 28,000 in 1930 and 24,000 in 1935. The decline in employment figures cannot be related too closely to the level of output in the industry. There was some improvement in productivity, particularly in the spinning branch of the industry in the 1930s, when there was a considerable degree of conversion to high-speed spindles.

The secular decline of the industry was, of course, due largely to the rise of the Calcutta jute industry. Like the Lancashire cotton industry, the Dundee jute industry of the 1930s could scarcely compete with the low-cost products of the Indian mills. Imports of jute manufactures from India into the United Kingdom almost doubled during the 1930s, and the share of United Kingdom consumption met by imports rose from 37 per cent in 1930 to 45 per cent in 1938. It is not surprising that one of the most discussed factors influencing the prosperity of the Dundee industry in the 1930s was the length of the working week in the Calcutta mills. Thus the breakdown in 1934 of the agreement by the Associated Mills of Bengal to restrict working hours and to seal redundant looms was rightly regarded as a serious blow to Dundee. Even the assistance of the swing to protectionism was denied to Dundee, as the Ottawa agreements, by adhering to the principle of imperial preference, safeguarded the United Kingdom market for the Indian jute manufacturers. 'The jute industry has, therefore, ' commented Silverman, 'changed from an industry whose primary interest was in its foreign markets to an industry primarily concerned with its home market.'[20]

Perhaps because of the degree of integration of the industry with other major sectors of the economy, shipbuilding was commonly regarded as the key to the Scottish economy. Yet in the base quinquennium 1925–29, a particularly good period by the standards of the twentieth century for exports of Scottish-built ships – and here we can be reasonably certain that the figures of exports through Scottish ports really do represent the whole export trade – these exports accounted for only 6·7 per cent of the value of total exports through Scottish ports. Thus the fact that by 1937 the exports had not recovered to even half the average of 1925–29 could not be interpreted as more than a minor element in the lagging Scottish recovery. What enables us to place the export of ships in the second category is, of course, the fact that, unlike most trades, this one continued vigorous recovery beyond the general peak of 1937. Moreover the well known lag of the shipbuilding cycle behind the general business cycle allowed the export trade in ships to play at least a minor role in dampening the effects of both slump and recovery. 1930, for example, was the best year for exports of ships in the whole inter-war period after 1923, and though the figure for 1931 showed a substantial fall it still represented one of the best years of the period. The lowest point in these exports was not reached until 1933, when recovery in other sectors was already under way. When it came, of course, the collapse of exports was catastrophic – to a mere 9 per cent of the average of the quinquennium 1925–29. Similarly, exports of ships continued their recovery into 1938 when most other trades turned downwards.

The loss of overseas markets in the 1920s was due to a large extent to the development, under strong protective policies, of shipbuilding in the countries which, before 1914, had been among the principal markets for the Scottish shipbuilding industry. 'An occasional liner is still built on the Clyde for foreign owners,' commented the *Glasgow Herald* in 1925, 'and during 1925 one of the finest vessels of that type was completed at Dalmuir for Italy; but France, Germany, Holland and Japan are all trying, and with unquestioned success, to have all their ships built in their own yards.'[21]

It was, of course, the third category of exports – those that failed to produce much significant recovery during the 1930s – that produced the most harmful effects on the Scottish economy as a whole. They had, as we have seen, accounted for 30 per cent of total shipments through Scottish ports in the late 1920s. Almost half this class was contributed by piece goods – manufactured woollen, linen and cotton cloth. For centuries these had been a mainstay of the Scottish export trade, but by 1937 they accounted together for only 4·6 per cent of exports through Scottish ports. Their failure to recover ground lost in the depression of the early 1930s was the most acute of all the principal categories of Scottish exports. In the case of cotton piece goods – though here the exports through Scottish ports may perhaps offer a particularly unreliable indicator of the total export of Scottish production – it was not so much a question of an incomplete recovery, or even of a failure to recover, as of a steady decline: an index of exports through Scottish ports based on 1925–29 = 100 had fallen to 51 in 1933 and 25 in 1938. The export trade in linen piece goods fell off drastically, largely because of the collapse of the American market. In 1929 the United States took 41·8 per cent of Scottish linen piece-goods exports.[22] There were particularly heavy reductions in the United States' imports of table damasks and handkerchiefs.[23] The woollen industry was, as we have seen, heavily dependent upon exports. By 1936 the trade with some markets, particularly Italy and Holland, had recovered fairly well after the depression of the early '30s, but other trades to Scandinavia, Belgium and the important United States market still fell short of 50 per cent of their 1928 levels.[24]

Exports of iron and steel manufactures – at 17 per cent of total exports the largest single item from Scottish ports in the late 1920s – showed perhaps the most disappointing performance of all the major export commodities. The downturn began as early as 1929; the trade remained at a level in 1931, 1932 and 1933 that was little more than one-third of its fairly modest peak levels of 1927–29; it showed only slight recovery during the mid-'30s; and it fell off again in 1938. Moreover, in one respect at least, the situation in the Scottish iron and steel industry was worse than these figures suggest. In the late 1930s these manufactured exports were based on a lower proportion of native raw materials. For many decades before the 1930s the Scottish iron and steel industry had been dependent to a large extent on imported pig iron, most of which came from the Cleveland district of north Yorkshire. This was supplemented by imports of foreign pig iron, of which there was a marked increase in the late '30s, particularly after the reduction of the import duty in 1937 from $33\frac{1}{3}$ per cent to $2\frac{1}{2}$ per cent. Imports of foreign pig iron into Scottish ports had averaged 120,000 tons per year in 1925–29. Falling to 29,000 tons in 1933, they rose to over 250,000 tons in 1937. Thus to a decline in exports of over 300,000 tons in the decade before 1939 must be added an increased import of 130,000 tons of pig iron. Recovery after 1935 was attributed in part to the agreement with the European steel cartel in July of that year, which gave British exporters a definite share of the international trade.[25]

This hasty survey of the principal elements in the export trade of Scottish ports during the 1930s – together they accounted for 81·9 per cent of total exports in 1925–29 – goes some way towards explaining the generally poorer performance of the Scottish contribution to the whole United Kingdom export trade. Not only did too small a proportion of the export trade show any sustained capacity to resist decline in the depression of the early '30s, but too large a segment of the whole trade failed to establish any significant recovery during the mid- or late '30s. With the possible exception of whisky, which, perversely, was a relatively small employer of labour, all these trades stemmed from major industries which were substantial employers of labour within the Scottish economy. Moreover most were industries for which the export market was of some importance.

What conclusions does this analysis point to concerning the role of exports in the depression of the 1930s in Scotland? It is clear, first, that a simple generalisation about the 'export bias' of the Scottish inter-war economy is a misleading oversimplification. Some of the major industries taking a significant share of the total trade through Scottish ports did not export a disproportionate share of their total output by the standards either of the whole of the United Kingdom or of Scottish industry generally. Second, it was, for the most part, these industries with a relatively low export commitment that suffered least in consequence of the depression of the early 1930s. Third, at the other extreme, the industries – primarily textiles – that were most heavily committed in the immediate pre-depression period to overseas markets fared worst during the 1930s: it was these industries, above all cotton, woollen and linen piece goods, whose exports fell most drastically in the early '30s and showed least ability to recover in the mid- and late '30s. Fourth, in a midway position, were industries like whisky distilling and jute which, with a substantial though not excessive commitment to the export market, enjoyed more success in recovering during the mid- and late '30s the ground lost in the early years of the decade. The overall picture is, therefore, a complex one. While far from denying the common belief in the importance of the export market in any analysis of the depression of the 1930s in the Scottish economy, it suggests nevertheless that there was such a wide range of experience even within the small number of principal industries in Scotland at that time as to make any simple generalisation virtually impossible.

Notes

1   While it is true that Scotland was severely affected by the depression, unemployment in the Scottish 'Special Area' was significantly lower during the mid-1930s than in any of the three other Special Areas. In May 1935, when 33·3 per cent of the insured workers of the West Cumberland Special Area were registered as unemployed, 32·3 per cent of those in the Durham and Tyneside area, and 37·5 per cent of those in the South Wales area, only 26·8 per cent of those in the Scottish area were unemployed. It would be unwise, however, to read too much into these comparisons: much depended on the exact boundaries of the areas, and strong feelings were expressed at the time in some cases about the exclusion from the Special Areas of some severely depressed districts. For general surveys of the low level of economic activity in Scotland during the 1930s see R. H. Campbell, *Scotland since 1707* (Oxford, 1965), pp. 249–75; and A. Slaven, *The Development of the West of Scotland, 1750–1960* (1975), pp. 183–209.
2   Scottish Economic Committee, *Scotland's Industrial Future* (1939), p. 19.
3   *Ibid.*, pp. 20–1.
4   *Glasgow Herald Trade Review*, 1936.
5   *Annual Statements of the Trade of the United Kingdom*.
6   For a fuller discussion of these statistics and the problems of interpreting them see M. W. Flinn, 'The overseas trade of Scottish ports, 1900–60',

Scottish Journal of Political Economy, 13 (1966).

7 Prepared by the London and Cambridge Economic Service, and published in B. R. Mitchell and P. Deane, *Abstract of British Historical Statistics* (Cambridge, 1962), p. 329.

8 There is a real problem here of comparing like with like. The only possibly relevant Scottish figures available for this purpose are Campbell's estimates of 'national income' (A. D. Campbell, 'Income', in A. K. Cairncross (ed.), *The Scottish Economy* (Cambridge, 1954), p. 50). The closest UK match for these figures seems to be those for 'total domestic income' in Feinstein's estimates (C. H. Feinstein, *National Income, Expenditure and Output of the United Kingdom, 1855–1965* (Cambridge, 1972), p. T6). The UK trade figures used are the official ones for domestic exports.

9 It is not, unfortunately, possible to make a comparison between Scotland and the United Kingdom of the ratio of exports of mining and manufactured goods to the value of the total output of these goods, since there are no annual estimates available of the value of the output of mining and manufactured products in Scotland for the period in question.

10 In calculating these percentages it has been assumed that all Scottish-mined coal and Scottish-built ships were exported through Scottish ports.

11 Board of Trade, *Industrial Survey of the South West of Scotland* (London, 1932), p. 171.

12 *Report of Jute Working Party* (London, 1948), p. 10.

13 H. Silverman, *Studies in Industrial Organisation* (1946), p. 146. When Silverman is more precise, however, he indicates rather lower percentages: twenty-four 'leading border manufacturers' together exported 43 per cent of their output in 1928 (p. 148).

14 Clydesdale Bank, *Survey of Economic Conditions in Scotland* (Glasgow, 1938), p. 15.

15 *Report of an Inquiry into the Alleged Existence of a Combine among the Manufacturers of Sewing Cotton* (Further Inquiry), Parliamentary Papers, 1920, XXIII (Cmd. 930).

16 *Report of the British Coal Delegation to Sweden, Norway and Denmark*, Parliamentary Papers, 1930–31, XV (Cmd. 3702) p. 4.

17 Clydesdale Bank, *Survey* (1934), p. 8.

18 *Ibid*. (1938), p. 5.

19 *Ibid*. (1935), p. 9; (1937), p. 11.

20 Silverman, *Studies in Industrial Organisation*, p. 255.

21 *Glasgow Herald Trade Review* (1925).

22 *Glasgow Herald Trade Review* (1929).

23 P. W. Bidwell, *Our Trade with Britain* (New York, 1938), p. 106.

24 *Scotland's Industrial Future*, p. 100.

25 *Glasgow Herald Trade Review* (1936).